Economic Security and the Origins of the Cold War,
1945–1950

14.50
3-7

ECONOMIC SECURITY AND THE ORIGINS OF THE COLD WAR, 1945–1950

ROBERT A. POLLARD

New York   Columbia University Press

Library of Congress Cataloging in Publication Data

Pollard, Robert A., 1951–
Economic security and the origins of the Cold War,
1945–1950.

Bibliography: p.
Includes index.
1. United States—Foreign economic relations.
2. United States—Foreign relations—1945–1953.
3. World politics—1945–1955. I. Title.
HF1455.P55 1985   337.73   85-3786
ISBN 0-231-05830-6
ISBN 0-231-05831-4 (pbk.)

Columbia University Press
New York   Guildford, Surrey
Copyright © 1985 Columbia University Press
All rights reserved

Printed in the United States of America

p 10 9 8 7 6 5 4 3 2 1
c 10 9 8 7 6 5 4 3 2

To My Mother

Contents

Preface

I BEGAN THIS STUDY as the United States was extricating itself from its longest and most unsuccessful war, and I am ending it as Americans are recovering from the deepest recession of the post-World War II era. The Vietnam War stimulated widespread public interest in the origins of the Cold War while our recent difficulties have caused many Americans to ask how we ever became so vulnerable to external economic developments. During the late sixties and early seventies, historians associated with the "revisionist" school raised the level of the national debate by reemphasizing the importance of economic factors in American foreign policy. Among other things, these scholars demonstrated that the United States assumed world-wide commitments after 1945 not just to stop Communist expansion, but to defend certain economic interests, both material and ideological, as well.

This study draws heavily upon the revisionists' insights, but breaks with them in its final assessment of American motivation and achievements. I regard the international economic achievements of the Truman administration as one of the great success stories of the twentieth century, not just for the United States but for the Western world as a whole. In contrast with the revisionist portrayal of an imperialist elite bent upon aggrandizing power in the service of world capitalism or narrow U.S. interests, I depict postwar American leaders—President Harry S. Truman, William Clayton, George Kennan, Dean Acheson, among others—as largely enlightened and responsible, willing to sacrifice short-term national advantage to long-term gains in Western stability and security. The Truman administration successfully integrated the Western economies in order to foster global (including U.S.) prosperity, stabilize the balance of power, and promote U.S. national security.

In this book, I focus upon the last objective because most Cold War studies have underemphasized the role of economic interdependence in upholding the Western alliance and American power. Indeed, successive Presidents since Truman have felt compelled to defend the multilateralist system for this very purpose. The United States must now pay an imposing price for the maintenance of an open economic order, but that price is worth paying, for the benefits of American economic leadership have greatly exceeded the costs.

The debts that I have accumulated since beginning this project are too numerous to acknowledge fully, but I wish to thank a few individuals whose support was especially important. First, I am indebted to Samuel R. Williamson, Jr., the Dean of the College of Arts and Sciences at the University of North Carolina and my thesis adviser, for providing continuing encouragement, advice, and criticism throughout the years it took to complete the dissertation. I also wish to thank Michael Hunt for his helpful suggestions in the later stages of the dissertation, as well as Otis Graham, William Leuchtenburg, and James Leutze for their extremely valuable comments in the oral examination. William Becker also deserves my thanks for offering moral support and substantive criticisms of the manuscript. It was a special pleasure to work with Bernard Gronert of Columbia University Press; no author could ask for a more kindly and helpful disposition from an editor. John Lewis Gaddis gave me excellent advice on revising the manuscript for publication, and I used his own work as a model of scholarship on the Cold War.

I also wish to acknowledge my debt to Samuel F. Wells, Jr., for helping support the research necessary to complete the dissertation and for bringing me to the Woodrow Wilson International Center for Scholars in Washington and its stimulating intellectual environment and excellent facilities. Among the Wilson Center scholars, I am especially grateful to Mary Furner for providing editorial advice, perspective, and humor; to Avi Shlaim for his comments on the interpretation of the Cold War, especially regarding Germany; and to Michael Hogan for his help on the Marshall Plan. Needless to say, any errors of fact or judgment are my own.

Among the many non-historians who were supportive, I should mention Jane Mutnick and Carla Borden for their help on the dissertation, and Steven Lagerfeld, who gave me the benefit of a keen editorial eye and a fresh perspective in numerous readings of the manuscript. Robert Stone, Judith Robb, and Carlton Conant offered able research assistance, and Diane Rivers helped type the manuscript when time was at a premium. And I would be truly remiss if I did not acknowledge the many "loans" that my brother Kemp floated me in graduate school.

The Harry S. Truman Library Institute provided financial support at critical junctures, and I am grateful for the professional assistance offered by the members of the library staff, notably Dennis Bilger, Harry Clark, Erwin Mueller, Elizabeth Safly, and Benedict Zobrist. Thanks to a generous grant from the Institute for Educational Affairs, I was able to spend several months rethinking some of the main issues addressed in this book, and Michael J. Lacey made it possible for me to remain at the Wilson Center during the last stages of the project.

Finally, I wish to thank my mother, Annemarie Zeilmann Pollard, for stimulating my interest in history, and for her support and love through many years of graduate studies, even though I did not become a medical doctor. This book is dedicated to her.

Washington, D.C.
June 1984

CHAPTER ONE

THE POLITICAL ECONOMY OF POSTWAR AMERICA

THE DEATH of the Bretton Woods system has been proclaimed many times since 1971, when President Richard M. Nixon formally decoupled the dollar from gold. But the spirit of the system and its offspring institutions survive, and its goals—a higher volume of world trade and growing international interdependence—have been largely realized.

In 1981, the United States exported about one-fifth of its industrial goods and two-fifths of its agricultural products, compared with about one-tenth for both indices during the 1930s. One-sixth of American employment in that year depended upon export markets while one-third of corporate profit derived from foreign trade and investment. The United States also imported more than half of its supplies of twenty-four of the forty-two most important raw materials. External developments now influence the domestic economy in many important ways. Fluctuations in the exchange rate of the dollar, for instance, can significantly affect the U.S. inflation rate, in addition to the balance of payments and domestic production.[1]

Yet for the first time since the 1930s, economic issues have emerged as a major source of discord in the West. Conflict over commercial discrimination, interest rates, and sanctions against the Soviet Union threaten the unity and resolve of the Western alliance as never before. To Americans accustomed to the steady growth and relative stability of the postwar era, moreover, the sudden vulnerability of the United States to oil embargoes, import competition, and volatile exchange and interest rates has come as a rude shock.

Many Americans have reacted by calling for the erection of steep trade barriers to protect industry and jobs in this country, but the probability of foreign retaliation has deterred Washington from demanding more than symbolic concessions from Japan and the West European countries. Aside from the economic infeasibility of protectionism, the United States remains wedded to the open and nondiscriminatory system established at Bretton Woods because the political and strategic costs of economic isolationism would be prohibitively high.

The ideas and institutions that govern the world economy today are a direct legacy of the Truman administration. Postwar American leaders—Harry S. Truman, Dean Acheson, William L. Clayton—deliberately fostered the economic interdependence of the major powers in order to ensure U.S. security and prosperity. Even with the momentous changes in the international economy since 1945, the system still functions largely as the postwar generation of policymakers anticipated it would.

The United States pursued an activist economic diplomacy after the war because American leaders enjoyed both the means and the will to exercise leadership of the global economy. While much of Europe and Asia lay in ruins, the United States in 1945 was producing almost half the world's goods. American officials keenly appreciated the leverage that U.S. economic power afforded them, and the lack of any immediate military threat to U.S. security encouraged a reliance upon economic power as the principal instrument of diplomacy.

A common set of beliefs, attitudes, and experiences informed American prescriptions for world peace and prosperity. Most U.S. leaders believed that international economic conditions had been largely responsible for the outbreak of world war, and that the United States needed to reform global planning and stabilization structures in order to prevent a recurrence of depression and war. "Nations which act as enemies in the marketplace cannot long be friends at the council table," Assistant Secretary of State William L. Clayton warned a group of Detroit businessmen in May 1945. "Most wars originate in economic causes," he argued, and the Roosevelt administration had designed the Bretton Woods agreements so that "all nations have free and equal access to the trade and raw materials of the world."[2]

This study focuses upon the American quest for "economic security" after World War II, that is, the Truman administration's effort to create an open world economic order that would serve U.S. strategic purposes. Most histories of the Truman era narrowly define national security policy in terms of defense budgets, conventional and atomic weapons, military force structures, and defense pacts. In contrast, the thesis of this work is that American leaders used foreign economic policy as the main instrument of U.S. security from 1945 to the eve of the Korean War.

While other historians have investigated postwar economic diplomacy, this is the first synthetic, "post-revisionist" interpretation of Truman's foreign economic and security policies. Soviet motives and policies in various areas of the world, and American perceptions of them, are subjected to extensive analysis in order to gain new insights into the origins of the Cold War. The impact of American policies upon other major actors in the postwar world economy, notably Britain, Germany, and Japan, receives considerable attention as well. Finally, bureaucratic and domestic political factors are weighed in an effort to develop a multi-causal explanation for American policies.

This chapter highlights the scholarly debate over U.S. foreign policy during the early Cold War and the place of this study within it. The remainder of the chapter analyzes the historical perspective of the postwar American leadership and the values and preconceptions that influenced their approach to economic problems.

The Historiographical Debate

Numerous historians, particularly those associated with the revisionist school, have drawn attention to the role of economic and ideological factors in the origins of the Cold War.[3] The revisionists have made an important contribution by demonstrating that the Truman administration regularly used trade and aid to attain certain political aims, notably the containment of Communism, and that conflict over economic issues was a critical cause of Soviet-American tensions. It is also true, as revisionist scholars claim, that many orthodox (and post-revisionist) works on the Cold War have under-emphasized the economic and ideological roots of American foreign policy.[4]

This study differs from the revisionists in several crucial respects. In the first place, certain revisionists, such as Joyce and Gabriel Kolko, claim that Washington's *primary* and *essential* "aim was to restructure the world so that American business could trade, operate, and profit without restrictions everywhere." These historians further contend that this aim "precluded the Left from power" in the industrialized countries and "required limitations on independence and development in the Third World."[5]

Actually, the American preference for an open and nondiscriminatory economic environment—the "Open Door"—was not a zero-sum
proposition. That is, U.S. foreign policy objectives were not necessarily achieved at the expense of other countries. The Bretton Woods
economic structure undoubtedly yielded handsome political and economic dividends for the United States, but this did not prevent other
countries participating in this system from making equally striking
gains. And as John Lewis Gaddis has argued, the "United States made
no systematic effort to suppress socialism within its sphere of influence."[6]

Second, this study attempts to integrate U.S. economic diplomacy
into the context of larger political and military objectives. Postwar
American foreign economic policy was not, as the Kolkos again contend, harnessed solely or even primarily to an effort "to sustain and to
reform world capitalism" through the expansion of foreign trade and
investment.[7] True, the opening of markets abroad enhanced business
profits, but this consideration was not foremost in the minds of policymakers. Instead, the Truman administration subordinated foreign economic policy to the preservation of democracy in Europe, the support
of friendly governments in the Far East, the containment of Soviet
power, and other political and strategic aims. The American quest for
prosperity went hand-in-hand with efforts toward a sounder world political and economic structure.

A corollary to this observation is that the American preoccupation
with the security implications of foreign economic policy preceded the
advent of the Cold War. The Bretton Woods system and early postwar
American foreign programs were not designed to punish the Soviet
Union. Rather, the United States opposed all forms, Left or Right, of
economic nationalism and autarky. The American commitment to a
stable and interdependent world economy necessitated the reconstruction of Western Europe with or without the presumed threat of Soviet
and Communist expansion.

Finally, this study attributes less coherence and design to American
foreign economic policies than do most revisionists.[8] To be sure, American officials agreed that the foundation of U.S. security and world
peace was a prosperous, multilateral international economic system.
Yet they often disagreed over how to translate principles into policies,
and competing domestic, bureaucratic, and political aims deflected
American leaders from a "pure" multilateralist course. There was more
than one path to the "reconstruction of world capitalism," to para-

phrase the revisionists, and postwar American policies were for the most part neither predictable nor inevitable. Indeed, the United States, despite years of wartime planning, was seriously unprepared for the economic chaos that followed the war.

Lessons of the Past

American foreign economic policy after World War II derived in large part from a resolution to profit from the lessons of the past. Underlying all of these lessons were the classical economists' assumptions that depressions gave rise to wars and that free, multilateral trade maximized international prosperity and peace.

Three historical experiences—the seemingly effortless workings of the nineteenth-century international economy, the problems of post-World War I finance and trade, and the Great Depression—shaped the thinking of American planners in the 1940s.[9] The thriving international economy and relatively peaceful political climate from 1815 to 1914 demonstrated the value of free trade, stable and convertible currencies based on gold, and minimal governmental interference (except for London's role as a financial center). The gold standard, as managed by the Bank of England, appeared responsible for the stability of currency exchange and prices and the steady growth in production and trade among the Western industrial countries. Britain further facilitated world liquidity and trade before World War I by eliminating most barriers to foreign imports and by balancing its huge current account surpluses with capital outflows.[10] The United States, on the other hand, played very little role in managing the international economy during this period:

> Up to 1914, dominant economic issues were argued in terms of domestic interests in a world taken as given, which U.S. action did little to affect, rather than in terms of economic theory or foreign relations. The British-dominated international economic system served American interests well.[11]

The First World War shattered this system, greatly expanding the functions of government in the West, unsettling the gold standard, breaking traditional patterns of trade, and signaling the decline of Europe in world trade and finance. Yet the Peace of Versailles failed to address major economic issues, and Great Britain, its export trade and invisible earnings (banking, shipping, insurance) disrupted, lacked the financial resources and the political will to revive the prewar monetary system. While the war had elevated the United States from debtor to creditor status, Washington was not prepared to accept economic leadership, thanks largely to Congressional opposition to the cancellation of Allied war debts and the reduction of trade barriers. Popular antipathy toward state management left responsibility for international lending, like much of public policy, in private hands.[12]

Stability in Europe returned for a time after American financiers, with the encouragement of officials in London and Washington, sponsored the Dawes Plan in 1924 and the Young Plan in 1929 in order to break the bottleneck of German reparations, and indirectly, Allied war debts to the United States. U.S. foreign investment in Europe ($7 billion of $10 billion world-wide, 1929) helped finance the continent's chronic trade deficit with, and war debts to, America. But the corporatist approach—private interests acting as the agents of official policy—did not resolve the key German problem.[13]

In effect, American bankers lent Germany funds to pay indemnities to the British and French who, in turn, used these same dollars to repay war debts they owed the United States. This Rube Goldberg-like contraption of world finance sputtered on until the onset of the Great Depression in the United States cut off the capital flow, helping activate a chain reaction of bank failures first in Europe, and then in the United States. When the system collapsed, there were few international institutions to cushion the fall.

The United States shared the blame for the world depression. American protectionism and recurrent trade surpluses during the 1920s had prevented European countries from paying off their war debts through trade, and the U.S. failure to regulate private loans to Europe encouraged highly speculative and irresponsible investment. Moreover, the Federal Reserve's tightening of the money supply during the early 1930s may have precipitated the financial crisis in Europe, while the notorious Smoot-Hawley Tariff of 1930 triggered a wave of protectionism world-wide.[14]

As prices fell and unemployment spread, the major industrial countries scrambled to protect native industries by raising barriers to foreign goods and devaluing their currencies. The crisis deepened in 1931 with the British suspension of sterling convertibility, the equivalent of a default for the many countries holding pounds as a reserve currency. The world monetary system began to disintegrate into a number of rival blocs, notably the self-contained, British "sterling" bloc and Germany's bilateral trading arrangements in Eastern Europe. From 1929 to 1932, world prices plunged 47.5 percent, the value of world trade by 60 percent, and employment in industrial countries by twenty-five million.[15]

During the late Hoover and first Roosevelt administrations, the United States largely spurned international cooperation. In 1933, President Franklin D. Roosevelt devalued the dollar and scuttled the London Economic Conference, which had been convened to stabilize currencies and to boost world trade and investment. Roosevelt believed that domestic recovery should take precedence over global stabilization. "The sound internal economic system of a nation," he stated, "is a greater factor in its well-being than the price of its currency." Later, the United States worked for currency stabilization through the 1936 Tripartite Agreement with Britain and France and for freer trade through bilateral reciprocal trade agreements. These lukewarm reforms came too late to reverse the downward spiral of world trade in the thirties. To make matters even worse, the economic nationalism and isolationism spurred by the depression reinforced the tendency of some countries, notably Germany in Eastern Europe, to use economic policy as an instrument of war and put a premium on competing political alliances. The abdication of American economic leadership during this period would later haunt U.S. officials.[16]

The Postwar Consensus

American policy makers in the forties drew several lessons from the events of the previous three decades. They concluded that American prosperity depended at least in part upon a thriving international economy, and that the federal government must intervene in the economy to preserve full employment and high income. The problem was that domestic objectives often conflicted with an optimum level of world trade. While American officials never resolved this dilemma, they agreed that Washington should take the leadership in creating postwar international institutions that would stabilize currencies, ease financial crises, and promote world commerce, as well as a new collective security organization that would deter aggression. A properly functioning system of world trade would foster interdependence among nations, they reasoned, thereby raising the price of aggression.

Conflict over economic interests probably had not been the main cause of the world war. Yet most American officials believed that the depression and despair of the 1930s had bred totalitarianism and militarism. "The next peace," Vice-President Henry Wallace stated in January 1941, "must take into account the facts of economics; otherwise, it will serve as the seedbed for aggression." In particular, the erection of closed economic blocs by fascist Germany in Eastern Europe, Japan in the Far East, and Britain in the Commonwealth countries had exacerbated economic rivalries and set the great powers on the road to war. Treasury official Harry Dexter White warned in 1942 that "the absence of a high degree of economic collaboration among the leading nations, will, during the coming decade, inevitably result in economic warfare that will be but the prelude and instigator of military warfare on an even vaster scale." This determination to avoid the mistakes of the past bore fruit in wartime planning. Assistant Secretary of State Dean Acheson observed in April 1945 that the distinguishing feature of American economic planning during World War II was "the wide recognition that peace is possible only if countries work together and prosper together. That is why the economic aspects are no less important than the political aspects of the peace."[17]

In addition to promoting traditional U.S. objectives—the freedom of the seas, national self-determination, and democratic government—American officials sought to build an "Open Door" world in which nations enjoyed equal opportunities for trade and investment. The assumption was that a nondiscriminatory environment would offer the benefits of peaceful economic competition, equal access to raw materials, and maximum efficiency through the principle of comparative advantage. The American commitment to the Open Door reflected more than commercial self-interest. "From its beginnings in the liberal democratic theory of John Locke and the laissez-faire economics of Adam Smith, American political and economic ideology has been grounded in the notion that maximum collective good will result from a society structured to permit freedom for individuals to compete in pursuit of their individual interests."[18] In the American view, this principle applied equally well to the international environment.

Generally, U.S. wartime planners favored private enterprise over state ownership of the means of production and commerce through private channels over state trading. Like most Americans who thought about such issues, these policymakers believed that steady economic growth under a modified capitalist system, rather than radical redistributive reforms under a socialist system, constituted the best way to remedy social ills.[19] In practice, this turned out to mean that U.S. foreign aid programs would emphasize increasing production and efficiency over the social transformation of recipient countries. While American officials after the First World War had relied primarily upon private and informal means to achieve similar policy aims, the Truman administration was inclined to make greater use of U.S. governmental agencies and multilateral institutions to implement foreign economic policy.

Well before the advent of the Cold War, American policymakers had identified the creation of an interdependent economic system as the basis of postwar American foreign policy. For most of the 1945–1950 period, economic instruments would serve as a partial substitute for a large military establishment. The principles, policies, and institutions established in these years would provide the foundation for American foreign economic policy over the next three decades, and the web of economic ties by which the Truman administration bound together the United States and its allies continues to sustain their collective security.

CHAPTER TWO

PLANNING FOR THE PEACE: BRETTON WOODS, POSTWAR RELIEF, AND SOVIET-AMERICAN RELATIONS, 1944–1945

THE BRETTON WOODS agreements of July 1944 establishing the International Monetary Fund and the World Bank marked the first major attempt by the United States to restructure the world economy. For almost three decades, the Bretton Woods institutions symbolized the American determination to maintain a world economic order based upon free trade and currency convertibility. More importantly, the 1944 conference was the foundation for later efforts to integrate the world economy under American leadership, and thereby to achieve economic security for the United States.

The Bretton Woods system was meant to be politically neutral, accommodating both capitalist and socialist countries. Yet thanks to the deterioration of Soviet-American relations soon after the war, the Soviet Union refused to participate in the new monetary and financial organizations. Moscow's failure to ratify Bretton Woods provides important insights into the origins of the Cold War.

Wartime economic planning had not focused on Soviet-American relations, and few foresaw the intense conflict that would develop between the putative superpowers after the war. Most American officials envisaged pragmatic cooperation among the great powers in the context of the United Nations Organization (UN) and tailored U.S. commercial policies to meet the needs of the Soviet Union and other state-trading countries. Washington, in short, attempted "to construct a new world economic order without first resolving the deep political differences which divided the United States and the Soviet Union."[1] American champions of free trade and multilateralism actually anticipated more problems with the United Kingdom (and other European industrial countries) than with the Soviet Union. As a result, economic planning at first focused on Anglo-American negotiation and cooperation in building a stable financial and commercial base for European reconstruction.

In pursuing these multilaterlist aims, the United States sought both to enhance its own prosperity and to secure world peace. It should come as no surprise that American ideals and self-interest coincided so neatly, for the primary goal of foreign policy, after all, is to serve the national interest. More surprising is the extent to which the Truman administration relied upon foreign economic instruments to promote American security, as well as American prosperity.

During the first months of the Truman presidency, policymakers found their economic tools woefully inadequate for the task. They had inherited highly ambiguous policies and principles from the Roosevelt administration, which had based its wartime planning upon postwar cooperation with the Soviet Union, rapid European reconstruction, and a strong revival of world trade. When none of these conditions was realized after the war, American policy floundered.

Roosevelt's Legacy

Wartime planners had strongly emphasized the link between foreign economic and security policies. Cordell Hull, Secretary of State from 1933 to 1944, embodied the commitment to Wilsonian internationalism and multilateralism more than anyone else in the Roosevelt administration. The moving force behind the Reciprocal Trade Agreements, Hull saw to it that the Atlantic Charter of August 1941 endorsed freedom of the seas, free trade, equal access for all nations to the raw materials of the world, and international collaboration in the economic field.[2]

Lend-Lease, which was designed to facilitate U.S. military and economic aid to its allies, also contained multilateralist provisions. At Hull's instigation, the British in Article VII of the Master Lend-Lease Agreement reluctantly pledged to dismantle the discriminatory commercial aspects of the imperial preference system. Hull sought not so much the dissolution of the British Empire as the elimination of *all* economic blocs since they had presumably helped cause the war. Despite his aversion to state-trading systems, the Secretary of State also favored Lend-Lease to the Soviet Union both to aid the Allied war effort and to include the Soviets in a postwar international commercial system.[3]

While Hull in principle abhorred all barriers to trade, most American officials, such as Harry Hawkins, Chief of the Division of Commercial Treaties and Agreements, drew a distinction between protectionism and discrimination. In American thinking, the protection of domestic producers through the use of high tariffs and other devices permitted the diversification of the national economy without directly injuring other countries. "The imposition of high, though non-discriminatory, trade barriers for the protection by a country of its own producers . . . is understandable and tolerable," Hawkins wrote in 1941. Yet the same officials regarded preference as a form of economic aggression, for it excluded certain countries from the benefits of equal access to raw materials, markets, and investment. In time, the aggrieved parties might seek to win by force what they had been denied by peaceful trade. Thus, Hull branded the 1932 Ottawa Agreements (that discriminated against dollar goods) as "the greatest injury, in a commercial way, that has been inflicted on this country since I have been in public life." The bilateralism practiced by Germany in Eastern Europe and Japan in East Asia during the thirties confirmed American suspicions that commercial discrimination would divide the world into competing, even warring blocs. (It apparently did not occur to American officials that U.S. discrimination against Japanese goods might have influenced Tokyo's decision to carve out a Co-Prosperity Sphere in the Far East.) Hull and Hawkins denounced the British Commonwealth preference system precisely because it seemed to foreshadow "trade warfare" between the United States and Britain.[4]

While the State Department largely handled commercial matters, the Treasury Department under Henry Morgenthau, Jr., took over financial planning, with a similar emphasis on economic security. Under Harry Dexter White's skillful direction, the Treasury began working on an international financial and monetary conference in late 1941. According to the White plan, which was released to the public in April 1943, each member nation would subscribe a small fraction of its currency to an international monetary fund (IMF) and a world bank (International Bank for Reconstruction and Development, or IBRD), which together would regulate currencies and distribute loans to needy countries. While the system entailed some loss of national sovereignty, it also promised to curtail the economic anarchy of the thirties.

The United States' economic supremacy would allow it virtual veto power in both organizations, but Morgenthau and White designed major roles in the system for Great Britain and the Soviet Union. Despite the minor part of the USSR in world trade, the Americans and the British wished to avoid the disastrous mistake made at Versailles of excluding a major power. In addition, the Treasury Department proposed a postwar reconstruction loan of $5 billion to $10 billion to the Russians as an incentive for them to participate in the system that many regarded as the precursor to the UN.[5]

The concept of "economic security"—the idea that American interests would be best served by an open and integrated economic system, as opposed to a large peacetime military establishment—was firmly established during the wartime period. Treasury planners sought to create a new monetary system that would benefit large and small, capitalist and socialist countries alike, for as Harry White put it, "prosperous neighbors are the best neighbors." Similarly, a State Department memo in February 1944 outlining postwar U.S. commercial policies stressed the link between expanded world trade and American prosperity and security. Without international agreement on an open economic order, the postwar period would "witness a revival, in more intense form, of the international economic warfare which characterized the twenties and thirties." The memo concluded by reiterating the familiar dictum correlating economic nationalism with war:

> The development of sound international economic relations is closely related to the problem of security. The establishment of a system of international trade which would make it possible for each country to have greater access to world markets and resources would reduce incentives to military aggression and provide a firm basis for political cooperation. Conversely, if such a system is not established, the international frictions which would result in the economic field would be certain to undermine any international security organization which might be created. Past experience makes it clear that close and enduring cooperation in the political field must rest on a sound foundation of cooperation in economic matters.[6]

Bretton Woods

Bretton Woods was specifically designed to provide the economic basis for international cooperation. On July 1, 1944, delegates from forty-four nations assembled at the opening of the UN Monetary and

Financial Conference at Bretton Woods, New Hampshire, the first such meeting since the abortive London Conference of 1933. Mindful of the need for bipartisan support, the Roosevelt administration appointed a delegation that included both Democratic and Republican Congressmen, an economics professor, and a banker, as well as State and Treasury officials.

In a welcoming message that was read to the assembled delegates, Roosevelt urged multilateral cooperation because "economic diseases are highly communicable." Echoing the Atlantic Charter, Morgenthau hailed the conference as "part of a broader program of agreed action to bring about the expansion of productivity, employment, and trade," and reminded the representatives that "economic aggression can have no other offspring than war." Creating a dynamic world economy, Morgenthau added, "is the indispensable cornerstone of freedom and security." If anything, Richard N. Gardner notes, American spokesmen exaggerated the economic roots of war. The aphorism of the day, "If goods can't cross borders, soldiers will," epitomized the simplistic, Hullian view that free trade and stable currencies almost alone could guarantee world peace.[7]

Few other governments shared the American conviction that liberal economic institutions held the key to world peace. For various reasons, the British, the Russians, and conservative American interest groups wanted to modify or abolish the Morgenthau-White plan. The British resented their displacement as the world's financial center, feared external interference with their domestic programs, and sought to retain the advantages of their special trading relationship with the Commonwealth. In addition to mere imperial pride, the British clung to their fading empire because they expected their trading partners to help them overcome the severe balance-of-payments problems anticipated in the postwar period.

To help alleviate their anxiety, the final version of the IMF agreement contained a "scarce currency" clause that, during the first few years after ratification, allowed a country with chronic payments difficulties (e.g., the United Kingdom) either to restrict its payments to a surplus country (e.g., the United States) or to devalue its currency. After that initial period, the American-controlled IMF could limit members' currency adjustments. When the British also tied ratification of the accord to a postwar loan from the United States, the American representatives quietly agreed. The British ultimately assented to the American proposals because they would depend heavily upon the United States for postwar reconstruction. Moreover, London had built up a fund of trust with Washington that it did not want to dissipate in disputes over financial issues.[8]

Since their country had never engaged in a significant volume of foreign trade, the Soviet representatives at the conference were bemused as the British and the Americans battled over various technicalities. The Soviet Union sought larger political objectives, such as recognition of its great power status, maximum influence in the IMF and IBRD at the smallest possible price, and assurance that the Bretton Woods system would not interfere with its internal policies. Morgenthau and White showed considerable sensitivity to Soviet feelings, in part because they anticipated heavy postwar exchange of American machinery for Russian raw materials, but mostly because the Roosevelt administration desired full Soviet cooperation both in war and in peace. White had insisted all along that "the Fund needs Russia."[9]

Consequently, the Soviets won the third largest subscription (contribution and voting power) in the IMF. In recognition of Russia's war losses, the Americans acceded to Moscow's demand for a 50 percent increase in its subscription to the Fund (from $800 million to $1,200 million). And when the Russian delegates temporarily refused to contribute an equivalent amount to the World Bank, Morgenthau arranged for the United States and other countries to compensate by increasing their shares. "The quota for the U.S.S.R. which was finally agreed upon," Raymond F. Mikesell, a participant, recalls, "bore little or no relation to its importance in world trade and was set almost entirely in recognition of its political and potential economic importance." The Russians finally increased their donation to the Bank on the last day of the conference, July 22, 1944. In his farewell address, Morgenthau praised the Soviet move and claimed that the conference marked the death of economic nationalism.[10]

The conference itself constituted only the first stage in the Bretton Woods Agreements, for the member states had to ratify the accords before they took effect. In the United States, a broad coalition of Congressmen, bankers, and businessmen fought Bretton Woods from the start. Conservative Congressmen suspected a liberal plot to create an international New Deal. The main foe of Bretton Woods, Republican Senator Robert A. Taft of Ohio, charged that the plan would usurp Congressional control over foreign lending, subsidize investment bankers, throw away the taxpayers' money, and endanger the domestic economy by underwriting unsound foreign loans. Instead of pouring dollars

down a "rathole," as Taft and fellow Republicans put it, the United
States should stick with bilateral aid mechanisms like the Export-
Import Bank (Eximbank).[11]

Similarly, the U.S. Chamber of Commerce and the Wall Street community, notably the American Bankers Association, feared tying the
American economy to volatile foreign ones. These groups suggested
that the United States should seek bilateral cooperation with the British
on postwar trade and currency stabilization before participating in
risky ventures like Bretton Woods. New York bankers meeting with
State Department officials in August 1944 urged exclusive reliance
upon sterling and the dollar, rather than the IMF, to stabilize monetary
markets. This "key-currency" proposal favored by conservative financial interests constituted the *status quo* of world finance.[12]

It bears asking at this point why the Roosevelt administration—not
known for boldness in international economic affairs—was willing to
gamble on the Bretton Woods institutions when conventional wisdom
dictated otherwise. Economic self-interest was part of the answer.
Spokesmen for Bretton Woods emphasized that the stabilization of financial and monetary markets increased demand for American exports,
created jobs at home, and safeguarded foreign investment. Massive
reconstruction was necessary to avert a cycle of revolutions world-wide,
they added, and without Bretton Woods, American taxpayers might be
saddled with a huge foreign aid bill after the war. "We must export
goods if we are to provide jobs for all of our workers," James F. Byrnes,
Director of the Office of Demobilization and Reconversion, explained
to Congress in January 1945, "but we cannot export goods unless others
have the dollars required to pay."[13]

More importantly, American officials believed that economic nationalism bred aggression. As Morgenthau explained in *Foreign Affairs*,
American isolationism would force needy countries back to "the old
game of power politics," and "power politics would be as disastrous to
prosperity as to peace." Bretton Woods, he added, provided a foundation for cooperation between capitalist and socialist countries. Morgenthau opened his testimony before the House Committee on Banking
and Currency in March 1945 by arguing that Bretton Woods represented a simple choice, "stability and order instead of insecurity and
chaos."[14]

Governmental officials succeeded in portraying opponents of Bretton
Woods as short-sighted isolationists, yet the administration clearly
overestimated the benefits of U.S. participation in the system. For one
thing, the successful operation of the IMF and the Bank required world

equilibrium (a rough balancing of international payments), a condition that was clearly lacking at the end of the war. Moreover, Congress was misled into believing that no major foreign aid programs would be necessary after Bretton Woods.[15]

What ultimately assured passage of Bretton Woods were the Allied victory in Europe, a number of tactical concessions by the administration to appease Congress, and the death of FDR. As Allied armies thrust into Germany from east and west during the winter of 1945, internationalist sentiment attained an irresistible momentum. The administration also made Bretton Woods more palatable to conservatives by announcing that the Congress need not vote appropriations because a windfall surplus in the Treasury would cover the American subscription to the Bank and the Fund.

In a further concession to critics, the Bretton Woods Act established a National Advisory Council on International Monetary and Financial Affairs (NAC) to oversee IMF, Bank, and Eximbank operations. This marked a major departure from the original conception of an impartial, internationally run Bank and Fund, for the creation of the NAC ensured that the United States would exercise *de facto* control over these institutions for many years to come. Roosevelt's sudden death in April temporarily quieted the more vociferous critics of his multilateralist programs, and by July 1945, the House and the Senate had passed Bretton Woods by comfortable margins.[16]

The Problem of Soviet Nonparticipation

While most other participants ratified the Bretton Woods accords by the deadline of December 31, 1945, the Soviet Union did not. Moscow's nonparticipation confused American policymakers because they expected that the Soviets would use the Fund and Bank to gain loans from, and trade with, the West. Although some officials thought the Russian absence would facilitate the workings of Bretton Woods, they regretted the blow to international understanding. Contemporary explanations stressed Soviet distrust of capitalist financial institutions and anger over the American delay in granting them a $6 billion reconstruction loan, but no one suggested the total breakdown in Soviet-American relations that one usually associates with the Cold War.[17]

Some historians have argued that the Soviets had reason to fear that Bretton Woods would interfere with their economic system. Lloyd Gardner, for instance, maintains that the IMF would have intervened "quite extensively" in Soviet policies, perhaps even retarding East European industrialization in order to retain export markets there for the West. Thomas Paterson describes Bretton Woods as part of a concerted American campaign, culminating in the Marshall Plan and German rehabilitation, to exert hegemony over Western Europe and the Middle East. Similarly, Gabriel Kolko believes that the United States sought control over the Bretton Woods institutions in order to promote American free enterprise and to defeat European socialism.[18]

Yet none of these scholars explains why the Soviets accepted the Bretton Woods agreements in July 1944, only to reject them in December 1945. After all, White and Morgenthau had intentionally built into the system specific provisions for state-trading and socialist economies, as well as disproportionate voting power for the Soviet Union. Nor did the Americans attempt to ensnare the Soviets and East Europeans into raw material production for the West, for the reconstruction aid that White, Morgenthau, and U.S. Ambassador to Moscow W. Averell Harriman recommended for the Soviet Union would have consisted largely of heavy capital equipment for industrialization.[19]

The best explanation for the Soviet repudiation of Bretton Woods is the sharp confrontation that had erupted between the Soviet Union and the United States in Eastern Europe during 1945. "Moscow's refusal to participate in the Bretton Woods monetary system or to relax trade barriers in the areas under its control," John Gaddis concludes, "was an effect rather than a cause of the Cold War."[20] Postwar American foreign economic policy was not driven by a strong anti-Soviet animus. Truman, in fact, inherited political and military policies from Roosevelt that inhibited a vigorous response to the perceived Soviet aggression.

Truman and his Advisers

Franklin D. Roosevelt's death on April 12, 1945, stunned the nation, but probably no one more than the new President, Harry S. Truman. After a decade in the Senate and eighty-three days as Vice-President, Truman could claim almost no expertise in foreign affairs. Roosevelt had excluded him not only from discussions on the atomic bomb, but also from virtually all executive conferences on foreign policy. "Thus, at a time of some of the greatest diplomatic crises in history," Robert J. Donovan observes, "Truman's knowledge of events derived mostly

from what he read in the newspapers and heard around Capitol Hill."
"The President said this morning . . . that he sat up late last night
reading the Yalta agreements again," Eben A. Ayers, the White House
assistant press secretary, recorded in his diary during late May 1945.
"He said every time he went over them he found new meanings in
them."[21]

Cabinet members, White House aides, and Congressional leaders at
first doubted Truman's ability to handle the job. Secretary of War
Henry L. Stimson commented in his diary on April 12 that "it was very
clear that he knew very little of the task into which he was stepping."
Truman's White House staff, which never exceeded thirteen, consisted
mostly of mediocre individuals who did not always serve the President
well. Yet Truman's vigor, receptivity, and willingness to make clear-cut
decisions soon impressed officials accustomed to Roosevelt's ambiguity
and single-handed control of foreign policy.[22]

Truman's ignorance of foreign affairs forced him to rely heavily upon
his advisers to interpret Roosevelt's policies. Initially, Truman's most
influential foreign policy advisers were Admiral William D. Leahy,
who remained as Chief of Staff to the Commander-in-Chief after Roosevelt's death, Averell Harriman, who quickly established a rapport with
Truman while visiting Washington in April 1945, and Secretary of the
Navy James V. Forrestal, a staunch anti-Communist and a superb administrator with the hard-nosed, forthright manner that Truman ad-
mired in men.

Leahy familiarized Truman with the most recent, unpleasant mes-
sages between Roosevelt and Stalin and recommended a tougher stand
against Russian misconduct in Eastern Europe, notably in Poland.
Harriman had foresaken his earlier optimism regarding relations with
Moscow and counseled a strictly *quid pro quo* approach to negotiations
with the Russians, whose presence in Europe he compared with a bar-
barian invasion. Having returned to Washington just before the visit of
Soviet Foreign Minister V. M. Molotov, Harriman advised the President to give Molotov a thorough dressing-down in their meeting of
April 23. While Stimson argued that Poland, the key issue of the day,
was a poor case by which to test Soviet behavior, Forrestal agreed with
Harriman that it was better to confront the Russians sooner than later
in Eastern Europe.[23]

Truman concurred with the hard-liners. In their April 23 meeting,
the President lashed out at Molotov for his government's alleged failure
to honor its agreements at Yalta concerning the self-determination and

independence of the Polish regime. Contemporary liberal critics and revisionist historians alike have claimed to detect a distinct shift in U.S. policy toward a tougher stance against Moscow following this episode. Truman's brusque, profane style of expression, these critics add, surely jarred Molotov, who was used to Roosevelt's affable, easygoing manner.

Yet Truman's stern lecture to Molotov did not signify a reversal of his predecessor's conciliatory relations with the Soviet Union. Rather, it served as a signal to Moscow that Washington felt events in Poland were now coming to a head and that the Soviets should make some gestures to appease Western opinion, if not implement substantive changes in the Soviet-backed Polish government.[24] On this and other major issues, Truman followed the outlines of Roosevelt's policies at least up to the surrender of Japan.

It was understandable that Truman suffered confusion over relations with the Soviet Union during his first months in office. While Roosevelt had resisted the advice of Harriman, Leahy, Churchill, and the hard-liners in the State Department, his last communications with Stalin and Churchill indicated a growing resolve to contain Soviet power and influence in Europe. Truman's seeming decisiveness in these matters disguised his uncertainty. "It was both his strength and his weakness that he had a simple view of right and wrong," Robert Donovan comments.[25]

Demobilization

Meanwhile, the unexpectedly rapid collapse of Germany in May and Japan in August 1945 caught the administration unprepared for a series of pressing foreign and domestic decisions.[26] The administration's preoccupation with domestic reconversion and the war against Japan, as well as Truman's desire to await completion of the American atomic program before informing Stalin of it, led the President to postpone the meeting of the Big Three at Potsdam until late July 1945.

Several domestic factors constrained the Truman administration's freedom of action in foreign policy. A lingering isolationism among Congress and the public, manifested in sentiment for rapid demobilization and against large-scale foreign aid and defense programs, limited the administration's ability to meet worldwide American responsibilities. The economic dislocation and high inflation attendant upon the end of the war, coupled with the President's own fiscal conservatism, discouraged experimentation at home or abroad. By the same token, the Republican Party, after so many years out of power, hardly welcomed major foreign policy initiatives by the unelected President.

The Second World War, to be sure, had destroyed the traditional bases of support for isolationism. The clear-cut nature of the Axis threat united the nation in a war of survival. Technological developments, especially long-range bombers and the atomic bomb, meant that the Atlantic and Pacific Oceans could no longer serve as moats that would protect the country from devastating attack by a determined enemy. The war also underscored the growing American dependence upon foreign sources of critical raw materials. Thus, the war experience undermined both the geographical and economic postulates of the old isolationism.[27] During the war Roosevelt had won the support of Republican leaders, notably Senator Arthur H. Vandenberg of Michigan, for a postwar collective security organization.

Still, isolationism was only transformed, not dead. Roosevelt had not prepared the American public for the postwar rift with the Soviet Union, quite possibly because he himself did not foresee it. Given the priority of the war effort, Roosevelt both understated the differences between Soviet and American postwar goals and failed to educate the public on his efforts to reach a compromise, as reflected in the implicit spheres-of-influence provisions of Yalta, that would accommodate the legitimate security aims of the major powers. The convening of the San Francisco UN Conference amidst the collapse of the Axis engendered a euphoria that did not lend itself to a sober appreciation of America's continuing responsibilities overseas. In time, a profound disillusionment, a revulsion for foreign affairs, and an exaggerated sense of betrayal by America's erstwhile ally, the Soviet Union, would overtake U.S. public opinion.[28]

The pell-mell demobilization of American armed forces after the war demonstrated the underlying strength of neo-isolationism. Forrestal and Secretary of War Robert P. Patterson, who had replaced Stimson in September, warned Truman in October 1945 that demobilization jeopardized the American strategic position in the world. Truman agreed, but felt that he could do nothing to stop it. In January 1946, Forrestal noted in his diary, the "Under Secretary [Dean Acheson] said [demobilization] was a matter of great embarrassment and concern to his own Department in their conduct of our foreign affairs."[29]

The Truman White House could not contain the overpowering public and bipartisan Congressional outcry—accompanied by riots at overseas military bases in January 1946—for the early return home of American soldiers. Only a serious foreign crisis could have reversed this trend, and, for the time being, the administration did not publicize its misgivings about Soviet behavior. American armed forces shrank from about twelve million in June 1945 to one-and-a-half million in June 1947 (see appendix, graph 1). Across-the-board cuts of specialists and experienced members of the armed forces eroded the military effectiveness of units even more than these figures would suggest.[30]

Meanwhile, legislation for Universal Military Training (UMT), which Truman, Forrestal, and Army Chief of Staff George C. Marshall promoted as the only satisfactory alternative to large standing forces, went nowhere on the Hill. The War Department, reflecting Army interests, continued to recommend UMT, rather than forces-in-being, as the mainstay of American defense in the atomic era on the grounds of fiscal prudence and military efficacy. Yet Congressmen and interest groups often voiced the suspicion that UMT was somehow un-American. In April 1946, Congress unenthusiastically extended the draft through March 1947, but forced the services to resort to voluntary recruitment between April 1947 and August 1948. The United States continued to maintain the largest navy and air force in the world and to retain a monopoly on the atomic bomb. But after one takes into account American commitments in occupied territories, the United States lacked the ground forces required to intervene in anything greater than a minor conflict, such as that over Venezia Giulia. Another result of demobilization and the failure of UMT was to highlight the importance of atomic weapons in defense planning.[31]

By both choice and necessity, the Truman administration relied more on economic than military power to achieve its foreign policy aims. Strategic planning reflected this emphasis. The Joint Chiefs did not approve a statement of general military strategy until mid-1947, nor a war plan until 1948, for they accepted the State Department's assessment that the main danger facing the United States was political rather than military. Similarly, the Army air staff did not fully accept the deterrent concept of powerful air forces in place and on the alert until 1947.[32]

Although the pace and scale of demobilization dismayed the President and his advisers, almost everyone agreed that major cuts in defense spending were in order. Administration officials perceived no immediate threat to U.S. security and feared that the continuation of wartime expenditures and deficits, or anything approaching them, would bankrupt the country. While the war had demonstrated the power of expansionary fiscal policies to spur enormous growth and high employment, Keynesian economics—in the sense of major compensatory spending to stimulate the economy—had made little headway among either the general public or Truman's Cabinet, which assigned priority to balancing the budget. Hence, the annual rate of military spending plunged from $90.9 billion in January 1945 to $10.3 billion during the second quarter of 1947 (see appendix, graph 3).[33] The cessation of hostilities would have prompted defense cutbacks in any case, but the fiscally conservative mood of the country, which Truman and his advisers shared, caused what in retrospect appears a precipitous dismantling of the American military machine.

No pervasive, national security "ideology" characterized U.S. military thinking in the early postwar period.[34] The disorganization, misconceptions, and infighting that had disrupted the military services during the war continued well into the postwar period. This does not mean that the military services did not engage in contingency planning for wars of the future, against Russia among other hypothetical enemies. Military planning, however, was not the same thing as actual defense programs, for the Truman administration did not believe that the Soviet Union posed a direct *military* threat to the United States at the end of the war. Instead, the containment doctrine that evolved from early confrontation with the Soviet Union would prescribe primary reliance upon the greatest American asset of all, its unrivalled economic power.

Reconversion, Inflation, and Party Politics

Before the United States could engage in ambitious economic programs abroad, it had to get its own house in order. Initially, economic planners feared that demobilization and reduced governmental spending would trigger massive unemployment reminiscent of the Great Depression. "Unless we develop domestic and foreign markets for something approximating 90 billion dollars' worth of goods and services on top of the present 100-billion-dollar rate of civilian output," an official in the Office of War Mobilization and Reconversion warned in late 1944, "unemployment will be unavoidable." Owing to the postwar aversion to governmental intervention in the economy, most officials and business leaders hoped that the expansion of American exports would help ease reconversion and maintain a high rate of economic growth.[35]

A sharp rise in unemployment in the summer and fall of 1945 heightened fears of a postwar depression and moved the administration to propose tax cuts to stimulate the economy. But government economists gradually realized that employment would rebound as the economy shifted from defense to consumer production. Inflation, fueled by wartime federal spending, public debt, enormous individual savings and pent-up demand for consumer goods, now posed the main danger to the economy.

Truman at first gave only lukewarm support to the anti-inflationary efforts of the Office of Price Administration (OPA), and Congress, which blamed governmental regulation for housing, meat, and other shortages, stripped OPA of its powers and cut taxes deeper than Truman had requested. As a result, double-digit inflation, coupled with countless strikes as workers sought to compensate for wages foregone during the war, plagued Truman's first years as President. Not until January 1946 did the President himself recognize that inflation, rather than unemployment, was his greatest domestic problem.[36]

The economy would influence the administration's foreign policy in subtle, but important, ways. Postwar inflation reinforced the widespread desire to cut governmental spending and programs. Spiraling prices also undercut the need for governmental promotion of exports in order to sustain the economy, for postwar inflation resulted from excess domestic and foreign demand for American goods at a time of high U.S. employment and production. Thus, excess domestic production did not, as some scholars claim, drive the United States into a desperate postwar search for overseas markets.

Congressional and party politics also constrained Truman's freedom of action. Republican strength in the Congress necessitated frequent and close consultation with Congressional leaders by the White House; the "imperial presidency" was not a product of the Truman era. The President also at first lacked the enthusiastic support of his own party. Truman's increasingly tough stance with the Soviet Union alienated liberal Democrats accustomed to the outwardly harmonious relations with that country while Roosevelt was President. Until early 1948, Alonzo L. Hamby notes, the feeling of most liberals was that Roosevelt could have preserved Allied unity and that Truman had broken with his predecessor's foreign policy.[37]

Domestic conditions limited the options available to the Truman administration in foreign policy. Although most Americans shunned isolationism, few welcomed the prospect of extensive intervention overseas. Given a choice, most of the public preferred foreign aid programs to a permanent U.S. military presence overseas, but economic problems at home did not encourage any bold ventures abroad. Besides, according to the administration's own experts, temporary U.S. relief programs in conjunction with the Bretton Woods institutions would be sufficient to meet the relief needs of most wartorn countries. Truman had every reason to believe that only limited aid programs were necessary—and politically feasible—in the early postwar period.

Early Postwar Relief Programs

The prerequisite for world peace, American policymakers believed, was the reconstruction of a stable, prosperous, and democratic Europe. Yet since wartime planners had failed to anticipate either the extent of European devastation or the obstacles to recovery, the relief programs of the 1945–46 period proved to be expensive failures.

Soon after the Bretton Woods conference had adjourned, American planners realized that European reconstruction and the revival of world trade would require more than structural reforms to reduce trade barriers and regulate currencies, especially since the Bank and Fund would take a year or more to begin operations. In August 1944, State Department officials determined that Europe needed additional Eximbank loans, increased private investment, and postwar extension of Lend-Lease, especially to the Soviet Union. Similarly, Eugene V. Rostow, then a professor at the Yale University Law School but formerly a State Department adviser on Lend-Lease, warned in October 1944 that if the United States did not *immediately* expand world credit, the ensuing economic warfare would "split the capitalist part of the world down the middle."[38]

Even then, the proposed remedies fell far short of European needs. In effect, governmental planners mistakenly believed that "priming the pump" of foreign economies would quickly restore normal private activity. Their optimism was unjustified for two reasons. First, stimulative fiscal measures, in this case foreign aid, could not by themselves restore the public confidence and private investment necessary to spur long-term recovery. Even if they had been operative in this period, the Bretton Woods institutions and multilateral trade agreements would have only provided the external preconditions for recovery.

Second, while American planners recognized the importance of private investment to European recovery, they had not created the mechanisms for a capital flow from the United States, the only potential source of major funding, to Europe. Most American investors were reluctant to sink capital in overseas ventures since the war had wiped out many of their foreign properties. The prospects for profitable investment in wartorn Europe looked particularly bleak. Also, since much of the investment of the twenties had been high-risk "hot capital" that later caused serious monetary problems, American planners had designed the Bretton Woods system to inhibit overseas capital movements while stimulating trade in goods and services. "The close collaboration between central bankers and governments that has characterized the postwar period," Richard Gardner states, "was neither foreseen nor even encouraged by wartime planners."[39]

Not surprisingly, the piecemeal European relief programs of the early Truman administration followed no coherent strategy. American officials remained strongly committed to the multilateralist concepts embodied in Bretton Woods, but these principles were not easily translated into practice.

UNRRA and the Politics of Relief

The story of the UN Relief and Rehabilitation Agency (UNRRA) illustrates the difficulty of implementing policy on the basis of ill-defined principles. Founded in 1943 by forty-four nations, UNRRA distributed about $4 billion in basic necessities to war victims over the next four years. Since the United States provided three-fourths of its funding, Americans headed and controlled its central organization, but not the local distribution of aid.[40]

The UNRRA programs in Soviet-occupied Eastern Europe, which received half of the aid, immediately became a source of controversy. The U.S. government and the American press charged that local regimes, at Soviet instigation, were using UNRRA for political purposes. Throughout 1945, American diplomats reported misuse of UNRRA supplies by the Soviet-backed (Lublin) Polish government to the disadvantage of supporters of the Western-backed (London) government-in-exile, as well as the diversion of supplies to the Red Army. Similarly, Ambassador to Czechoslovakia Laurence A. Steinhardt charged the

Soviets in the fall of 1945 with misleading the Czechoslovak public about the source of UNRRA supplies, using UNRRA to secure local political advantage, and siphoning off aid for the Red Army. The United States also resisted attempts by the Yugoslav government to control distribution of UNRRA supplies because American diplomats claimed that Tito's army consumed much of the aid.[41]

Not all reports were so critical. In July 1945, for example, Harriman told Washington that current information was inadequate to make a firm judgment on the alleged Soviet abuses of UNRRA in Poland and Czechoslovakia. American observers in Yugoslavia during August reported no evidence of political discrimination despite some inequities in distribution due to transportation problems. Though some irregularities occurred, Thomas Paterson concludes, most charges against UNRRA operations in Eastern Europe were spurious, and the program fairly and efficiently assisted innumerable destitute Europeans.[42]

The administration was at first reluctant to make a vigorous public defense of UNRRA, in part because of the program's unpopularity. The State Department ultimately supported $250 million in UNRRA aid to the Soviet Union in August 1945 after the Soviets accepted greater UNRRA control and supervision of operations in their sphere. Yet Congress repeatedly attached burdensome restrictions to UNRRA appropriations and threatened to end American participation in the program altogether.

Implementing the program proved no easier than steering the legislation through Congress. In one instance, Secretary of State James F. Byrnes had to order the Bureau of the Budget to expedite funding of UNRRA when the BOB appeared to be balking. Wary of public opposition to controls, Truman did not reinstitute food rationing in 1946 when American grain shipments to UNRRA recipients fell short, and instead opted for a largely unsuccessful voluntary program for food conservation. Still, American food deliveries provided the margin of survival for many Europeans.[43]

In August 1946, the administration moved to terminate UNRRA by the end of the year, ostensibly because European food shortages had eased. But disappointment over the minimal political leverage that UNRRA had afforded the United States in Eastern Europe undoubtedly played a role as well.[44] In American eyes, an experiment in international cooperation had failed, and henceforth, the United States favored bilateral foreign aid programs that it could control.

Lend-Lease

The cancellation of Lend-Lease did far more than UNRRA to exacerbate Soviet-American tension. Altogether, the United States furnished about $11 billion in Lend-Lease to support the Soviet war effort. To facilitate the flow of aid, President Roosevelt ordered Lend-Lease authorities to waive standard procedures in examining Soviet aid requests. Roosevelt also rejected suggestions by Harriman and others late in the war that the United States demand Soviet concessions for Lend-Lease. Like the British, the Soviets received military material under Lend-Lease without formal obligation for repayment. The Soviets, however, neither expressed appreciation for this special treatment nor acknowledged American requests for military information.[45]

Unconditional Lend-Lease was already on the way out when the Soviets tried to gain postwar reconstruction aid through Lend-Lease. Congress had expressly prohibited the use of Land-Lease for this purpose. When negotiations over a postwar Russian loan stalled, the Roosevelt administration in May 1944 devised an amendment under section 3(c) of the Lend-Lease agreement by which the Soviets could *buy* non-military items in the Lend-Lease pipeline for postwar rehabilitation. Moscow, hoping for a reconstruction loan, ignored the proposal, but Molotov's request in January 1945 for a $6 billion credit on the same generous terms as Lend-Lease met a frosty welcome. Leo T. Crowley, head of the Foreign Economic Administration, made the case for a strict segregation of Lend-Lease—a war supply program—from postwar reconstruction, especially since the Soviets had yet to accept the 3(c) proposal. After further wrangling with the Soviets over the terms of a loan, Harriman and Secretary of State Edward R. Stettinius, Jr., agreed that the United States should withdraw the 3(c) proposal and cut back industrial shipments under Lend-Lease to the Soviet Union.[46]

Roosevelt subsequently approved Crowley's recommendation to eliminate most postwar reconstruction aid under Lend-Lease, with certain exceptions, and the State Department informed the Soviets to this effect in March 1945. While the withdrawal of section 3(c) did not signify a reversal of U.S. policy toward Russia, it did serve notice to Lend-Lease administrators that "legal limitations would require substantial adjustments in all programs when hostilities in Europe ceased."[47]

Even had Roosevelt lived, Congress probably would have further restricted Lend-Lease to Russia. Just two days before Roosevelt's death, Vice-President Truman cast the deciding vote that broke a Senate deadlock over the very issue of whether recipients could use Lend-Lease for postwar reconstruction. (Without Truman's intervention, *all* nonmilitary Lend-Lease shipments to Russia would have ceased.) A spirit of ecomony then pervaded Washington, and Congress subjected foreign aid requests to greater scrutiny as the war against Japan accelerated. Due to its privileged position during the war, the Soviet Union received special attention. While the United States had curtailed Lend-Lease to Great Britain beginning in the summer of 1944, Lend-Lease shipments to Russia peaked in May 1945. Cutbacks in Lend-Lease during the spring of 1945 were bound to have a greater impact upon the Soviets than the British even if the intent were not to discriminate against one or the other.[48]

Nonetheless, Truman seriously blundered when he signed Crowley's memo of May 11, 1945, which caused an immediate cut-off of all Lend-Lease aid, including shipments in progress, for Soviet and other allied operations in Europe. The President apparently did not fully realize the diplomatic implications of so sudden and drastic a decision. The Soviets at first feigned "complete surprise," but accepted the American decision. Stalin did not object so much to the fact of Lend-Lease termination as to the "brutal" manner in which it was done. In June, Soviet Foreign Trade Commissar A. A. Mikoyan complained to Harriman that the abrupt end of Lend-Lease seemed to mark a shift from the cooperative spirit of Yalta. Harriman countered that the Soviets had had a year to act upon the 3(c) offer, and that Congress had mandated termination beginning on VE day.[49]

Lend-Lease was an irritant in Soviet-American relations rather than a decisive precipitant of the Cold War. American representatives had repeatedly emphasized that Lend-Lease was strictly a military aid program that would cease upon the end of hostilities. Besides, the Soviets eventually received large Lend-Lease supplies to fulfill their war needs in the Far East, as well as a "pipeline agreement" for postwar Lend-Lease purchases. If anything, the Soviets may have welcomed the American *faux pas* in May 1945, for it gave them an opportunity to charge the new administration with reversing Roosevelt's policies and to demand more liberal terms for postwar aid. As early as the fall of 1945, some Soviet officials were hinting that compensation even for industrial items furnished under Lend-Lease was unlikely since their country had already paid for Lend-Lease in blood.[50] The lack of a Lend-Lease settlement has plagued Soviet-American economic relations to this day.

The Eximbank, European Recovery, and Aid to Russia

Whereas UNRRA and Lend-Lease did not easily lend themselves to political uses, the Export-Import Bank did. Congress had established the Eximbank in 1934 in order to promote U.S. exports, but the "coming of World War II saw a shift in Eximbank's policies in the direction of U.S. foreign policy and the strategic interests of the U.S. Government." In the postwar period, Herbert Feis wrote in the July 1945 issue of *Foreign Affairs*, the United States would refuse to extend credit to those nations "which may seem either to threaten our own safety, or to wish to dominate others, or to be wedded to oppression."[51]

Following the defeat of the Third Reich, American officials realized that Europe would collapse without some financial mechanism to replace Lend-Lease. Officials of the Foreign Economic Administration (FEA) observed in May 1945 that the United States was furnishing altogether about $7 billion a year in nonmilitary Lend-Lease and that postwar foreign reconstruction needs would equal or exceed that figure. Without such aid, they predicted "grave political instability in Europe, . . . a marked decline in employment and production in the United States, . . . and the seeds of another world war." Given the inadequacy of postwar Lend-Lease and UNRRA, the Bretton Woods institutions, private investment, and foreign reserves, the FEA officials recommended a multi-billion dollar increase in Eximbank lending authority.[52]

The White House in July 1945 asked Congress to increase Eximbank assets from $700 million to $3.5 billion. Significantly, the State Department at that time favored a $1 billion credit to the Soviet Union for the year beginning July 1945 and another $1–2 billion credit to the Soviets for the following year if Congress authorized additional funds. In approving the White House request, Congress facilitated a Russion loan by repealing the Johnson Act of 1934, which forbade both governmental and private loans to countries that had defaulted on their obligations to the United States.[53]

Several factors led the Eximbank to concentrate most of its resources in Western Europe. American businessmen and economic planners had earlier assumed that Soviet trade was necessary to bolster peacetime American exports, production, and employment. But the postwar surge in West European imports and in domestic U.S. demand eliminated the danger of depression for the near term. As the economic rationale for a Russian loan lost force, political factors, particularly the desire to influence Russian policies in Eastern Europe and to shore up beleagured West European governments, assumed increasing importance.

The State Department's *de facto* domination of the NAC, which coordinated Eximbank, IMF, and Bank operations, accentuated the political orientation of the Eximbank. In a September 1945 memo to FEA head Crowley, who was also Chairman of the Eximbank, Secretary of State Brynes (who had replaced Stettinius in July) stressed "the importance of relating [the Eximbank's] program to the framework of the foreign policy of the United States." Byrnes also requested regular State Department participation in the NAC since it was "essential that financial aid for reconstruction go hand in hand" with commercial policy.[54]

Budgetary pressures helped cause the evolution of the Eximbank into a political weapon. In January 1946, the NAC staff committee estimated that urgent foreign loan needs for 1946 exceeded the Eximbank's lending capacity by $1.5 billion. Setting aside the Russian loan would largely eliminate the need for extra Congressional funding.[55] With its limited resources, the Eximbank would focus its efforts in West European countries whose recovery would do most to revive world trade.

The Politics of Foreign Economic Policy

Wartime planners had sought a stable and peaceful world order structured on American economic principles. Anything less, they had reasoned, would reinstitute the prewar cycle of depression, economic rivalry, and war. The UN, it was hoped, would provide the collective security apparatus necessary to deter aggression. To meet its responsibilities in the UN, its extensive occupation duties, and its other foreign commitments would have required the United States to maintain unprecedentedly large armed forces after the war.

Yet public war weariness, budgetary pressures, and the seeming absence of any serious military threat made the Truman administration drastically scale down American military might. American policymakers confidently believed that the United States could utilize its massive economic power to persuade or compel other countries to adopt the multilateralist principles embodied in Bretton Woods. These principles presumably offered a neutral basis by which countries could peacefully and fairly compete for the world's resources. A politically free, economically open world order would also eliminate the roots of war.

The Soviet erection of a relatively closed sphere of influence in Eastern Europe appeared to challenge American plans. Aside from the repugnance felt toward the repressive political systems that the Soviets sponsored there, American decision makers feared that Soviet economic policies might encourage the formation of closed economic blocs in Western Europe and elsewhere. Yet in the initial postwar period, American leaders failed to challenge Soviet hegemony in Eastern Europe or to mobilize America's economic power behind an effective program for West European recovery.

CHAPTER THREE

COLD WAR IN THE SOVIET SPHERE: AMERICAN POLICIES IN EASTERN EUROPE, THE RUSSIAN LOAN, AND CONTAINMENT DOCTRINE, 1945–1947

THE OPENING SHOTS of the Cold War were fired over Eastern Europe. Underlying the controversy over this region was a fundamental difference between Soviet and American concepts of security. To the Russians, security dictated extraordinary measures to control the political and economic destiny of Eastern Europe, while to the Americans, the nearly closed Soviet sphere seemed to threaten the open and integrated economic order upon which U.S. hopes for peace and prosperity rested.

Historians differ on the roots of U.S. policy toward Eastern Europe. According to the orthodox interpretation, the crux of the problem was the Red Army's imposition of unrepresentative governments in certain East European capitals. Thus, the orthodox historians argue that the Truman administration's policies marked a defensive reaction to Soviet political repression in the East European countries; economic issues played little or no part in the conflict.

In contrast, most revisionist historians portray Stalin as a patriotic Russian statesman who simply sought to achieve traditional czarist security aims in Eastern Europe. According to this view, the unwillingness of the Truman administration to grant the Soviets a sphere of influence in Eastern Europe precipitated the Cold War. Some revisionists, such as Joyce and Gabriel Kolko, further claim that American efforts to establish an Open Door in the region—open to U.S. trade, investment, and political influence—was the main cause of Soviet-American tensions.[1]

Yet American leaders were not categorically opposed to spheres of influence. They realized that the United States was almost powerless to influence events in Eastern Europe as long as Soviet armies remained there to exercise the will of the Kremlin. U.S. interests in the region were in any case too small to justify a diversion of American resources from more important areas, such as Western Europe.

Nor did the United States deny the right of the Soviet Union to safeguard its security interests in Eastern Europe after the war. A traditional sphere of influence—in which Moscow exercised control over the major strategic and foreign policy decisions of its client states, but did not interfere with their internal policies—was acceptable to Washington. A Soviet protectorate that brought to mind memories of the prewar Nazi system was not. As U.S. diplomat Charles E. Bohlen noted in 1947, Washington's wartime agreements with Moscow clearly indicated that "we were not attempting to deny to Russia the perquisites of a great power, namely that she has a certain primary strategic interest in the countries that lie along her borders. It has been the abuse of that right which has caused most of the trouble we have had."[2]

Without question, disputes over political issues, particularly the status of the Polish government, lay at the heart of East-West tensions. But conflict over trade and aid further aggravated relations between Washington and Moscow, and this chapter will focus on the manner in which the confrontation over economic issues helped stimulate the development of a containment doctrine. In brief, American officials feared that a Soviet bloc in Eastern Europe would spawn a multitude of equally closed blocs in Western Europe and elsewhere, replicating the very conditions that had given birth to World War II.

In at least one regard, the Americans shared the blame for the tragedy of Eastern Europe. During and immediately after the war, U.S. policy was marked by vacillation and confusion, as American policymakers vainly sought a postwar accommodation with the Soviet Union that would not compromise the independence of the East European countries. The Roosevelt administration's tactic of deferring political and territorial issues until the end of the war did not help matters. On Poland, Roosevelt attempted an impossible balancing act between the Soviets and the (London) Polish government-in-exile. In the end, he inadvertently alienated the Soviets without gaining a satisfactory settlement for the London Poles. Key issues remained unresolved when FDR died. As Vojtech Mastny puts it, "It was not so much an open clash of interests as their dangerously indefinite and elastic nature that jeopardized the wartime alliance in the long run."[3]

Roosevelt compounded the problem for his successor by concealing the realities of Soviet power and Anglo-American concessions in Eastern Europe from the American public. Officials in the Roosevelt administration believed, rightly or wrongly, that public aversion to power politics constrained them from revealing the agreements reached at the wartime conferences. Yet the American effort to sustain the wartime alliance may have been doomed from the start. As Soviet diplomat Maxim Litvinov told CBS correspondent Richard C. Hottelet in Moscow during June 1946, the "root cause" of East-West confrontation was "the ideological conception prevailing here that conflict between Communist and capitalist worlds is inevitable." When Hottelet asked what would happen if the West were suddenly to grant the Kremlin all of its current foreign policy aims, Litvinov answered, "It would lead to the West's being faced, after a more or less short time, with the next series of demands."[4]

Soviet Goals in Eastern Europe

Much of the debate on the origins of the Cold War really concerns the question of Soviet motivation. Even in the improbable event that the Kremlin were to open its archives to scholars, a consensus on this problem would be unlikely. Nonetheless, most historians agree that postwar Soviet policies in Eastern Europe were the product of reconstruction needs, traditional foreign policy objectives, Stalinist ideology, and internal political imperatives.

Soviet reconstruction needs were immense, for the German invasion had devastated European Russia. By the end of the war, the Soviet Union had suffered 20 million dead and the destruction of 1,710 towns, 70,000 villages, and 5 million homes. "In their retreat," a Soviet scholar wrote in 1946, "the Germans left zones which can simply be described as deserts." In 1945, production in the formerly occupied territories reached only 30 percent of prewar levels. With the cut-off of Lend-Lease, the Soviet Union lacked the foreign exchange to pay for badly needed imports. Although industrial productivity rapidly recovered, a terrible drought in 1946 caused widespread hunger and pushed living standards below even the Russian norm.[5]

In order to help restore its economy, the Soviet Union extracted major concessions from the East European countries. During the war, the Soviets had blocked a British-backed plan for an East European economic federation and instead established a series of bilateral agreements with East European governments-in-exile. Once they had liberated the region from Nazi rule, the Soviets seized reparations from Rumania and Hungary, expropriated sizeable assets in occupied countries as German "war booty," and gained a controlling interest in numerous joint-stock companies.

The Soviet Union also determined the nature and direction of trade in its newly won empire. The East European countries had engaged in minimal trade with Russia during the 1930s, but Soviet commerce with the region soared after the war. While Western countries still traded extensively with Eastern Europe (an average of $1.3 billion annually, 1947–1949), the Kremlin used its political clout to secure highly favorable, bilateral trade agreements that discriminated against the West and exacted a heavy price from the satellites. From the American perspective, the Soviets were apparently replacing the former German economic bloc in Eastern Europe with their own.[6]

An alternative interpretation holds that many of the economic reforms in Eastern Europe were not imposed by the Soviets, but sprang from indigenous sources. As Barbara Ward noted at the time, the nationalization of heavy industry in Central and Eastern Europe had begun in the prewar era, and the decision of postwar governments to accelerate the process enjoyed broad popular support. Immediately after the war, Soviet intervention in the satellite countries was largely opportunistic and uncoordinated, varying with local circumstances. Moscow, according to this view, had no master plan for economic revolution in Eastern Europe.[7]

Revisionist historians further argue that the Soviet quest for clearly defined spheres of influence in Europe, if fulfilled, might have fostered stable and harmonious relations among the great powers. The Kremlin's demand for primary influence in Eastern Europe, they believe, derived from the centuries-long Russian quest to build a buffer zone of allied Pan-Slav states against foreign aggression. At Yalta, Stalin asserted that a strong and friendly Poland was essential to Russian security because enemies had so often used Poland as a corridor for invasion. Since the Western allies had tacitly accepted his position in wartime negotiations, the revisionists contend, the later Anglo-American challenge to Moscow's sphere aroused latent Soviet fears of capitalist encirclement and triggered a further tightening of control over the satellites.[8]

This interpretation does not explain several crucial aspects of Soviet policy. In the first place, Western statesmen viewed the Red Army's advance into Eastern Europe with mixed emotions. While they hailed the defeat of Nazism, officials in Washington and London sought the early withdrawal of Soviet troops from the "liberated" East European countries, for Russian expansionism, whether carried out by a czarist or a Soviet government, threatened the balance of power in Europe.

What is more, the Soviets sought power and influence in Eastern Europe far in excess of their security requirements. "If indeed it be true . . . that the motive force of postwar Soviet policy was a desire for security," Eduard Mark asks, "why did the Soviets act as though security was inseparable from domination?" Soviet expert Charles Bohlen provided a partial answer in October 1945, when he observed that "from all indications the Soviet mind is incapable of making a distinction between influence and domination, or between a friendly government and a puppet government."[9]

The Soviet crackdown in Poland, Rumania, and Bulgaria immediately after the war cannot be explained by the Kremlin's apprehension of an attack from the West. The United States maintained only small garrison forces on the continent after VE Day and did not systematically use the U.S. atomic monopoly to press for Soviet concessions in Eastern Europe or elsewhere. Stalin in any event secretly demobilized the Soviet armed forces from 11,365,000 in 1945 to 2,874,000 in 1948, roughly twice the American total. This gave the Soviets an overwhelming edge in ground forces in Europe, without suggesting that Moscow anticipated imminent aggression from Western countries. Moreover, Soviet research on an atomic bomb was well under way by the Potsdam Conference in July 1945.[10] Neither traditional security concerns nor American "atomic blackmail" can fully account for Soviet policies before the Marshall Plan.

Revisionists generally portray Stalin's foreign policy as cautious and opportunistic. Yet Stalin's treatment of the London Poles was neither flexible nor tolerant. During the war, Stalin summarily rejected their plea for the restoration of territories seized under the Nazi-Soviet Pact of 1939, when Poland, after all, had been the victim of Hitler's (and Stalin's) aggression. The Soviets later imposed a highly unrepresentative government and an unfavorable commercial treaty upon a country that had suffered enormously during the war.

Stalin's argument regarding Poland as an invasion "corridor" also does not hold up well. Russian control of Poland in 1812 and 1914 had not prevented invasions from the West; nor did the Soviet annexation of eastern Poland in 1939 stop Hitler's armies in 1941. Corridors open both ways. After the war, Stalin may have viewed Poland as an entrance to Germany, and Eastern Europe as an opening to the West.[11]

The reconstruction of the Soviet Union and the industrialization of Eastern Europe did not necessarily rule out continued Western trade and investment in the region. Marxist-Leninist doctrine did not dictate autarkic policies. "Soviet trade during the 1920's and 1930's," one expert observes, had been "of a distinctly multilateral character." The Soviets probably excluded Western businessmen from Eastern Europe after 1945 because they interfered with Soviet economic exploitation of the region, not because their presence was truly incompatible with socialist reform.[12]

A fundamental misconception about the U.S. economy also inhibited the Soviets from vigorously pursuing American trade and aid. Kremlin leaders, notably Stalin, assumed that the United States would face a crisis of over-production after the war. Thus, Molotov's request in January 1945 for a $6 billion loan rudely implied that the Soviets were doing the Americans a favor. Although Eugene Varga, the eminent Soviet economist, argued in 1946 that the collapse of capitalism was not imminent, he failed to dissuade the Kremlin and was forced to recant. The Soviets spurned economic ties with the United States because they were "acutely sensitive to economic dependence as a harbinger of political dependence." In addition, the Soviets expected Anglo-American commercial rivalry to precipitate a major war between the capitalist powers, from which socialism would emerge triumphant.[13]

Just as Stalinist ideology came to dictate an autarkic economic program, the nature of the Kremlin's decision-making apparatus helped to foreclose a policy of peaceful coexistence with the West. Stalin's habit of surrounding himself with fawning sychophants, Yugloslav envoy Milovan Djilas noticed, ensured few challenges to the infallibility of his judgment. In an October 1944 interview with Edgar Snow, Soviet diplomat Maxim Litvinov corroborated Djilas' point when he complained that Stalin's main foreign policy advisers—Molotov and his deputies, Andrei Vyshinsky and Vladimir Dekanozov—knew nothing about the West and reinforced Stalin's prejudices. Despite repeated signals from London and Washington, Vojtech Mastny observes, "Stalin himself did not seem to accept readily the disturbing proposition that his subjugation of East-Central Europe would necessarily lead to a clash with the West."[14]

In a later conversation with British correspondent Alexander Werth, Litvinov claimed that Stalin and his advisers knew they had options in Europe, but deliberately chose a provocative policy:

> By the end of the war, [Litvinov] said, Russia had had the choice of two policies: one was to "cash in on the goodwill she had accumulated during the war in Britain and the United States." But *they* (meaning Stalin and Molotov) had, unfortunately, chosen the other policy. Not believing that "goodwill" could constitute the *lasting* basis for any kind of policy, they had decided that "security" was what mattered most of all, and they had therefore grabbed all they could while the going was good—meaning the whole of eastern Europe and parts of central Europe.[15]

Stalinist ideology perhaps did not allow for the possibility of lasting cooperation with the West. As Stalin explained to Tito and Djilas in April 1945, "This war is not as in the past: whoever occupies a territory also imposes on it his social system. Everyone imposes his own system as far as his army can reach. It cannot be otherwise." Stalin's minimum aim in Europe was probably a security zone in the eastern half of the continent; his maximum aim, a demilitarized Germany and a politically fractured Western Europe, susceptible to Moscow's pressure. As Mastny argues, the readiness of Roosevelt and Churchill to accede to Soviet demands in Eastern Europe only fed Stalin's appetite for more. David Holloway adds:

> The Soviet leaders differed among themselves in their assessment of how the capitalist world would develop, but they all seem to have shared the belief that the conflict between capitalism and socialism would sooner or later lead to a new world war. . . . The postwar years, in other words, were viewed by the Soviet leaders as a prewar period, and this reinforced the conclusion that the Soviet Union should once again give priority to increasing its military power.[16]

Internal political developments also shed light on Soviet foreign policy. In one view, the Kremlin moved quickly after the war to keep the Soviet population isolated from Western influences and to reinstate prewar discipline with the object of rebuilding the economy and restoring the authority of the Communist Party. An alternative explanation holds that while Stalin wished to maintain good relations with the West, he adopted provocative policies in order to retain the good graces of the militant wing of the international Communist movement. In either case, Western imperialism served as a convenient pretext for Stalin's reassertion of power within the Soviet Union and for the suppression of national autonomy in Eastern Europe after 1947.[17]

U.S. Interests in Eastern Europe

Soviet policies in Eastern Europe challenged the American program for a free-trading, open world order. U.S. economic interests in the region, however, were minimal. Before the war, American assets in Eastern Europe had amounted to only $560 million, 12 percent of the U.S. investments in Europe and 4 percent of U.S. investments world-wide. Similarly, American exports to the East European countries ($62 million annually, 1936–38) represented only 2.1 percent of total American exports. Postwar trade consisted largely of free UNRRA shipments.[18]

Revisionist historians generally concede that U.S. economic interests in Eastern Europe were minor before the war, but argue that American policymakers and businessmen hoped to develop and exploit that market after the war. For this reason, they argue, the United States aggressively challenged Soviet hegemony in the region. Of particular interest were U.S. petroleum companies. MAORT, a Hungarian subsidiary of Standard Oil of New Jersey (SONJ), alone was responsible for about one-third of all oil production in Europe. Soviet seizure of American-owned oil fields as "German" war booty or reparations, as well as the nationalization of the industry by local governments, enraged U.S. oil company executives, but the State Department could do very little to help.[19] In a July 1946 meeting at the State Department, for instance, a SONJ official complained that Rumanian Communist authorities, in collusion with the Russians, were squeezing his company out of business. He demanded that the government retaliate, adding that "the U.S. was rapidly losing face because of its complete acquiescence to the Russians." Yet William L. Clayton—the Assistant Secretary of State for Economic Affairs who was the main proponent of liberal business ideology and free trade in the administration—counseled patience for the time being:

> [I]n light of the present situation in Eastern Europe, we must take a realistic attitude. [Clayton] described in considerable detail the history of our negotiations with Russians regarding

Eastern Europe, and the necessity we have encountered of making compromises all along the way in order to get the armies out of the occupied territories so that rehabilitation can be started.[20]

Businessmen's complaints about governmental inaction perhaps missed the point. The administration could do little to recover American assets in the Soviet zone and so instead concentrated its efforts in areas, namely Western Europe, where long-term U.S. interests and the prospects of success were greater. Nonetheless, the confusion in the State Department was real, for U.S. policymakers were torn by conflicting objectives—to sustain the wartime alliance with the Soviet Union, yet to uphold political and economic freedoms in Eastern Europe.

U.S. Relations with Poland, 1945–1947

American relations with East European governments varied with each country's foreign policy orientation, internal political system, and policy toward U.S. business interests. An examination of American relations with Poland and Czechoslovakia shows that the Truman administration was more interested in preventing total Soviet domination of those countries than it was in extending the U.S. economic sphere into Eastern Europe.

Before Yalta, the Roosevelt administration had attempted to remain neutral in the dispute between the London Poles and the Soviets. A case in point was the episode of the Warsaw uprising during August and September 1944. While the Nazis slaughtered thousands of Polish rebels, the Red Army sat by the Vistula and refused to allow Western airdrops to the besieged Poles until it was too late. Although Roosevelt reprimanded Stalin, the President simultaneously urged Stanislaw Mikolajczyk, Premier of the Polish government in London, to make concessions to the Soviets on territorial and political issues. At Yalta in February 1945, the President accepted the Curzon Line and a Polish government dominated by the Soviet-backed Lublin Poles in return for Stalin's promise to sponsor free elections.

The Soviet failure to stage such elections or to reorganize the Polish government to American satisfaction provided the setting for Truman's lecture to Molotov in April 1945. Truman's words apparently fell on deaf ears, for Moscow's interference in Polish politics increased. When the Soviets announced in early May that they had imprisoned sixteen leaders of the anti-Nazi Polish underground, negotiations between the London Poles and Moscow came to a standstill. Yet the President feared that further delay would help to consolidate Communist rule, and following Harry Hopkins' talks with Stalin in June 1945, Truman scaled down U.S. demands for the reorganization of the Polish government. In recognizing the reconstituted Polish government in early July 1945, Truman tacitly acknowledged predominant Soviet influence in that country.[21]

American policymakers at first expected that economic aid would exercise a moderating influence upon the new Polish government. Poland received more UNRRA aid than any other country except China, and the State Department encouraged Polish applications for surplus property and Eximbank credits. American confidence in Polish good faith soon waned. By the fall of 1945, Warsaw was engaging in practices—discrimination against U.S. trade, expropriation of foreign property, and a crackdown on the free press and pro-Western political parties—that American observers believed bore the stamp of the Kremlin.[22]

Officials in Washington were tempted to attach stiffer conditions to Polish aid. In September 1945, for example, Acting Secretary of State Dean Acheson informed Arthur Bliss Lane, the Ambassador in Warsaw, that Eximbank credits would be thereafter contingent upon Polish acceptance of Article VII of Lend-Lease, which is to say a non-discriminatory commercial policy. State Department officials sometimes insisted upon this principle even when it hurt friends of the United States. In a November 1945 meeting in Washington, Vice Premier Mikolajczyk, by then a member of the reorganized Warsaw government, pleaded for American economic aid as "one of the most important steps to insure that the Polish people could regain their independence." Elbridge Durbrow, the Chief of the Division of Eastern European Affairs, explained that the United States would withhold such aid as long as the Soviet government sought "to bring about an economic bloc in Eastern Europe by concluding bilateral treaties which in effect tend to exclude all other countries from having an equal opportunity to trade in the area." To the unhappy surprise of the Polish government, which had requested more than $500 million in aid, the State Department decided in late November 1945 to limit American aid to less than $100 million.[23]

But the United States had not yet written off Poland, for two reasons peculiar to that country. First, the Western-oriented parties and the press retained some freedoms through the first half of 1946. As Irving Brant, correspondent for the *Chicago Sun*, reported to Truman in January 1946 following a two months' visit to Poland:

> No Polish government, conservative or radical, will do anything Russia dislikes. There is no indication of actual supervisory control, directly or through the Polish Communists. . . . Polish Communists, though pro-Soviet, are Poles first. . . . as long as Communists are prominent in the government they are an insurance against Russian intervention. . . . [Nationalization of heavy industry] had extensive roots in prewar Poland. . . . liberal American credits offer the only assurance of genuine Polish independence. . . . I don't think we should push the Poles too hard as they climb the democratic ladder. They will stay on it, and keep climbing, if we help them through their economic difficulties.[24]

More importantly, Western Europe desperately needed Polish coal to fuel its industrial recovery, at least until German mines reopened. In early 1946, the Poles asked for U.S. credits to purchase railway equipment needed for shipping coal to Western Europe. Warsaw met American conditions for aid by endorsing multilateral commercial principles, reaffirming the most-favored-nation (MFN) status of the United States, and promising compensation for nationalized American property. In April 1946, the United States reciprocated with a $40 million Eximbank loan and a $50 million surplus property line-of-credit to Poland.[25]

Yet by the late summer of 1946, American policymakers had concluded that Poland was largely lost to the Soviets and that free elections were impossible. As Ambassador Lane repeatedly argued, the Polish situation "boils down in the last analysis to [a] decision as to what our policy is going to be towards [the] Soviet Union." In a cable to Acheson from the Paris Peace Conference in August 1946, Byrnes stated the new American line:

> the time has come when we should endeavor by all fair means to assist our friends in western Europe and Italy . . . rather than to continue to extend material aid to those countries of eastern Europe at present engaged in the campaign of vilification of the United States and distortion of our motives and policies.

Byrnes' speech at Stuttgart on September 6, 1946, which among other things challenged the legitimacy of the Oder-Western Neisse line separating Poland and Germany, also demonstrated that U.S. interests in

Germany had assumed priority over those in Poland and Eastern Europe.[26]

Hereafter, the United States offered aid to Poland on a strictly *quid pro quo* basis. Further American credits were tied to resolution of the compensation issue and continued Polish exports of coal to Western Europe. In December 1946 meetings in Washington, the State Department discouraged the Polish representatives from applying for another Eximbank loan and suggested they appeal to the IBRD instead. Although the United States unblocked Polish assets in U.S. banks in exchange for an inconclusive compensation agreement, the Polish ministers went home largely empty-handed.[27]

The Polish government was caught in a vicious circle. Warsaw could not meet American demands until it had dollars, but the only source of dollars in the short run was American aid. Meanwhile, Polish reconstruction lagged. The only way out of this dilemma lay in expanded coal exports to Western Europe. But as Polish Minister of Industry Hilary Minc explained to Acheson in December 1946, the U.S refusal to extend sufficient cotton credits forced Poland to commit a large portion of its coal exports to buy expensive Soviet cotton. Minc added that "Poland did not wish to be absorbed either politically or economically in the Soviet system," and instead sought close relations with both the East and the West. Acheson replied that

> [the United States] was not prepared to make extensive loans and economic arrangements with countries which appeared to be accepting this help merely for the purpose of building up a domestic economy which would be joined to the closed economic system of the Soviet Union. The form of government which a nation had was, of course, its own affair but it was of vital importance to the United States in considering the extension of help to any nation whether or not the economy of that country was to be an important factor in raising the whole level of the economy in Europe and this hemisphere or whether it was to join a system, the operation of which was either of no benefit to the rest of the world or an actually depressing factor.[28]

Throughout 1947, Polish officials pleaded for American aid so that Poland would not be drawn further into the Soviet orbit. Responding to Polish reports of near-famine conditions, the State Department initially considered Poland eligible for a share of the administration's $350 million post-UNRRA relief program. Yet in July 1947, an American agricultural mission concluded that Poland could meet its food needs without U.S. help. An agronomist who had accompanied the mission later reported otherwise to Llewellyn Thompson, Chief of the Division of Eastern European Affairs. But Thompson, who represented the hardline, political wing of the State Department, turned aside the agronomist's stories of Polish misery with a curt rejoinder. "Those countries which actively opposed the policies of this Government," he said, "were obviously the first to be excluded."[29]

The intensification of the Cold War during 1947 led to an equally tough-minded American policy on a World Bank loan to Poland. The Poles had applied in 1946 for a three-year, $600 million loan. The State Department argued that the Bank should extend no more than a total of $75–100 million to East European countries given the greater needs and importance of West European and other countries. The IBRD generally took the position that "only economic considerations shall be relevant to its decisions," Emilio G. Collado, the U.S. executive director of the Bank, wrote NAC Chairman John Snyder in November 1946. Yet the Bank had to consider "the broad trade, financial, and investment policies of the borrower" as they might affect the prospects for repayment, and on those grounds, Collado recommended delaying action on the loan applications by Poland, Czechoslovakia, and Yugoslavia.[30]

Under Secretary William Clayton, voicing the sentiments of the more pragmatic, economic wing of the State Department, disagreed. Although Poland had abstained from the Marshall Plan, Clayton supported a Bank loan in July 1947 because it would boost Polish coal exports to the West and reduce Soviet influence in that country. To resolve the issue, the Vice-President of the World Bank approached Llewellyn Thompson in September 1947 to ascertain the State Department's position on a $47 million loan to increase Polish coal production. The Bank felt that the dividends to Western Europe outweighed the risks posed by Soviet control of Poland. (Significantly, financiers in New York, the major source of Bank capital, were willing to back the loan.) Thompson promised an early decision, but the State Department took no action on the proposal for months. Eventually, the Bank quietly dropped the matter.[31]

The freezing of American aid to Poland in 1947 coincided with a brutal crackdown on non-Communist political groups in Poland and a further shift of Polish trade toward the East. The Communist takeover of the Polish government was probably proceeding on its own timetable, with American policies having only a marginal effect. Neutrality, in any case, was never a viable option for the Poles. Both Washington and Moscow demanded that Warsaw choose sides; the outcome was never in doubt, given the Soviet occupation of Poland. The fate of Polish-American relations was poignantly illustrated in October 1947, when British and American diplomats helped Mikolajczyk, the key moderate in the government and the last great hope of the West, flee for his life by concealing him under a pile of boxes in the back of a truck.[32]

U.S. Relations with Czechoslovakia, 1945–1947

The collapse of Czechoslovakian democracy had an even deeper impact upon American perceptions of the Soviet Union. Unlike Poland, Czechoslovakia enjoyed a strong tradition of representative government and a developed economy left largely intact after the war. The Czechoslovak strategy pursued by President Eduard Beneš and Foreign Minister Jan Masaryk of building bridges between East and West was at first successful, in part because it served both Soviet and American purposes.

The State Department hoped to incorporate Czechoslovakia into the multilateral system, especially to benefit West European recovery. American diplomats, to be sure, felt misgivings about the December 1943 Soviet-Czech treaty of mutual assistance, the presence of Communist and leftist elements in the Prague government, and Soviet interference with the UNRRA program there. On the whole, however, U.S. relations with Czechoslovakia remained satisfactory through most of 1945. And in early October, Stalin surprised Truman by accepting the President's proposal for a mutual U.S.-Soviet troop withdrawal from Czechoslovakia on December 1, 1945.[33]

The October 1945 Czech nationalization decree, affecting sizeable American investments, complicated economic relations with Washington. Already in September, the State Department, accepting the advice of Ambassador Laurence A. Steinhardt, had persuaded the Eximbank to withhold a $300 million loan from Czechoslovakia until Prague agreed not to discriminate against American trade and investment. Following the Red Army's withdrawal in December, Byrnes indicated that Czechoslovakia would soon receive a $25–35 million loan and $50 million in surplus property credits, in addition to cotton credits. Yet the Czechoslovak failure to follow up on American overtures in early 1946 prompted concern in Washington that Soviet influence, manifested in the economic radicalism of the Prague government, was as strong as ever.[34]

As in Poland, the compensation issue posed an intractable problem for Czechoslovakia: compensation required dollars, but the only source of dollars, given the dislocation of postwar trade and the scarcity of hard currency in Europe, was U.S. aid. In February 1946, Byrnes still favored a loan in order to prop up moderate political parties in Czechoslovakia. Yet Steinhardt adamantly opposed it because "a large American loan to any foreign Government in which the Communist Party is strongly represented will be availed of them indirectly to entrench their position and extend their grip." The ambassador recommended postponing aid and trade agreements until general elections in Czechoslovakia were held in late May 1946.[35]

Compared with Poland, the political situation in Czechoslovakia was considerably more gratifying from the American perspective. Steinhardt reported that the May elections, which gave the Communists an unexpectedly large (38 percent), if not decisive, plurality, were conducted fairly. The United States immediately offered the new government, headed by Communist Prime Minister Klement Gottwald, $50 million in surplus credits and $20 million in cotton credits. While Communist domination of the government upset American officials, they took comfort in the fact that free elections were possible at all, and that Beneš and Masaryk remained in office. Byrnes felt the Czechs "have shown greater willingness to negotiate than Poland." The compensation issue remained the only serious obstacle to harmonious relations.[36]

Just as in the case of Poland, Czech-American relations deteriorated after the Paris Conference in August 1946. Byrnes deeply resented the Czech delegates' applause when Soviet representative Andrei Vyshinsky insultingly charged that the United States sought to enslave Europe through a policy of handouts. This and other evidence of Prague's subservience to Moscow led the United States to suspend the surplus sales and terminate the Eximbank negotiations in mid-September.[37]

Czech officials, Communist and non-Communist alike, desperately sought to mend relations with the United States over the next year despite a marked heightening of the Cold War. Soon after the suspension of the Eximbank talks, Gottwald impressed Steinhardt as entirely sincere when he promised to moderate criticism of the United States in the Prague press and to facilitate agreement on the compensation issue. Masaryk later told Steinhardt that

> Gottwald had stated categorically at meeting of Cabinet that there "must" be a "prompt settlement" of American claims arising out of illegally seized and nationalized properties and a discontinuance of newspaper articles offensive to US. Gottwald had informed Cabinet that he had given strict orders that objectionable newspaper articles were to cease and that he was taking it upon himself to see that his orders are carried out.[38]

The Czech press thereafter showed greater restraint, and in December 1946, Masaryk promised about $30 million in compensation for U.S. property once Czechoslovakia's foreign trade revived. As Beneš explained to the American ambassador, Communist cabinet ministers had matured in office, even to the point of showing bourgeois tendencies. Prague followed Moscow's line in international conferences, Beneš added, only in order to preclude Soviet interference in Czechoslovakian internal affairs. The Gottwald government requested a further Eximbank cotton credit in February 1947 and participated in the Paris Conference on the Marshall Plan in July 1947 until the Kremlin forced its withdrawal. As late as November 1947, when Washington had largely given up on Czechoslovakia, the Prague regime, including top Communist ministers, repeatedly proposed a settlement of the compensation issue tied to American cotton credits and a commercial treaty. The available evidence supports the conclusion that Czech Communists, as well as moderates like Beneš and Masaryk, sought to maintain a precarious balance between East and West, albeit with an emphasis on good relations with their eastern neighbor.[39]

The ultimate fate of the East European countries lay in the hands of the Soviet Union, but American intolerance of Czechoslovakia's tilt toward Moscow undoubtedly exacerbated the problems of the Prague government. Steinhardt, whose cables carried weight in Washington, believed that Prague, like Moscow, responded best to toughness, and that a generous U.S. aid policy would only encourage Czechrecalcitrance. The ambassador interpreted Gottwald's conciliatory actions in October 1946 as proof that Byrnes' suspension of aid talks had "restored respect of the Czechoslovak Government for US," rather than as a manifestation of Prague's longing for autonomy from Moscow.[40]

Similarly, Steinhardt regarded the Czechoslovakian departure from the Paris Conference on the Marshall Plan in July 1947 as "irrefutable evidence" that "Soviet control of Czech foreign policy since end of war has been substantially complete." He recommended that the United States precipitate an economic crisis by cutting off all aid to Czechoslovakia, apparently forgetting that the State Department had already done so. Curiously, the ambassador felt that Prague officials—who supposedly had no control over their own foreign policy—would realize the error of their ways once the Czech masses—who supposedly had no voice in a Communist-dominated state—demonstrated against the government. The U.S. Embassy in Prague accordingly rebuffed the conciliatory overtures of the Gottwald government in late 1947. American policies probably pushed Czechoslovakia further into the Soviet camp.[41]

Why did Steinhardt's convoluted reasoning gain currency in the State Department? The key to U.S. policies toward Eastern Europe lay in Soviet-American relations. By late 1946, policymakers in Washington were certain that the Soviet Union controlled most developments in Eastern Europe, and that U.S. policy toward specific East European countries should be integrated into a broader containment strategy. As Secretary Byrnes stated in November 1946, "we must help our friends in every way and refrain from assisting those who either through helplessness or for other reasons are opposing the principles for which we stand."[42]

Neither economic nor political factors alone can explain U.S. policy toward Eastern Europe during this period. American trade and investment in Eastern Europe were too small to justify a major confrontation with the Soviet Union. On the other hand, the U.S. commitment to Atlantic Charter principles cannot fully explain Washington's alarm over Soviet hegemony in the region. The United States had recognized Soviet dominance in Eastern Europe during the war and was generally willing to deal with unrepresentative regimes as long as they seemed amenable to democratic reform. Rather, it was the combination of political repression and economic exclusiveness in Eastern Europe that so alarmed American officials, for the Soviets were seemingly replacing the Nazi bloc with their own. Moscow's attempt to create a closed sphere of influence appeared to thwart the integration of a Europe linked to the United States through multilateral economic institutions. In response, the United States gradually sealed off Eastern Europe from Western aid, trade, and technology.

The Russian Loan and Soviet-American Trade, 1945–1946

The deteriorating U.S. relations with Eastern Europe paralleled those with the Soviet Union. Policymakers in Washington had initially hoped to work out a *modus vivendi* with the Soviet Union that would preserve the main features of the Open Door yet allow for the special need of state-trading economic systems and meet Soviet security needs in Eastern Europe. Despite Harriman's warning in April 1945 that "the Soviet Union, once it had control of bordering areas, would attempt to penetrate the next adjacent countries," State Department officials generally minimized disturbing reports from the field and continued to counsel a policy of firm, but not unfriendly, pressure on Moscow until early 1946. Many top policymakers, including the President himself, entertained the illusion that the Soviets might support Western-style parliamentary governments in Eastern Europe if only the Americans could win Stalin's good favor. As Truman told his staff upon returning from the Potsdam Conference:

> Stalin was one, [Truman] said, who, if he said something one time, would say the same thing the next time; in other words, he could be depended upon. [Truman] did not feel the same way about Molotov . . . or Vyshinsky.[43]

Yet once the evidence of Soviet repression in Eastern Europe became overwhelming, American officials retaliated by cutting off U.S trade and credits. Remembering the economic warfare practiced by Germany and Japan during the 1930s, American decision makers probably exaggerated the political and strategic threat posed by Soviet state-trading and bilateralism.[44] They also overestimated the willingness of Soviet leaders to compromise their principles in order to gain U.S. aid.

The foremost instrument of American policy was the Russian loan. Following Molotov's request for a low interest, $6 billion loan in January 1945, Harriman argued that "we should do everything we can to assist the Soviet Union through credits in developing a sound economy." An improved Soviet standard of living would yield a "more tolerant" foreign policy. Harriman, however, believed that the price of a Russian loan should be political concessions in Eastern Europe.[45]

Meanwhile, Secretary of the Treasury Henry Morgenthau was pressing for an extremely generous $10 billion loan with no strings attached, in part to maintain high domestic employment. The Russians, he suggested, could repay the loan with shipments of strategic raw materials.[46] Several factors militated against Morgenthau's proposal. Congress had already ruled Lend-Lease ineligible for postwar reconstruction purposes and was unlikely to approve special legislation for Russian credits along the lines of the British loan. Only the Eximbank or World Bank, therefore, could offer a loan to Russia. Yet the World Bank would not begin operations until mid-1946, while the Eximbank, controlled by the State Department, would not extend a loan until the Soviets relaxed their grip on Eastern Europe. Even if the State Department approved the loan, domestic interests, notably mining companies, would not welcome massive raw material imports from the Soviet Union. In any event, it was unlikely that the Soviets could export enough to sustain a very large loan. By April 1945, the State Department had trimmed the proposed Eximbank loan down to $1 billion.[47]

Although the administration would not publicly announce the death of the Russian loan until April 1947, the State Department quietly suspended consideration of Russian credits in late 1945. In January 1946, the NAC discussed shifting the $1 billion earmarked for Russia to other uses given the shortage of bank reserves. The State Department, however, insisted that the bank officially reserve funds for Russia until the summer of 1946, partly to retain an economic lever for bargaining purposes.[48]

The Soviets did not vigorously press for a loan, probably because they believed that American overproduction would eventually force Washington to grant them more generous terms than the Eximbank would. In his first mention of credits in November 1943, Harriman had perhaps reinforced Soviet expectations of a postwar capitalist crisis by stressing the importance of Russian purchases to U.S. full employment. The Soviets also had an ideological stake in self-sufficiency. "The steady rise in all branches of Soviet industry is ensured by planned economy," a Soviet writer in *Foreign Affairs* boasted. "With a planned economy there is no need to be afraid of postwar unemployment crises or depressions." The Soviets also may have preferred German reparations over a loan from Washington, reasoning that it was better to take from the conquered than from the United States, which might ask for embarrassing concessions.[49]

The loan question was academic as long as the erstwhile allies could not settle such basic issues as Lend-Lease. The Soviets' extraordinarily dilatory tactics in the Lend-Lease negotiations suggested to American diplomats that Moscow cared little about economic ties with the United

States, except on extremely advantageous terms. "Whether observers were commenting on Stalin, Molotov, or other Soviet officials," Thomas Paterson states, "the pervasive judgment was that the Soviet diplomatic style inhibited the negotiating process and eroded goodwill."[50]

Washington's efforts on behalf of postwar Soviet-American trade proved equally fruitless. At the end of the war, U.S. officials hoped commercial ties would promote greater cooperation with the Soviet Union. American businessmen, lured by the volume of Lend-Lease exports, eagerly anticipated a huge postwar Soviet market for capital equipment and consumer goods. But by late 1945, as U.S. businessmen enjoyed strong domestic demand and a seller's market in world trade, their enthusiasm waned.

Will Clayton and the economic divisions of the State Department continued to favor Soviet participation in the UN-sponsored International Trade Organization (ITO), the commercial counterpart to Bretton Woods designed to expand world trade and employment. While Clayton believed the role of the Soviet Union in world trade would remain minimal, Soviet participation might lend prestige to the ITO. Furthermore, the prospect of American trade (financed by an Eximbank loan) would presumably encourage the Soviets to cooperate on other matters.[51]

Harriman sharply challenged Clayton. Tariff reductions had little relevance to a state-trading economy, the ambassador argued in late 1945, although the Soviets might make "fictitious" concessions in order to win Western acquiescence on other points. When Acheson suggested that the United States offer MFN status to the Russians if they promised to import an agreed minimum of U.S. goods, Harriman countered that the plan was woefully "unrealistic." The Russians desperately needed our goods already. "The problem," he said, "is to get them to contribute to the world economy something even half way commensurate to what they expect to get out of it." Specifically, Harriman felt the United States should press the Soviets to cease their economic exploitation of Eastern Europe.[52] American diplomats in Moscow argued that the Soviets had no faith in a long-term, peaceful relationship with the West based on commercial ties. As an embassy attaché put it, the "end of the military war inaugurates a period of economic and political warfare" against the West.[53]

The prospect of a reconstruction loan never significantly influenced Moscow's policies. Acheson assured the Soviets in May 1946 that the

Eximbank still reserved $1 billion for a Russian loan, even if it no longer formally set aside the funds. But President Truman's equivocal public remarks on the loan must have aroused Soviet suspicions and further weakened the American bargaining position.[54]

By the end of 1946, Soviet-American negotiations on aid and trade had reached an almost irrevocable deadlock. American diplomats now commonly interpreted Soviet abstention from Bretton Woods and the ITO as evidence of Soviet determination not only to maintain absolute independence in foreign affairs, but to destroy those institutions.[55]

Kennan and Containment

The Soviet oppression of Eastern Europe clearly alarmed U.S. policymakers, but American misgivings about Soviet conduct lacked co-herent expression until George F. Kennan formulated the containment thesis.[56] From the vantage point of the American Embassy in Moscow, Kennan felt ill-disguised contempt toward Washington's effort to accommodate the Kremlin while affirming Atlantic Charter principles. In particular, Kennan feared that the American endeavor to reconstruct the whole of the continent would gain the United States nothing in Eastern Europe while diverting attention from more vital interests in Western Europe. As he comments in his memoirs, "We were thus in danger of losing, like the dog standing over the reflecting pool, the bone in our mouth without obtaining the one we saw in the water."[57]

In mid-February 1946, Kennan, then running the embassy in Harriman's absence, received a telegram asking him for an analysis of Stalin's recent election speech. "The more I thought about this message," Kennan recalls,

> the more it seemed to be obvious that this was "it." . . . It would not do to give them just a fragment of the truth. Here was a case where nothing but the whole truth would do. They had asked for it. Now, by God, they would have it.[58]

Kennan's five-part "long telegram" began by arguing that the Soviet foreign outlook postulated an unremitting hostility against the West. The wartime alliance did nothing to reduce historic fears of capitalist encirclement:

> Soviet party line is not based on any objective analysis of situation beyond Russia's borders; . . . it arises mainly from basic inner-Russian necessities which existed before the recent war and exist today.
>
> At bottom of Kremlin's neurotic view of world affairs is traditional and instinctive Russian sense of insecurity. . . . And [the Russian rulers] have learned to seek security only in patient but deadly struggle for total destruction of rival power, never in compacts and compromises with it.[59]

In combination with Marxist-Leninist ideology, Kennan continued, the current phase of Russian expansionism was "more dangerous and insidious than ever before." The Kremlin used Marxism, "the fig leaf of their moral and intellectual respectability," and the capitalist encirclement thesis to justify the increased military and police power of the Russian state. But the spokesmen of the Soviet party line, Kennan added ambiguously, were not entirely disingenuous; they had come to believe their own propaganda:

> There is good reason to suspect that this Government is actually a conspiracy within a conspiracy; and I for one am reluctant to believe that Stalin himself receives anything like an objective picture of outside world. . . . Inability of foreign governments to place their case squarely before Russian policymakers . . . to my mind is most disquieting feature of diplomacy in Moscow, and one which Western statesmen would do well to keep in mind if they would understand nature of difficulties encountered here.[60]

The Soviets, according to Kennan, favored peaceful coexistence only as a breathing spell to recover from the war and as a low-cost means to subvert the West:

> In summary, we have here a political force committed fanatically to the belief that with US there can be no permanent *modus vivendi*, that it is desirable and necessary that the internal harmony of our society be disrupted, our traditional way of life be destroyed, the international authority of our state be broken, if Soviet power is to be secure.[61]

Given the impressive resources at the command of the Kremlin and the inflexibility of its outlook, what could the West do? Kennan first reassured Washington that the Soviets would respond to the logic of force, if not the logic of reason. The West was still collectively stronger than the Soviet Union, and the Kremlin had yet to consolidate its rule. Kennan then recommended further diagnosis of the Soviet system "with same courage, detachment, objectivity . . . with which a doctor studies an unruly and unreasonable individual." Above all, the administration needed to educate the public about the realities of Soviet power and intransigence, to secure its allies against Communist subversion, and to project a more positive image of American society to the world.[62]

Interestingly, Kennan's telegram, generally considered the harbinger of the containment doctrine, offered no concrete recommendations for U.S. policy, other than a plea for the reeducation of the American public. Nowhere in the telegram, for instance, did Kennan prescribe greater economic or military aid to countries threatened by a Communist takeover. Nor did Kennan's famous "X" article in the July 1947 issue of *Foreign Affairs* clarify the distinction between political and military containment. Kennan evidently did not recognize the full implications of his own thesis.[63]

The telegram, to Kennan's surprise, created a sensation in official Washington. Unfortunately, the ambiguity of Kennan's thesis allowed for varying interpretations. The author had not intended to imply that negotiations with the Soviets were futile or that Soviet foreign policy was unalterably dedicated to war according to some set timetable. Yet some policymakers, notably Secretary of the Navy James V. Forrestal, seized upon its more militant passages to justify much tougher policies against the Soviet Union and a general escalation in U.S. defense programs. Others were more restrained. While Kennan's "predictions and warnings could not have been better," Acheson comments in his memoirs, "we responded to them slowly."[64]

Containment Deferred

Indeed, the Truman White House did not implement Kennan's containment doctrine for more than a year. The story of the Clifford-Elsey report illustrates the gap between official thinking and action in this period. In the summer of 1946, President Truman ordered Clark M. Clifford, his special counsel, to prepare a study on Soviet-American relations. The senior officials whom Clifford and his aide, George M. Elsey, consulted generally painted an even gloomier picture of Soviet intentions and capabilities than had Kennan. Secretary of War Robert P. Patterson warned that "we must envisage the possibility of the U.S.S.R. adopting open use of armed forces on a global scale." He called for the development of "long range air power, supplemented by atomic and long range weapons, and adequate ground forces to hold and seize key areas." Similarly, the State Department recommended the integration of all foreign economic, political, and defense programs for the purpose of deterring Soviet expansion. "The local dimensions of any question were secondary or even tertiary in the grand scheme of the incipient East-West conflict," Daniel Yergin observes. The final report denigrated negotiations with Moscow and fell just short of predicting imminent war between the superpowers.[65]

Yet when Clifford submitted the report to the President in September 1946, Truman said it was too "hot" to be circulated and locked away all the copies in his office safe. The President did not necessarily disagree with the report, but he realized that the public and the Congress were still unprepared for either an open confrontation with the Soviet Union or a military buildup so soon after the war. Coming right after his firing of Commerce Secretary Henry A. Wallace, moreover, publication of the report might have triggered a liberal backlash. And Truman himself remained ambivalent about what action to take. As he wrote former Vice-President John Nance Garner in September 1946, "There is too much loose talk about the Russian situation. We are not going to have any shooting trouble with them but they are tough bargainers and always ask for the whole earth, expecting maybe to get an acre."[66]

For all the rhetoric about the Soviet threat, the administration sat on its hands. Although Admiral Leahy and others had warned Truman that the armed forces were gravely undermanned and could not handle more than a minor crisis, demobilization and defense cuts continued apace. Nor did the atomic program accelerate. Truman claimed in October 1946 that the United States had stationed no bombs in overseas bases, meaning that American silver-plated bombers could not reach Russia in a general war. Truman told his Cabinet that "he did not believe there were over a half-dozen [atomic bombs] in the United States, although, he added, that was enough to win a war." David Rosenberg has discovered that the U.S. atomic arsenal in the summer of 1946 consisted of no more than seven Mark III (Nagasaki-type, "Fat Man") weapons. As late as April 1947, the newly operative Atomic Energy Commission told Truman that the armed forces still had very few bombs, none of them ready to be used, and that military bomb assembly teams were unprepared for a crisis situation.[67]

In the months preceding the Truman Doctrine, Forrestal repeatedly complained that American diplomatic commitments greatly exceeded military capabilities. Yet for both political and bureaucratic reasons, Pentagon policies and programs continued to lag behind containment doctrine. The unification struggle had exhausted much of the military establishment's credibility on the Hill, as well as in the White House. Budgetary pressures also encouraged the administration to pin its hopes on a national defense built around atomic weapons, however few, and around UMT, however chimerical. The Clifford-Elsey report itself recognized that American aid and trade remained the mainstay in the battle against Communism.[68] Even with the failure of economic diplomacy in Eastern Europe staring them in the face, Truman and his top advisers continued to believe that economic power could achieve most vital U.S. foreign policy aims.

The Legacy of Eastern Europe, 1945–1947

The conflict over Eastern Europe engendered a climate of mutual mistrust that set a lasting pattern for future Soviet-American relations. While American economic and strategic interests in the region were minor, the diplomatic stakes were nonetheless high. Policymakers in Washington regarded Soviet behavior in Eastern Europe as a crucial test of the Kremlin's intentions in Europe and elsewhere.

The Truman administration never threatened to use its military power to force a Soviet pullout from Eastern Europe because the position of the Red Army was impregnable and the limits of American power dictated concentration of strength in Western Europe. The economic weapon appeared to be the only appropriate and available instrument by which the United States could maintain a foothold in Eastern Europe and block further expansion of Soviet influence in Europe. Economic pressure, however, only intensified Soviet suspicions of the United States and helped precipitate a further crackdown on the satellite nations after 1946.

Political and strategic considerations, in particular the need to promote recovery in Western Europe, ultimately shaped American policies in Eastern Europe more than did the abstract principles of the Open Door and the Atlantic Charter. The Soviet sphere of influence in Eastern Europe provided evidence that the Kremlin was unwilling to participate in multilateral institutions, and that the American quest for an open world order embracing the entire developed world would never be realized.

The Soviet bloc also seemed to threaten U.S. economic security. If the industrial countries of Western Europe could not be assured of free access to the markets and raw materials of Eastern Europe, they might be tempted to create their own exclusive trading bloc. Aside from the potential harm this could cause American business interests, such an arrangement smacked of the autarkic practices of the prewar era. Soviet protectionism, state trading, and other "unfair" economic tactics reminded American leaders of the competitive and antagonistic environment that had led to the Second World War. As the U.S. Minister to Budapest reported in February 1946,

> It is increasingly evident that USSR through successive and individually tentative steps bids fair to advance steadily in this area and elsewhere in Europe much as Nazi Germany advanced through the late thirties. . . . In relatively short time Hungary will become an economic colony of USSR from which western trade will be excluded and in which western investments will be totally lost.[69]

The United States could have satisfied Soviet demands in Eastern Europe only by renouncing traditional American ideals and wartime objectives. Yet by agreeing during the war to a large, but undefined, Soviet sphere of influence in Europe, the Western allies misled Stalin about their requirements in postwar Europe. As Vojtech Mastny concludes, "Russia's striving for power and influence far in excess of its reasonable security requirements was the primary source of conflict, and the Western failure to resist it early enough an important secondary one."[70]

Early postwar relations with Eastern Europe and the Soviet Union provided American officials with important lessons about the nature of Soviet power and the steps required to contain it. Ironically, Stalin's quest for security in Europe helped to bring about the very anti-Soviet coalition that his diplomacy was meant to forestall.

CHAPTER FOUR

RECOVERY AND CRISIS
IN WESTERN EUROPE,
1945–1947

AMERICAN PREDOMINANCE in Western Europe was almost unchallenged after the war. Here Washington could implement with few constraints the multilateralist program—freer trade, currency convertibility, financial integration—developed during the war. Yet this very fact encouraged a dangerous complacency on the part of most American officials, who were preoccupied with problems in Central and Eastern Europe, the Near East, and elsewhere. Concerned officials focused on Western Europe only long enough to deal with immediate problems. The region did not command the full attention it deserved until the winter of 1947, when economic collapse threatened to engulf America's main overseas trading partners. Even then, Washington needed several months to devise a coherent course of action.

American policies in Western Europe, unlike those in Eastern Europe, assumed no consistent pattern before the Marshall Plan, largely because U.S. policymakers initially misunderstood the nature of the economic problems there. The threat to American interests in London and Paris was far more difficult to define than in Warsaw and Budapest, where the Red Army posed a tangible danger. Western Europe's problems, unlike those of Eastern Europe, were largely indigenous, and American multilateralism did not offer any quick and easy remedies for them.

Due to the U.S. tradition of nonintervention in European affairs and a strong popular distaste for power politics, Washington was slow to secure its sphere of influence in Europe. During the war, the fear of an isolationist backlash against U.S. participation in a world organization had inhibited Roosevelt from accepting a sphere-of-influence agreement in Europe with Stalin and Churchill. American officials hoped instead to win a Wilsonian peace based on self-determination, collective security, and multilateralism. Even after Soviet designs on Eastern Europe became clearer and U.S. leaders accepted the necessity of restoring a balance of power in Europe, Washington never sought to dominate its allies as Moscow did in its zone. Indeed, France, Britain, and the Benelux countries had to coax the United States into accepting its responsibilities as a great power. The American sphere of influence in Europe was an "empire by invitation."[1]

American Interests in Western Europe

The American reluctance to fill the power vacuum in Western Europe is surprising since the stakes there were substantial. During 1947, the West European countries—here broadly defined as the Marshall Plan participants minus Germany—accounted for about one-third of all American exports, roughly the same as during the late 1930s. The dollar value of American exports to this area almost quintupled from a $1.1 billion annual average during the 1936–38 period to $5.3 billion in 1947.[2]

The weakness of European export industries facilitated the U.S. penetration of new foreign markets after the war. While the U.S. share of world trade increased from one-seventh in 1938 to one-third in 1947, the European share dropped from roughly one-half to one-third. And whereas one-fourth of U.S. imports had come from the West European countries from 1936 to 1938, their share of the American import market fell to one-seventh in 1947. The region as a whole suffered a staggering $5 billion trade deficit with the United States for 1947 alone, with the United Kingdom registering a $900 million shortfall and France $770 million.[3]

Despite the seemingly small part that foreign trade played in their country's gross national product, U.S. economists, business leaders, and policymakers recognized its growing importance. In April 1945, the Truman administration estimated that exports were responsible, directly or indirectly, for five million to six million jobs. Imports served the equally useful purpose of lowering domestic prices to consumers, increasing competition, and furnishing raw materials that were either scarce or unavailable in the United States. The world trade disequilibrium alarmed American experts because they believed that the United States could not maintain its profitable export trade if it did not expand imports as well. Otherwise, America's customers would at some point exhaust the foreign exchange, gold, and credits needed to finance their trade deficits.[4]

Yet Washington tended to focus upon long-term multilateral goals, rather than the payments difficulties and production shortfalls that plagued Europe immediately after the war. This orientation stemmed in part from a deep-seated bias against governmental intervention in the free market economy, and in part from a shortsighted desire to hold down foreign aid costs. For instance, wartime planners had anticipated that private U.S. foreign investment would help offset European trade deficits, but American direct investment in Europe grew slowly after the war, from $1.2 billion in 1940 to just $1.7 billion in 1950. In the meantime, total European direct investment in the United States rose from $1.6 billion to $2.2 billion, thereby cancelling out whatever benefits Europe might have derived from new American investment.[5]

There was another reason why the Truman administration moved so slowly to correct the trade imbalance: no powerful constituency pressed for expanded imports. In fact, the administration faced pressure to boost exports. Despite the huge trade surplus, American businessmen complained that the government did not do enough to protect and promote U.S. export markets and foreign investment. As one businessman testified before a Senate subcommittee in the spring of 1945, "We need some highgrade American salesmen in our diplomatic corps who are trained in smelling out a market, no matter where it is or what it is, and who relate that market to some product that American manufacturers can supply."[6]

Similarly, Ambassador-at-Large William S. Culbertson, the spokesman for a Special Economic Mission that traveled to liberated areas in late 1944, had recommended the creation of a quasi-governmental organization called the "Corporation" to meet the needs of U.S. businessmen abroad:

> It is not possible for American nationals to engage in foreign production and foreign distribution in the world as it is today without the active support of the American Government. . . . Until economic liberty without any discrimination is accepted by the nations, the American Government should exert the pressure necessary to remove types of barriers, sometimes intangible, which are . . . beyond the reach of traditional diplomatic methods. . . . It is obvious to anyone who knows the Foreign Service of the United States that a substantial and influential portion of its personnel is not interested in international economic policy.

While promising to improve the caliber of its overseas representatives, the State Department flatly rejected Culbertson's proposals for the corporation and collaboration with specific business interests. In addition to resenting the potential intrusion of a rival agency onto their turf, the gentlemen at Foggy Bottom believed that the corporation would contradict the administration's policy of "removing government restrictions and returning trade to private enterprise." Foreign governments might retaliate with restrictions on trade.[7]

Businessmen's complaints about government inaction continued after the war. In an April 1946 meeting at the State Department, for instance, members of the influential National Foreign Trade Council argued that the administration should use its foreign aid programs as "bargaining power" to win nondiscriminatory trade and investment treaties from recipient countries. Private groups were prepared to invest $3 billion annually overseas, the General Motors representative to the NFTC claimed, but "they do not feel at the present time that they have a guardian in the government." The GM official acutely observed that "Bretton Woods provides only a balancing mechanism for foreign trade." In order to compensate for American trade surpluses, massive U.S. foreign investment was necessary if Washington were not "to pump this amount indefinitely in the form of government loans."[8]

Few Truman administration officials, however, thought aid to business was necessary or desirable. A rarely stated, but implicit, premise of American foreign economic planning in this period was that the restoration of prewar patterns of trade and investment, in the absence of governmental interference, would almost by itself spur rapid world recovery. Having already established the multilateral foundations for world recovery, the United States—so this reasoning went—needed to extend only temporary limited aid to Europe. The UN, the Bretton Woods institutions, and the European countries themselves would bear the main burden for reconstruction and stabilization. Thus, while President Truman recognized in July 1945 that European recovery was foundering, he ruled out anything more than a supervisory role for the United States in relief efforts. As the President instructed Secretary of State Byrnes, "Concerted action by the European countries themselves . . . will be of major consequence in reestablishing the economy of liberated nations."[9]

Until May 1946, the administration generally favored multinational, as opposed to unilateral U.S., aid programs. In April 1946, for instance, State Department officials criticized a proposal to establish a centralized European economic organization because the authors of the memo

> have apparently lost sight of the over-riding consideration that the rehabilitation and stabilization of Europe, like that of any other region of the world, is the primary responsibility of the United Nations. . . . Moreover, fitting the proposal firmly within the framework of the United Nations would serve to mitigate the conceivable dangers which otherwise might be involved with respect to the possible political and economic domination of Europe by the Soviet Union and even by a resurgent Germany.[10]

This is not to say that American aid to Western Europe before the Marshall Plan was trifling. U.S. government grants and credits to Western Europe totalled $554 million in 1945 and $2,752 million in 1946, 28 percent and 48 percent of total American foreign aid, respectively.[11] True, Washington usually tied grants and credits to the purchase of American goods and services and to various commercial concessions that sometimes restricted European freedom of action and exacerbated European payments difficulties. Yet American policies were not the fundamental cause of Europe's economic troubles. No amount of American aid, in the absence of the extensive reform of European institutions, could have solved the staggering problems of those war-torn countries.

The European Crisis, 1945–1946

The West European economic crisis stemmed from deficiencies in trade and productivity, both of which were reflected in payments deficits. Before the war, the pattern of trade and payments had rested on three main supports. First, Great Britain—thanks to its large "invisible income" (foreign investments, shipping, and insurance)—had been able to maintain a heavy import surplus with other European countries. The liquidity provided by exports to Britain in turn had paid for continental Europe's purchase of manufactured goods from the Ruhr. Finally, these export earnings permitted Germany to buy raw materials from neighboring and overseas countries.[12]

The war shattered this delicate relationship. For one thing, the collapse of German production crippled intra-European trade. With German manufacturing capacity and East European primary production greatly reduced, continental Europe was forced to turn to overseas suppliers, particularly the United States, for capital equipment, foodstuffs, raw materials, and consumer goods. Moreover, the wartime shipping losses and liquidation of foreign investments sharply curtailed the invisible earnings of European countries, notably Great Britain. And continental Europe, even if it increased production in excess of domestic demand, could no longer count on a large export trade with Great Britain.

Europe now suffered huge deficits in overseas trade, roughly $5 billion in 1946 and $7 billion in 1947. While foreign investment earned $500 million annually, other transactions, such as shipping and overseas defense expenditures, deepened European current account deficits by about $1 billion annually. World inflation, reflected in import prices, aggravated European problems. As a UN study concluded in 1948, "The adverse balance of payments with the rest of the world, together with the attendant dearth of hard currencies required to maintain imports, is, beyond question, the most critical feature of Europe's current economic situation."[13]

Many European countries faced internal inflationary pressures as well. Great Britain kept prices fairly stable through controls, but prices in Italy and France soared after the war. Inflation, whether suppressed or not, distorted the allocation of resources within domestic markets. In most countries, agriculture and luxury goods production absorbed a larger share of national income than they had before the war, draining resources from heavy industry. Inflation also posed a dilemma in relation to foreign trade that became cruelly familiar to Americans during the late 1970s: European currencies were overvalued at the end of the war, but devaluation would have raised the prices of imports at the same time that it encouraged exports. What served the purposes of trade equilibrium, in other words, fueled domestic inflation.[14]

The underlying cause of European problems was low productivity. The war had depleted the working capital of European industry, especially in the occupied countries. Nazi exploitation had also left manpower exhausted and demoralized; postwar labor productivity, a UN report estimated, sank to 40–50 percent of prewar levels. The shortage of hard currency, moreover, cut imports of essential raw materials. Adding to this the terrible damage done to transportation, communications, and housing during the war, the outlook for European recovery was grim.[15]

Nonetheless, European industry, in contrast to the aftermath of World War I, staged a vigorous comeback during the first eighteen months after the war. For fifteen European countries, industrial production rose from 60 percent of 1938 levels in the second half of 1945 to 83 percent in the last quarter of 1946. The degree of restoration varied widely by country. By the latter period, France had almost equaled, and the United Kingdom had exceeded, prewar production. Italy, on the other hand, had recovered to only two-thirds of its 1938 level, while the three western zones of Germany—the industrial heartland of continental Europe—limped along at a disastrous one-third of prewar levels, slumping to one-fourth of prewar production in the first quarter of 1947. Yet excluding Germany, European industry as a whole roughly matched antebellum levels by late 1946.[16]

The recovery was regrettably short-lived. Bad weather and a coal shortage precipitated (but did not cause) a severe recession during the winter of 1946–47. The rehabilitation of the European countries during 1945–46 had entailed the rapid depletion of stocks of raw and semi-finished materials. With the prewar pattern of trade and payments disrupted, European countries lacked the hard currency to pay for imports of these materials. In late 1946, the European economies ground to a halt.[17]

The European countries had by this time entered into a series of two hundred bilateral trade and payments agreements that were designed to conserve scarce currencies and gold and to balance intra-European trade. This eased the immediate settlements problem posed by the inconvertibility of European currencies, but bilateralism also placed restraints upon the volume and character of intra-European trade. Given the grave shortage of hard currency and gold reserves, a country with an export surplus could not extend large amounts of credit to a country with an import surplus. A close balancing of accounts was therefore necessary. Bilateralism denied European countries the opportunity to buy or to sell goods on the most advantageous terms, held down the volume of intra-European trade below prewar levels, and discouraged long-term recovery. Once protectionist measures were instituted, moreover, they proved difficult to remove: "Home production formerly encouraged to save foreign exchange might now require protection against competition from abroad," William Diebold, Jr., observes. "Import barriers originally imposed to save dollars might be maintained to keep out goods from other European countries as well."[18]

This trend toward bilateralism and state-trading naturally alarmed American officials, who remembered where such a course had led Europe in the recent past. American efforts to unravel this tangle of trade restrictions made good political and economic sense from a long-term perspective. Yet the flow of Lend-Lease, Eximbank, surplus property and other aid was drying up just as European recovery began to stall in late 1946. Since UNRRA relief was limited to severely crippled, war-torn countries such as China, Italy, and Greece, most West European countries, notably Britain and France, were excluded from one of the few grants-in-aid programs of the early postwar period. Meanwhile, the Bretton Woods institutions remained inactive.[19]

What Western Europe needed most was a program of large-scale reconstruction aid and regional economic integration. Otherwise, these countries could never hope to compensate for losses of invisible earnings or replace manufactured imports from the United States. Only Washington could provide the aid and the impetus for reform necessary for European recovery. Until the Marshall Plan, however, American planners focused narrowly upon short-term relief and long-term structural reforms without sufficient attention to mid-term reconstruction.[20]

An alternative interpretation has it that West European recovery was under way well before the arrival of substantial American aid. In this view, the United States, by disguising Open Door imperialism as moral idealism, took advantage of temporary European distress and lured those countries into the American economic orbit. Presumably, the main object of U.S. policy was to rescue capitalism.[21]

One may safely dismiss this interpretation. Europe's recovery after the war was by no means assured, and her needs were many. American officials were hardly enthusiastic about assuming the additional financial burdens of new aid programs. Of course, Truman administration officials were aware of the dividends that would eventually accrue to the United States from the integration of Western Europe into the American sphere. But in the period before the Marshall Plan, they did not clearly understand the steps necessary to further U.S. aims in the region, or at least acted as if they did not understand. Anglo-American negotiations leading to the British loan illustrate the limited scope of U.S. planning.

The British Loan and the Decline of the British Empire, 1945–1947

By 1945, the United States and Great Britain had developed a special relationship built upon cultural ties, economic interdependence, and military alliance in two world wars. Yet the superficial amity of wartime relations concealed an undercurrent of rivalry and resentment stemming from divergent national interests and goals. And while most policymakers in Washington and London were unaware of it, the British Empire was rapidly decaying. U.S. officials imposed economic conditions that accelerated the decline of the Empire. "The essential fact of the Anglo-American relationship was that it was not a symmetrical one," Robert Hathaway states. "Great Britain needed and relied upon the Americans much more than the United States depended on Britain."[22]

The war had stripped away many of Britain's most important external assets: "The country had lost one-quarter of its prewar national wealth and had been forced to liquidate one-half, or $8 billion worth, of its foreign investments, while its external debt had increased. By the close of 1944 British exports had dropped to one-third of their prewar volume."[23]

With their country incurring huge trade deficits late in the war, the British were reluctant to adopt American multilateralist programs. The conflict between British and American policies first publicly surfaced in the Bretton Woods negotiations. In Parliament, an unlikely coalition of Tories and socialists worked to maintain the discriminatory imperial system. To them, joining Bretton Woods meant going into the American orbit as a junior partner. British officials, U.S. Ambassador to London John G. Winant noted, expressed concern "about the ability of the United States to maintain a high level of employment," and hence imports, during peacetime. What assurance, they asked, did Britain have that American isolationism would not reemerge after the war, just as it had after World War I? Free trade, critics added, might worsen the British external position and act as a brake on social change.[24]

Even the British business community, traditionally a friend of free trade, had embraced protectionism. Remembering the steep American trade barriers against British goods during the 1930s, British businessmen were unhappy at the prospect of exchanging the certain advantages of the preference system for the uncertain advantages of freer trade. As Winant explained, the British believed they had sacrificed far more than the Americans during the war. Restrictive commercial practices, such as state trading in bulk grain purchases, seemed a sensible expedient until recovery was assured.[25]

American negotiators met British objections halfway in the drafting of the Bretton Woods agreements. London's representatives signed the accords only after receiving assurances that the United States would give them a postwar loan. Britain also obtained the right to impose trade and currency restrictions if she faced chronic payments difficulties. American officials pledged reciprocal tariff concessions and certain steps, such as generous Lend-Lease settlements, to restore world equilibrium.

Other, more informal understandings at Bretton Woods were equally important. John Maynard Keynes made clear that his country expected the United States, as the world's chief creditor nation, to maintain high domestic production and employment (to encourage imports) and to sponsor an International Trade Organization (ITO) that would reduce commercial barriers. The British generally refused to discontinue the sterling system and other restrictive practices until the United States reciprocated by opening its own ports to foreign merchants.[26]

Ironically, after all the lip-service Americans had given to free trade, the U.S. Congress refused to endorse the multilateral principles— maintenance of high domestic employment and production, reduction of trade barriers, elimination of cartels, and regulation of state trading—that would lay the basis for the ITO. Instead, the Congress merely approved extension of the Reciprocal Trade Agreements (RTA), a cumbersome procedure granting the Executive authority to negotiate bilateral tariff reductions. Some American officials, such as Ambassador Winant, recognized the inconsistency of the American position and tried to correct it.

Yet by the fall of 1945, the Congress and the public had turned against outright grants of foreign aid and demanded concrete concessions from aid recipients. Congressional approval of RTA, in fact, came only after prolonged lobbying by the administration. Many Congressmen were highly critical of the British welfare state and quailed at the thought of following the British socialists' "path to economic ruin." The replacement of Henry Morgenthau as Secretary of the Treasury by the more conservative Fred M. Vinson in July 1945 marked a parallel shift within the administration away from bold economic initiatives abroad.[27]

Representatives of Great Britain and Canada, which was also suffering a severe dollar shortage, were quick to note the American double standard. They asked why their countries should give up the benefits of the preference system when the United States had yet to adopt a consistent position on multilateralism and the ITO. The best American officials could do was to propose a compromise measure that fell between bilateralism and multilateralism.[28]

In any case, the British soon crumbled before American pressure. During talks at London in August 1945, British negotiators tried to separate financial issues—the loan and Lend-Lease—from commercial ones—preference, import restrictions, and convertibility—while American officials sought to link U.S. aid with British trade and currency concessions. Lord Keynes insisted he wanted "the same economic world as did the US but he kept hinting and on several occasions virtually threatening that if the US was not inspired the British would probably choose a bilateralistic course and that if the British swung to state trading they would have an important influence on many parts of the world."[29] Assistant Secretary of State William Clayton was not impressed. Reporting to Washington on August 17, 1945, he contended that "the British are putting up a very determined front to cover a basically very weak financial position with a very serious outlook."[30]

President Truman's sudden cancellation of Lend-Lease the following day called the British bluff. Though the United States had begun curtailing Lend-Lease to Britain in mid-1944 and had cut off most military supplies in May 1945, Whitehall had expected continuation of the non-military pipeline in accordance with an informal understanding reached at Potsdam. Prime Minister Clement R. Attlee could barely conceal his sense of betrayal and outrage in a brisk message to the President:

> the maintenance of the physical flow of supplies from the United States . . . is necessary for the maintenance of the living conditions of this country. You have probably also been informed by Mr. Clayton of the general financial position in which we find ourselves because our war effort took a certain shape as part of the combined war plans. . . . We have realized that . . . we shall henceforward have to pay for the urgent supplies that we need from the United States. Therefore it is hardly necessary for me to assure you that if these supplies for the next month come forward to us, . . . they will be paid for.[31]

Truman's reply was abrupt and hardly reassuring. The President was keenly aware of Congressional opposition to the use of Lend-Lease for reconstruction purposes. Truman's ignorance of Roosevelt's wartime commitments and his insensitivity to London's distress further disposed him against a generous interpretation of British rights under Lend-Lease.[32]

The Anglo-American Financial Agreement of December 1945 extracted numerous painful concessions from the British. As Attlee complained to Winant, the agreements forced his country to give up the escape clauses won at Bretton Woods. After December 31, 1946, the British were obliged to end the sterling area dollar pool and quantitative import controls (QRs) on American goods. In addition, Britain was required to restore sterling convertibility in mid-1947, that is, to allow countries enjoying export surpluses with the United Kingdom to exchange sterling for scarce dollars. Finally, the agreement compelled the United Kingdom to scale down the vast sterling balances accumulated by other countries during the war, presumably to facilitate the transition to a multilateral currency regime. Yet due to numerous loopholes, only the provisions concerning QRs and sterling convertibility would pose major problems for the British.[33]

In return, the British received a low-interest $3.75 billion loan designed to meet short-term payments problems. In a supplementary agreement, the United States also wiped out the British wartime Lend-Lease account of $20 billion and sold over $6 billion worth of surplus property and pipeline (postwar) Lend-Lease equipment for just $650 million, with the same liberal provisions for repayment as those for the loan. Convinced by Keynes that Britain had no other recourse, the House of Commons ratified Bretton Woods, the Lend-Lease settlement, and the financial agreement in December 1945 after a stormy debate.[34]

However unwise certain of the multilateral obligations appear in retrospect, one cannot agree with revisionist characterizations of the loan agreements as an American plot to bankrupt Britain and capture her foreign markets. It is true that Clayton confided to Bernard Baruch, "We loaded the British loan negotiations with all the conditions that the traffic would bear." But the context of this statement is crucial: Clayton surely stressed the advantages of the loan to the United States because the Anglophobe Baruch was the foremost opponent of a large loan to Britain. The terms of the loan also compared favorably with those offered by the Eximbank, which imposed higher interest charges and required recipients to buy American goods. And if the Truman administration's policies contributed to the collapse of the British Empire, they certainly did not cause it, for the rot was already well advanced before the war ended.[35]

U.S. policymakers, in fact, wished to preserve the special relationship with Britain and only pressed for concessions from London because experts on both sides of the Atlantic overestimated her economic and military strength after the war. In the public debate, American officials offered three main arguments for the loan agreement, with varying emphasis depending upon their audience. To businessmen, internationalists, and the general public, they pointed out that Britain was a major importer of American goods, and that the cooperation of the British Commonwealth was essential for the success of U.S. multilateralism. "The third reason was seldom publicly advocated by government officials," Thomas Paterson states, "but became prominent in the congressional debates: Britain was a valuable ally."[36]

During the prolonged Congressional consideration of the loan, the architects of foreign economic policy learned a sobering lesson. Despite an intense effort to educate the public on the economic benefits of the loan, multilateralism never stirred the popular imagination. The loan, in fact, faced stiff opposition in Congress on both political and economic grounds. Some Congressmen feared that the loan, by reinforcing the alliance with Britain, contravened the internationalist spirit of the UN. Others felt that Britain had sufficient economic resources to stand on her own feet, that her socialist government was the main barrier to recovery, and that the United States had already done enough to help Britain during the war. Even stalwart backing for the loan by business groups could not rally Congressional support.[37]

What finally won Congressional passage of the loan agreement was the belated realization, amid deepening tension in Soviet-American relations, that Britain was America's best friend in the struggle against Communist expansion. Officials responsible for ushering the loan through Congress, such as Under Secretary of State Dean Acheson, deplored this tendency. But as Republican Representative Christian Herter of New York reported to Clayton in May 1946 after the Assistant Secretary had consulted with Republican Congressmen, anti-Communism was an effective rallying cry. "I find that the economic arguments in favor of the loan," Herter wrote, "are on the whole much less convincing to this group than the feeling that the loan may serve us in good stead in holding up a hand of a nation whom we may need badly as a friend because of impending Russian troubles." Clayton replied, "I am sure you are right in your analysis."[38]

Yet aside from the loan, the United States took few steps to solidify military and diplomatic ties with Britain immediately after the war. During Byrnes' tenure as Secretary of State, ambiguity and uncertainty characterized Anglo-American relations. Byrnes decided in the summer of 1946 to forsake Eastern Europe and concentrate American resources upon the reconstruction of Western Europe. But he did not consistently act upon this resolution.[39]

The shortcomings of Anglo-American cooperation were most apparent in the military field. U.S. reluctance to share information on atomic energy with Britain, culminating in the McMahon Act of August 1946, seemingly violated wartime agreements and "retarded cooperation in the whole field of strategic planning." Military officials naturally desired an alliance with Britain in event of war, but did not expect significant help from Britain or any other ally during the initial stages of hostilities. During the summer of 1946, the JCS for the first time recommended efforts to conclude formal military alliances with friendly nations. Even then, the military chiefs warned that the United States should be prepared to fight alone, for it could not rely upon any of its allies. Only in late 1946 did American military officials take steps to coordinate strategic planning with their British counterparts.[40]

What explains the American neglect of Britain? Most American officials believed that war with Russia was not imminent, and that Western Europe was secure. Moreover, many of them suspected London's motives; some believed, for instance, that the British were exploiting the Soviet threat to win American protection for their overseas Empire. Finally, a number of U.S. planners felt ill-concealed disdain toward British capabilities.[41]

In any event, the administration had greatly oversold the degree to which the agreements of December 1945 would reduce British trade barriers, open up world trade, and restore West European stability. Exaggeration of the loan's benefits would soon return to haunt the administration. The British external situation, after a robust expansion of exports during most of 1946, rapidly deteriorated in the latter part of that year. Reduced invisible income, unexpectedly high expenditures overseas, mounting trade deficits, and ambitious domestic programs forced Britain to draw down the loan faster than scheduled. The short-lived experiment in sterling convertibility (July to August 1947) virtually exhausted the remainder of the loan. By the summer of 1947, the British payments deficit had grown 50 percent larger than it had been in 1946.[42]

The loan had failed, and once again, Europe was clamoring for more American aid. After the Republican resurgence in the autumn of 1946, the administration could scarcely count on enthusiastic Congressional backing for additional foreign aid programs. The administration had learned that economic self-interest did not impress Congress and the public as much as the specter of Communist aggression. As a result, multilateralism would play less and less a role in official advocacy of trade and aid programs.

Containing Communism in France and Italy

Political factors guided American policies in France and Italy more than they did in Great Britain. In particular, the seeming risk of Soviet-inspired Communist coups in those countries spurred Washington officials to mount ever larger rescue aid programs. Lacking a coherent program for the reconstruction of Europe as a whole, the Truman administration would blatantly, but effectively, intervene in French and Italian politics by extending emergency loans to non-Communist governments just before national elections in the spring of 1946.

Until the Marshall Plan, France was the linchpin of American policy in Europe, for most American planners hoped that France would replace Germany as the main power on the European continent. Presumably, Paris would work with London and Washington to rebuild the shattered European economies and contain the Soviet Union. This plan would both restore the balance of power on the continent and appease French fears of a renascent Germany. From Washington's perspective, the contribution of France, as well as Italy, to a new Europe was more political than economic: to combat Communism and to reestablish moderate democratic governments in the U.S. sphere of Europe.[43] There were several problems with the American plan, not the least of which was that Washington officials grossly underestimated the importance of Germany to general European recovery.

They also may have misunderstood the roots of Communist influence in Western Europe. Both Paris and Rome harbored strong Communist parties, neither of which were simple creatures of Moscow. In the European experience, democracy had not been most closely associated with capitalism, as it was in the United States, but with socialism. And in postwar France and Italy, the Communist Party seemed to be the heir to democratic socialism. As the country that had done the most to defeat Hitler, the Soviet Union appeared to be the most progressive nation, the model and inspiration for socialists everywhere. (Stalin's crimes were as of yet not widely known.) Thus, despite important differences between the French and Italian Communists and their Soviet mentors, the West European parties strictly followed Moscow on foreign policy issues, for instance by attempting to disrupt the Marshall Plan with strikes and demonstrations in the fall of 1947. It is perhaps understandable, then, that U.S. policymakers should sometimes exaggerate the degree to which national Communist parties reflected the will of the Kremlin.[44]

Vigorous U.S. leadership was in any event sorely lacking during 1945 and 1946. Left to their own devices, Britain, France, and Italy scrambled to protect native industries, making little progress toward a viable regional economy. At times, Washington's policies exacerbated their problems. The American tendency was to take back with one hand what the other had given away. At the same time that it was offering billions in relief to Western Europe, for example, the United States sought commercial concessions from Paris and Rome that they could ill afford to grant. Until the winter 1947 crisis forced a reevaluation, American policies toward these countries followed an erratic and drifting course.

A shift in U.S. policies toward France and Italy was imperative, for American interests there were substantial. U.S. exports to France, for instance, soared from $472 million in 1945 to $817 million in 1947, the latter figure representing an almost sixfold increase over the 1936–1938 average. Italy imported about 40 percent less from the United States, but like France, Italy was an important component in European recovery. Both countries, however, suffered severe trade deficits with the United States. With only $63 million in exports to the U.S. in 1946, for instance, the French deficit came to $646 million; Italy's deficit was $302 million.[45] As their hard reserves diminished, France and Italy increasingly relied upon the United States to finance imports. But U.S. aid was running out just as European recovery stalled in late 1946.

U.S. Aid to France, 1945–1947

The French experience illustrates the *ad hoc* nature of American aid programs in continental Europe. Following the Allied liberation, living conditions in France deteriorated to levels worse than those during the German occupation, and recovery commenced only in late 1945. The termination of Lend-Lease in September 1945 put France in almost as awkward an economic position as Britain. Recognizing the grievous French capital and manpower losses during the war, the National Advisory Council in 1945 committed $550 million in Eximbank funds to cover pipeline Lend-Lease shipments to France. In return, American diplomats demanded that France, under its Article VII obligations, reduce trade barriers, restore trade to private channels, and generally lessen governmental interference in the domestic economy.[46]

In the autumn of 1945, French officials, wary of a worsening external position, reluctantly agreed to the American principles to expedite an Eximbank loan, but refused to take concrete action until equilibrium was restored in Europe. In addition, Ambassador Jefferson Caffery explained, the Paris government sought "recognition of France by US as an economic power entailed to same considerations as the UK." Caffery recommended that Washington hold out for more meaningful concessions than the verbal assurances that the French had offered in exchange for a loan. Subsequently, the State Department in early 1946 ruled out a special loan for France while keeping open the possibility of a large Eximbank loan. "An approach to Congress for a credit to France, along lines of British loan," Byrnes decided, "is not practicable."[47]

French diplomacy during the early postwar period did not improve the chances for a big loan. The French resented and envied the power and wealth of their American liberators. Like their British counterparts, French nationalists who hoped to retain the advantages of their trading empire resisted the American prescriptions for freer trade and reduced governmental intervention in the economy. The strength of the Communist Party in postwar France also meant that the United States could not easily recruit Paris into the Western coalition. In France, journalist Alexander Werth observed, "Anti-Soviet feeling was, on the whole, slower to develop than in Britain or the USA." The prickly conduct of General Charles De Gaulle in his talks with Truman in August 1945 further disinclined the administration from offering special aid to France, even to one of its foremost non-Communist leaders.[48]

Political crisis, rather than economic hardship, softened the U.S. negotiating posture. The collapse of the De Gaulle government in January 1946 and the deterioration of the French financial position, Ambassador Caffery warned, could redound to the advantage of the Communist Party in the May and June elections. Interestingly, Caffery now argued, with scarcely a reference to reciprocal concessions, that "the loan France will request of US should be weighed in terms of its political importance."[49]

Caffery's point was not lost on the State Department, notably Will Clayton, who sought a $650 million to $750 million Eximbank loan to France, in addition to a comparable amount of surplus property credits, to combat Communist influence in that country. Meeting in late April 1946, the National Advisory Council quietly killed the Russian loan and considered shifting the funds earmarked for that purpose to France. Meanwhile, Treasury Secretary Vinson served notice to Léon Blum, the visiting French Ambassador-Extraordinary and leader of the French Socialists, that the chances for U.S. aid would be greatly improved if his party would join an anti-Communist coalition and oust the Communists from important economic posts in the Cabinet.[50]

Events in May 1946 forced the NAC to reach a quick decision on the French loan. The French elections were rapidly approaching, and the Communist threat appeared more ominous than ever. The War Department, after receiving President Truman's approval, authorized U.S. military movements in the event of a Communist coup.[51]

The NAC met again on May 24 to discuss the French loan. Clayton asked for a $650 million credit before the French national elections in June, but Eximbank Director William McChesney Martin, Jr., demurred, citing a shortage of bank funds and the needs of other worthy applicants for aid. Federal Reserve Governor Marriner S. Eccles added that using Eximbank funds for political, as opposed to purely economic, purposes violated the bank's charter, "It would be unfortunate," Eccles stated, "to make a loan to influence an election in a particular direction."[52]

Clayton admitted that he "had great difficulty in separating political from economic considerations in thinking about Europe." The Assistant Secretary at first awkwardly tried to make the case for a massive loan to France on economic grounds alone, but then laid his cards on the table. "England and France form the key to the whole Western European situation," Clayton told his colleagues, and their stabilization was necessary to save "Western Europe from a collapse." With only the Eximbank Director dissenting, the NAC approved a $650 million loan to France. The United States and France quickly reached agreement on the loan, Lend-Lease, surplus property, and other matters in May 1946. Washington secured few concrete economic concessions in these negotiations, although Paris pledged cooperation with American efforts to expand world trade.[53]

The crisis in Paris temporarily subsided after May 1946. Caffery attributed the Communists' setback to Byrnes' firm stand against Molotov during the spring of 1946 at the Paris Council of Foreign Ministers. Byrnes, the ambassador claimed, had convinced the French electorate that "perhaps the Cossacks won't get here after all." Apparently, too, the Comintern had instructed the French Communist Party to strike a lower profile.[54]

Yet as France slid into another economic crisis during the fall, Caffery predicted a renewed Communist bid for power. The Communist success in the November 1946 elections and the fragility of French governments in subsequent months seemed to confirm Caffery's worst fears. In February 1947, the Ambassador reported:

> Posing to the average Frenchman as the strongest defender of his fatherland, especially against the German "menace" and "international capital," the Soviet Trojan horse in France is so well camouflaged that millions of Communist militants, sympathizers, and opportunists have been brought to believe that the best way to defend France is to identify French national interests with the aims of the Soviet Union. . . . The Comintern "brain trust" here is more active and bolder than at any period since the liberation.[55]

Bilateral transfusions of American aid neither cured French economic problems nor drew France securely into the Western camp. The failure of the early postwar aid programs to put France on a sound footing was not due to American parsimony. U.S. governmental grants and credits grew from $149 million in 1945 to $1,158 million in 1946, the latter figure representing the largest American outlay for any country in Western Europe.[56] Simply put, the problems of France and Italy could not be solved without the integration of the West European—including German—economies.

U.S. Aid to Italy, 1945–1947

American relations with Italy paralleled those with France in at least one major respect: the level of U.S. aid depended as much, if not more, upon American perceptions of the threat posed by the local Communist Party as upon actual physical need. Italy had lost only about 8 percent of her industrial capacity in the war, but thanks to raw material shortages and heavy destruction of her transportation network, Italy's industrial production in 1945 dropped 29 percent from 1938 levels. Agricultural output fell 63 percent over the same years. "In the devastation inflicted by the war," H. Stuart Hughes concludes, "Italy suffered more heavily than any Western nation except Germany."[57]

As a former Axis belligerent, however, Italy held a "low priority position" in American aid programs. The result was a policy of benign neglect. In accordance with "the policy of encouraging the Italian Government to stand on its own feet," as the British put it, the Allied Commission for Italy gradually turned over economic responsibilities to the hapless Italian government during late 1945. At a time when Italy could not pay for essential imports, Byrnes pressed the Rome government to return foreign trade to private channels, but offered little hope for dollar credits. Italy was the second largest recipient of UNRRA aid ($418 million) in Europe, but this and other civilian relief could not satisfy Italy's tremendous hunger for capital goods and raw materials.[58]

During early 1946, the Italian government headed by Christian Democrat Alcide De Gasperi repeatedly submitted applications for a $940 million Eximbank loan. The Italians forthrightly based their case for a loan on political grounds. American aid, they implied, would hurt the Communist Party in the summer elections. Yet Eximbank officials in a March 1946 meeting of the NAC firmly rejected the Italian request because the bank had hitherto resisted political loans to high-risk clients. In this instance, even Clayton "observed that a loan to Italy will be a political loan and he wondered whether the Export-Import Bank should make a political loan which none of the Council's members believe will be repaid." Meeting a month later, the NAC recommended indirect Treasury Department aid totaling about $100 million, but again postponed consideration of an Eximbank loan.[59]

By May, however, Clayton was pleading for an emergency $100 million Eximbank loan to Italy. Ostensibly, State Department officials favored Eximbank aid to alleviate the grave recession in Italy, but with the June elections approaching, the political dividends of such aid were probably foremost in their minds. Clayton himself conceded that the loan would be little more than a gesture of goodwill to the Italian people. As Soviet-American relations soured, U.S. policymakers increasingly measured aid programs in terms of Cold War politics. The National Advisory Council, however, was one step behind the State Department and refused to help Italy as it had France, partly because the NAC members harbored strong doubts about Italy's ability to repay.[60]

Meanwhile, a Congressional subcommittee killed the proposal for Treasury Department aid to Italy. An ex-enemy country did not deserve grants-in-aid, the Congressmen reasoned. Clayton and Secretary of the Treasury John W. Snyder, who succeeded Vinson in June 1946, finally won Congressional consent to Treasury aid in July, but Italy did not receive the first $50 million of these funds until October 1946. In addition to this and UNRRA aid, the United States gave Italy a $25 million cotton credit, $160 million in surplus property credits, and forty Liberty ships for a nominal price.[61]

This trickle of aid did virtually nothing to stem Italy's soaring inflation, staggering trade deficits, and political instability. Negotiations on the Eximbank loan had yet to commence in the fall of 1946 when American officials belatedly recognized the severity of Italy's crisis, now accompanied by civil disorder and Communist resurgence. Following settlement of the Treasury aid issue, the NAC staff at last recommended a $100 million Eximbank loan to cover "Italy's urgent import needs during the next few months." During a visit to Washington in January 1947, De Gasperi won assurances of the Eximbank loan, increased grain shipments, post-UNRRA and other aid, "coupled with the intimation that his government would enjoy still greater favor in Washington if the Communists were no longer in it."[62]

Italy received far less American help than France, and what little Rome received did not come in time to avert the winter 1947 crisis.[63] American officials simply did not rate the needs of an impoverished, underdeveloped, ex-enemy state very highly in comparison with problems elsewhere. The stopgap American aid programs in Italy and France delayed, for a dangerously long interval, the recovery of Europe as a whole, as well as the fulfillment of the American multilateral program.

Failure of Early Postwar American Aid Programs

There were some promising developments in this period, but far more occasions for despair. The Geneva General Agreement on Tariffs and Trade (GATT) in 1947, for instance, opened up world trade and helped compensate for the failure of the ITO.[64] But in the short run, reduced American trade barriers did little for European nations that were incapable of producing enough for home consumption, let alone for export. Moreover, the scaling down of European protectionism actually accentuated their payments problems by encouraging a larger inflow of American products.

American aid did not fill this trade gap. Americans sometimes pointed to the $15 billion in paper assets that the World Bank commanded. Supposedly, the Bank would meet European needs when U.S. aid ran out. In fact, the Bank held only $3.2 billion in real assets to finance European reconstruction, and virtually none of this was forthcoming before or during the 1946-1947 crisis. The Bank was just beginning to operate, and its cumbersome procedure for loan applications discouraged aid requests.[65]

American aid programs to Western Europe were not only too little, but too late as well. By the time Britain was able to draw upon the $3.75 billion loan, inflation had sharply reduced the quantity of U.S. goods this sum could buy. France received more timely, if less ample, aid than Britain, but Italy did not receive substantial help until she had already plunged into a painful recession. In no case did the haphazard and *ad hoc* American aid programs help recipient countries avert the downturn of 1946–47. At best, U.S. aid cushioned their fall.

Some foresighted Americans, such as William Clayton, recognized that before long, the United States would have to intervene on a massive scale to revive the European economies. Yet for the time being, certain prejudices inhibited bold action. For instance, spending limitations—both those dictated by Congress and those self-imposed by the Truman administration—constrained planners from undertaking the large-scale, medium-term reconstruction program that Europe needed. American officials were also reluctant to act because they expected the Europeans to rely upon their own resources or, if worse came to worst, upon the Bretton Woods and other UN institutions.

The unhappy American experience in Western Europe raised doubts about these operating principles. True, Washington gained considerable leverage over individual countries once it abandoned the multinational (UN) approach to foreign aid after mid-1946 and embarked on bilateral aid programs. But the United States still exercised little control over intra-European economic relations. After all the billions Washington had spent, the West European countries erected a maze of barriers to multilateral trade and finance that bore a disturbing resemblance to prewar restrictions.

The prospects for a multilateral world economy seemed to fade during this period. Eastern Europe enjoyed only nominal autonomy, and Western Europe had become tangled in a thicket of bilateral treaties. American economic security—based upon an open and cooperative economic system in postwar Europe—was in jeopardy.

American officials realized that West European reconstruction could not await the advent of ideal economic conditions. Attention turned to the linchpin of the European economy, and the main impediment to its recovery: Germany. "The outstanding feature of the aftermath of the Second World War," a UN report in 1948 stated, "was the collapse of production in Germany." The postwar decline of German trade "exercises a heavy depressing influence on the entire European trade picture."[66] But rehabilitation in Germany would prove even more difficult than it did in Western Europe.

CHAPTER FIVE

INDECISION IN GERMANY, 1945–1947

A MERICAN POLICYMAKERS were slow to realize how much Europe's survival depended on German recovery. Germany, the heartland of Europe, almost bled to death while the Allies fought over its future. And the clumsy and incremental process by which U.S. officials arrived at a policy for Germany suggests none of the purposeful action that one might expect of a world power bent upon empire-building in Europe.

From the very first, American planning in Germany was pulled in two directions. On the one hand, wartime planners wished to disarm and neutralize the former Reich. Germany would be stripped of heavy industry, if not actually pastoralized, and shorn of large tracts of territory, if not fully partitioned. On the other hand, the American multi-lateral program called for the reconstruction of German industry and its integration into the West European economy. The conflict between these tendencies was never quite resolved before early 1947. Even after European recovery had clearly assumed precedence over German disarmament in American policy, Washington faced stiff resistance to its plans in Germany from other interested powers, East and West.

American Interests in Germany

The United States had fought in two world wars to preclude German hegemony over Europe. In later years, Americans would have difficulty remembering the revulsion that they had felt toward Germany in 1945 following the Nazis' savage persecution and slaughter of captive populations. In cooperation with other nations, American officials resolved to punish war criminals and stamp out every vestige of Nazi power and influence.

More importantly in the long term, the United States sought the elimination of German militarism. Like the French and Russians, many American officials feared the early revival of German military might and aggression and favored the indefinite occupation of Germany by the Allied powers.[1] The American prescription for a peaceful Germany included economic reforms as well. Wartime planners believed that world depression, protectionism, and state control of the economy had engendered and sustained fascism. By restructuring the German economy, the victorious Allies presumably could eliminate the conditions that had given birth to internal repression and external aggression in Germany.

Official Washington never reached agreement during the war on how to realize the general objective of a peaceful, democratic, and implicitly capitalist Germany. Clearly, a crippled Germany would impede European recovery. Yet reconstructing and integrating the German economy into Western Europe ran directly contrary to the impulse of many wartime planners to destroy German war potential.

Before the war, Germany had been one of America's important, but not primary, trading partners. U.S. exports to Germany during the 1920s had averaged about $350 million annually, or almost one-seventh of all exports to Europe. With the onset of the world depression, Hitler endorsed nationalist policies designed to reduce dependence on imports. American exports to Germany fell two-thirds during the 1930s to about $125 million, or less than one-ninth of total U.S. exports to Europe.[2]

Not surprisingly, trade revived very slowly after the war. Her economy shattered, Germany (including the Soviet zone) in 1946 imported only $83 million worth of American goods in 1946, as against a pathetic $3 million in exports (the comparable figures for 1947 were $128 million and $6 million). U.S. government grants and credits rose sharply from $26 million in 1945 to $300 million in 1946 and $417 million in 1947, but Germany's overall commercial situation remained dismal.[3]

Prewar American investment in Germany had been small compared with that in other major industrialized nations. It was even less likely that Americans would sink capital in postwar Germany. The war had wiped out many U.S. properties, and the Russians did not hesitate to seize those that had survived in their zone.

The Truman administration, moreover, did little to encourage the return of American capital. The State Department, for instance, initially blocked the International Telephone and Telegraph Corporation from reestablishing operations in Germany. Immediately after the Nazi surrender, the War Department had appointed an IT&T vice-president as a Brigadier General in the U.S. occupation organization in order to survey the communications industry in the American zone. The State Department, however, claimed that the appointment undermined U.S. decartelization policy in Germany:

> In view of the program for the military control and industrial disarmament of Germany, and the policies of this Government with respect to the termination of German participation in international cartels and combines and the elimination of private restrictive agreements affecting international trade, the State Department regards these developments as undesirable.[4]

IT&T's trials in Germany had only begun. In late 1945, the Soviets seized two IT&T plants in eastern Germany as "war booty." More exasperating yet was the decision by the War Department's Office of Military Government of the United States for Germany (OMGUS) to allow local German authorities to determine the rate at which industrial plants, including IT&T affiliates, could resume production in the U.S. zone. The devastation and uncertainty in European markets led the founder of IT&T, Colonel Sosthenes Behn, to confide in February 1946 that he had "liquidated every foreign property that he could as fast as he could."[5]

Although private American interests were too small to influence national policies in Germany, the American stakes in general European recovery were considerable. And both as a supplier of coal and manufactured goods and as a trading partner, Germany held the key to the economic health of Europe. The collapse of German production was the main source of contraction in intra-European trade and European overseas exports. Since German coal and manufactured goods were unavailable, European countries were forced to squander precious hard currency on imports of these goods from overseas countries, notably the United States. A UN report in 1948 concluded that Europe could restore a balance-of-payments equilibrium only by increasing its own industrial production and by cutting overseas imports.[6] German reconstruction, U.S. officials would belatedly realize, offered the solution to both problems.

The Morgenthau Plan and Roosevelt's Vacillation on Germany

No country in Europe had more unused industrial capacity than Germany. Why, then, did the United States block German reconstruction? Part of the answer lies in the roles of Franklin Roosevelt and Henry Morgenthau in wartime planning on Germany.

The ascendancy of the Morgenthau Plan in American policy for Germany was short-lived, but two years passed before a clear alternative emerged. Morgenthau's program for Germany has found few latter-day defenders, and for good reason. In addition to German disarmament, the Secretary of the Treasury favored the prompt and wholesale deindustrialization of the defeated power. By pastoralizing and decentralizing the German economy, Morgenthau hoped to eradicate the socioeconomic structure that had nurtured Nazism.

It mattered little to Morgenthau that modern Germany had never been able to feed itself. Like many New Dealers, including President Roosevelt, Morgenthau subscribed to the naive agrarian notion that cities give rise to unnatural and aggressive behavior while the countryside is the fount of mankind's better impulses.[7] From this, Morgenthau concluded that reducing the German people to subsistence farming would make them more peaceful and constructive members of the world community.

Morgenthau was unwilling to acknowledge the economic dangers that a nonproductive, let alone pastoralized, Germany would pose to Europe and America. His plan to strip the Ruhr might put eighteen or twenty million Germans out of work, Morgenthau admitted to Roosevelt in September 1944, but it "ought to go a long way towards solving the economic future of England." The victors, Morgenthau added, should "transplant" all Nazi-inculcated Germans between the ages of twenty and forty "to some place in Central Africa where you can do some big TVA project." When Harry White, the architect with John Maynard Keynes of Bretton Woods, asked what would happen to the millions of unemployed, Morgenthau replied that the President would feed them from the Army's soup kitchens. Morgenthau was inflexible on the issue of the Ruhr. "I am for destroying [the Ruhr] first and we will worry about the population second," he told White and other Treasury officials in September 1944. "Why the hell should I worry about what happens to their people?"[8]

A Treasury memo of January 1945 further warned that "the building up of Germany as a bulwark against Russia and communism will inevitably lead to a third World War." The United States should help transfer heavy industry from Germany to neighboring countries and harness the remaining German production to European reconstruction. Europe, according to the memo, did not need a strong industrial Germany, and "a 'soft' peace" would not necessarily "facilitate the growth of democracy in Germany." Treasury officials also opposed reparations from current production, as opposed to once-and-for-all capital removals, because that "would require immediate reconstruction of the German economy."[9]

Despite furious opposition from the State and War Departments, Morgenthau dominated U.S. policy toward Germany while his close friend Franklin Roosevelt was alive. The President appeared to endorse the Morgenthau Plan by accepting provisions for a harsh German settlement in the Quebec Agreement, which Churchill and Roosevelt signed in September 1944. Later in the month, Roosevelt also approved a tough, interim version of JCS 1067, the directive on U.S. occupation policy in Germany, which called for denazification, demilitarization, financial reform, minimal relief, and strict economic controls.

Treasury's victory was nevertheless a Pyrrhic one, for nowhere was the President's ambiguity and confusion more apparent than in his handling of the German question. Roosevelt soon qualified his support for the Morgenthau Plan following public criticism of the agreement in the United States during the 1944 campaign. Having overplayed his hand, Morgenthau now faced a backlash from the State and War Departments, which began to mobilize Congressional opposition to the Treasury Plan. Roosevelt, unable or unwilling to find firm ground to stand on, ordered a postponement of any important decisions on the treatment of Germany for the duration of the war. Roosevelt also wavered in his support for JCS 1067 before his death.[10]

As it was, the final version of JCS 1067 contained numerous loopholes. General Lucius D. Clay, the head of OMGUS and an avowed critic of economic dismantling, wrote in June 1945 that "like all general directives, JCS 1067 can be interpreted in many ways."[11] Even admirers of FDR would be hard pressed to make the case for the President's handling of the German question.

With Roosevelt's passing, Morgenthau's influence, as reflected in American policies on both Germany and the Russian loan, waned. Just as it took more than a year before the Truman administration fully repudiated the Russian loan, however, vestiges of the Morgenthau Plan survived well into 1946. Harry Truman felt little enthusiasm for either Morgenthau or his plan, but the new President lacked alternative courses of action. Truman neatly summarizes early postwar American priorities in his memoirs. Germany was to be disarmed, but left "with sufficient means to provide a minimum subsistence level without sustained outside (which could only mean American) relief."[12] In practice, the goal of disarmament, requiring curbs on German industry, would not be easily reconciled with the goal of self-sufficiency.

American Hopes and Fears: Yalta and Potsdam

Memories of the interwar years haunted the American officials charged with wartime planning for Germany. If the Allies had occupied Germany after World War I, some reasoned, the German people would have learned the costs of aggression, and Hitler could never have exploited the German hunger for vengeance with such telling effect. One product of this line of thought was the American support for the unconditional surrender and military occupation of Germany. Yet the wartime conferences never resolved other, more difficult issues, such as territorial partition and the level of German industry, let alone the future of German society and government.

The Allies' decisions on the reparations issue were especially ambiguous. Having borne the brunt of the fighting and the greatest destruction during the war, the Russians demanded reparations from Germany both to reconstruct their economy and to eliminate German war potential. Most American policymakers favored German reparations for Russia, but they also feared a repetition of the Dawes and Young Plans of the 1920s, in which U.S. loans had effectively paid for German reparations and Allied loan repayments. "We were most anxious," Edward R. Stettinius, Jr., later said of the period before Yalta, "to avoid the disastrous experience of reparations after World War I."[13]

As early as the Moscow Conference of October 1943, Secretary of State Cordell Hull declared that the United States wished to limit German reparations to levels consistent with a healthy "postwar world economic and political order." An American position paper added, "Reparations should not be relied on as a major instrument of control over Germany's military power." A major source of later difficulties was the disagreement over how to define a "fair" standard of living for postwar Germany. While the Americans used neighboring countries as a benchmark, Harriman noted immediately after the Moscow Conference, the Soviet "measure of Germany's capacity to pay reparations in goods and services appears to be based on the concept that the Germans are not entitled to a postwar standard of living higher than the Russians."[14]

At Yalta in February 1945, Roosevelt forthrightly explained to his Russian hosts that the United States had no intention of lending Germany money as it had in the 1920s.[15] The Americans agreed at Yalta to consider $10 billion as a basis for discussion on German reparations to Russia, but the British refused to accept this figure. The failure to reach a firm figure on German reparations at Yalta later offered President Truman and Secretary of State Byrnes a loophole to justify lesser deliveries to Russia, especially in retribution for Russian depredations in Eastern Europe.[16]

During the interval between Yalta and Potsdam, American perceptions of the German problem shifted considerably. Destruction was greater than anticipated. The U.S. zone, American planners belatedly realized, could never be economically self-sufficient, and reparations from current production and excessive dismantling would wreak havoc in the U.S. sector. Potential remedies included U.S. subsidies (a most distasteful prospect), the revival of German industry (still frowned upon), or an agreement among the Allies to treat all zones of Germany as an economic unit. By default, the Americans seized upon economic unification as the solution to their problem. Washington also concluded that a revival of German coal production was essential for European rehabilitation.[17]

The German and Polish issues dominated the agenda at the Potsdam Conference (July 17 to August 2, 1945). Before the United States would recognize the Polish government and the new Polish frontier with Germany, it called for a reduction in the Soviet share of German reparations. Poland's annexation, with Soviet blessings, of the agriculturally rich, eastern arm of Germany especially irritated Truman, since the United States now had to ship food to its zone at a time of domestic shortages. The flood tide of refugees from the eastern sections of Germany heightened the distress in the American zone and reinforced U.S. opposition to a large reparations settlement.

The main American protagonist on German policy, however, was not the President, but his Secretary of State, James F. Byrnes.[18] At Potsdam, Byrnes insisted that the occupying powers take reparations primarily from existing assets, rather than from current production on a year-by-year basis. The object here was to avoid saddling Germany with a huge reparations burden, either in the form of a cash debt or reparations-in-kind, such as the Allies had imposed after World War I. The Americans also demanded that German exports, before being applied to the reparations account, should be used to pay for imports of food and other goods necessary for subsistence. In other words, the victors could not extract reparations from the U.S. zone until the minimum needs of the local population were met. This formula would help hold down U.S. occupation costs and preclude an American subsidy of reparations. The Soviets objected to the American "first-charge" principle for its seeming preference for German over Soviet welfare. But as Byrnes flatly informed Molotov, "There will be no reparations until imports in the American zone are paid for."[19]

A compromise on the reparations issue was finally struck during the last days of the conference. Byrnes and Ernest Bevin, the British Foreign Minister, won Molotov's grudging consent to the principle that each zonal commander would determine the amount of materials suitable for reparations. The Soviets tacitly agreed to drop the $10 billion reparations figure in exchange for the American *de facto* recognition of the Polish frontier with Germany and the entry of the Soviet-backed Polish delegation into the UN. Stalin also accepted the first-charge principle after the Soviets gained 25 percent of the machinery and other goods eligible as reparations in the western zones.[20]

By almost any measure, Potsdam was a disaster. The Big Three reached no firm decision on the future of Germany. The Protocol did not take full account of the massive German population shift westward, the need of neighboring countries for German manufactured goods and coal, the limited utility of dismantled capital equipment for Soviet (and other countries') reconstruction, or the difficulty of implementing denazification. Although the Big Three agreed that an Allied council based in Berlin should treat the dismembered country as an economic unit, the agreement on zonal reparations undermined this principle.[21] For the sake of appearances, the Americans pretended to recognize an unacceptable regime in Poland while the Soviets pretended to give up most of their claims to German reparations. These pretenses contributed nothing to later Soviet-American cooperation.

Implementing Potsdam: Lucius Clay and the View from OMGUS

The Allied debates at Potsdam and later conferences over German reparations and level of industry were meaningless as long as the former Reich lay prostrate. During the first postwar years, for instance, Germany never came even close to the minimum levels set by the Allies for steel capacity. The reason is not hard to find: the war had devastated the country. An estimated four-and-one-half million Germans died during the conflict. There were two million cripples in the western zones alone. Ten million homes were destroyed or severely damaged. To compound the housing and food shortages, eleven to twelve million Germans fled from Eastern Europe and the territories annexed by Poland, mostly to the western zones. Whole cities, including 95 percent of urban Berlin, lay in ruins. Bridges, waterways, and railways were broken and paralyzed. The Ruhr's coal production dropped from a prewar figure of 400,000 tons a day to just 25,000. And in U.S.-occupied southern Germany, where much light industry and consumer goods production were concentrated, industrial output plummeted to just 5 percent of prewar levels. An entire nation was hungry, afraid, and traumatized by defeat.[22]

No one was more impressed by German suffering than General Lucius D. Clay, head of OMGUS and proconsul of the American zone. An intense and disciplined Army technocrat who had directed the logistical operations of the Normandy invasion, Clay quickly took command over virtually every aspect of political and economic life in the U.S. zone. A British high official commented after a hard bargaining session with Clay, "He looks like a Roman Emperor—and acts like one." The son of a Southern senator of the Reconstruction era, Clay inherited an almost unquestioning faith in American-style democracy, tempered only by a deep-seated bias against central authority. From the start, Clay encouraged the growth of local assemblies and parties in the American zone. "In the summer of 1946, when the rest of Germany had hardly begun to emerge from utter chaos," a journalist commented, "the American Zone looked [like] a neat little model Confederacy."[23]

When Clay had left Washington in the spring of 1945 for Europe, he knew next to nothing about JCS 1067 and other wartime planning for Germany. He was in any case soon disinclined to implement the harsher features of the directive, for the destruction in Germany astounded him. Short-term relief and reconstruction seemed more important than the long-term disarmament of Germany. Clay wrote Byrnes in April 1945 that "several years will be required to develop even a sustaining economy to provide a bare minimum standard of living." The general opposed inflexible economic controls, heavy reparations, and a harsh peace, for while believing that Germany must know defeat, he favored "the holding out always of a ray of hope to the German people."[24]

One reason why Americans like Clay favored a revival of German production lay in the mentality and background of the experts imported from the United States:

> not a few of the industrialists were so beset with production problems of the moment and so imbued with the American philosophy of production that they would have found it most difficult to cut drastically the capability of the industries they were supervising. . . . It [restricting production] went contrary to all habits of thought in the Western world, in which it is practically a religion to encourage more and better production and to promote higher standards of living.[25]

The zealousness of these officials in the service of German reconstruction helped serve the foremost short-term goal of U.S. policy in Germany, namely, the minimization of occupation costs. It now appeared that even the minimum standard of living envisaged for Germany in the Morgenthau Plan would be difficult to attain.[26] To be sure, security against German aggression remained the primary goal, but in the absence of either clear objectives from Washington or an integrated Allied policy, occupation expenses assumed over-riding importance. The U.S. zone was especially susceptible to high costs, for southern Germany was a net importer of food, raw materials, heavy machinery, and semifinished goods. To pay for these goods, Army officials wished to revive light industries and consumer goods production, which in turn required a restoration of intra-German and European trade.

Lucius Clay had another compelling reason to worry about these expenses: the Army was forced to pay for the German occupation out of its own budget at a time when Congress was eager to slash defense spending. For this reason, the War Department had fruitlessly sought to transfer its occupation duties to the State Department as early as October 1945.[27] Not surprisingly, the Army's financial burden in Germany led to sharp differences between the Pentagon and the State Department on German policy.

Economic considerations initiated the shift of American policy toward a "softer" settlement in Germany. The resumption of German industrial production was necessary to reduce occupation costs and to spur West European reconstruction. A secondary goal in Germany was the containment of Soviet influence in Europe. Some time would elapse, however, before the twin American goals of multilateralism and containment would converge.

Soviet Goals in Germany

Soviet policies did not at first appear to threaten American interests in Germany, for the Kremlin was more cautious and opportunistic in Germany than in Eastern Europe. "It was, indeed, in Stalin's approach to Germany," Isaac Deutscher observes, "that the conflict between his nationalism and his revolutionism was sharpest, and that the nationalist, one might say the anti-revolutionary, element dominated longest."[28] Stalin's main diplomatic goal during the war had been to prevent a separate peace between the Western Allies and the Third Reich.[29] Moscow's aims in postwar Germany were more fluid. The Soviets above all sought German disarmament and heavy reparations. But like the Americans and the British, the Soviets alternately endorsed and backed away from the dismemberment and deindustrialization of Germany.[30]

As in Eastern Europe, Stalin set both minimum and maximum aims in Germany. Having secured a grip on Eastern Europe, Stalin hoped at least to retain full control over eastern Germany, and at most to infiltrate a unified but neutralized Germany. The latter objective may seem illusory until one remembers that Stalin had received assurances from no less an authority than President Roosevelt that American troops would withdraw from Europe soon after the war. Beginning in early 1945, the Soviets apparently acted on the premise that Allied unity in occupied Germany was unlikely, if not impossible. As two scholars on Soviet occupation policy in Germany comment, "Taken together, the various clauses of the Potsdam Protocol furnished guarantees that the Soviets would be able to control their own occupation zone for their own purposes. Yet, the treaty provisions also provided opportunities for extending Soviet influence throughout the entire German territory."[31]

Stalin's ambitions in Germany, however, never amounted to a master plan, and Soviet policies followed an erratic course both during and after the war. Despite their later portrayals of the Kremlin's behavior, most American policymakers at the time recognized the inconstant and evolutionary nature of Soviet policies in Germany. Conflicting policy aims also caught the Soviets in a painful dilemma. Ambassador Caffery, for example, reported from Paris in July 1946 that Soviet recognition of the western Oder-Neisse as the new Polish-German frontier had bolstered the Polish Communists, but had undermined the German Communists. And when Molotov sought to win German support by announcing in that month that his country opposed separation of the Ruhr and the Rhineland, he inadvertently undercut the French Communists.[32]

The most dramatic shift occurred in Soviet reparations policy. As an economic and emotional issue, reparations rated high on Moscow's agenda. In the spirit of the slogan, "Reparations for Fulfillment of the Five-Year Plan," the Russians stripped their zone of virtually all movable capital plant, regardless of its utility. Altogether the Soviets extracted about $1.6 billion (prewar value) in industrial plant from their zone, in addition to $600 million in raw timber and countless millions more in railway equipment, agricultural goods, and consumer goods. Much of the seized machinery lay rusting in railway sidings for months due to railcar shortages and bureaucratic blundering.[33]

Paralleling the American experience, an intense battle over German policy raged within the Kremlin well into 1946. The Soviets ultimately chose a strategy of reparations from current production because it promised a more efficient and prompt delivery of goods than a capital removal program. In addition, reviving the industry of the eastern zone helped win the loyalty of German workers and provided a base for the possible economic and political penetration of the western zones.[34]

Soviet policies were for the most part successful. Recovery in the eastern zone was rapid, and the Russians gained direct control over one-half of all industrial output in their sector. Up to 1949, the Soviets received deliveries worth $2.5 billion from eastern Germany. They also imposed social reforms, such as the dispossession of the landed Junker class, that destroyed the foundation of the traditional political system. Through creation of the Socialist Unity Party (SED) in April 1946, the Soviets set the stage for the destruction of alternative political parties as well. In 1948–49, the SED began purging Social Democrats from its ranks; the Communists would soon assume almost complete control over the party.[35] With the collapse of Allied cooperation in Germany, the Soviets resolved to rebuild eastern Germany in their own image, confirming American suspicions of a Soviet design to shut out Western influence from their sphere.

Still, the inconsistency of Soviet policies before 1947 suggests that Moscow enjoyed no more foresight, and exercised no more control over events in Germany, than did Washington. The exigencies of the occupation encouraged the Soviets, like the Americans, to put off long-range decisions on Germany. The longer both sides vacillated, the more their respective zones drifted apart.

Reparations Again: Soviet-American Conflict in Germany

The bitter disputes between the allies over German reparations were largely the product of the ambiguous and inconclusive decisions reached at Potsdam. Important in their own right, reparations assumed special importance because they became linked to Russian reconstruction, American occupation costs, European recovery, and German disarmament and rehabilitation. The story of the reparations issue is complex, but deserves telling for what it says not only about great power diplomacy, but also about the workings of the U.S. foreign policy bureaucracy.

Harry Truman abhorred the very idea of reparations. Mindful of the post-World War I debacle over reparations, Truman in May 1945 instructed Edwin W. Pauley, his representative on this issue, that reparations should never again render Germany dependent upon American "charity." Similarly, in August 1945, when Pauley was about to return from the Moscow reparations talks, his White House liaison advised him to emphasize in public statements "that the desire of the American people has been fulfilled and that reparations mistakes following the First World War have been avoided."[36]

At Potsdam, a further objective of U.S. policy was to protect the industrial assets of the western zones, particularly the Ruhr (under British administration), from the clutches of the Russians, who were plundering their own zone. Thanks to Byrnes, the Americans were successful.[37] Soviet transgressions in the eastern zone, however, were a less important determinant of American policy than the failure of the Allied Control Council (ACC) to establish central administrative agencies. The absence of these agencies—for transportation, coal and power, the postal service, and other functions—worked to the particular disadvantage of the United States. Without them, American officials could not obtain free access to the resources of the other zones, notably the raw materials and food of the eastern zone and the coal and machinery of the Ruhr. As a result, the U.S. zone accumulated large trade deficits, necessitating heavy American subsidies. Finally, in May 1946, Lucius Clay suspended dismantling and reparations deliveries from the U.S. zone to all recipients, including the Soviets.[38]

Certain American officials, such as Under Secretary of State Dean Acheson, regarded Clay's decision as just retribution against the Soviets for their alleged failure to cooperate in the ACC. Most historians have also portrayed the American suspension of reparations deliveries as a flashpoint in the Cold War. This interpretation is not entirely convincing, for Clay himself privately acknowledged that his action was pointed as much against the French as the Soviets.[39]

American authorities publicly justified reparations suspension as a measure to spur German recovery. Yet reparations probably did not retard reconstruction, except insofar as they dampened German morale. After all, German heavy industrial capability at the end of the war greatly exceeded civilian needs. Germany probably could have afforded the reparations that the Soviets and the French were demanding without undue suffering. (In any event, actual reparation deliveries fell far behind schedule.) In addition, a reading of the Potsdam Protocol indicates that the Soviets were at least technically correct "in maintaining that the delivery of reparations from the Western zones did not depend upon settlement of other matters," including the American first-charge principle.[40]

American officials at first did not fundamentally disagree with the Soviets on the postwar German level of industry (and hence, the availability of reparations). A case in point is the (Calvin) Hoover Report of September 1945. In this report, the American definition of an "average standard of living," calculated at three-fourths of the German production figures in 1938, would have reduced Germany to the levels of 1932, a year of grave depression, mass unemployment, and disastrous political developments.[41] Similarly, the United States often sided with the Soviet Union against Britain in negotiations over German steel production. The figures finally agreed upon by the Allies in early 1946 set German steel capacity at about 18 percent below the lowest levels of the Great Depression. The premise of these agreements was that much German industrial plant was war-related.[42]

If Cold War considerations were not the *primary* factor in his decision, why, then, did Clay end dismantling and reparations in the American zone, and later promote fusion with the British and French zones? In the first place, Clay *believed*—the reality may be another matter—that until the four Allies agreed upon an economic program for Germany, the United States in effect would be subsidizing the other zones through reparations. "We are struggling with a collapsed economy which cannot be revived piece-meal," Clay wrote in April 1946. While the U.S. zone contained the greater part of Germany's scenic beauty, Clay wryly noted, it enjoyed few economic resources. The American zone, for instance, held less than 2 percent of Germany's coal. Consequently, OMGUS demanded that the Allies agree to pool German economic resources and establish central administrative agencies before the United States would resume reparations deliveries. As Clay explained in May 1946,

> The postwar level of industry to be left Germany, which serves as a basis for reparations, is based on treatment of Germany as an economic unit. Its execution under other conditions would be absolutely impossible as it would leave economic chaos. It would particularly affect the U.S. zone which has no raw materials and would create a continuing financial liability for the United States for many years. . . . If economic unity is obtained, there is no reason why the reparations plan should not be implemented promptly.[43]

Nonetheless, there was, as Acheson and others discerned, a Cold War logic to Clay's decision, for the Soviets and the Americans fundamentally differed over what it meant to treat Germany as an "economic unit." To the Soviets, this meant state planning and control over most aspects of German economic life. To the Americans, this meant free trade and enterprise within the whole of Germany, with minimal centralized direction of the economy. Unless the Soviets and Americans could reach some compromise on this issue, their negotiations on trade, reparations, and other matters were bound to stagnate. As a prescient member of Pauley's staff predicted in August 1945, "The handling of reparations depends on the way the military commanders settle the economic unity of Germany."[44]

The impasse over the economic unity issue ultimately led to the collapse of the reparations talks and to a steady erosion of mutual trust in the ACC. In the meantime, Soviet border restrictions in Germany unpleasantly reminded Americans of the plight of the satellite nations in Eastern Europe. Secretary of War Robert Patterson concluded in July 1946 that the Soviets used reparations to advance the takeover of subject countries; the economic benefits of reparations were secondary. Soviet socialization of the eastern zone also suggested that the Kremlin sought to restructure the German economy in a way that differed markedly from the American free-enterprise concept. By September 1946, U.S. officials estimated, the Soviets had expropriated 80 percent of the industrial property in their zone, including plants cleared of complicity with the Nazis and assets owned in whole or in part by American nationals.[45]

Clay, however, did not consider Soviet-American differences to be irreconcilable. After all, the suspension of dismantling and reparations deliveries affected the French as much as the Soviets. Contrary to his recollections in his memoirs, Clay at the time blamed the Soviets less than the French for the impasse in the ACC. "It is difficult to find major instances of Soviet failure to carry out agreements reached in quadripartite government of Germany . . . ," Clay reported in July 1946. "French unwillingness to enter into agreements relative to governing Germany as a whole makes it difficult to place blame on Soviet."[46]

When Assistant Secretary of War for Air W. Stuart Symington took an around-the-world tour in July 1946 and interviewed General Douglas MacArthur in Japan, General George C. Marshall in China, and General Clay in Germany, Clay stood out as the maverick:

> It was from General Lucius Clay in Berlin the first counter thinking to the heavy anti-Russian sentiment characteristic of previous opinions on our trip around the world. [sic]
> Clay felt that the Russian story was not being reported accurately. He said there were incidents of arrest and detention, but that there were also comparable incidents of Americans picking up Russians and holding them over a period. . . .
> Clay felt the Russians antagonized the "old school" diplomats, because they were rude and did not have social graces. . . .
> General Clay felt the situation was far from hopeless and could be worked out. He said he agreed with General Bedell Smith . . . that the Russians could not possibly fight us for 15 years (Clay first said 5 was his guess), and would never try until they were actually making the atomic bomb. . . .
> General Clay felt that Western capital was essential [for German recovery], but agreed the amount and nature of the arrangements had to be controlled, else the new German economy would be controlled from the outside, which appeared to be the present French idea, and which would lead to the same old problems.[47]

A desire to cut U.S. occupation costs perhaps best explains Clay's unilateral action of May 1946, but there were perhaps two additional motives for his decision. First, he may have wished to prompt Washington to reappraise its hitherto lenient policy toward France. Clay also may have calculated that the suspension of reparations would pressure the Soviets into taking a clear position on the economic unity issue, which in this context meant lining up with the Americans against the French in the ACC on the issue of central administrative organs.

If this were the case, Clay's tactics backfired. The Soviets never joined in a concerted effort against the French in the ACC, and the State Department was slow to support Clay. In fact, State Department representatives, who were then in the process of mobilizing a Cold War consensus within the administration, welcomed Clay's initiative primarily because they believed it would force a showdown with the Soviets in Germany.[48]

Clay's differences with the State Department should not obscure his devotion to the establishment of American-style capitalism and democracy in Germany. With Washington's blessing, he discouraged local German efforts to expropriate private industry in the western zones and forced the British to cease socialist experimentation in the Ruhr once the British and American zones were fused. Clay also embraced Konrad Adenauer and the Christian Democratic Union (CDU/CSU), which endorsed a variety of hardy individualism, free enterprise, and federalism akin to the American system. In contrast, Clay's relations with Kurt Schumacher and the Social Democratic Party (SPD), which stood for nationalization of heavy industry and a strong central government, were cordial but cool. In this regard, Clay was in accord with most American policymakers, including Forrestal and Patterson, who believed that radical social reforms, notably the socialization of industry, would impair European reconstruction.[49]

And in this one respect, Clay's decision in the spring of 1946 perfectly served the dual purposes of American economic security and Kennan's containment strategy. The main danger to Western interests in Europe, Kennan had argued in his long telegram of February 1946, lay in social and economic conditions that bred despair and revolution. On these very grounds, Clay had opposed stripping "peaceful" industries for reparations as early as January 1946. Similarly, Robert D. Murphy, U.S. political adviser for Germany, warned in February 1946 that the Soviets, by exploiting French differences with the United States, were laying the foundation for both German Communist infiltration of the western zones and a close affiliation between the new Germany and the Soviet Union. The increasingly militant German Communist and Soviet rhetoric during this period, of course, did nothing to calm American fears on this score.[50]

By itself, the Soviet-American conflict over German reparations was not a major cause of the Cold War.[51] Both sides later used the reparations imbroglio as a symbolic issue by which to emphasize their differences in Germany. But at the time, it was less significant. Once the Soviets found that capital removals from their zone were wasteful, they shifted to a policy of reparations from current production. This meant that Moscow halted dismantling and began to rebuild industry in the eastern zone. The interruption of capital removals from the American zone in the spring of 1946 could not have greatly upset the Soviets, for they had always looked most enviously upon the resources of the Ruhr in the *British* zone.

The Soviets faced a dilemma, however. Capital removals were less helpful than a long-term program for reparations from current production. Yet this implied a revival of German industry in the western zones. What most alarmed the Soviets was not their exclusion from access to western reparations, but their exclusion from control over the Ruhr. The Soviets were not alone. The French, three times victims of German aggression in three generations, regarded German deindustrialization and disarmament as the centerpiece of their postwar security policy.

Franco-American Conflict and Anglo-American Cooperation in Germany

France posed more immediate and concrete obstacles to American goals in Germany than did Russia. In particular, French opposition to German central administrative organs—the instruments of economic unity and eventual self-government envisaged at Potsdam—frustrated American hopes for the restoration of the German economy, the reduction of occupation costs, and the reunification of Germany.[52] As we have seen, Clay's decision to suspend dismantling and reparations deliveries was aimed as much against the French as the Russians. Some historians, indeed, attempt to explain Clay's decisions in Germany almost exclusively in terms of his reaction to French obstructionism.[53]

For several reasons, however, the French never threatened vital U.S. interests in Germany as much as the Soviets did. The French argued that the Allies should settle the status of the Ruhr, the Rhineland, and the Saar—which had provided Germany with the resources to fight two world wars—before restoring the German economy and government. Since the State Department regarded a strong France as the linchpin of a revived Western Europe, it initially sided with Paris against OMGUS.[54]

The State Department was also more sensitive to the domestic constraints upon French foreign policy. Washington policymakers understood that the moderate, pro-American Paris governments of the early postwar years depended upon precarious parliamentary coalitions pitted against a powerful Communist party. Thus, it was recognized that French diplomats could neither withdraw territorial demands on Germany nor appear to side too openly with the Anglo-Saxon powers against the Soviet Union.[55]

Washington, moreover, enjoyed considerable political and economic leverage over France. In late 1946, for example, the United States cut food shipments to the French zone in Germany in retaliation for French obstinacy on the administrative issue.[56] U.S. grants and credits to France itself offered an additional incentive for Paris to cooperate on German issues.

The Americans were ultimately able to dominate developments in the western zones because they could enlist the support of the British, whose policy in Germany was largely compatible with that of the United States. Churchill had acquiesced in the Morgenthau Plan at Quebec in September 1944 only with the greatest reluctance, and he was partly responsible for Roosevelt's gradual shift toward a more lenient German policy in early 1945. Like OMGUS under Clay, the British occupation authorities under General Sir Brian Hubert Robertson favored from the outset a relatively high productive level and standard of living in postwar Germany.

On the other hand, the British took Potsdam's provisions for German decartelization more seriously than the Americans or French and sought to nationalize some key industries in the Ruhr, such as steel and coal. The Americans bitterly opposed nationalization because it allegedly disrupted production (coal output in 1946 was only 40 percent of prewar levels), raised occupation costs, retarded European recovery, and paved the way for socialism in Germany. Faced with mounting occupation expenses and economic problems at home, the British succumbed to U.S. pressure and scrapped structural reforms in their zone.

On most issues, the British and Americans shared common ground. The British zone, comprising the populous and industrial, but heavily damaged, regions of the Ruhr, the Rhineland, and Northern Germany, was by far the most expensive to administer, costing about $400 million in 1946 alone. Like the Americans, the British needed food and raw materials from the east to sustain the population in their zone, and therefore joined the Americans in pressing for German economic unity. Furthermore, Robertson, like Clay, recognized the impossibility of reconstructing Europe without reviving Germany and feared Communist political infiltration of the western zones. In late July 1946, the British government accepted Byrnes' proposal for the economic merger of the British and American zones.[57]

The creation of the Bizone won French cooperation where milder diplomatic tactics had failed. Anxious lest Anglo-American planning go ahead without consideration of their interests, French Foreign Ministry officials privately assured Ambassador Caffery in September 1946 that they would discuss merging their zone with the Bizone some time after the November 1946 elections in France.[58] Still, the State Department hesitated to pressure Paris, for despite the importance of German reconstruction to West European recovery, "the maintenance of France in the western camp outweighed all other considerations." In setting German policy, State Department planners temporarily prevailed over Clay. Though personally close to Secretary Byrnes, Clay was not always well informed on Foggy Bottom's thinking. He was deeply embarrased in late 1946, for example, when Washington failed to inform him that Byrnes had agreed in October to the French proposal for the economic merger of the Saar with France.[59] In fact, one of the main purposes of Byrnes' speech at Stuttgart in September 1946 was to reassure Clay that the State Department finally intended to break French recalcitrance.

The Stuttgart Speech and Bizonal Fusion

The genesis of Byrnes' speech lay in Clay's memo of July 1946 entitled "Summary of United States Policy and Objectives in Germany." Clay's objective was to justify OMGUS' "soft" interpretation of JCS 1067 and Potsdam. The United States, he began, sought the disarmament, denazification, and democratization of Germany. Heavy industry should be limited until the UN was satisfied that Germany no longer posed a threat to world peace. Yet Clay ruled out a large reparations program, for he felt the first-charge principle should govern the economic relations of the U.S. zone until economic unity was achieved. While Clay urged American de facto approval of the Polish annexations and the French claims to the Saar, he adamantly opposed the dismemberment of the Ruhr and the Rhineland.[60]

Clay's thesis on the purposes of the American occupation rested upon psychological premises that were diametrically opposed to those of Morgenthau. As Clay stated,

No country can regain its self-respect nor progress to maturity in democratic processes in the presence of large occupying forces. No country will recognize its own guilt over a period of years if it lives in economic squalor under the shadow of mighty occupying armies. Basically, the most important objective to the peace of the world is to create a democratic state in Germany which can be received in confidence as a member of the United Nations. This objective can be accomplished best with a minimum of outside control and with token forces, provided that the occupying powers stand firmly together so that Germany will recognize that any deviation from Allied objectives will bring swift retribution.[61]

While bureaucrats in Washington blocked publication of Clay's policy statement, Byrnes' speech at Stuttgart on September 6, 1946, incorporated most of Clay's ideas, word-for-word in some places.[62] In addition to ratifying Clay's policies in Germany, Byrnes sought to break the deadlock that had developed within the ACC over implementation of the Potsdam provisions for a central administration of the German economy and government. Like Clay, the Secretary of State held the French responsible for the deadlock, and the outraged French public reaction that followed Byrnes' speech indicated that the message was not lost on them. Byrnes was also trying to reassure friendly German officials that Americans would not "become disgusted with the trend of events in Europe and withdraw as we did after the last war." As Byrnes explained to Secretary of the Treasury John W. Snyder soon after delivering the Stuttgart speech,

> The German officials appointed by our people in the American zone felt that if we were going to leave it was useless to rely upon any plan we had for restoring the economy of the people and establishing local governments. The argument was daily made that while the Soviets would remain, the Americans would leave. We had to declare our views on this problem and also on the boundary questions which would influence our decisions as to economic problems.[63]

So, too, the Bizone initially represented an effort to force the French and Russians to face the economic unity issue. The Bizone originated in Byrnes' July 1946 invitation to each of the three other powers to merge its zone with the American sector in order to create an economic union. At this point, the Americans were not ready to form a new German government. In August 1946 talks with the British, Clay insisted that "economic integration of zones must exclude any implication of political integration." Economic agencies were to be geographically dispersed, moreover, "to avoid implication we are establishing western

German capital." Byrnes, in explaining his Stuttgart speech to French Foreign Minister Georges Bidault a month later, also denied that the United States desired a strong central government in Germany. Instead, the Americans promoted Bizonia as an economic magnet to draw the four zones together. Thus, Washington did not, as some historians have contended, seek to divide Germany politically. "As so often in the history of the Cold War," one scholar observes, "the conclusions suggested by the actual records are rather more mundane than those advanced by committed historians."[64] Only later, following the further deterioration of Soviet-American relations, did the United States pursue the *political* integration of western Germany.

Point of No Return: The Decision to Rebuild Germany

By a subtle and incremental process, the United States had become committed to the reconstruction of Germany by early 1947. The logic of American multilateralism prevailed over the reformist impulse to remake German society anew. The "core of the thing," as James Forrestal put it in a telephone conversation with columnist James Reston in March 1947, "is are you going to try to keep Germany a running boil with the pus exuding over the rest of Europe, or are you going to try to bring it back into inner society."[65] Later, the Truman administration's decision to integrate German industry into the West European economy through the Marshall Plan set in motion a chain of events that resulted in the division of Germany and Europe.

A lesser, but symbolically important, casualty of the Cold War in Germany was Edwin Pauley. President Truman had appointed Pauley in April 1945 as head of the American delegation to the Moscow Reparations Commission because, in Truman's words, "the position required a tough bargainer, someone who could be as tough as Molotov." A hard-boiled oil producer and leader of conservative California Democrats, Pauley was not one to look kindly upon Soviet interests in Germany or anywhere else. Indeed, Pauley stoutly resisted Soviet reparations demands at Moscow and during later negotiations in which he served as the President's personal representative on reparations.[66]

Yet Pauley, in one of the strangest ironies of the Cold War, emerged as the Truman administration's foremost champion of curbs on German industry, even when most interested American officials and businessmen were tilting in the other direction. While a foe of the Morgenthau

Plan, Pauley opposed obtaining reparations from current production because that would have meant rebuilding the very plants that had supplied the Nazi war machine. Pauley acknowledged that industrial dismantling in Germany might cut overall European productivity. But "sometimes," he argued in December 1946, "there are things more important than efficiency—for example, peace and security."[67]

By late 1946, Pauley's views were clearly out of favor. He had already lost key bureaucratic battles with OMGUS and the State Department, which as early as October 1945 had begun whittling away at his authority over reparations policy. Truman tried to kick Pauley upstairs by nominating him Secretary of the Navy in early 1946, but the Senate rejected him because of his oil interests. Although Pauley remained in the White House, Truman remarked to his Cabinet in February 1947 that Pauley "has no status now." A month later, he resigned from his reparations post.[68]

With Pauley's passing, few forces remained in the administration to slow the momentum of German reconstruction. The Morgenthau Plan was now fully repudiated, and reparations were a dead letter. Germany no longer posed a security threat to the United States; the economic vacuum in Central Europe did. By September 1946, the State and Treasury Departments were encouraging American businessmen to purchase goods manufactured in the U.S. zone, both to boost local industry and to cut occupation costs.[69] The United States sought economic fusion of the western zones as quickly as possible, for Germany was to abet European recovery.

The process of recovery, however, was dishearteningly slow. Germany had not shared in the economic boomlet of 1946, and the severe winter of 1946–47 reduced a large portion of the German people to near-starvation. The Bizone officially came into being on New Year's Day, 1947, but the impact of Anglo-American cooperation upon German productivity was not readily apparent.[70]

By the spring of 1947, American policymakers had recognized that they could no longer deal with the German problem in isolation from other U.S. interests in Europe. German reconstruction and West European recovery, American officials realized, were interdependent. And Russia now appeared a major obstacle to U.S. plans. Charles Bohlen recalls that Stalin, meeting with newly appointed Secretary of State George C. Marshall during the Moscow Council of Foreign Ministers in March 1947, expressed indifference toward the early completion of a settlement on Germany. Marshall concluded that Stalin, looking over Europe, saw that the best way to advance Soviet interests was to let matters drift. . . . This was the kind of crisis that Communism thrived on. All the way back to Washington, Marshall talked of the importance of finding some initiative to prevent the complete breakdown of Western Europe.[71]

With the enunciation of the Marshall Plan in June 1947, American policymakers would promote a stable and prosperous Germany as a buffer to Soviet expansion. Yet the decisions and events leading to the rehabilitation of Germany predated the actual outbreak of the Cold War, and one can hardly discern an anti-Soviet logic to U.S. policies in Germany before early 1947. American interests in West European recovery would have required a revision of policies in Germany even if the Truman administration had not realized the value of mobilizing a West German state in the service of the United States in the Cold War. Indeed, insofar as a containment strategy animated U.S. policy during 1945–46, it favored the reconstruction of Britain and France before Germany since Germany's place in a peaceful, multilateral world order appeared uncertain at best. Even in Clay's case, decisions were made through improvisation rather than design. The confusion and vacillation of *both* Soviet and American policies in Germany before early 1947 suggest that neither power willed or foresaw a confrontation in that country.

The very structure of the peace probably doomed great power cooperation in Germany. By agreeing to a quadripartite occupation before reaching agreement on other basic issues, the wartime leaders were setting the stage for conflict in Germany. A stable agreement that would have been acceptable to all four powers is difficult to imagine.[72]

The reparations issue illustrated the fragility of the quadripartite approach. The United States above all sought to avoid subsidizing German reparations, but when Clay cut off reparation deliveries, he appeared to favor German over Soviet and French reconstruction. (The British generally followed the Americans on this issue.) The Soviets could only gain the huge reparations they sought for domestic reconstruction by rebuilding German industry in their zone (for reparations from current production); surrendering exclusive control over their sector in order to gain access to the Ruhr was out of the question. But when Moscow chose the former course, consolidating control over economic and political life in eastern Germany, it forfeited any remaining claims to reparations from the western zones. Like the Russians, the

French sought reparations for domestic reconstruction, but their country's recovery, however much they disliked it, depended upon a revival of German production and trade.

The Potsdam agreements, then, were grossly flawed. Each party to them—and France, incidentally, was not fully a party to it—could bend the provisions of the treaty to suit certain national needs. The French, for instance, could indefinitely delay creation of a central government in Germany, while the Americans could curtail industrial dismantling in, and reparations deliveries from, their zone at will. The Russians, by the same token, could unilaterally redraw the Polish-German frontier, suppress pro-Western political parties and exploit the economy in their zone as long as the four occupying powers could not agree on a final settlement for German reunification.

Above all, Potsdam never clarified which, if any, decision-making body would exercise supreme authority over the German economy. While the ACC was supposed to enforce economic unity in Germany, the reparations agreement clearly undermined this principle. "Few understood clearly what had been wrought at Potsdam," John Gimbel observes. Even within national delegations, participants had begun to quarrel over the meaning of the Potsdam agreements before the conference adjourned in August 1945.[73]

While the special circumstances of the German occupation posed major obstacles to cooperation in Germany, the Cold War in Eastern Europe rendered a lasting settlement in Germany almost inconceivable. Soviet and American policies assumed the character of position warfare after late 1946, with each action generating a reaction. With no unifying concept to govern Allied policies in Germany, each power sought to recreate national institutions in its zone. American economic might ultimately succeeded in imposing unity upon the western zones where diplomatic persuasion had failed. But by incorporating the western zones within its sphere, the United States appeared to threaten Soviet control over the eastern zone, prompting a series of Cold War confrontations over Germany.

The Truman administration had now made three major decisions in Europe: to cut off Eastern Europe and the Soviet Union from American trade and capital, to restore West European productivity and commerce, and to reindustrialize Germany. Until the enunciation of the Truman Doctrine, however, the administration lacked a coherent thesis by which to rally the public and the Congress behind a sustained program for European reconstruction.

CHAPTER SIX

THE TRUMAN DOCTRINE: GREECE, TURKEY, IRAN, AND U.S. INTERESTS IN THE NEAR EAST

THE SPECTER OF failure haunted American foreign policy-makers at the beginning of 1947. The extensive cooperation with the Soviet Union that American leaders had foreseen late in the war seemed an impossible dream less than two years later, and America's main allies in Europe were in desperate trouble. Britain and France, the expected pillars of economic strength and political stability in Western Europe, had plunged into a deep recession while Germany remained in ruins.

Few Americans, however, cared about the plight of Europe. The mood of the country favored budget cuts and retrenchment in foreign policy. As the Republican-controlled 80th Congress assembled in Washington in January 1947, the White House faced stubborn resistance to any new ventures in foreign policy. Even if Americans had been less weary of international problems, the Truman administration had yet to devise a comprehensive program for European reconstruction. And before they could tackle European problems, American policymakers had to confront a series of crises in the Near East.

The Iranian and Turkish Straits Crises, 1945–1946

American involvement in the Near and Middle East had been limited before the war, but this would quickly change as the strategic and economic importance of the region's oil reserves became apparent. The Allies' ability to control most of the world's oil resources had been a significant ingredient in the victory over the Axis. Yet the vastly increased appetite of the world for oil and the decline of Western Hemisphere reserves, notably in the United States, led to acute fears of postwar shortages among Washington planners. Officials in the State, Navy, and Interior Departments, as well as the Senate's Truman Committee investigating defense mobilization, agreed that achieving secure foreign oil rights was critical to the national security. "In all surveys of the situation," Herbert Feis, the State Department's Economic Adviser, observed, "the pencil came to an awed pause at one point and place—the Middle East." Saudi Arabian oil production, which U.S. companies controlled, soared from 66,000 long tons in 1938 to 11.8 million long tons in 1947.[1]

It was for this reason that the Truman administration, notably the State Department's Office of Near Eastern and African Affairs, viewed Soviet pressure on Iran (and, to a lesser extent, Turkey) with such alarm. Washington valued a stable Iran as a buffer between Russia and the Persian Gulf. As Secretary of State Cordell Hull advised President Roosevelt in August 1944, "it is to our interest that no great power be established on the Persian Gulf opposite the important American petroleum development in Saudi Arabia."[2]

But oil was not the whole story. Washington did not always actively abet the expansion of oil companies into the Near East. Instead, much of U.S. policy in the region can be explained in terms of classic balance of power considerations. The erosion of British power in the Near East created a power vacuum that invited Soviet and American expansion. As early as the fall of 1945, the Attlee government was planning a total military withdrawal from the region, but the threatened resignation of the British Chiefs of Staff forced a hasty abandonment of this idea. The Truman administration was aware of British distress and began to consider assuming British responsibilities in the area, notably Greece, well before the enunciation of the Truman Doctrine in March 1947.[3]

Washington regarded the crises in Iran, Turkey, and Greece as test cases of Soviet intentions and U.S. resolve. As in Eastern Europe, the Munich analogy was central to American thinking: if the United States did not stand up to Russian expansion in peripheral areas, it would invite aggression in areas of greater strategic importance, such as Germany. Despite intense Anglo-American competition over the oil wealth of the Gulf and Washington's desire to dissociate itself from British colonialism in the Middle East, the United States and Great Britain shared a desire to exclude Soviet influence from the Near East. Consequently, the Roosevelt and the Truman administrations informally agreed to respect British oil rights in Iran, while London accepted U.S. dominance in Saudi Arabia, Kuwait, and Bahrain, where American oil companies were firmly entrenched.[4]

The main source of friction in Iran was Moscow's support for separatist groups in the northern part of the country against the Teheran government. The Kremlin's apparent objectives were to create a security buffer and to win oil concessions in Iran. But as Averell Harriman had observed in the fall of 1944, the only countries that the Soviets appeared to regard as friendly were those that they could dominate.[5]

The British and the Soviets had occupied Iran in August 1941 to protect its rich oil fields from the Nazis and to open a supply line from the West to the hard-pressed Red Army. Under the 1942 Tripartite Treaty between Iran, Britain, and Russia, the occupying countries agreed to respect Iranian sovereignty and to withdraw their forces no later than six months after the defeat of the Axis. (Washington made similar pledges when it signed the Declaration on Iran at the Teheran Conference in November 1943.) The U.S. role in Iran was more modest, although numerous American supply troops and military and economic advisers served in the country. The U.S. Persian Gulf Command, eventually numbering 30,000 men, transported 7.9 million long tons of imports into Russia between 1941 and 1945, over half of which consisted of Lend-Lease goods, including 180,000 trucks and 4,900 airplanes.[6]

In order to counterbalance British and American influence, Teheran invited U.S. oil corporations to expand their concessions, but the State Department offered only lukewarm encouragement to the American companies and generally respected Soviet interests in northern Iran. When Moscow in October 1944 openly backed the radical Tudeh Party, which was demonstrating against the central government, Washington gave words of support to Teheran, but no more. "As in Southeastern Europe," Bruce Kuniholm writes, "it seemed that in Iran the State Department was on the verge of granting the Soviets in fact what it was denying them in principle: a sphere of influence."[7]

Just as in the case of Eastern Europe, however, the Americans had second thoughts about Soviet expansion in the Near East as the war neared its end. At Potsdam in July 1945, the Americans and British proposed a withdrawal from Iran at the earliest possible date, but Stalin demurred, citing the Declaration on Iran. Technically, Stalin was correct, for a troop pullout would not be required until March 1946, six months after the defeat of Japan. But the Soviets' blatant intervention in Iran's internal affairs, particularly their support for the rebellion in the northern provinces, did appear a clear violation of the 1943 accord. The situation reached crisis proportions in November 1945, when the 75,000-man Red Army supplied weapons to rebels in Azerbaijan and prevented the 3,000 troops of the Iranian garrison there from suppressing the revolt. Despite repeated requests by Secretary of State Byrnes for an immediate withdrawal of all foreign troops, the Russians refused and in December hailed the proclamation of autonomous Kurdish and Azerbaijani republics in their zone of Iran.[8]

Two developments in late 1945 reinforced American suspicions of Moscow. First, U.S. policymakers learned from captured German documents that Moscow, in a secret protocol to the Nazi-Soviet Nonaggression Pact of 1939, had expressed a strong interest in gaining a warm water port in the Persian Gulf area. This revelation deepened American concern that the Kremlin sought something more than an economic foothold in northern Iran. A Soviet note in late November 1945, implying that the Red Army might remain in Iran beyond the March 1946 deadline, further alarmed Truman and Byrnes.[9]

Meanwhile, Turkey was having its own problems with the Russians. The Soviets had massed troops along the Turkish borders and were demanding the revision of the 1936 Montreux Convention on the Straits (Dardanelles and Bosporus), as well as major territorial concessions from Ankara. At the Moscow Council of Foreign Ministers in December 1945, Stalin revealed that the Soviet Union sought to annex the Armenian and Georgian portions of eastern Turkey (altogether, a 180-by 75-mile area) and to gain military bases at the Straits. Byrnes, in Truman's estimation, failed to respond vigorously enough to Soviet provocation in Turkey and Iran at the Moscow Council. "There isn't a doubt in my mind," Truman reportedly told Byrnes when he returned to Washington in January 1946,

> that Russia intends an invasion of Turkey and the seizure of the Black Sea Straits to the Mediterranean. Unless Russia is faced with an iron fist and strong language another war is in the making. Only one language do they understand—"how many divisions have you?"
> I do not think we should play compromise any longer. . . .
> I'm tired of babying the Soviets.[10]

The Iranian government, with Washington's backing, lodged a complaint against Moscow before the UN Security Council on January 19,

1946. While its deliberations embarrassed the Russians, the Security Council could not take effective action because of the Soviet veto power. When the deadline withdrawal of March 2, 1946, came, all British and American troops had long since left Iran. The Soviets, on the other hand, retained a large army in what Moscow called "disturbed areas," including Azerbaijan. Reports of major Soviet troop movements in northern Iran and in the area bordering Turkey in early March outraged Byrnes, who resolved to "give it to them with both barrels."[11] As a signal to the Kremlin, Secretary of the Navy James Forrestal dispatched the battleship *Missouri* to Istanbul on March 22.[12]

The UN Security Council reopened debate on Iran on March 25, but tensions began to ease in early April, after Moscow and Teheran reached a compromise on the oil and troops issues. The Soviets promised to withdraw their forces in early May and to avoid interference in Azerbaijan. The Iranians, in turn, agreed to the establishment of a Soviet-Iranian joint-stock oil company with 51 percent Soviet ownership. (The Iranian parliament, the Majlis, ultimately rejected this concession in October 1947.)[13]

Although Washington did not undertake major new military commitments in the region, the twin crises significantly influenced official U.S. perceptions of Soviet intentions. The Joint Chiefs of Staff had all along favored a vigorous response to Moscow's provocation in the Near East. In March 1946, Secretary of State Byrnes had asked the JCS to assess the threat to the United States and the British Commonwealth if Turkey were to accede to Soviet demands in the Straits. The Chiefs discounted the traditional Russian quest for warm water ports as an explanation for Soviet behavior and concluded that the Soviets sought exclusive control over the Straits and the Persian Gulf. If the massing of Soviet troops on Turkey's frontier led to violence, the JCS hoped the British would be prepared to assist the Turks militarily—if necessary, by committing British forces. The JCS did not recommend, and the Truman administration did not offer, direct American military aid to Ankara at this time.[14]

When the Soviets continued to demand revisions of the Montreux Convention during the summer of 1946, however, American resolve stiffened. In mid-August, State, War, and Navy Department representatives drafted an important statement of U.S. policy on the Turkish issue. This paper helped set the stage for the gradual escalation of American commitments in the region over the following months. "In our opinion," the memo began, "the primary objective of the Soviet

Union is to obtain control of Turkey." If Turkey were to fall, the Soviets would gain "control over Greece and over the whole Near and Middle East." Given the inability of the UN to provide substantial aid, the Turks would not stand up to the Russians without clearcut American support. "The only thing which will deter the Russians will be the conviction that the United States is prepared, if necessary, to meet aggression with force of arms," the authors of the memo concluded. Foreshadowing the Truman Doctrine, they recommended that the United States "resist with all means at our disposal any Soviet aggression and in particular, . . . any Soviet aggression against Turkey."[15]

Truman approved the August 1946 policy statement because, he told Forrestal and Acheson, "we might as well find out whether the Russians were bent on world conflict now as in five or ten years." The State Department soon sent a note to the Soviets rejecting their proposals for joint control of the Straits by the Black Sea powers and the establishment of Russian bases near the Straits. In late September, Forrestal announced the stationing of a permanent naval force in the Mediterranean. For the most part, however, U.S. diplomatic initiatives in the eastern Mediterranean were accompanied by military restraint.[16]

American support for Iran was also equivocal, and the Teheran government did not disguise its disappointment. Throughout 1946, the Iranians invited bids by American companies for new oil concessions as a counterweight to British and Soviet influence. But the State Department again did not encourage the oil companies, both because it respected Britain's sphere of interest in Iran and because it wished to avoid any appearance of self-interest. Similarly, when Prime Minister Ahmad Qavam suggested in August 1946 that he soon intended to order army troops to reoccupy Azerbaijan—still controlled by an autonomous, Russian-backed, radical regime—U.S. Ambassador George V. Allen hesitated to give anything more than verbal support. Part of the reason for Allen's reticence was his suspicion that the enigmatic Qavam, who was performing a precarious balancing act between the Tudeh Party and the Shah, was unreliable. But equally important, Allen was under orders from Washington to avoid provoking the Soviets.[17]

Finally, in October 1946, Allen took matters into his own hands and persuaded the Shah to make Qavam purge his government of Tudeh members. When the United States followed this up in November 1946 with $10 million in credits for military supplies and the prospect of an

Eximbank loan as well, Qavam ordered the army to reoccupy Azerbaijan. In December, the Azerbaijani and Kurdish autonomous republics, which had never enjoyed much local support, suddenly collapsed.[18]

American political influence in Iran was now considerable, but U.S. business did not immediately follow the flag, partly because Washington did not want it to do so. In January 1947, for instance, U.S. diplomats discouraged Standard Oil of New Jersey (SONJ) officials from visiting Iran in order to investigate crude oil production and pipeline construction in conjunction with the Anglo-Iranian Company. As Loy Henderson, chief of the Office of Near Eastern and African Affairs (NEA), stated, it was "difficult if not impossible . . . to control the activities and particularly the discussions of oil men once they were in Iran." (Consequently, the State Department permitted the SONJ representatives to visit only specified areas of Iran.) Even after Washington extended another $25 million in military credits to Teheran in June 1947, Allen told the Iranians that U.S. interest in Iranian oil remained minimal. As John Jernegan of NEA later put it, Iran differed from Greece and Turkey in that Iran, with the continued British presence, did not require direct U.S. intervention. In fact, Teheran might be best off if it did not unequivocally join the Western camp.[19]

The Iranian and Turkish crises soon passed, but the effects were important and lasting. It is clear, John Oneal argues, that "the challenge as perceived by the Truman administration was not only economic in nature, probably not even primarily so, nor limited to the immediate geographical region." Instead, Washington viewed the concurrent crises in Turkey and Iran in the global context of Soviet-American relations. Truman later described the Soviet notes on the Straits as "an open bid to obtain control of Turkey," that, if successful, would have led to aggression elsewhere. For Under Secretary Dean Acheson, who would be a critical decision maker in the Truman Doctrine episode, the crises over Turkey and Iran cast the Greek situation in an entirely new light. Until the fall of 1946, Acheson had discouraged Greek overtures for an increased American commitment. But "the importance which the Near East had assumed in Acheson's thinking as a result of the crises of the previous spring and summer," his biographer, David McLellan, explains, "now prepared him to overlook the failings of the Greek government if that was necessary to salvage it from collapse."[20]

The Greek Civil War, 1944–1946

Acheson and other American officials had good reason to fear involvement in Greek troubles. U.S. economic interests in the country were minimal. The German occupation had been prolonged and destructive, with over a half million Greeks dying in the war. Greece also suffered enormous material losses during the war.[21]

Now a bitter and bloody civil war, with roots in prewar feuds and rivalries, threatened to consume what little of the country had survived. On one side lay the National Liberation Front (EAM) and its military arm, the National Popular Liberation Army (ELAS). During the war, the EAM had attracted a diverse following of approximately one million Greeks, while the ELAS, which numbered 50,000 troops by October 1944, was by far the most effective resistance group. Although the Greek Communist Party (KKE) dominated the coalition, EAM-ELAS nonetheless encompassed virtually the entire political spectrum from extreme leftists to reformist republicans. Pitted against the EAM was an equally diverse group of royalists, conservative landowners and businessmen, and moderate republicans loosely associated with the government-in-exile and Greek King George II.[22]

The "First Round" of the civil war broke out between ELAS and loyalist forces in October 1943 and continued until February 1944, when a temporary truce was arranged. Most historians of the subject agree that EAM would have readily won majority support in a democratic referendum at the end of the German occupation in October 1944. As it happened, a coalition government, including elements from the EAM, the government-in-exile, and rightist resistance forces, was established under British auspices in that month, only to collapse in December. On December 4, 1944, a "Second Round" (December 1944 to February 1945) of fighting erupted between ELAS and forces loyal to the national government and the king. Within days, more than two British divisions joined the loyalists in the struggle against ELAS in Athens.[23]

The decision by Churchill in December 1944 to support the unpopular regime in Athens with military force was probably a mistake, for "his protestations notwithstanding, in Greece Churchill set out to combat not merely Communism but the entire republican camp." London soon became associated with the royalist cause. Confident that a show of force could quickly restore the prewar political order in Greece, Churchill compounded his error by dispatching too small an army to handle the Greek revolt. While the British had subdued the rebels in major Greek cities by January 1945, EAM-ELAS, increasingly dominated by the KKE, retained a strong base in the countryside, from which it would launch a counter-offensive and "Third Round" in the spring of 1946.[24]

Meanwhile, Washington tried to maintain a hands-off policy toward Greece. During the war, Secretaries of State Hull and Stettinius had refused to involve the United States in Greek affairs other than to provide some aid to Greek guerrillas fighting the Germans. The Americans had no desire to become tainted with the power politics that Britain had traditionally practiced in the region. Despite their open distaste for the Greek government, however, U.S. policymakers for the most part suppressed their unhappiness with London due to the close ties that had developed between the two English-speaking countries during the war. And some State Department officials were not displeased to see the British suppress the Greek Communists.[25]

The Soviet Union, in accordance with the informal spheres-of-influence agreement on the Balkans reached by Churchill and Stalin in October 1944, also generally respected British dominance in Greece. "There is no evidence," William Hardy McNeil wrote in October 1946, "that EAM or the Greek Communist Party received any instructions from Russia during the first years of the war." At most, the Russians provided moral support; even the Russian military mission established in Greece in August 1944 extended no material aid or direction to the leftist guerrillas. Churchill, in fact, thanked Stalin at Yalta for keeping his distance from Greek affairs.[26]

Most American policymakers nonetheless held Moscow responsible for the fighting in Greece and genuinely feared that a rebel victory would threaten important U.S. interests. If the Greek Communists seized power, Washington believed, they would eventually become Stalin's wards. As American diplomat Charles Bohlen has observed, the KKE lacked the ideological independence of Tito's Communists. Until Yugoslavia broke ranks with the Soviet Union in 1948, "every Communist party in the world not only was patterned after that of the Soviet Union but was also the subservient instrument of Moscow policy." Moreover, Moscow did not maintain perfect neutrality toward Greece after 1945. During 1946 and 1947, Soviet propagandists regularly denounced British and American intervention in Greece and called for an EAM-ELAS victory. In early 1947, a UN commission confirmed charges that Albania, Bulgaria, and Yugoslavia were giving shelter and arms to the Greek rebels. No wonder, then, that the Truman administration suspected a Russian connection. Yugoslavia and Bulgaria also had designs on Greek territory, and the KKE's willingness to discuss cessions of territory to those countries called into question the rebels' motives. If the Communists so readily surrendered Greek territory, might they not also grant naval bases to the Soviets?[27]

Until the fall of 1946, however, American officials remained reluctant to become entangled in Greek affairs. The rampant corruption and venality of the Tsaldaris regime, coupled with its violent repression of opposition parties and gross violation of civil liberties, repelled even friends of the Athens government, such as U.S. Ambassador Lincoln MacVeagh. As Paul A. Porter, head of a U.S. fact-finding mission to Greece, discovered, Greek officials hoped to substitute foreign aid for reform and reconstruction. Greece had already squandered the better part of several hundred million dollars in foreign assistance, including $362 million in UNRRA relief and a $25 million Eximbank credit concluded in January 1946. Yet the Greeks, believing that their sacrifices in the war entitled them to still more help, boldly asked Secretary of State Byrnes for $6 billion in July 1946. Byrnes refused to offer further financial support until the Greeks initiated currency stabilization and other reforms. Even as the Greek civil war intensified during the summer of 1946, the Americans spurned Greek aid requests. When a Greek economic mission to Washington in August 1946 demanded $175 million in further Eximbank credits, Acheson, then Acting Secretary in Byrnes' absence, turned them aside. The Greek government, he informed Truman, "has not used any of the $25 million credit made available to it nearly eight months ago." A new loan would not "solve the basic economic or political difficulties of Greece, and would ultimately add to its financial problems."[28]

The American position began to shift in September and October 1946, following the August decision by the Truman administration to back Turkey with diplomatic support and a naval show of force. In mid-September, Under Secretary of State Will Clayton, writing on behalf of the State-War-Navy Coordinating Committee (SWNCC), recommended the lifting of restrictions on American sales of military equipment to Greece, Turkey, and Iran. Replying from the Paris Conference on September 24, Byrnes concurred:

> The situation has so hardened that the time has now come when . . . the implementation of our general policies requires the closest coordination. In a word we must help our friends in

every way and refrain from assisting those who either through helplessness or for other reasons are opposing the principles for which we stand.

I have in mind particularly two countries which it is of the highest importance for us to assist, Turkey and Greece.[29]

Just as the United States began systematically cutting aid to Eastern Europe, it began increasing aid to friendly countries in the Near East (and Western Europe). The State Department also drew up new policy statements on Greece, Turkey, and Iran. In mid-October 1946, Acheson informed MacVeagh, the department sensed that

strained international relations focusing on Greece may result in early major crisis which may be a deciding factor in future orientation of Near and Middle Eastern countries. It is of importance to US security that Greece remain independent . . . , and we are prepared to take suitable measures to support territorial and political integrity [of] Greece.[30]

In a revised policy statement of October 21, 1946, the Office of Near Eastern and African Affairs (NEA) argued that Greece and Turkey were critical to the containment of Soviet influence in the Eastern Mediterranean. While sharply critical of the Athens government's repressive practices, NEA saw no alternative to supporting the present government given the alleged Soviet military assistance to satellite proxy forces and, through them, the Greek rebels. Before extending aid, however, NEA recommended that the United States obtain pledges from the Greek government to broaden its political base and to drop its irredentist claims on neighboring countries. In return, the United States would permit limited military sales and encourage Eximbank and World Bank loans to Greece.[31]

Yet after this flurry of activity, official enthusiasm for aid to Greece cooled once again. Byrnes ordered MacVeagh to "discourage extravagant hopes in Greek Govt quarters." In order to avoid provoking the Soviets, Acheson explained to the American Ambassador in November 1946, the United States would supply only limited economic aid to Athens, while Great Britain would remain responsible for providing military matériel and advice. Acheson confidentially told MacVeagh in December 1946 that the department expected a delay of at least two or three months before Congress would appropriate new funds for foreign aid programs.[32]

The Greeks did not help their cause. The visit of Greek Prime Minister Constantine Tsaldaris to Washington in January 1947 left Byrnes "unfavorably impressed by Tsaldaris's lack of precision." Acheson later ridiculed the Greek leader as "a weak, pleasant, but silly man," obsessed by hopes of augmenting Greek territory at the expense of its neighbors. Later in the month, the Eximbank even considered suspending the balance ($13 million) of its $25 million loan to Greece.[33] The American commitment to Greece before February 1947 was by no means unequivocal.

When George C. Marshall replaced James F. Byrnes as Secretary of State in late January 1947, the United States had gained very few of its objectives in Greece. "Since the liberation of Greece from German occupation," Thomas Paterson observes, "the United States had given it $181,500,000 in assistance, but the impact of the aid had been minimal." In February 1947, Paul Porter reported that the Greek economy was in much worse shape than expected. Despite a looming financial crisis, the Greek government was unwilling to cut spending or improve tax collection. Only further American aid could save Greece from bankruptcy and collapse, Porter warned. Later in the same month, Mark F. Ethridge, the U.S. representative on the UN Commission of Investigation in Greece, predicted that the Soviets, having found "Greece surprisingly soft," were about to spring "an all out offensive for the kill." Yet Washington felt almost powerless to act. While the department was giving urgent attention to Greek problems, Marshall informed MacVeagh, it was "handicapped by lack of authority so far as Eximbank and Federal Reserve are concerned."[34]

Meanwhile, signs of the further decline of British power were unmistakable. A British White Paper in January 1947 reported that a shortage of manpower and capital were holding down exports and production to a disastrously low level. The $5 billion in loans secured from the United States and Canada just a year earlier were almost exhausted, forcing London to reduce the armed forces by over 300,000 (out of 1.5 million). But the worst was yet to come. A shortfall in coal production and a succession of blizzards paralyzed more than half of British industry by February 7, 1947. A new White paper on February 21, which *The Times* of London labeled "the most disturbing statement ever made by a British government," forecast unremitting hardship for the foreseeable future. Observers on both sides of the Atlantic recognized that Great Britain, if still a major power, was no longer a *world* power. Continental Europe also suffered from the severe weather, and the economic crises of France and Italy portended Communist Party gains. It was in this setting that the British delivered two notes to the State Department on

February 21, 1947, announcing that they would be unable to retain responsibility for the security of Greece and Turkey after March 31.[35]

Although the timing of the British notes surprised them, the Americans had had ample warning of British distress. What is more, "American policymakers were hardly the innocents abroad that the British imagined them," Lawrence Wittner observes. Following dire warnings of an impending Greek collapse from MacVeagh, Porter, and Ethridge, Under Secretary Acheson had forwarded a memo on the "Crisis and Imminent Possibility of Collapse in Greece" to Secretary Marshall on February 21, just hours before the British emissaries arrived.

The British, the Eximbank, and the World Bank, Acheson noted, were all unable to meet the most pressing financial needs of Greece. "It was understood when the British loan was made last year," Acheson continued, "that no further requests for direct loans to foreign governments would be asked of Congress." But the Greek situation demanded drastic action: "If we are to act at all, we recommend presenting a special bill to Congress on an urgent basis for a direct loan to Greece, stressing the fact that if inflation and chaos are not prevented within the next few months, the gravest consequences will ensue and the country will be beyond our help."[36]

According to Joseph M. Jones, a speechwriter for the State Department, Marshall asked Acheson to prepare a bill for economic and military aid for Greece *before* the British notes arrived later that day.[37] In any event, the British notes accelerated the American decision-making process, setting in motion the bureaucratic machinery that would produce the Truman Doctrine.[38] Before administration officials could deal with the Greek rebels, however, they would have to deal with the U.S. Congress.

Domestic Politics and the Truman Doctrine

The large margins by which the Congress approved the major foreign policy legislation of the Truman administration have led some historians to assume that the national legislature seldom posed a significant barrier to executive policies. Thomas Paterson argues that Congress sometimes

> made Truman work hard for his legislation, but it trimmed budgets only slightly and usually left him free to exercise

American power as he wished in the early Cold War years. . . .
on the whole, Truman got what he wanted from Congress, and
Congress did not control foreign policy. When its reaction was
very critical, . . . that criticism itself paralleled existing administration thinking.[39]

Yet officials in the White House and the State Department took
Congressional opposition quite seriously. The administration's alarm
over the Congress becomes more understandable when one considers
the fate of its foreign economic and budgetary proposals in early 1947.
Joseph Jones later recalled that from the vantage point of the State
Department, it appeared as if "the entire structure of United States
foreign economic policy built up since 1934 was in jeopardy of nullifica-
tion by Congress." The 80th Congress took steps to raise tariffs, end
the Reciprocal Trade Agreements program, curtail the Eximbank's
right to extend reconstruction loans, and block creation of the International Trade Organization. The President's proposed budget for
the fiscal year 1948 also ran into rough weather. Committed to tax
cuts, spending reductions, and smaller government, the Republican-
controlled Congress slashed $3 billion from Truman's already lean bud-
get of $37.7 billion. Only the intervention of Republican Senator
Arthur H. Vandenberg, the chairman of the Foreign Relations Committee, headed off these efforts, and then only after the White House
pledged to meet the Republicans halfway.[40]

Concern over Congressional parsimony permeated administration
thinking on foreign policy. On February 24, 1947, the very day on
which the British Ambassador formally announced his country's impending withdrawal from Greece and Turkey, Secretary of the Navy
Forrestal lamented the impact of Republican budgetary constraints on
American foreign policy. "The next eighteen months look to me to be
about the most critical that this country has ever faced," he wrote, "and
to deny Marshall the cards to play, when the stakes are as high as they
are, would be a grave decision." President Truman himself caught the
budget-cutting fever. Lunching with his Cabinet on February 24, he
pledged additional cutbacks in future years. The President's goal was
"a postwar budget between 25 and 30 billion," Forrestal noted, "but
. . . this would have to be accomplished gradually and not by disor-
derly and drastic measures."[41]

The domestic political environment, then, was at the forefront of
American officials' minds when the British made their announcement.
Joseph Jones, unaware of the crisis building over Greece and Turkey,

captured the administration's mood in a memo for the files he wrote on February 26, 1947. While Western Europe and other important areas teetered on the brink of political and economic collapse, Jones noted, the President and other officials were struggling with the Congress to win approval for already inadequate foreign aid and trade programs:

> Congress and the people of this country are not sufficiently aware of the character and dimensions of the crisis that impends, and of the measures that must be taken . . . if disaster is to be avoided. The people and Congress do not know the incomparably greater cost to them if the chief supporters of our trade and political policies around the world are forced to abandon us, if the United States should be obliged to shoulder directly responsibilities that are now only contingent, for peace and security in all parts of the world. The State Department knows. Congress and the people do not know.[42]

Recalling prewar isolationism, and hoping to head off further Congressional budget-cutting, the administration decided to portray the situations in Greece and Turkey in apocalyptic, globalist terms. A more sober approach was unlikely to win Congressional approval for new foreign aid programs. In a February 27 meeting with Congressional leaders called by the President, Marshall's unemotional presentation of the problems in the Near East left his audience unimpressed. As Acheson recalls,

> My distinguished chief, most unusually and unhappily, flubbed his opening statement. In desperation I whispered to him a request to speak. This was my crisis. For a week I had nurtured it. These congressmen had no conception of what challenged them; it was my task to bring it home. Both my superiors, equally perturbed, gave me the floor. Never have I spoken under such a pressing sense that the issue was up to me alone. No time was left for measured appraisal. In the past eighteen months, I said, Soviet pressure . . . had brought the Balkans to the point where a highly possible Soviet breakthrough might open three continents to Soviet penetration. Like apples in a barrel infected by one rotten one, the corruption of Greece would infect Iran and all to the east. It would also carry infection to Africa . . . , and to Europe through Italy and France. . . . The Soviet Union was playing one of the greatest gambles in history at minimal cost.[43]

Senator Vandenberg, like most of those present, was shocked by Acheson's statement. "If you will say that to the Congress and the country," he told Truman, "I will support you and I believe that most of its members will do the same." It was at this point that the drafting of the Truman Doctrine speech began. From the beginning, the administration regarded the Truman Doctrine as less a diplomatic announcement than a call to action to the American people. The President's speech would be, as Clark Clifford put it, "the opening gun in a campaign to bring people up to [the] realization that the war isn't over by any means."[44]

The officials entrusted with the drafting of the Truman Doctrine speech sought to use anti-Communism to galvanize Congressional and public support for aid to Greece and Turkey. A special subcommittee of the SWNCC addressed the question of how best to present the President's message in a February 28 meeting. The War Department representative stated that "the only thing that can sell [the] public is [the] necessity of holding the line[;] Communism versus Democracy should be [the] major theme." Still, the SWNCC group did not wish the President to appear too hostile to the Soviet Union because that would needlessly offend liberal Democrats. "There are ways of making [the] situation perfectly clear," Llewellyn Thompson, Chief of the State Department's Division of Eastern European Affairs, stated, "without specifically mentioning Russia." Administration officials could privately emphasize the Soviet danger to Congressmen and others, "but not in official pronouncements." To undercut charges of militarism, the economic components of American aid should receive more attention than military aid. The President, the group agreed, should also downplay the importance of Anglo-American cooperation in the region. The "sweeping globalism of the Truman Doctrine," one historian of Anglo-American relations states, ". . . was to some extent a response to and a rejection of these suspicions that the United States was merely standing in for Great Britain."[45]

Not everyone in the administration recommended framing the request for aid to Greece and Turkey in the unequivocal and stark terms that the SWNCC subcommittee favored. Its language made George Kennan, then teaching at the National War College in Washington, "extremely unhappy." Kennan believed that the Soviet threat to Greece, let alone Turkey, was political rather than military, and he suspected that "the Pentagon had exploited a favorable set of circumstances in order to infiltrate a military aid program for Turkey into what was supposed to be primarily a political and economic program for Greece."[46]

White House aide George Elsey also doubted that this was "the occasion for the 'All-out' speech." The administration had had too little time to prepare for the speech, and there had been "no overt action in the immediate past by the USSR which serves as an adequate pretext for the 'All-out' speech." The Greek case was too "abstract," and "an 'All-out' speech will have a divisive effect if delivered too soon." Finally, Elsey feared that a presidential statement of this type could destroy the forthcoming Moscow Council of Foreign Ministers. From Paris, en route to Moscow, Secretary Marshall and Charles Bohlen agreed that "there was too much flamboyant anti-Communism in the speech."[47]

The White House, however, reasoned that "the Senate would not approve the doctrine without the emphasis on the Communist danger." As Truman told his Cabinet on March 7, the Truman Doctrine "means [the] U.S. is going into European politics. It means the greatest selling job ever facing a President."[48]

Before a joint session of Congress on March 12, 1947, President Truman asked for $400 million in economic and military aid to Greece ($250 million) and Turkey ($150 million). While he deemphasized the military portions of the aid package, only $128,150,000 of the requested $400,000,000 consisted of economic and financial aid. Truman also implied that the United States would support other nations threatened by Communist takeovers, whether through internal subversion or external aggression:

> The very existence of the Greek state is today threatened by the terrorist activities of several thousand men, led by communists. . . .
> There is no other country to which democratic Greece can turn.
> The extension of aid by this country does not mean that the United States condones everything that the Greek government has done or will do. . . .
> I believe that it must be the policy of the United States to support free peoples who are resisting attempted subjugation by armed minorities or by outside pressures. . . .
> I believe that our help should be primarily through economic and financial aid which is essential to economic stability and orderly political processes. . . .
> Should we fail to aid Greece and Turkey in this fateful hour, the effect will be far-reaching to the West as well as to the East. . . .
> The seeds of totalitarian regimes are nurtured by misery and want. They spread and grow in the evil soil of poverty and strife.[49]

Congressional reaction to the speech was generally favorable, but still not entirely satisfactory from the viewpoint of its architects. As Acheson states in his memoirs, the standing ovation that Congress gave the President was "a tribute to a brave man rather than unanimous acceptance of his policy." While his message elicited strong support from the news media, a State Department survey of public reaction found that a large minority of liberal Americans objected to the Truman Doctrine's allegedly militaristic tone and to the administration's failure to take the problem to the UN.[50]

The anti-Communist thrust of the Truman Doctrine was expected to win greater support from conservatives and former isolationists. "They don't like Russia, they don't like the Communists, but still they don't want to do anything to stop it," Representative Carl Vinson of Georgia told Forrestal the day after the speech. "But they are on the spot now, and they all have to come clean." Still, many conservatives, such as Republican Senator Robert A. Taft of Ohio, questioned the cost of the aid program and the seemingly open-ended commitment to further aid programs that Truman's speech implied. Echoing the concerns of many Americans, columnist Walter Lippmann warned that the temptation to "reinforce every theater, to fill every vacuum of power and restore at one and the same time the whole shattered economic life of Europe and Asia" could only dissipate American strength.[51]

While liberal and conservative critics never seriously threatened the aid programs, administration officials could not let their dissent go unchallenged, for they hoped to use the Truman Doctrine to build a lasting consensus behind an activist foreign policy. As newsman James Reston told Forrestal the day after Truman's speech, the "really disturbing thing is that the Congress of the United States is simply not ready to have this country take over the leadership which it was obviously intended to take over."[52]

With Marshall attending the Moscow CFM, Dean Acheson faced the Senate Foreign Relations Committee as the administration's key spokesman beginning on March 13. He quickly mastered the debate. Publicly, Acheson downplayed the universalism of the Truman Doctrine and focused attention upon economic reconstruction rather than military aid. By avoiding a direct attack on the Soviet Union, Acheson disarmed liberal critics of the doctrine. He also denied that the United States had any intention of sending troops to Greece or of underwriting British obligations. The United States intervened in the Near East, the Under Secretary declared, only because the UN would not act as quickly as the crisis required.[53]

In executive testimony before the same committee, administration officials stressed the strategic stakes involved in the Near East, particularly in Turkey, more than they had in the public presentations. "Greece and Turkey are a strategic line," Ambassador MacVeagh instructed the committee members on March 28. "If they [the Soviets] break that down, the whole Near East falls and they pick the lock of world dominion." Senator Vandenberg was especially quick to learn. The "fall of Greece, followed by the fall of Turkey," he stated, "would establish a chain reaction around the world which could very easily leave us isolated in a Communist-dominated earth." When pressed on April 1 on the question of who should control the Straits, Acheson stressed the containment of Russia. "It is not that we are trying to control it," he stated. "We feel that it is very important that the Soviets should not control it. . . . That is why that area is so important." As Republican Senator Henry Cabot Lodge of Massachusetts stated, "this is not primarily a relief mission or an economic mission, it is a strategic mission."[54]

Perhaps the most effective argument brought forward by the administration centered around national prestige and presidential credibility. The Senators sensed that a turning point had been reached, and that America's image in the world required them to rally around the President. "Congress' acceptance of Truman's definition of the crisis," Walter LaFeber observes, "marked the point in the Cold War when power in foreign policy formulation began shifting rapidly from Capitol Hill to the White House." "We are confronted . . . with the fundamental fact," Vandenberg declared, "that if we desert the President of the United States at the moment[,] we cease to have influence in the world forever." Republican Senator Wallace H. White, Jr., of Maine agreed. "Wherever the fault may be, if there is fault, . . . I do not see how we . . . can leave the President in this situation," he stated. "I think we have got to go along with him."[55]

The administration's tactics worked. The Congress subjected the Truman Doctrine to little further scrutiny. The Senate approved the bill on April 22 by a margin of 67 to 23; the House followed on May 8 by 287 to 107. Truman signed it into law in late May.[56]

For the first time, the Truman administration had attained unity, discipline, and purpose in its foreign policy. The accession of George C. Marshall as Secretary of State had much to do with this. Byrnes had spent 350 of his 562 days as Secretary abroad, leaving much of the daily business of the department in Acheson's able hands. But Byrnes' relations with Truman were tenuous, and Byrnes tended to address issues in an *ad hoc*, crisis-oriented manner. Broad U.S. goals, notably in the economic sphere, were never clearly defined. In contrast, Marshall brought military habits into State, clearly delegating authority within the department, and maintained close personal ties with Truman. "No other American in our history can be imagined who could have taken over command from General Washington at Valley Forge," Acheson later wrote. "It was, indeed, an act of God that made him chief adviser to the President and head of the State Department in the no less critical winter of 1947."[57]

The Greek-Turkish crisis also witnessed a change of mood in the White House. Truman now appeared more self-assured as Chief Executive. As he later told press aide Eben Ayers, the Truman Doctrine and its immediate aftermath "marked the beginning of his own foreign policy." "The image of the confused, uncertain, accidental President was changing to one of a confident, self-assured leader," one historian has noted. Speechwriter Jones observed on the day of Truman's March 12 speech before Congress: "The message was in my opinion momentous not only for its content, but for the *way* in which the Government functioned in the crisis: fast, brave, and clean. It seemed to me as though it marked our passing into adulthood in the conduct of foreign affairs."[58]

Interpreting the Truman Doctrine

The administration still had to define the precise policies it would follow in foreign affairs. Everyone recognized that the Truman Doctrine signified much more than an American commitment to Greece and Turkey. In internal meetings and public discussions, the administration had put forward numerous reasons for American intervention in Greece and Turkey: to protect the independence of those countries; to rally and to unify the American people against the Soviet threat; to preserve Western access to the raw materials and trade of the Near and Middle East; to maintain Western control over strategic areas in the Eastern Mediterranean; and to affirm American support for friendly countries faced with internal rebellion or external aggression. Clearly, the United States could not simultaneously fulfill all of these obligations.

Dean Acheson assumed the duty of setting American priorities in foreign policy. In the early stages of planning for the Truman Doctrine,

American policymakers had decided to delay asking for funds for other needy countries until aid to Greece and Turkey was secured. But already on March 5, 1947, Acheson, observing that the situation in Greece and Turkey "is only part of a much larger problem growing out of the change in Great Britain's strength and other circumstances," asked SWNCC and the Treasury department to consider what other countries might require analogous aid.[59] To Acheson and others, the significance of the Truman Doctrine lay as much in its impact upon the morale and security of Western Europe as in its impact upon Greece and Turkey. Even George Kennan, for all his dislike of the Truman Doctrine's rhetorical excess, supported Greek and Turkish aid because of its salutary effect upon Western Europe.[60]

Alert observers quickly discerned the outline of future administration policy. In a telephone conversation with James Forrestal on March 13, for instance, James Reston speculated that "if you followed this policy [the Truman Doctrine] to its logical conclusion," then "something in the neighborhood of fifteen or twenty billion dollars in the next four years" would be in order. Forrestal agreed, implying that the main concern of the administration—even of its senior naval official— remained the restoration of European production and world trade:

FORRESTAL:
We've had a lot of high-level, penthouse economic free trade, etc., but the guts of it is can a little guy buy silk in Japan and sell it in New York and make a dollar? . . . And are we going to build a heavy steel industry here to supply the lack of steel, when there's an industry in Germany lying fallow when it could supply Europe? . . .

RESTON:
I think that was the only weakness in what was otherwise a magnificent statement of the President . . . namely, . . . that the [only] people who were going to get help were the people who were in desperate straits and who had an armed minority at their border; whereas I would like to have seen him indicate that you can fight Communism in other ways—in economic ways—by a positive policy of lending, and so on.

FORRESTAL:
Of course the thing has to be a part of a global pattern. . . . the only way that you can get the American taxpayer back to believe is to let these people produce.[61]

Despite its emphasis upon Greece and Turkey in both the speech and the aid bill, the Truman Doctrine was primarily an instrument of economic containment in *Europe*. This is not to say that other factors, notably the establishment of American power in the Eastern Mediterranean and the Middle East, would not prove important in the long term. But at the time, the Truman administration was not eager to assume these new responsibilities, which could only distract attention from the main theater of action in Europe. While Acheson's lecture on the strategic importance of Greece and Turkey may have impressed Congressional leaders, his argument did not excite keen interest among military officials. In fact, the JCS did not become directly involved in the decision-making process leading to the Truman Doctrine. In one of their few comments on the subject, the Joint Chiefs strongly backed military aid to Turkey but concluded that "this assistance involves political, economic and psychological factors which are primary as compared to the military factor."[62]

The course of events following passage of the Greek-Turkish legislation also demonstrates the administration's reluctance to broaden American commitments in the region. The United States established a permanent, but limited, naval task force in the Mediterranean and avoided a further expansion of the U.S. military presence in the region. When the British, who had already withdrawn 8,000 troops from Greece, announced in the summer of 1947 that they would evacuate their remaining 5,000 men and cut their occupation forces in Italy, Marshall showed uncharacteristic anger. The Secretary of State complained that Whitehall was "far too casual or freehanded in passing the buck of the international dilemma to US with little or no consideration for the harmful results." Forrestal and Secretary of War Kenneth C. Royall, who had replaced Robert Patterson in July, agreed that the British pullout seriously threatened Greek security and concluded that there "appears to be no course of action open to the United States which would fully offset the adverse effects of this move." The administration considered dispatching American troops to Greece. Yet, as Marshall told the Senate Foreign Relations Committee in March 1948, the President ultimately decided against this step because of the difficulty of fighting on the treacherous Greek terrain, the small number of ready combat divisions in the U.S. Army, and the need to conserve American strength for more important theaters of war. In the end, U.S. pressure kept British troops in Greece until 1954.[63]

Meanwhile, British Foreign Minister Ernest Bevin had won Marshall's assent in September 1947 to the convening of Anglo-American talks "for the purpose of arriving at a 'gentlemen's understanding'" in the Near and Middle East. British and American military officials met secretly at the Pentagon during the fall of 1947. While the talks were symbolically important, few substantive agreements were reached. The United States affirmed its support for the security of the region against external aggression and agreed to assume primary responsibility for economic aid, while the British promised to maintain a military presence there. The two allies also agreed to exclude the Soviets from military bases in former Italian colonies. In effect, the United States relaxed its traditional anti-imperialist policy in recognition of the fact that British forces, by stabilizing the region, performed a vital service to the United States. In any event, the Pentagon talks of 1947 did not evince an eagerness on the part of the Americans to take on additional duties in the region, with the exceptions of Greece and Turkey.[64]

The Greek civil war dragged on bloodily until October 1949, when the Yugoslav decision to seal the Greek border, Soviet nonsupport, and sustained offensives by the regular army finally doomed the guerrillas. Ironically, Stalin himself, perhaps fearing that a growing American presence in Greece would endanger the Soviet sphere of influence in Eastern Europe, in 1948 attacked Tito for his adventuristic support of the Greek rebels against the Kremlin's orders. Isolated within the Communist movement and denounced even by the KKE, Tito felt compelled to desert the Greek guerrillas and to come to terms with the Athens government and the West a year later. The National Security Council determined in early 1949 that the United States should "relax export licensing controls in favor of Yugoslavia" because "Tito's successful heresy strikes at the roots of Moscow's complete control . . . of the Russian satellite empire."[65]

Still, American leaders never stopped believing that the Greek rebels were pawns of the Kremlin and that, as a corollary, the victory of the Greek regulars in 1949 constituted an American triumph against the Soviet Union and international Communism.[66] The reasons for the American misunderstanding of the Greek civil war are fairly simple. Until that point, Communist national movements had demonstrated a remarkable degree of allegiance to Moscow. If the Communist regimes of Yugoslavia, Albania, and Bulgaria aided the Greek rebels, the Greek revolution must be part of the Kremlin's master plan for world conquest, or so official thinking went. Another factor that predisposed the Truman administration to emphasize the monolithic nature of Communism, of course, was the receptivity of the Congress to that theme.

The pervasiveness of anti-Communism in official thinking helps explain the peculiar course of American programs in Greece from 1947 to 1949. In the Truman Doctrine speech, the President had maintained that economic aid and reform held the key to defeating the rebel insurgency. Truman at first restricted the advisers of the U.S. Army Group in Greece to a supply role and denied repeated requests by Athens for an expansion of its army. But after the Greek National Army (GNA) suffered numerous battle defeats during the fall and winter of 1947–48, the administration relented and permitted a major buildup of Athens' forces. (By November 1948, government troops outnumbered the rebels by 263,000 to 23,000.) Beginning in November 1947, American advisers assumed virtual command of the GNA, as well as many functions of the government. In effect, the United States adopted a military solution to the Greek problem, substituting the annihilation of the enemy for the reform of the social and economic conditions that had fostered the insurgency in the first place. Despite some success in rebuilding the country's transportation system and improving public health, the U.S. economic aid program in Greece foundered. Recovery was extremely slow, and reform, notably of the notorious taxation system, almost nonexistent.[67] In Greece, economic containment was not the main instrument of U.S. policy.

In some ways, the Truman Doctrine set an unfortunate precedent. Anti-Communism increasingly came to permeate American political discourse and foreign policy. Soon after delivering his March 1947 speech, the President, reacting to the discovery of Soviet spy rings in Britain, Canada, and the United States, set up loyalty and security procedures in order to purge the government of "disloyal elements" and to steal the anti-Communist issue from the Republicans. In doing so, Truman may have unwittingly fueled the growing alarm in the country over Communist subversion.[68]

After March 1947, American officials seldom felt free to justify multilateral programs on their own merits. Instead, they felt compelled to demonstrate that foreign aid programs and other economic agreements served to contain the Soviet Union. In time, an increasing proportion of foreign aid would consist of military or military-related material for this purpose.

Yet, as John Lewis Gaddis has argued, most historians have exaggerated the significance of the Truman Doctrine. The administration had already made the decision to contain the Soviet Union in 1946. It was forced to publicize the containment doctrine in the Truman Doctrine speech in March 1947 because the Greek-Turkish crisis, unlike previous confrontations with the Soviet Union, necessitated Congressional approval of large-scale appropriations. Despite the President's universalist rhetoric, the administration had neither the inclination nor the means to police the world against Communism. And even with the enunciation of the Truman Doctrine, the administration lacked a concrete plan of action. Given continued constraints on the budget, American containment before the Korean War largely took the form of political and economic efforts to bolster Western Europe, rather than military measures to threaten the Soviet Union. The Truman Doctrine, in short, did not herald either the militarization of American society or the commitment of the United States to contain Communism everywhere.[69]

The Truman Doctrine did pave the way for the Marshall Plan. The Moscow CFM in March and April 1947 convinced Secretary of State Marshall that a solution to the German problem required the exclusion of the Soviets from the negotiating process. Time was of the essence, Marshall told a national radio audience on April 28, and West European survival could no longer await great power agreement. "The recovery of Europe has been far slower than had been expected," he stated. "Disintegrating forces are becoming evident. The patient is sinking while the doctors deliberate. So I believe that action cannot await compromise through exhaustion."[70]

The SWNCC subcommittee that Acheson had appointed in March foreshadowed the future course of American aid programs in its report of April 21, 1947. The group estimated that American world exports for 1947 ($16.2 billion) would exceed imports ($8.7 billion) by about $7.5 billion. Private long-term loans and private and governmental short-term credits together would finance only $450 million of the U.S. surplus. The World Bank ($300 million), hard reserves of foreign buyers ($1.2 billion), and private remittances ($750 million) would still leave a $4.8 billion shortfall for the U.S. government to finance. American aid programs, however, would begin tapering off in the following year. "The conclusion is inescapable," the SWNCC subcommittee stated, that "the world will not be able to continue to buy United States exports at the 1946–1947 rate beyond another 12–18 months." Even if the United States were to maintain foreign financing at its current level, it would be inadequate "to the accomplishment either of world economic stability and the type of world trading system which is the object of our trade policy, or of the political objectives in several critical countries." A sharp decline in American exports, accompanied by a slackening of domestic demand, could send the United States into a deep recession.[71]

By the winter of 1947, American officials realized that the crisis in Western Europe demanded immediate attention. When the Greek-Turkish crises offered a convenient tool to build a sustained U.S. commitment to Western Europe, they seized it. Before a public and Congress unaccustomed to thinking in terms of power politics and uninterested in international economic problems, the administration felt it necessary to emphasize certain aspects of the situation in that area—the Balkan countries' support for the Greek Communists—and to deemphasize others—the dubious nature of the Greek government. In failing to temper the rhetorical excesses of his March 12 speech, Truman unleashed forces over which he would eventually have little control; the Truman Doctrine, like Kennan's containment thesis, became harnessed to purposes that its authors had neither intended nor foreseen. Yet for the first time, the President enjoyed a mandate for European reconstruction.

CHAPTER SEVEN

THE MARSHALL PLAN: INTERIM AID, THE EUROPEAN RECOVERY PROGRAM, AND THE DIVISION OF EUROPE, 1947–1949

THE EUROPEAN CRISIS in the spring of 1947 threatened to destroy the Truman administration's program for economic security. Washington officials feared that if economic conditions continued to deteriorate, the West European governments might succumb to Soviet influence, if not outright Communist takeovers. At the very least, Western Europe might pursue protectionist, beggar-thy-neighbor policies, in turn reducing American exports, weakening the already fragile structure of world trade and finance, and undermining the economic foundations of the peace.

The containment policy outlined in the Truman Doctrine provided a rationale for American intervention in Europe, but it did not offer positive and practical solutions to the purely economic problems of Western Europe. The U.S. pledge to fight Communism did not warm British homes, feed French workers, or open German waterways. Even in June 1947, when Secretary of State George C. Marshall announced the plan that would bear his name, the Truman administration lacked a coherent program for European reconstruction.

The "Marshall Plan" enunciated in the Secretary's speech was not a fixed program for action. By inviting the European countries to initiate their own plan for recovery, Marshall opened the door to significant foreign participation in the planning and implementation of the aid program. Due to its unprecedented cost and scope, moreover, the European Recovery Program was subject to greater domestic pressures than earlier foreign economic legislation. Itself the product of numerous competing influences, the Marshall Plan was all things to all men: humanitarian relief program, prop to American exports, weapon against international Communism, antidote to West European radicalism, and instrument for European integration.

The European Crisis and the Origins of the Marshall Plan

The European Recovery Program (ERP) grew out of an increasing sense of anxiety among American officials that Western Europe was nearing political and economic collapse. The surprising recovery of 1946 had been followed by a sharp drop in production and trade during the bitter winter of 1947. These problems worsened in the spring. Western Europe faced a huge balance-of-payments deficit with the outside world, particularly the United States (an estimated $4.25 billion in fiscal 1948) and raw materials suppliers.[1] British insolvency caused special problems, for that country's traditional import surplus with the continent had supplied the foreign exchange earnings necessary to pay for European imports from the Americas and other areas. Factories shut down when stocks of raw and semifinished materials, notably coal, ran out, while inflation, currency inconvertibility, and the proliferation of protectionist commercial agreements crippled intra-European trade.

In April 1947, a SWNCC subcommittee reported that the European dollar gap required a vast infusion of American aid. A new program of U.S. assistance was imperative because existing relief programs were tapering off at the time of greatest European need. The State Department estimated in May 1947 that while aid by the U.S. government, including IBRD and IMF disbursements, would finance the export of $6.2 billion of goods and services in 1947, this figure would shrink to $4.6 billion in 1948 and $2.7 billion in 1949. Neither the World Bank nor private American banks could meet West European deficits, explained Bank President John J. McCloy in an April 1947 speech. The sums were too large, and financial institutions refused to extend what they considered economically unsound loans to accomplish political objectives.[2]

Following his return from the Moscow Council of Foreign Ministers at the end of April, Secretary of State Marshall instructed George F. Kennan, then teaching at the National War College in Washington, to establish a Policy Planning Staff (PPS) that would formulate the principles for a European reconstruction program. (Marshall created the PPS, he told the Cabinet, because there had been a "notable lack of central planning on American policy.") Kennan's group contributed its preliminary report on European reconstruction on May 23. The PPS felt that the root of European instability lay in the after-effects of war rather than in Communist activities. While Europe itself must initiate a new cooperative recovery program, the United States could help by using aid to open up major production bottlenecks, such as the German coal industry. The Soviet bloc countries could participate, but only if they agreed "to abandon the exclusive orientation of their economies." The PPS concluded with a plea for a deemphasis of anti-Communism in U.S. policy.[3]

On May 8, 1947, Under Secretary Dean Acheson defined the principles of a new aid program in a major address on the European economic crisis before the Delta Council at Cleveland, Mississippi. To answer domestic and foreign criticism of the Truman Doctrine's allegedly single-minded anti-Communism, Acheson stressed the positive U.S. commitment to European reconstruction. Acheson first described in vivid detail the destruction wrought by the war in Europe and the consequences of its inability to pay for desperately needed American goods. Just to maintain current imports, the European countries needed about $5 billion per year in additional hard currency. International institutions were incapable of handling the crisis, he explained, and only the United States had sufficient resources to help. But even with its impressive assets, America needed to concentrate its "emergency assistance in areas where it will be most effective in building world political and economic stability . . . [and] in fostering liberal trade policies . . . ," notably in Western Europe and Germany. "European cooperation," he stated, "cannot await 'compromise through exhaustion,' and . . . we must take whatever action is possible immediately, even without full Four Power agreement, to effect a larger measure of European, including German, recovery."[4]

In a May 27 memo, Under Secretary for Economic Affairs William Clayton, recently returned from Europe and shaken by the deteriorating conditions there, argued that the United States had seriously understated European recovery problems. He recommended a three-year program of aid at $6–7 billion per year. But Clayton, remembering the negative public and Congressional reaction to UNRRA, believed the United States should carefully supervise the program. *"The United States must run this show,"* he wrote.[5]

At this point, the administration had not decided such important matters as the size and duration of a recovery program or the scope of European participation in it. In his famous speech at Harvard University on June 5, Secretary of State Marshall simply called for a European initiative in a joint recovery effort and pledged American assistance. As of yet, there was no "Marshall Plan," for policymakers had not resolved the differing approaches among the various proposals for European reconstruction. The countries that the SWNCC subcommittee had identified as most deserving of American aid in its report on April 21, for example, did not correspond closely with the eventual ERP recipients. Similarly, the preliminary, hastily prepared PPS report of May 23 dealt with principles for European reconstruction rather than a concrete program, and had only a limited impact upon Marshall except for its recommendation of a European initiative. Indeed, the PPS did not deliver a final version of the report until late July 1947, and by then it was superceded by events. Finally, in stressing European self-help, Marshall seemed to reject Clayton's suggestion for direct U.S. control over the recovery program.[6]

If they lacked a specific plan to rescue Europe, American officials at least shared the conviction that drastic action was necessary to secure American multilateralist aims on the continent. Already in early 1947, key European countries were turning to bilateral treaties and other restrictive measures to hold down imports from the dollar area. In preliminary discussions with Clayton in late June 1947, for instance, British Cabinet officials threatened to pursue bilateral trade agreements—which on the scale they mentioned would have doomed the Marshall Plan—if they did not receive special interim aid and other concessions.[7] In the American view, rescuing Europe required more than just another injection of dollar aid; it called for the full integration of the European economy.

The Soviet Response to the Marshall Plan

In time, the Marshall Plan would polarize Europe into hostile blocs, but American policymakers were at first undecided about the roles of the Soviet Union and Eastern Europe in a recovery program. To be sure, Washington wished to contain Soviet power and influence. Yet both American and European planners were accustomed to thinking of the continent as an economic unit and viewed East-West trade as a key element in West European reconstruction.

U.S. officials did not welcome, but nevertheless did not entirely rule out, Soviet participation in the Marshall Plan. American aid, they reasoned, could perhaps counteract the Soviet hold over the East European countries; at the very least, the West would retain access to their raw materials and markets. On May 24, 1947, George Kennan advised Secretary Marshall to "play it straight" with the Russians. If the Russians responded favorably, the West could "test their good faith." If not, the Russians would exclude themselves. Most importantly, Kennan recalls arguing, "we would not ourselves draw a line of division through Europe." In a meeting of State Department heads of offices on May 28, Clayton contended that the inclusion of the East European countries was unnecessary, for they needed Western goods so badly that they would export coal and grain to Western Europe no matter what. Yet the group, siding with Kennan's PPS, decided to permit East European participation, "provided the countries would abandon [the] near-exclusive Soviet orientation of their economies."[8]

The prospect of reconstruction aid must have tempted the Kremlin. By June 1947, the Soviets knew that heavy reparations from western Germany and credits from the United States would not be forthcoming. The Soviets had already stripped eastern Germany, and the capacity of the war-ravaged East European countries to provide reparations and trade was limited. Only the United States could offer critical supplies of machinery, technology, and food. Some administration officials fully expected Soviet participation. Secretary of the Navy James Forrestal, an outspoken anti-Communist who chafed at the thought of aid to Russia, exclaimed at a Cabinet luncheon shortly after Marshall's speech that "there was no chance of Russia's *not* joining in this effort."[9]

Despite some initial skepticism, Moscow on June 22 accepted the Anglo-French invitation to confer in Paris and promised to cooperate as long as the United States did not intervene in its internal affairs. Yet in the opening meeting on June 27, Soviet Foreign Minister V. M. Molotov instantly aroused the suspicions of his British and French counterparts, Ernest Bevin and Georges Bidault. Molotov suggested that the three ministers should test the seriousness of Marshall's proposal by boldly asking Washington the exact sum of money that it was prepared to offer the European countries. On the next day, Molotov added that rather than investigate the prospects for European self-help, the needy countries should simply forward their aggregate aid request to Washington and await a reply. This procedure, Bevin and Bidault protested, fell far short of the coordinated European plan envisaged by Marshall. As a French diplomat privately put it, "The Soviets want to put the United States in a position where it must either shell out dollars before there is a real plan or refuse outright to advance any credits." On June 30, Molotov rejected a compromise offered by the British and French and reiterated his demands of the previous meetings, whereupon Bevin accused him of demanding a "blank check" from the United States. Unwilling to make any concessions for American aid, the Kremlin apparently had instructed Molotov to pull out of the conference. During the last session on July 2, Molotov denounced the Western ministers and warned of a division of Europe into two camps. Subsequently, the Soviets forced the East European representatives to leave Paris.[10]

Why did the Soviets quit the Paris talks? Undoubtedly the Russians would have had to release economic statistics and allow some American inspection of their country. But Moscow rarely furnished candid data, and American probing would only have confirmed what almost everyone already knew: the Soviet Union was weak. Also, even if, as Molotov predicted, the U.S. Congress had rejected the plan because of Soviet participation, the Americans would then have taken the blame and the plan might have failed. If Congress had approved the plan, on the other hand, the Soviets would have gained reconstruction aid for themselves and their dependencies.

Some historians stress the economic vulnerability of the Russian sphere in Eastern Europe. Thomas G. Paterson, for instance, argues that the Soviets rejected the Marshall Plan because it would have signified a return to the *status quo ante bellum* in which Eastern Europe traded food and raw materials for Western machinery and consumer goods. Given the precarious Soviet hold over the region, he adds, "a massive influx of American dollars would certainly have challenged the Soviet position."[11]

Yet neither side in 1947 anticipated or desired an interruption of the mutually profitable East-West trade. There is little evidence that American capitalists hungered after this market, and U.S. planners cared most about Eastern Europe as a source of trade and raw materials for *Western* Europe (see chapter 3). Nor did the Russians have good reason to disrupt the traditional pattern of intra-European trade. Foreign trade had never figured largely in Soviet planning, and the East European economies did not complement Moscow's needs well. Czechoslovakia excepted, most specialized in agricultural and unprocessed goods of which the Soviet Union usually enjoyed a surplus. The Soviet satellites, on the other hand, depended upon Western trade for recovery. Thus, Western trade with, and investment in, Eastern Europe would not have necessarily conflicted with Soviet *economic* goals in the region, certainly not to the point of warranting Soviet rejection of the Marshall Plan.[12]

Strategic and political needs, on the other hand, help explain Soviet fears of American influence in Eastern Europe. Moscow was determined to create a buffer zone against invasion from the West, but it had yet to secure allegiance from its dependencies when Marshall proposed a new recovery program. The anxious men in the Kremlin, Adam Ulam and Isaac Deutscher have speculated, may have interpreted the increasingly militant rhetoric of American spokesmen following the Truman Doctrine as the first step in a campaign to lure the East European countries out of the Soviet bloc. Indeed, the Poles and Czechoslovaks at first resisted Soviet pressure to withdraw from the Paris conference.[13]

Ideology also militated against Soviet participation in the Marshall Plan. Obviously, the Kremlin did not want to help save capitalism in Western Europe. The Soviets, who equated economic control with political mastery of Eastern Europe, probably regarded the American goal of an open, free-trading, economically integrated Europe as a thinly disguised challenge to their sphere of influence.

In an "economic defense of Stalin's autarky," the Soviets gradually sealed off Eastern Europe and set up self-sufficient, "nationalist" economies and a bilateral trading system. During the 1930s, when the terms of trade had turned against primary goods and made imported machinery prohibitively expensive, Soviet planners had concentrated on the extraction of natural resources and the production of capital goods over consumer commodities. By the time the Red Army pushed into Eastern Europe, the Soviet experiment had become locked into an iron law of "Marxist"—or rather, Stalinist—economics, and Soviet and local Communist authorities began to apply the now orthodox operating procedures to the satellites. Ideological and bureaucratic imperatives thus overrode economic rationality and the specialization of labor. Countries as small as Albania constructed expensive and inefficient steel mills in deference to Stalin. In the mid-1950s, Comecon, the Soviet bloc's counterpart to the Marshall Plan, would finally abandon the irrational Stalinist model in favor of increased competition and trade with the West. But in 1947 the Marshall Plan probably seemed to challenge the Soviet promise of industrial growth and economic autonomy for the underdeveloped East European states.[14]

A combination of strategic, political, and ideological factors led to the Soviet repudiation of the Marshall Plan. Economic issues played a smaller role. The Soviet withdrawal from the Paris talks was inevitable only in the sense that the absence of a general political settlement in postwar Europe, notably in Germany, precluded economic cooperation between East and West.

The German Question Revisited, 1947–1948

Solving the German problem was an essential requisite for European recovery.[15] By early 1947, several factors—the desire to lower occupation costs, the dependence of Western Europe upon German recovery, the failure of quadripartite control, and the decision to contain Soviet power and influence in Europe—all had committed the United States to the reconstruction of western Germany. But this prospect alienated France and other friendly European countries, not to mention the Soviet Union and the East European countries, which had suffered so grievously at the hands of Nazi Germany. Moreover, the State Department still expected France to act as the centerpiece of a new continental balance of power. The Truman administration needed to find a solution to the German problem that would serve simultaneously to resolve disagreements within the American government over occupation policies, reduce West European opposition to German reconstruction, and integrate the industrial giant of Europe into the U.S. orbit.[16]

At first, American efforts focused upon raising the permitted level of industry in the Bizone. This was largely a symbolic political gesture designed to boost German morale and appease Congressmen disgruntled with the high cost of the occupation. In February 1947, for example, a presidential mission chaired by Herbert Hoover blamed the March 1946 limits on German industry for high occupation costs and European stagnation and warned, "We can keep Germany in these economic chains but it will also keep Europe in rags." Actually, German production had not even reached the March 1946 ceiling when Hoover issued his report.[17]

Nonetheless, the British and Americans agreed in July 1947 to raise the German level of industry to roughly 1936 (as opposed to 1932) levels of production. The total ceiling on German steel *capacity* (not to be confused with actual *production*, which was lower), rose from 7.5 to 11.5 million tons, of which 10.7 million tons lay in the Bizone. Anglo-American agreement was achieved only after long and acrimonious negotiations over the Ruhr and German coal during the spring and summer of 1947. In the end, the United States picked up most British occupation costs in exchange for American predominance in the Bizone, which meant among other things the end of efforts to nationalize the German coal industry. In July 1947, the administration also replaced JCS 1067 with a new directive (JCS 1779) that reaffirmed the first-charge principle, Clay's halt to reparations deliveries, and other measures designed to revive the German economy.[18]

The French forced the British and Americans to delay announcement of the Bizonal agreement. Bidault complained in July 1947 that the Anglo-American *fait accompli* seemed to confirm Communist charges that the United States favored German over French reconstruction. Paris demanded the internationalization of Ruhr industries, guaranteed access to German coal (at prices below the prevailing market rate), and the restoration of reparation deliveries.[19] French petulance sorely tested the patience of Secretary of State Marshall, who told the French Ambassador in July 1947 that a Soviet-dominated Germany—the likely consequence of indefinite stagnation—posed a greater danger to France than did a reconstructed Germany linked to the West. The United States, Marshall made clear, intended to revive German production in order to cut Bizonal imports and occupation costs.[20]

Under Secretary Clayton later voiced suspicions, with some basis in fact, that the French were using the security argument to suppress German competition. In tripartite exploratory discussions in London during August 1947, John Gimbel observes, the French revealed that "their main objection to the bizonal level-of-industry plan was that it threatened the Monnet Plan's projected steel production figures." The French hoped that control of German coal and limits on the Ruhr would translate into industrial supremacy in Europe. In August 1947, Paris finally approved the higher production levels in the Bizone after the Americans agreed to reconsider the French position on the Ruhr in later negotiations.[21]

In the meantime, the State Department again faced formidable opposition to its plans from General Lucius Clay and the Army. The policymakers at Foggy Bottom believed that the United States needed to meet the French halfway on the Ruhr if the pro-Western Paris government were to remain in power. State's seeming appeasement of the French infuriated the mercurial Clay, who threatened to resign in July 1947. Marshall and Under Secretary of War (later named Army Secretary) Kenneth C. Royall reassured Clay that his hard-won agreement with the British on Bizonal production would remain intact although some concessions would be necessary to win French participation in the fledgling European recovery program.[22]

In early August, Royall himself caused a major flap by publicly suggesting that the United States was not obliged to consult with the French on the Bizonal plan, a rebuke that the Quai d'Orsay did not take lightly. Under Secretary of State Robert Lovett, among others, thought that the time had now come for the State Department to take over the occupation duties in Germany from OMGUS and the War Department. In Lovett's opinion, they were blocking State's plan for the balanced use of German resources for European recovery as a whole.[23]

Yet as State Department officials further contemplated assuming Clay's job in Germany, they became increasingly sympathetic toward the OMGUS head. "Faced with the financial responsibilities that accompanied administrative responsibilities in Germany," John Gimbel notes,

> the State Department moved toward a position it had prevented the Army from taking for more than two years: it became more critical of France's aims and objectives regarding Germany and the future of Europe, and it finally concluded that France's territorial and economic demands were, in fact, incompatible with any program that would have Germany achieve a viable economy in the future.[24]

Evidence of Washington's growing dissatisfaction with the French surfaced in the summer of 1947, as the Conference on European Economic Cooperation (CEEC) opened at Paris. Amid indications that the CEEC was about to "produce little more than 16 'shopping lists' for which the United States would be expected to pay the bill," Lovett informed French Ambassador Henri Bonnet that the Europeans would have to show a greater willingness to help themselves before the Congress would appropriate more foreign aid. In particular, he warned that the American people would not support an expensive new aid program if France and other potential beneficiaries of U.S. largesse sought to impose a punitive peace on Germany.[25]

From Washington's perspective, it seemed terribly wasteful for France to build new steel mills when the smokestacks of the Ruhr remained dormant. Lovett instructed American representatives in Paris to put "primary emphasis on efficient utilization of existing capacity rather than on capital development." Since the largest amount of idle capacity by far lay in Germany, the Truman administration had pinned its hopes for European recovery on the restoration of German industry.[26] Thus, the State Department's revised position paper on the aid program in late August 1947 stressed European self–help through "elimination of bottlenecks" and "full use of existing or readily repairable capacity." Long-term capital development would receive secondary consideration. The State Department would "not agree to system of allocations of German resources or U.S. aid which would postpone German recovery until full recovery [of] other countries has been assured."[27]

The French reluctantly came to accept the American viewpoint. When the Council of Foreign Ministers reconvened in London (November–December 1947), the Western allies had already given up on a quadripartite German settlement. As Communist-led strikes rocked France, Paris' representatives secretly expressed interest in the formation of a West German state and a western security alliance. Not surprisingly, Molotov's pleas for reparations and a unified Germany fell on deaf ears, and the conference ended amid bitter recriminations between the Russian minister and his three Western counterparts. With the Russians finally out of the picture, the way lay open for a fusion of the three western zones.[28]

During the first session (February–March 1948) of the tripartite London Conference on Germany, however, the French refused to merge their zone with the Bizone until the British and Americans approved international control of the Ruhr and a security pact against Germany. Marshall felt that French fears of aggression from that corner were unfounded. "As long as Germany is occupied," the Secretary of State argued, "it will not be able to develop the prerequisites of military power."[29]

But to win French agreement to trizonal unification, Washington in early March submitted a draft plan for an international control agency for the Ruhr. Ambassador Douglas also quietly assured British, French, and Dutch officials that the United States would pledge itself to a security arrangement against German aggression. The U.S. Ambassador told the Europeans that "it was very unlikely that American forces would be withdrawn from Germany for a long time—until the threat from the east had disappeared." On March 6, 1948, the first session concluded with an agreement by the participants to reconstruct the western zones of Germany under ERP.[30]

Upon resumption of the London Conference during April and May 1948, American negotiators rejected French proposals for permanent limits on German industrial capacity. But the French received assurances that U.S. troops would remain indefinitely in Germany and that Washington would soon associate itself with the Brussels Pact (ratified in March 1948). In a final conference report on security, the United States reiterated its pledge to maintain occupation forces in Germany until peace was secured in Europe.[31]

Due to steadfast opposition by Clay and the Army, the French won fewer concessions on the Ruhr. As Army Secretary Royall complained to Marshall in May 1948, the proposal for an International Authority for the Ruhr (IAR) violated the Bizonal fusion agreement, under which General Clay had won supreme authority over the resources of the Bizone. The Congress would rebel, Royall shrewdly intimated, if the Ruhr authority, the Economic Cooperation Administration (ECA), or some other interloper were to infringe upon Clay's domain. The State Department agreed that the United States must control the Ruhr in order to ensure the self-sufficiency of the Bizone. But, Lovett chided Royall, the Bizonal agreement was subordinate "to the subsequent and overriding policy of the President and Congress" as expressed in ERP, "which covers the [European] economic problem as a whole."[32]

In discussions on the IAR in late May, the State Department again struck a careful balance between the French and the War Department. State officials managed to soothe French feelings without committing the United States to anything more than a supervisory body, as opposed to international ownership and management of Ruhr industries. As Paul Nitze later instructed Ambassador Douglas during the London Conference on the Ruhr (November–December 1948), the chief American aim in the IAR was not so much the containment of Germany as a "larger degree of Western European cooperation and economic integration" and a "more effective utilization of the Ruhr resources . . . for the common good."[33]

The State Department used the Marshall Plan as a means both to win French (and other allied) consent to German reconstruction and to break the deadlock in the American government over German policy. In that sense, John Gimbel is correct in defining the Marshall Plan as a "crash program to dovetail German economic recovery with a general European recovery program in order to make German economic recovery politically acceptable in Europe and in the United States."[34] Yet Gimbel is only partially correct, for the domestic debate over the Marshall Plan focused more on the Soviet threat than on Germany.

Domestic Politics and the Marshall Plan

During 1945–46, American officials had been able for the most part to discount domestic factors in the formulation of foreign relief programs. But the unprecedented size and nature of the Marshall Plan required a concerted effort to educate the public, appease interest groups, and reassure the Congress that this program, unlike its predecessors, would work.

Although public opinion rarely exercised a direct influence over foreign policy, the Truman administration needed strong public backing for the Marshall Plan in order to win large appropriations from the Republican-controlled 80th Congress. Despite an initially favorable reception, popular support for the Marshall Plan was thin and unreliable, and the administration knew it. Indeed, Marshall instructed the State Department not to publicize his Harvard speech at home because he knew the public was not ready for another great foreign undertaking so soon after the Truman Doctrine. The President also took the unusual step of not endorsing the plan for three weeks after Marshall's speech. A State Department study dated June 13, 1947, found that while press and radio comment on Marshall's address was mostly positive, "nearly all agreed that *an intense effort would be required to convince a reluctant Congress and public that heavy expenditures would be needed.*"[35]

The administration, in part due to a disagreement within the State Department over how to handle publicity, did not communicate its message well. In late June 1947, speechwriter Joseph Jones noted widespread confusion in the news media over the Secretary's proposal. "Everyone is asking: Does the Marshall Plan mean that the Truman Doctrine is abandoned?" Jones hoped Marshall would clarify that "there is a straight line running from the Truman Doctrine to the Marshall Plan."[36]

While most upper-income and educated individuals and most farm and labor organizations favored the Marshall Plan, many big businessmen did not. "Leaders of industry," a departmental study discovered in December 1947, "have particularly withheld support—notably in the cases of steel, automobiles, and oil." The authors of the study identified businessmen as the only "real resistance" to the Marshall Plan, but feared that their influence upon a Congress already wary of the costly reconstruction program could be decisive.[37]

Generally, the Congress would not support a recovery effort unless absolutely assured that the European countries would put American aid to good use. A common complaint was that European countries had done little on their own to cure internal economic problems.[38] A substantial number of Congressmen also insisted upon strict limits on the size and duration of a European program, and demanded that German reconstruction accompany any aid program. Republicans especially protested against pouring dollars into what some termed a "rathole" and others, more charitably, an "international New Deal." They maintained that an agency independent of the State Department should run the aid program on sound business principles.[39]

At Senator Vandenberg's urging, President Truman in late June 1947 appointed three prestigious commissions on the Marshall Plan. Headed by Secretary of Commerce W. Averell Harriman, Secretary of the Interior Julius A. Krug, and Council of Economic Advisers (CEA) Chairman Edwin G. Nourse, the three groups were instructed to study the feasibility of the Marshall Plan and its impact upon the American economy and natural resources. A private Committee for the Marshall Plan to Aid European Recovery (CMP), led by former Secretary of War Henry L. Stimson, organized newspaper advertisements, speaking engagements, and petition and letter campaigns in close cooperation with the State Department. The CMP was especially successful in mobilizing the support of prominent businessmen. Other powerful interest groups, such as the American Federation of Labor, the Veterans of Foreign Wars, and the American Farm Bureau Federation strongly endorsed the program as well.[40]

Events in Europe during the summer of 1947 forced the administration to seek special "Interim Aid" from the Congress before submission of Marshall Plan legislation. The plight of Britain was in some ways the most worrisome, for American officials regarded it as the linchpin to European trade. In the first half of 1947, the outflow of British reserves rose to an average of $300 million per month, compared with $70 million during all of the third *quarter* of 1946. The $5 billion in loans that the United States and Canada had advanced in early 1946 were nearly exhausted. Indeed, a dollar shortage threatened the entire fabric of world multilateral trade. Convertibility of sterling, which began July 15 under the Anglo-American Financial Agreements, so quickly drained British dollar reserves that London was forced to stop trading dollars for sterling on August 20, 1947.

Yet aid to Britain, already the recipient of so much U.S. aid, posed special difficulties with the Congress. As a subcommittee of the National Advisory Council concluded, the administration had to persuade the Congress and the public that it had permitted British suspension of sterling convertibility "only as a temporary, emergency measure," and that the British commitment to eventual nondiscriminatory trade remained intact. Although American officials were sympathetic toward the British in their time of troubles, Washington retaliated against the suspension of sterling convertibility by freezing the funds remaining in the British loan account and by excluding Britain from consideration for Interim Aid.[41]

A special aid package was critical, Clayton and the PPS believed, for without it, Western Europe might collapse before Congress could act upon Marshall Plan legislation. "The margin of safety, in Europe, both from an economic and political viewpoint, is extremely thin," the PPS stated in August 1947. Yet State Department officials observed "very strong" Congressional opposition to a *fait accompli* along the lines of the Truman Doctrine.[42]

In late September, Truman told Congressional leaders that France, Italy, and Austria required $597 million in emergency aid to survive the coming winter, and on October 23, 1947, the President called for a special session of Congress to begin November 17. Truman asked the Congress to consider anti-inflation measures in conjunction with Interim Aid, a political tactic meant to embarrass the Republican majority for its dismantling of price controls in 1946.[43] For the most part, the administration avoided explicit reference to the Soviet Union during the special session, although it made clear that without Interim Aid, the French and Italian Communist parties would probably triumph in forthcoming elections. "The future of free nations in Europe hangs in the balance," Truman explained in a message to Congress on November 17. "The future of our own economy is in jeopardy."[44]

By now, anti-Communism had gathered a momentum of its own, and the nation's legislators needed no prompting on this point. Even before the special session convened, columnist William S. White noted, "The Marshall Plan appears to draw its greatest strength now not from any special feeling that other peoples should be helped for their own sake, but only as a demonstration against the spread of communism." Congressmen returning from Europe were often skeptical about the extent of European distress, but not the Communist threat. Members of the influential Herter Committee commented "that they had observed no real starvation during their travels, and, that if it were not for the communist menace spreading its poisonous tentacles across western Europe the Committee's interest in the Marshall Plan would be anything but enthusiastic." Pundit Arthur Krock added that "the Herter

Committee is inclined to the belief that any Marshall Plan can have assured returns in security values only, that its economic future is unsound."[45]

Meanwhile, the Harriman Committee's report, released on November 7, sought to alleviate widespread fears that the U.S. aid program would fuel domestic inflation. Challenging "the idea . . . that we need to export our goods and services as free gifts, to ensure our own prosperity," the committee reported that "the immediate economic danger to the United States is inflation." Yet through fiscal restraint, this country could dampen domestic demand and still provide $12.7 billion to $17 billion in aid to its European allies over four years. The European recipients, in turn, needed to stabilize their currencies, cut trade barriers, expand production, and deemphasize long-term capital formation and welfare programs.[46]

In October 1947, the CEA had also reported that a large-scale aid program need not be inflationary. Privately, the CEA and the Harriman Committee were not nearly so sanguine about the government's ability to curb inflation as their reports suggested. But potential difficulties were glossed over in the name of political expediency.[47]

Events in Europe deepened the apprehensive mood in Washington. An upsurge in Communist activity raised the question of whether American aid would end up benefiting forces that were unfriendly to the United States. In September, the State Department's Advisory Steering Committee on ERP argued that "if the virus of totalitarianism spreads" to France and Italy, "it would be almost impossible to prevent its engulfing all of western Europe."[48]

These fears proved unfounded, for the Communist strikes of the fall were a sign of weakness rather than strength. In early November 1947, the PPS declared that "the political advance of the communists in Western Europe had been at least temporarily halted," and "the Soviet Government neither wants nor expects war with us in the near future." The victory of moderate forces in French elections and the failure of Communist strikes in France and Italy during the autumn of 1947 were major American victories. "The advance of Communism has been stemmed," Marshall told the Cabinet on November 7, "and the Russians have been compelled to make a reevaluation of their position." The "Commies are losing ground," Senator Vandenberg exulted to his wife, and "this seems to be the time for us 'to make hay.'"[49]

Interim Aid passed through the Congress with relative ease, partly because the administration had subtly linked foreign aid with anti-

Communism, and partly because many Congressmen were holding their fire for the larger aid program. By December 15, both houses of Congress had approved Interim Aid by large margins. France, Italy, and Austria received grants totalling $522 million (increased to $577 million in March 1948). In addition, the NAC decided in December, after consulting with Congressional leaders, that London could resume drawing against the $400 million remainder of the British loan. The United States also assumed the full costs of the German Bizone.[50]

The passage of Interim Aid by no means ensured the success of the Marshall Plan. In an election year, many Republican (and Democratic) Congressmen worried that ERP would feed inflation and delay realization of a long-awaited tax cut. Indeed, even Robert Lovett and Secretary of the Treasury John Snyder had privately grumbled in June 1947 that the estimated $5 billion required for the first year of ERP was an "astronomical" sum that the Congress would never accept. Representative Christian Herter of the House Foreign Affairs Committee, Senator Robert Taft, and a group of twenty "revisionist" Senators organized by Republican Whip Kenneth Wherry hoped either to cripple ERP with amendments or at least to cut the funds for the plan by one-third. The Republican legislators were also unwilling to countenance the large volume of East-West trade and the extensive U.S. tariff reductions that the State Department regarded as crucial to multilateral commerce. Furthermore, presidential hopefuls like Taft and other loyal Republicans certainly did not wish to credit Truman with a major diplomatic coup. As Vandenberg lamented in November, "It is next to impossible to keep any sort of unpartisan climate in respect to anything. Politics is heavy in the air."[51]

On December 9, 1947, President Truman requested $6.8 billion for the first fifteen months of ERP and $17 billion for the first four years. The sixteen member states of the CEEC, plus the western zones of Germany, would be eligible for aid. Truman asked Congress to complete legislation by April 1, 1948, just as Interim Aid funds would run out—and just before the Italian elections. Truman later observed that the $17 billion amounted to only 5 percent of the costs of World War II and 3 percent of national income in 1948 (see appendix, graph 2). Yet compared with the peacetime federal budgets of the 1930s, the figure was enormous.[52]

The administration launched a concerted campaign to win over Congressional leaders. Maintaining close liaison with Marshall and Lovett, Senator Vandenberg undertook the responsibility for overcoming the opposition of his Republican colleagues to the European program. In December 1947, for instance, Vandenberg suggested that the Committee for the Marshall Plan should recruit "top-level business executives" to testify in favor of ERP before the Senate Foreign Relations Committee, which Vandenberg chaired. The Senator from Michigan also persuaded the White House to trim the initial appropriations to $5.3 billion for the first twelve months, eliminate the requirement for a four-year authorization, and strengthen a "self-help" proviso whereby the President could terminate aid to uncooperative aid recipients.[53]

The White House yielded to Congressional pressure on the administration of ERP. Republicans had demanded that an agency independent from the State Department—later named the Economic Cooperation Administration (ECA)—run the European aid program. Secretary of State Marshall apparently deferred to the Hill on this issue because he anticipated, not incorrectly as it turned out, that the State Department would be able to exert considerable influence over the aid agency. Senator Vandenberg, disturbed by press reports that the White House was considering Will Clayton as the head of ECA, also persuaded Marshall that Congress would more likely approve ERP in an election year if an individual "from the outside business world with strong industrial credentials and *not* via the State Department" were to direct the ECA. Eventually, Paul Hoffman—an executive of the Studebaker Corporation, one of Vandenberg's Michigan constituents, and a Republican—was chosen to head ECA.[54]

Administration spokesmen sought to overcome any lingering Congressional recalcitrance by promoting the Marshall Plan as a security measure. Secretary of Defense James Forrestal, in a memo to Truman in December 1947, had outlined a reply to critics of foreign aid:

> In general, my answer . . . is that you have to look at our own security not merely in terms of great military power or of wealth (the Spain of Philip II had both, and so did Rome, but both went down the drain) but rather in terms of these objectives: High domestic production, a balanced budget, a sound currency, and adequate and expandable defense organization resting upon diversified domestic industry, restoration of the balance of power in the world . . ., and finally making it clear to Russia that no one is going to take over Hitler's job of trying to run the world.[55]

Similarly, Marshall testified in January 1948 before the Senate Foreign Relations Committee that the European Recovery Program, by restoring the European balance of power, would fulfill American objectives in World War II. As Marshall put it, "the way of life we have known is literally in balance." Without ERP, America risked a third world war that would require "tremendous appropriations for national security." Secretary of the Army Royall, claiming that American combat strength (not counting occupation troops) was 60 to 70 percent deficient, warned that he would recommend the training of 160,000 more troops and the addition of $2.25 billion to the current military budget of $11 billion if the Congress did not approve the aid program.[56]

The economic security argument made it easier for Republicans (and economy-minded Democrats) to accept spending billions on the Marshall Plan. To avoid the "me-too" label, Republicans modified ERP without destroying the program: no domestic price controls as Truman had wanted, an independent agency to run ERP, a requirement that recipient countries partly compensate the United States with strategic raw materials for the national stockpile, and additional aid to China. By letting the Republicans take credit for cost-cutting and other amendments to ERP, the administration won bipartisan support for the program. As a result, no fundamental differences developed between Democrats and Republicans in voting on ERP through all of its legislative stages.[57]

What finally secured passage of ERP, however, was the war scare of March 1948. During the fall and winter of 1947–48, the press, notably the Alsop brothers in the mass-circulation *Saturday Evening Post*, had already fueled speculation on the possibility of an all-out war with the Soviet Union. The Western allies had also begun informal military discussions on the Soviet threat, and on February 22, 1948, Marshall praised British Foreign Minister Ernest Bevin's proposal for a West European defense pact as "our great hope." When the Prague coup in late February was followed by the mysterious death on March 10 of Jan Masaryk, a symbol of Czech democracy, Marshall decried the "reign of terror" in that country. On March 5, General Clay, known as one who did not frighten easily in the face of Soviet provocation, alarmed official Washington by reporting that war could come with "dramatic suddenness." Americans' worst suspicions about Soviet intentions were seemingly confirmed. On March 13, the Senate, by a vote of 67 to 17, authorized $5.3 billion for ERP in its first year.[58]

The tide had turned. A Cold War consensus was finally emerging. Congress now accepted the responsibility of the United States to rebuild Western Europe. The war scare helped ERP pass through the

House Foreign Affairs Committee, the last major hurdle before ratification, on March 17, by a margin of 11 to 8. The committee, rejecting Representative Herter's proposal to reduce aid for the first year to $4.5 billion, accepted exactly the sum requested by the administration. Before long, there was a stampede to hop on the bandwagon. Even Herbert Hoover endorsed the Marshall Plan on March 23. On March 30, the House by 329 to 74 authorized a $6.2 billion omnibus foreign aid bill that included funds for China, Greece, and Turkey. Following a House-Senate conference, Truman signed the Foreign Assistance Act of 1948 on April 1, 1948. The administration succeeded in keeping cuts in the appropriations bill in June 1948 to a minimum. Altogether the United States would commit $12.4 billion, mostly in the form of grants, to European recovery over the next four years.[59]

The war scare of 1948 did not radically alter the political balance; rather, it catalyzed forces in being. Before the crisis, the Congress almost certainly would have supported some sort of truncated ERP for the first year of operation. Still, anti-Communism provided the crucial agent that brought together Republicans and Democrats on the size, timing, and nature of the Marshall Plan. In January 1948, columnist James Reston had detected "a touch of isolationism"—a desire to be rid of European troubles—even among internationalist Congressional supporters of ERP. "If it hadn't been for the activity of Communists in Europe," Reston wrote regarding the massive strikes during the fall of 1947, "there would never have been a program of this magnitude, and if they were to lie low for a while even now, the Administration would be in serious trouble." In his usual melodramatic way, Senator Vandenberg told his Senate colleagues on March 1, 1948, that "communism threatens all freedom and all security, whether in the old world or in the new, when it puts free people anywhere in chains. . . . The iron curtain must not come to the rims of the Atlantic either by aggression or by default."[60]

The bipartisanship forged in the debate over ERP survived even the 1948 presidential election, albeit with a great assist from Joseph Stalin in instigating the Berlin blockade during the summer of 1948. As early as November 1947, Clark Clifford had suggested that the President could enhance his election prospects by taking a more visible role in foreign policymaking. "In times of crisis," Clifford wrote, "the American citizen tends to back up his president." The special session of Congress offered Truman this opportunity. He personally delivered a message to the Congress on Interim Aid on November 17, 1947, the first day of the special sesssion, and a month later, he sent another important message on the Marshall Plan to Capitol Hill. The Czech coup and the war scare of March 1948 also worked to the President's advantage, particularly by helping isolate former Commerce Secretary Henry A. Wallace, the Progressive Party candidate for President, on the left. When Wallace adopted a benign view of Soviet motives in the Czech coup, the White House branded him a dupe of the Kremlin and the American Communists. The charge stuck, and as a result, many liberals returned to the mainstream of the Democratic Party. The Berlin blockade just as effectively silenced the Republican challenger, Governor Thomas Dewey of New York, on foreign policy questions. While domestic issues—notably, Truman's success in revamping the New Deal coalition and in pillorying the "do-nothing" 80th Congress— probably decided the election, Truman's unchallenged preeminence as leader of the Western alliance did much to refurbish his image among the voters.[61]

The Truman administration did not create the March 1948 or Berlin crises, but it did exploit the fears aroused by them. If American officials sometimes resorted to hyperbole in order to assure Congressional passage of the Marshall Plan, they did so out of genuine alarm over events abroad. In any case, the Cold War politics of 1948 had only limited objectives; once the crises subsided during the summer of 1948, American resolve fell far short of full-scale rearmament.

The Abortive Rearmament of 1948

American military preparedness did not keep pace with the proliferation of U.S. diplomatic commitments after World War II. The heated and sometimes militaristic rhetoric generated by the March 1948 war scare has prompted some scholars to exaggerate the shift in U.S. defense planning and force structure during this period. Daniel Yergin, for instance, states that the "events in Czechoslovakia provided impetus to move to a new level of military preparedness."[62] In fact, the crises of 1948 only exposed the limitations of American conventional military forces, the over-reliance of U.S. military planners upon atomic power, and the shortcomings of economic containment.

It is true that the March crisis gave rise to a momentary enthusiasm in Washington for increased defense spending. Addressing a joint session of Congress on March 17, 1948, President Truman denounced the "pattern" of Soviet aggression and Communist subversion in Czechoslovakia, Finland, Greece, and Italy. Truman also expressed support for the Brussels Pact and called for early Congressional approval of the Marshall Plan, Universal Military Training, and selective service because "we have learned the importance of maintaining military strength as a means of preventing war." In testimony before the Senate Armed Services Committee on March 17, Secretary Marshall also invoked the memory of Munich in pressing for prompt passage of ERP and defense measures. "Diplomatic action, without the backing of military strength, in the present world can only lead to appeasement," he stated. Two days later, he equated Soviet policy with "the high-handed and calculated procedure of the Nazi regime."[63] The Congress approved ERP and restored the draft in April 1948, but again rejected UMT although Truman and Marshall had repeatedly promoted it as the mainstay of a strong national defense.[64]

The military services sought to capitalize on the spring crisis by demanding a sharp boost in defense spending. Their case was by no means unreasonable, for the administration's $9.8 billion military budget for FY 1949 was draconian by almost any measure. In a February 1948 White House presentation, for instance, Maj. Gen. Alfred M. Gruenther, who headed the Joint Staff advising the JCS, argued that the services, particularly the Army, suffered acute shortages of combat-ready troops. The shortfall of Navy personnel had already immobilized 107 ships and by the end of 1948, the Army shortage would reach 165,000. "He emphasized that the employment of anything more than a division in any area would make partial mobilization a necessity," Forrestal recorded.[65]

Truman's March speech emboldened the military services to press for several billion dollars' worth of supplemental appropriations. "The President commented that every department of the government now has gone warlike," an aide noted in late March. Truman favored only a $1.5 billion supplement to the FY 1949 budget, with an emphasis upon increased ground troops and UMT, for the Bureau of the Budget had convinced him that a major expansion in military expenditures would fuel inflation and require deficit spending. Yet after intense lobbying by the services, Truman agreed to meet the Pentagon part way. On April 1, 1948, Truman requested $3 billion (subsequently raised to $3.2 billion) in supplemental defense appropriations from the Congress, including $775 million more for aircraft procurement.[66]

The debate within the administration over the defense budget had just begun, however. Forrestal had persuaded the JCS to drop their original $9 billion supplemental request by promising that he could increase the supplement before Congress from $3 billion to $3.5 billion. Proponents of air power in the Congress and the administration, notably Air Force Secretary W. Stuart Symington, also demanded increased funding for air procurement and a 70-group force. Truman instead favored a gradual and balanced military buildup stressing defense mobilization capabilities over standing forces. When Forrestal later failed to persuade the services to accept the President's guidelines, Truman told his staff that he was "getting damn sore" at the Secretary of Defense. The President also blamed the "three muttonheads" in the Department of Defense—Forrestal, Symington, and Royall—for undermining UMT by stirring up Congressional support for their own pet projects.[67]

The armed services gained $3.2 billion in supplemental appropriations in May 1948, but they had won a Pyrrhic victory. On May 13, 1948, President Truman summoned Forrestal, the service secretaries, the three Chiefs of Staff, and top budget officials to the White House. Truman announced his intention to withhold the procurement funds that the House had designated for a 70-group Air Force. Moreover, the Commander-in-Chief put a ceiling of $14.4 billion (excluding $600 million in stockpiling) on the FY 1950 defense budget.[68]

The Berlin crisis beginning just a month later, in June 1948, further exposed the weakness of American forces, as well as, some would argue, the absence of a strategic concept in U.S. military planning. While the United States deployed several dozen B-29s to forward bases in England during July and August 1948, none of the so-called "atomic bombers" had been modified to carry atomic weapons. Washington never seriously considered the use of armed convoys to break the Berlin blockade, in part because the Army could not spare a sizeable contingent of combat troops. Postwar demobilization had so weakened American forces that the United States could not negotiate as an equal with the Soviets on Berlin, argued Colonel Frank Howley, the U.S. commandant in that city. "We are . . . so weak now physically," he wrote at the height of the crisis in late June, "that it is an invitation for the Russians to destroy us and to walk all over us, and to do what they want to do without consultation."[69]

Yet Truman, thanks to Budget Director James E. Webb, held the defense budget for FY 1950 to only $14.4 billion (exclusive of stockpiling), compared with the JCS request for $23 billion. While NSC 20/4, the major U.S. policy review that was completed in November 1948, warned that a war could erupt as a result of a "Soviet miscalculation" of

U.S. capabilities and intentions, it "emphasized the importance of safeguarding the domestic economy and left unresolved the extent of the resources that should be devoted to military preparation." The replacement of Forrestal by Louis A. Johnson as Secretary of Defense in March 1949 reinforced the budget-trimming tendencies in the administration. The President, in fact, would be in the process of seeking further cuts in the FY '50 defense budget when the Korean War broke out in June 1950.[70]

Perhaps the major flaw in Truman's budgetary philosophy was that it set defense spending levels according to what the President and the Budget Bureau determined the economy could withstand, rather than what the administration's own foreign policy commitments seemed to require. The strength of his approach was that it provided the President with a consistent rationale by which to restrain air power zealots and save tax dollars by stretching out rearmament—at least until the Korean War shattered the illusion of preparedness. Moreover, the President's tight-fisted stance toward the Pentagon followed logically from the American tradition of civilian rule and from the administration's concept of economic containment as the first line of U.S. defense.

Implementing the Marshall Plan, 1948–1949

American policymakers and legislators alike believed that the Marshall Plan offered them an unprecedented opportunity to reform European institutions. Recalling the failure of earlier U.S. aid programs, Congressmen were especially eager to put European recovery on a self-sustaining basis, if necessary through wholesale intervention. As Senator Henry Cabot Lodge bluntly declared during an executive session of the Committee on Foreign Relations on Interim Aid in November 1947,

> God knows this Marshall Plan is going to be the biggest damned interference in internal affairs that there has ever been in history. We are being [sic] responsible for the people who stay in power as a result of our efforts. . . .
> I don't think we need to be too sensitive about interfering in the internal affairs of these countries. We are in it up to our necks, and almost everybody except a few political leaders will be damned glad to see us interfere.[71]

Certain revisionist historians, notably Joyce and Gabriel Kolko, have seized upon such evidence to argue that the Marshall Plan was an instrument of American imperialism. The main danger to American interests in Europe, these historians claim, lay not in the Soviet Union, but in vibrant Leftist parties dedicated to social reform and to autarkic, national capitalist policies that threatened to exclude American trade and capital from Europe. The Congressionally mandated "counterpart funds," which were matching funds in local currencies controlled by Washington, presumably "gave Washington substantial power to exercise over the internal economic plans and programs of the European states and attained one of the most fundamental aims of American policy."[72]

The major object of the Marshall Plan, according to the Kolkos, was to benefit American businessmen and the conservative, propertied classes in Europe. Thus, executives from large U.S. corporations filled key ECA positions, and certain interest groups, such as the oil, shipping, and farm lobbies, forced ECA to favor American procurement and services. The Congress, the Kolkos add, amended ERP legislation in order to expand raw material production in European colonial dependencies and guarantee the free access of American business to those areas. And while the European bourgeoisie flourished, the working class allegedly lost ground during the Marshall Plan. "The economies of Europe," the Kolkos charge, "were *intentionally* manipulated to *lower* living standards, create new unemployment, and sharpen inequality—a time-tested capitalist cure for an inflationary economy and an essential aspect of their concept of 'recovery.'"[73]

A closer examination of the Marshall Plan reveals that this interpretation has little to recommend it. In the first place, Charles Maier has demonstrated that Leftist parties and working-class groups were not very militant or powerful in Western Europe after World War II, especially when compared with the post-World War I period. The Christian Democratic parties—grouped around Konrad Adenauer in western Germany, Alcide De Gasperi in Italy, and the MRP (*Mouvement Républicain Populaire*) in France—sapped support from the Left immediately after the war by offering socialist alternatives to Communism. European business groups, meanwhile, helped defuse class conflict by improving working conditions and adopting progressive managerial methods. Whether as a result of a genuine amelioration of living conditions or of some more subtle form of cooptation, the Left did not directly challenge the supremacy of management after the war. Even Communist leaders, notably French party head Maurice Thorez, endorsed harsh labor discipline until rank-and-file militancy in the wake of the bitter winter of 1947—and orders from Moscow, perhaps—required the leadership to adopt a more confrontational stance against big business (and the Marshall Plan) during 1947 and 1948. Generally, economic issues played a lesser role in West European politics than before the war, and the boundaries of political debate narrowed. The West European experience to some degree paralleled the American one during the New Deal and the Second World War: conflict over the distribution of income and other fundamental questions was adjourned so that workers and managers alike could harness their energies to increasing productivity. Labor's wage restraint made a major contribution to Europe's (and America's) phenomenal growth rate over succeeding decades. (A second major factor was the willingness of the United States to underwrite European deficits for several years after the war.) The point to bear in mind is that the tendency of West Europeans to defer social conflict for the sake of economic growth—what Maier calls the "politics of productivity"—was well entrenched *before* ECA administrators arrived in Europe.[74]

ECA's ability to intervene was far less than raw dollar figures might suggest. The more industrialized a recipient country, the less impact American aid had upon it. For example, the U.S. contribution to new French industrial projects from mid-1948 to mid-1951 equalled roughly $150 million, about one-fifth of the total. In Great Britain, ECA paid for less than one-eighth ($420 million) of the total new investment. In most instances, European governments found it fairly easy to circumvent ECA guidelines, and the aid agency generally ended up approving national economic plans.[75] European officials often manipulated American fears of economic collapse and political upheaval in order to minimize U.S. intervention. During 1948–49, for instance, the United States persuaded the ERP countries to devalue their currencies and to lower intra-European trade barriers—something that European planners wanted to do anyway—but failed to make them significantly reduce discrimination against dollar-area goods.[76]

Although counterpart funds theoretically gave the United States greater power to shape national policies, the political utility of the funds also proved limited. True, Washington required London to apply all but $3 million of its $1.7 billion in sterling counterpart toward debt reduction. But the British themselves did not object to this arrangement, which in any event precluded ECA from meddling extensively in British internal affairs. In France, where ECA released over $1 billion, or 84 percent of total counterpart, for investment purposes, the opportunity for American control over local projects appeared greater. "But here," Hadley Arkes has found, the Monnet Plan was the dominant factor. France either had the projects staked out or had full control of the administrative machinery that was developing them. According to informants who were in France as members of the ECA mission, the American role was usually one of providing an official source of financing for projects that, for one reason or another, could not be included in the French budget. . . . In no meaningful sense was the pattern one of ECA participation in the drafting of the project.[77]

The chronic instability of Paris governments deterred the Americans from pressing very hard for monetary and financial reforms. After the centrist Schuman government fell in July 1948 (despite special U.S. wheat shipments to France), the ECA released additional counterpart funds in the fall to prop up the shaky Queuille government. State Department and ECA officials, acutely unhappy over Paris' failure to control inflation and balance the national budget, threatened to withhold counterpart aid. Yet following the British devaluation of the pound, a new surge of inflation and other domestic problems brought the French government to its knees in November 1949, and the NAC decided to release additional counterpart funds to assist its successor.[78]

The opportunities for American interference in Italy were greater. During March 1948, the United States signaled that it would cut off ERP aid if the Communists took power in the April elections. In light of the precarious Italian political situation, the ECA, Eximbank, and Department of Agriculture (as well as the World Bank) accelerated U.S. aid to that country in the spring of 1948. Partly due to American efforts, the Communist coalition was defeated. Yet the very fragility of the Rome government prevented the Americans from pushing for major internal reforms in Italy.[79]

Examples of British obstruction of European economic integration and other American multilateralist aims are legion. After the unsuccessful experiment in sterling-dollar convertibility in 1947, the British were the main obstacle to a liberalized system of multilateral payments. Moreover, when Washington sought to restrict East-West trade during the late 1940s, London cultivated commercial relations with Eastern Europe and signed a far-reaching trading pact with the Soviet Union. But because of the close political-military ties between the two countries, ECA never considered terminating aid to Britain. The British sterling crisis during the summer and fall of 1949 forced the Americans to abandon hope for any early British reduction of trade restrictions. American intervention in Britain was confined to slowing, without reversing, the progress of social welfare programs.[80]

ECA interference was most common in the weakest of the ERP nations, especially Greece and Turkey, where the aid programs under the Truman Doctrine legislation already dictated heavy American involvement. But if anything, the ECA, with a mandate to disband by 1952, and with personnel drafted in large part from the ranks of corporate America, passed up chances to intervene in the industrialized ERP countries. Biased as many ECA officials were by training against centralized government, they exhibited little of the traditional bureaucratic instinct to enlarge and perpetuate their organization:

> Intervention, for the ECA, was a sometimes thing. As a principle it was repugnant; as a concept it was elusive. Where it was recognizable and effective, as in Greece and Turkey, it was of little consequence as far as European recovery was concerned. And in the more industrialized countries, where all the ambitions of the Marshall Plan would stand or fall, intervention was either unworkable in practice or simply unnecessary.[81]

Instead, ECA put its weight behind supranational institutions that furthered European economic integration, such as the first Agreement for Intra-European Payments and Compensations (AIEPC, established in 1948), the European Payments Union (EPU, 1950) and the European Coal and Steel Community (ECSC, 1951). Although full trade liberalization remained unfulfilled, trade accelerated sharply in 1950 with the reduction of intra-European tariffs. The United States endorsed the Schuman Plan (which led to the ECSC), despite its cartel-like qualities, because the prospect for Franco-German cooperation in the coal and steel industries promised major political dividends, notably eventual French acceptance of West German rearmament and membership in NATO. What is more, the Americans supported West European commercial integration, culminating in the European Economic Community (EEC, or Common Market) in 1957, even though it entailed discrimination against outside countries, including the United States. Washington, in short, did not press the ERP countries to adopt truly multilateralist policies because the immediate political advantages of regional economic integration seemed to outweigh the theoretical benefits of the Open Door.[82]

Nor did ECA act as the servant of special interests. The Congress had created a presumption in favor of American agricultural, shipping, and other private interests in ERP procurement. Yet despite pressure from the Coal Exporters' Association and coal-state Congressmen, the ECA in 1949 sharply cut its financing of high-priced U.S coal exports to

Europe as continental coal production revived. Congress, responding to the shipping industry and organized labor, forced the ECA in 1949 to transport 50 percent of each class of cargo in U.S.-flag ships, a requirement that raised the price of commodities imported by the ERP countries. But without the efforts of the ECA, the costs could have been higher. As Administrator Paul Hoffman told the Senate Foreign Relations Committee in 1949, his agency sought to promote free trade and did not fear European competition and imports. Unless Congress expressly ordered the ECA to do otherwise, it would seek out the cheapest supplier in procuring ERP goods.[83]

The ECA acted as a dike against the floodtide of special interests. Generally, the Congress supported the aid agency, for its main objective, after all, was to restore European production at the least cost to the U.S. taxpayer. And where the Congress did impose presumptions in favor of American interest groups, the ECA often found ways to thwart its intent.

East-West Trade, 1947–1949

The most important case in which the administration circumvented Congressional guidelines was East-West trade, where the political needs of the Alliance would prevail over export control aims. In effect, U.S. policymakers pursued a two-track policy entailing tough controls on U.S. trade and weak restraints on West European commerce with the East. During 1945–46, American officials had regarded economic penetration as a way to loosen the Soviet grip on Eastern Europe, but by mid-1947 they had largely given up on this tactic. The main aims of the U.S. control policy when Marshall delivered his Harvard speech were to limit the export of strategic equipment and technology to the Soviet bloc and to ensure West European access to scarce materials in Eastern Europe.

At this point, the Truman administration relied mostly upon informal constraints on trade. In August 1947, for instance, an official of the Allis-Chalmers Manufacturing Company explained to State Department officials that his company was "reluctant" to supply machinery for a steel plant to Czechoslovakia because "it was likely that the steel mill in question would work for the Soviet Union." Llewellyn Thompson, chief of the Division of Eastern European Affairs, declined to prohibit the sale outright, but expressed concern that sales to East

European countries might deprive friendly West European countries of scarce machinery. Evidently relieved, the business executive stated that since there was some shortage of steel equipment, he would recommend cancellation of the sale.[84]

In late 1947, as Congressional sentiment for a systematic embargo on U.S.-Soviet bloc trade mounted, the Truman administration redoubled its efforts to seal off the Soviet Union and its satellites from Western trade and technology. The first controls had applied to items that either had obvious military uses or were in short supply. Since the volume of American trade with Eastern Europe was already quite low, the State and Commerce Departments did not feel that strict controls were necessary. The Policy Planning Staff determined in November 1947 that loopholes under current export regulations were too small to warrant major revisions. If anything, American officials charged with framing new controls policy worried lest the new rules impose unnecessary red tape upon U.S. business and governmental agencies.[85]

In December 1947, however, the National Security Council (NSC), responding to Congressional pressure, recommended the application of stricter controls to all U.S. exports of strategic and scarce materials to Europe in order to stop the transshipment of prohibited U.S. goods from Western Europe to the Soviet bloc. The NSC's "R" procedure for export controls mostly restrained trade in military-related materials, such as those that the Atomic Energy Commission identified as essential to the production of atomic weapons. Yet by declaring all of Europe as a recovery zone to which the export controls applied, NSC Director Sidney Souers observed, the "R" procedure theoretically achieved "total control of shipments to Eastern Europe without apparent discrimination."[86]

During 1948 the administration cut most remaining U.S. economic ties with the East European satellites. Poland, still a major beneficiary of Western aid and trade, was the main victim of the American crackdown. In January 1948, World Bank President John J. McCloy told State Department representatives that certain Commerce, NAC, and Bank officials wished to cancel a $40–50 million loan for mining equipment to Poland, but reneging on the loan might call into question the Bank's already dubious status as an apolitical institution. The ERP countries, moreover, needed Polish coal. Under Secretary Lovett suggested a way out: since Wall Street would probably frown upon a loan to a Soviet satellite, sales of bonds in the United States to finance the Polish loan would languish. On these "economic" grounds, McCloy could disavow the Polish mining project. The Poles, Lovett reasoned, needed hard currency so badly that they would sell coal to the West with or without a loan. Besides, he added, Poland hardly deserved special consideration, for as a member of the Cominform, it was officially dedicated to the destruction of the Marshall Plan.[87]

Later that month, when the Polish Ambassador complained that the Bank had stiffened its terms for a loan, a State Department official explained that the Bank, while an international institution, had to consider the salability of its bonds. The continuing inability or unwillingness of the Polish government to provide compensation for nationalized U.S. property or to settle its Lend-Lease debt had not reassured American investors. The Polish Ambassador retorted in April 1948 that his government could not normalize relations with the United States until it received a Bank loan. Warsaw never received the loan and it resigned from the Bank in 1950, but as Lovett had predicted, Poland continued to export large quantities of coal to the West.[88]

American policy toward West European trade with the Soviet bloc was decidedly different. Washington knew that, at least in the short run, such commerce was essential to West European recovery. "Trade is necessarily a mutual affair," Charles Bohlen wrote in March 1948 to a Congressman who had complained of large British steel exports to the Soviet Union. "Trade between Eastern and Western Europe, now reduced to 30 per cent of its prewar level, must be expanded if the economic recovery of Western Europe is to be assured."[89]

Secretary of State Marshall favored further restrictions on strategic exports to the East, but he convinced the Cabinet in late March 1948 that a sharp cut in intra-European trade was neither desirable nor feasible. The State Department estimated that from April 1948 to June 1949, West European imports from the Soviet sphere would total $1.2 billion, consisting mostly of food, coal, and timber products. The volume of imports would rise in succeeding years, and to "replace them from other sources would be in some cases impossible." Cutting off West European exports of manufactured goods would slow, but not prevent, the completion of long-range industrial projects in the Soviet bloc. Without East-West trade, Foggy Bottom also contended, the United States and its allies would lose access to certain strategic materials, such as manganese, chrome, and platinum, which were available in large quantities only in the Soviet Union. In the view of the State Department and the National Security Resources Board, the Commerce Department's zealous campaign against East-West trade contradicted the intent of the Second Decontrol Act, which only authorized selective trade restrictions. In a June 1948 meeting of the NSC, Lovett stated that he was "more interested in getting manganese from Russia than in denying baby bottles to Russia." Later in the month, the Commerce Department agreed to relax East-West controls.[90]

The ERP countries in any case resolutely defied the rigid export controls that the U.S. Congress wanted to impose upon East-West trade. To the West Europeans, especially the British, trade with the Eastern bloc offered substantial economic benefits, as well as the possibility of some residual political influence in the East. The West Europeans also adopted a more relaxed attitude than the Americans toward the export of items with potential military utility. The Truman administration soon recognized that very strict limits on East-West trade would curtail European recovery and alienate America's allies, and that a tough controls policy would fail in any event.[91]

Trade statistics testify to the consequences of the dual American policy toward East-West trade. U.S. exports to the Soviet Union and Eastern Europe dwindled to almost nothing ($2 million) in 1951, at the height of the Korean War. In contrast, West European (including West German) sales to the Soviet bloc in that year totalled $682 million, over one-half of the 1938 level and about two-thirds of the postwar peak of $994 million in 1949.[92]

In most cases, the ECA and other agencies of the U.S. government did not intrude upon European internal and external affairs, except when crisis conditions or overwhelming pressure from the Congress dictated otherwise. The Congressional mandate for the Marshall Plan, consisting largely of general codes rather than rigid imperatives, was sufficiently loose to allow considerable discretion by ECA administrators. As a result of the anti-bureaucratic mood of the Congress, ECA officials were not held responsible for the actual distribution of most American aid in the ERP countries. The ECA proved to be an efficient and flexible instrument for European recovery.[93]

Evaluating the Marshall Plan

How successful was the Marshall Plan? In the ERP legislation, the Congress had established four aims for Europe: a strong production effort, the expansion of foreign trade, monetary and financial stabilization, and European "unification." The greatest achievements occurred in production. A key contribution of the Marshall Plan was the high rate of investment in Western Europe during the life of the program, through both direct ECA aid and counterpart funds. From 1947 to 1951, the ERP countries' collective gross national products grew from $120 billion to almost $159 billion, a 32.5 percent increase. By the end of the Marshall Plan in December 1951, West European industrial production was 35 percent higher than the 1938 level, compared with a goal of 30 percent. While agricultural output fell slightly short of projections (11 percent above prewar in 1951, vs. 15 percent planned), it still showed strong improvement over 1947. The one big disappointment was the $300 million ECA investment-guaranty program, which was designed to encourage private U.S. investment in Western Europe. Only 10 percent ($31.4 million) of the funds were ever used because U.S. business resisted investing in unsettled Europe.[94] Nonetheless, the ERP countries made impressive productivity gains.

The record for financial and monetary stabilization was mixed. In order to fight inflation, the ECA required certain ERP countries— notably Norway, Denmark, and the United Kingdom—to commit a large proportion of their counterpart funds toward the reduction of national debt or budgetary deficits. Despite some taming of inflation during 1948–49, prices rose sharply by the third quarter of 1950 and continued to rise thereafter, thanks to the Korean War. As Imanuel Wexler has noted, the ECA could never reconcile "the inherent conflict between the financial stabilization objective and the need to stimulate large-scale investments so as to increase production." Finally, in mid-1950, a choice was made to emphasize defense-oriented investment and production over the control of inflation. By the end of the Marshall Plan "much of the ground gained in the fight against inflation during its first two and a half years had been lost. The quest for a firmly maintained internal financial stability remained largely unfulfilled."[95]

Trade was the only area where the Europeans cooperated extensively. Payments difficulties—the product of the web of bilateral agreements spun after the war, the shortage of hard currencies, and the inconvertibility of currencies—had blocked the expansion of trade. Although Washington had at first sought a rapid return to multilateralism, the disastrous British experiment in sterling convertibility in 1947 convinced U.S. officials that *regional* trade and payments liberalization was the prerequisite to eventual currency convertibility and free trade. Thus, the ECA accepted the European Payments Union, which greatly facilitated *intra*-European trade, as the first step toward European integration. By 1951, intra-European commerce had risen to 36 percent above the 1938 level, while West European exports to the outside world had grown to 66 percent above the prewar level. The liberalization of intra-European trade, however, "entailed an element of discrimination against non-EPU members, particularly the dollar area." Bilateral payments arrangements, exchange controls, and quantitative import restrictions remained the rule. Indeed, the EPU never solved Western Europe's payments disequilibrium, and the ERP countries as a whole were unable to restore currency convertibility until the late 1950s. The regionalism born in the Marshall Plan years never gave way to a full integration of trans-Atlantic trade, as the Common Market became a permanent feature of the world economy.[96]

The record on integration, or as Congress had vaguely called it, "unification," was thus the least satisfactory. Aside from the reduction of trade barriers, the Benelux customs union, and the newly emerging European Coal and Steel Community, the basic structure of the West European economy remained unchanged. Economic integration was confined largely to the commercial sphere, and then only to a fraction of the ERP countries. (The Common Market, established in 1957, excluded Great Britain, Scandinavia, and other countries.) Political unification remained a pipedream.[97]

The larger goal of West European economic viability was not achieved for many years, for the ERP countries continued to require foreign assistance. Indeed, the Marshall Plan in a sense did not really end in December 1951. The Mutual Security Program provided Western Europe with vast U.S. military aid throughout the 1950s. Yet economic viability in the sense that Congress defined it was perhaps an unrealistic goal, and one could argue that the Marshall Plan laid the groundwork for eventual West European self-reliance.

Critics have charged the Marshall Plan with widening the rift between East and West, dampening the prospects of East-West trade and other interchange, and decreasing the chances for German reunification. But this may be confusing cause and effect: the American decision to aid Western Europe was a reaction to Soviet-American confrontation rather than a source of it.[98]

On balance, the Marshall Plan was a remarkable success. Its most important achievement was to restore West European self-confidence and to lay the basis for a long-term political, economic, and military association of the United States with Western Europe. True, American decision makers had to compromise certain principles in order to ensure the survival of Western Europe. For example, they supported regional organizations in Western Europe—notably, the EPU and the ECSC—that departed significantly from the open economic environment that Cordell Hull, Will Clayton, and other devotees of pure multilateralism had espoused. But the American willingness to compromise bore fruit in later years, as the miraculous recovery of the ERP countries led to a gradual loosening of economic restraints and to a boom in North Atlantic trade and investment beyond the fondest hopes of wartime American planners. The success of the Marshall Plan, moreover, laid the basis for a durable, bipartisan American consensus behind multilateralist policies that would survive the Republican victory in 1952.

Finally, the Marshall Plan and associated American policies helped alleviate, if not solve, the most critical problem of Europe in the twentieth century: Germany. The recovery program helped to rebuild western Germany, set the foundation for a viable West German state, and integrated that country into the Western alliance. If the United States deserves some of the blame for dividing Germany, it also deserves some of the credit for eliminating Germany as the main threat to European security and stability. The Marshall Plan facilitated the rapprochement between France and Germany after the war, and, in conjunction with the Monnet Plan, inextricably entwined western Germany in a network of multilateral institutions and agreements.

The United States had achieved its main economic security goals in Europe by 1950: the reconstruction of Western Europe in an American-centered multilateral system, the alignment of Germany with the West, and the containment of Soviet power in Europe. Significantly, the Truman administration realized these objectives chiefly through the use of economic instruments, rather than military power. In securing its own interests in Europe, the United States helped rebuild Western Europe as a viable entity in world politics. That was no small achievement.

CHAPTER EIGHT

U.S. ECONOMIC DIPLOMACY IN EAST ASIA: THE FALL OF CHINA AND THE RECONSTRUCTION OF JAPAN, 1945–1950

THE STORY OF U.S. policy in East Asia during the Truman era is full of ironies. Although the Pacific War had originated in the competition between Japan and America over the markets and resources of the Far East, the United States took steps after the war both to reconstruct Japan and to secure Japanese economic interests in the region. And while the United States had fought the war in the Far East firmly resolved to subjugate Japan and to elevate China to great power status, just five years after VJ Day it was equally determined to restore Japan as a regional power and to undermine China. Finally, while American planners consistently ranked Europe above Asia in strategic importance, U.S. troops became engaged in the first shooting war of the Cold War in Korea, a peripheral corner of Asia.

American Interests in East Asia

The key goals of the United States in East Asia at the end of the war were to eradicate Japanese militarism, prevent Japanese domination of the regional economy, and restore China as a sovereign power. Secondarily, the United States sought to contain Soviet expansion, accelerate the decolonization of Southeast Asia and other European dependencies, and preserve East Asian markets for American business. As in Europe, U.S. economic policies served larger political and strategic objectives, in this instance the integration of East Asia into the world economy.

Both before and after the war, American economic interests in Japan greatly exceeded those in China despite the widespread and enduring popular belief in the fabled China market. During the 1930s, the United States registered about three times more trade and investment in Japan than in China. American exports to Japan, for instance, averaged about 7.6 percent of all overseas sales during the prewar decade compared with 2.3 percent for China. Neither China nor Japan offered strategic raw materials that the United States could not obtain elsewhere. Interestingly, the bulk of American exports to Asia (more than $1.4 billion out of $1.8 billion in 1947) went to countries—notably, the Philippines, Southeast Asia, and British India—that received little attention in Washington during the late forties.[1]

Crude economic statistics, however, say less about U.S. policy toward the Far East during the 1940s than political and strategic factors. Since the enunciation of the Open Door policy in 1899, the United States had opposed the division of China into spheres of influence and had sought equality of access by all nations to Asian markets. The brutal Japanese attack on China during the 1930s offended the moral sensibilities of many Americans and aroused latent U.S. fears of Japanese hegemony in East Asia. Moreover, Tokyo's alliance with Berlin and Rome came at a time when the United States had all but entered the war against the Axis in the European theater. American policymakers recognized Japan's need for foreign sources of raw materials and markets and regarded it as natural that she should turn to the Asian mainland for them. But the means that Tokyo's leaders chose—military force, the establishment of puppet regimes, and the attempted creation of an exclusive sphere of influence—violated basic principles of international law and threatened Western access to East Asian markets. The United States progressively shut off strategic raw material supplies and war-related exports to Japan during 1940–41 while funneling ever-larger amounts of aid to Nationalist China. Tokyo responded with the attack on Pearl Harbor.[2]

The Yalta System and the Decline of Nationalist China, 1945–1947

Wartime American planners believed that the underlying cause of the war in Asia was Japan's imposition of a closed and restrictive economic regime—the abortive "Greater East Asian Co-Prosperity Sphere"—upon its weaker neighbors. Determined to eradicate Japanese domination of East Asia, the United States initially pinned its hopes for stability in postwar East Asia upon a strong Nationalist China. The steady decline of the Kuomintang (KMT) government, however, threw U.S. policy into disarray until 1948, when Washington adopted an alternative strategy.

Cold War considerations did not greatly influence the relations of the powers in Asia before 1948. Until then, the Western countries and the Soviet Union sought to develop a new balance of power in Asia, based upon agreements at the Yalta Conference of February 1945 that signaled the end of English and Japanese dominance in the Asia-Pacific region and the rise of American and Soviet power.[3] At Yalta, the Soviets won a *de facto* sphere of influence in Northeast Asia. In exchange for their pledge to enter the war against Japan and their recognition of the Nationalist Chinese government, the Soviets were allowed to reclaim territories (South Sakhalin Island and the Kuriles) and privileges (railway rights in Manchuria, the leasehold at Port Arthur, and the internationalization of Dairen) that czarist Russia had lost after the Russo-Japanese War of 1904–05. The United States, as the major combatant against Japan, in effect gained the right to sole occupation of that country, control over South Korea, and military bases throughout the Pacific.

In contrast, China won almost nothing concrete at the secret conference other than the retrocession of Formosa. Despite serious doubts about the viability of Nationalist China, the Big Three recognized the Kuomintang regime of Chiang Kai-shek as the sole legitimate government of China. They maintained the pretense that China was a great power because they hoped it would serve as a buffer between Russia and the West.[4]

Wartime planners had not fully reckoned with the chaos and weakness of China under Chiang. The KMT was in many ways its own worst enemy, and its eventual collapse was due almost entirely to internal causes.[5] The recipient of extensive U.S. aid during the war, the Nationalists enjoyed vast military superiority over the Chinese Communists (CCP) in 1945. Altogether, from the end of World War II to mid-1949, Chiang's government obtained more than $2.8 billion in economic and military aid from the United States, in addition to $.25 billion from other countries.[6] The KMT also received invaluable logistical aid and huge stores of surplus military equipment from the United States. With all of these advantages, few observers doubted that Chiang would prevail over the Communists for at least several years.[7]

Three factors accounted for the surprisingly rapid decline of the Nationalist regime. Chiang's decision to occupy most of North China and Manchuria, against the recommendation of his American advisers, greatly over-extended the communication and supply lines of the Nationalist armies and set the stage for a series of devastating Communist counteroffensives beginning in the spring of 1947. Chronic disunity and factionalism within the KMT paralyzed the government and undermined its diplomatic credibility, notably with the United States. Finally, the almost incomprehensible corruption and ineptitude of the Kuomintang resulted in disastrous economic developments, such as the more than 2,000-fold rise in retail prices from July 1937 to June 1945, which destroyed the social and political basis of the old regime.[8]

The Truman administration never reached a satisfactory solution to the China problem. Further aid to the KMT was indeed distasteful, but the alternatives remained unclear. The prospect of abandoning America's main wartime ally in Asia and extending either *de facto* or *de jure* recognition to an isolated Communist guerrilla organization appeared highly unattractive. The result of American ambivalence was a limited aid program that pleased neither side in the Chinese civil war. With little expectation of either a KMT victory or a lasting truce, President Truman dispatched George C. Marshall on a mission to China in December 1945 in hopes that he might stave off further CCP advances, stem Soviet influence in China, and deflect domestic criticism of the administration's China policy.[9]

The Marshall Mission was probably doomed from the start since neither the Communists nor the Nationalists could reconcile themselves to the coalition government that the United States favored. Both sides repeatedly violated U.S.-backed ceasefires. And in Washington, the case for American mediation in the civil war lost much of its urgency once Marshall ascertained that Moscow was not supplying major aid to the CCP and that the Red Army was pulling out of Manchuria. As U.S. officials became increasingly disillusioned with the venal Nationalist regime, even nonmilitary aid to Chiang was called into question.[10]

Marshall had initially favored a $500 million loan to shore up Chiang's regime, and Congress earmarked Eximbank credits for that amount in August 1946. But he changed his mind when Chiang renewed full-scale hostilities against the Communists during the summer of 1946. The KMT had already squandered an $83 million Eximbank loan and over a half billion dollars' worth of UNRRA relief. Unless Chiang implemented comprehensive reforms, Marshall advised Washington, the United States should cut off all further aid. Marshall's return to Washington to become the new Secretary of State in January

1947 further darkened the prospects for aid to the KMT. Marshall indicated to a Chinese official in February 1947 that the Eximbank would not give the Nationalists more help "as long as the intransigent clique surrounding the Generalissimo was still in authority."[11]

Even if a more savory non-Communist regime had replaced the KMT, it would have had trouble enacting all of the internal reforms— taxing the rich, redistributing land, stabilizing the currency—that Washington desired in China. In retrospect, the Truman administration's attempt to establish the Open Door in war-wracked China appears especially ill-advised. In January 1946, for example, the National Advisory Council informed the embattled KMT government that the Eximbank would not extend a large loan until the Chinese agreed to open up trade on a nondiscriminatory basis. However reasonable Washington's demands might have seemed in peacetime, its efforts on behalf of foreign private enterprise during the civil war offended Chinese of almost every stripe. (Even Chiang had fiercely resisted the reentry of U.S. business into China after the war.) The KMT's grudging concessions to Yankee business lent support to Communist charges that the Nationalists kowtowed to Washington.[12]

As the fortunes of the KMT declined, U.S. officials were faced with the difficult question of how to deal with the Communists without undercutting the Nationalist government. American relations with the CCP had remained friendly as long as the common struggle against Japan existed. In March 1945, CCP leader Mao Tse-tung had told an American diplomat that the United States "is not only the most suitable country to assist [the] economic development of China; she is the only country fully able to participate." To be sure, Chinese Communist suspicions of American intentions in China were aroused soon after the war, as the United States showed a distinct tilt toward the KMT. Yet CCP-U.S. relations did not seriously deteriorate until the summer of 1946, when Washington agreed to sell $1 billion worth of surplus war supplies to the Nationalists. It was at this point that Marshall's efforts to establish a truce in the Chinese civil war completely broke down. Although most American officials—Marshall, Truman, Acheson—believed that the Chinese Communists might remain independent of Moscow, they were unwilling to nurture ties with the CCP as long as some hope remained that non-Communist forces might stabilize China.

For their part, the Communists probably did not expect to form a lasting friendship with the country that they regarded as the capitalist archfoe. Instead, Mao may have hoped to obtain American neutrality in the civil war and, eventually, diplomatic recognition, if not aid, from Washington. Nor could the Communist leaders afford to appear too cordial toward the Americans lest they offend their vigilant Soviet ally.[13]

Soviet Aims in East Asia

Soviet aims and policies in postwar East Asia were conservative but opportunistic. The Soviets met their Yalta commitments and generally respected the KMT's prerogatives until Chiang's final retreat from the mainland in 1949. Like Washington, Moscow apparently did not foresee an early CCP victory. Moreover, the Kremlin probably did not anticipate or desire sustained competition with the United States for influence in China. The Middle Kingdom, as mysterious and complex in Russian eyes as in American, was to serve as a buffer between Soviet interests in Northeast Asia (North Korea and Manchuria) and Western interests in the Pacific and Southeast Asia.

The Red Army stripped Manchuria of much of its industry in late 1945 ostensibly to gain war booty from Japan, but another probable objective was to ensure that China, whether under KMT or CCP control, would remain weak for some time. Soviet military aid to the CCP consisted mostly of light arms. There are many indications that Stalin did not welcome the emergence of a rival power center in the world Communist movement.[14]

Still, the strains that developed between Moscow and Yenan did not preclude cooperation and support. Stalin's embrace of the Chinese Communists was both less intimate and less suffocating than in the case of the East European parties. The CCP did not need a great deal of direct Soviet aid to defeat the KMT and probably appreciated Moscow's desire not to provoke the United States. Open Soviet support might have prompted greater U.S. intervention in the civil war. If the Chinese Communists' maximum goal in the 1945–1947 period vis-à-vis the United States was American abandonment of the KMT and recognition of the CCP, their minimum aim was a limited American presence in postwar China. In the latter sense, they were successful.

Relying on economic and military aid, Washington failed to secure a stable and pro-Western China. The years 1945–1947 were a time of retrenchment for the United States in Asia as the Truman administration concentrated its energies and resources in Europe. The seeming intractability of the civil war in China, the gross decadence of the

Kuomintang regime, and limitations upon American resources all worked to minimize American intervention in China. By early 1947, after U.S. officials had all but given up hope of resuscitating the KMT regime, Japan had replaced China as the focus of American policy in Asia.

The American Occupation of Japan, 1945–1947: MacArthur and the Japanese Conservatives

The American experience in Japan differed from that in Germany in important ways. With the other powers only nominally involved in the occupation, the United States exercised virtually unrestricted control over Japan. The Cold War also arrived in Japan much later than in Germany, with the result that strategic factors initially played a lesser role in shaping U.S. policies in Japan than they did in Germany and Western Europe. Another peculiarity of the Japanese occupation was the existence of a national government that continued to function when the war ended and significantly influenced U.S. policies.

Nonetheless, the American experiences in Japan and Germany were similar in one major respect: the absence of firm guidance from Washington produced vacillating and ineffective reconstruction policies in both countries. As in the case of Germany, planning for the occupation of Japan was marked by a sharp division within the U.S. government. One faction, associated with Under Secretary of State Joseph Grew and other State Department experts on Japan (nicknamed the "Japan Crowd"), believed that Japan's militarism was an aberration brought on by the Great Depression and sustained by a small and eradicable martial clique. By rooting out the influence of the armed forces, revising the constitution to release liberal forces while retaining the Emperor in power, and integrating Japan into a multilateral world economy, this group hoped to set Japan back on the democratic and peaceful path that it had presumably followed in the 1920s. Until roughly the spring of 1945, this tendency prevailed in planning for postwar Japan.[15]

Following the death of President Franklin D. Roosevelt in April 1945, the influence of the Japan Crowd waned. A second group, including Secretary of State James F. Byrnes, Assistant Secretary Dean Acheson, and State Department experts on China (dubbed the "China Crowd"), took control over much of America's Asia policy. They regarded Japanese aggression as the inevitable product of deep-seated, "feudalistic" tendencies in the Japanese social structure, political system, and culture and concluded that the mission of the United States was to upend Japanese society and implant American values and institutions at every level of Japanese life.[16]

The Potsdam Declaration, with its ambiguous assurances regarding the status of the emperor in postwar Japan, represented a tenuous compromise between these two tendencies. But with the formulation of the U.S. Initial Post-Surrender Policy (SWNCC 150) in September 1945, the hardliners gained the ascendancy. During this second stage of U.S. policy toward Japan (summer 1945 to spring 1948), American authorities sought to demilitarize and democratize Japan by thoroughly reforming Japanese institutions. Yet American policymakers never resolved the basic tension between the comparatively mild Potsdam statement, which most U.S. occupation officials (and Japanese) regarded as the basis of the peace, and the harsher SWNCC 150 policy.[17]

However much American officials may have disagreed over other matters, there was no dispute about the dire condition of the postwar Japanese economy. The war had killed an estimated 1,850,000 Japanese and left 40 percent of Japan's urban areas destroyed or seriously damaged. In 1945, industrial production plunged to one-third of the 1934–1936 average. Harvests were poor, and the newspapers reported death by starvation. With the collapse of the Empire and the return of six million soldiers and civilian repatriates, unemployment soared to thirteen million in 1946. Shorn of overseas territories, denied access to foreign sources of food and raw materials, and lacking the means to sustain exports, Japan faced a bleak and uncertain future.[18]

The main U.S. policy statements on Japan were weighted in favor of demilitarization over reconstruction. SWNCC 150 called upon General Douglas MacArthur, the Supreme Commander for the Allied Powers ("SCAP," used hereafter to refer to MacArthur's staff and the occupation regime), to disarm the Japanese armed forces, try war criminals, and dissolve large financial and industrial establishments. The United States would not pay for Japanese reconstruction. In contrast with the quadripartite occupation of Germany, SCAP would administer Japan as one unit.[19]

The United States had agreed at Potsdam that an eleven-power Far Eastern Commission (FEC) in Washington would oversee the demilitarization and occupation of Japan. To the extent that the State Department, if not SCAP, catered to the FEC, it did so to win international backing for American policies in Japan. A quadripartite Allied Control

Council in Tokyo also had theoretical power to supervise SCAP, but MacArthur barely acknowledged its existence. Hoping to avoid the thicket of problems that OMGUS was facing in Germany, SCAP intended to exercise almost exclusive control over Japan. Yet "American policymakers," Charles Neu has commented, "did not envisage Japan as part of the postwar balance of power in East Asia. Japan was to be, as General MacArthur phrased it, the 'Switzerland of the Pacific,' while China was to serve as the stabilizing force in that region."[20]

The U.S. occupation bore the peculiar stamp of the Supreme Commander, who combined an unshakable faith in the righteousness and universality of American institutions with an equally intense conviction that fate had chosen him to impose Christian values upon the Japanese nation.[21] Aloof and isolated from Japanese society, MacArthur issued far-reaching edicts on every aspect of Japanese life, but did little at first to foster recovery. For a conservative, he showed remarkably little concern over the potential growth of revolutionary movements and parties in Japan. In March 1947, MacArthur would casually and prematurely announce the fulfillment of his mission in Japan and call for an early peace treaty.[22]

In order to "democratize" Japan, SCAP pledged twin campaigns to transform Japanese political and economic institutions.[23] The economic reform program, which concerns us here, focused on dissolving the *zaibatsu*, which were highly concentrated industrial and financial combines controlled by an extended *zaibatsu* family. The *zaibatsu* enjoyed the advantages of tightly knit "relationships among the affiliated firms by means of holding companies, interlocking directorships, and mutual stockholdings." In addition, the *zaibatsu* could call upon enormous financial resources from commercial banks that the combines could use to control whole industries.[24] In a sense, the American deconcentration policy was designed merely to restore prewar conditions by reversing the mergers that the Japanese government had dictated during the war. (The "Big Four" of the *zaibatsu*—Mitsui, Mitsubishi, Sumitomo, and Yasuda—had increased their share of total paid-in capital from 10.4 percent in 1937 to 24.5 percent in 1946.) In Germany and Japan, Eleanor Hadley has observed, the United States followed a similar policy toward cartels:

> The Allied assumption in the case of both countries was that giant enterprises, benefiting greatly by a policy of foreign aggression, had supported the leadership directing the foreign aggression. . . . But more fundamentally, the charge was that

the political climate that suited such giant structures was not equality but hierarchy, not individual rights and liberties but their suppression.[25]

SCAP's assault upon the *zaibatsu*, then, was consistent with the Truman administration's liberalization of postwar economic institutions around the world. Yet SCAP's reforms and objectives collided head-on with the goals of conservative Japanese leaders, who feared the revolution from above as much as any from below. The growth of state power during the Depression, notably over the economy, had alarmed the capitalist and landowning classes, whose ideal political system dated from the Meiji Restoration of the late nineteenth century. Elements of the elite, in fact, had pressed the Emperor to sue for peace as early as February 1945 (the "Konoe Memorial") because they feared that continuation of the war would erode the social order and end in a Communist revolution.

After the war, the conservative coalition rallied around Yoshida Shigeru, an Anglophile Cabinet minister of the 1920s associated with the Konoe Memorial group. Yoshida, who would serve as the Foreign Minister or Prime Minister in every Japanese Cabinet but one during the first postwar decade, sought to preserve the emperor system and the prewar national polity (except for the excessive power of the military), if necessary by brutally suppressing revolutionary movements. In addition, Yoshida and his allies favored reconstruction along capitalist lines, restoration of the *zaibatsu*, and Japanese partnership with the Western powers.[26]

The conservatives found much to disparage about the U.S. occupation in the early postwar years. The reforms initiated by MacArthur struck Yoshida and his colleagues as dangerous recipes for social ferment. Widespread strikes and Leftist agitation, culminating in massive protest marches in May 1946, heightened their fears of a Communist takeover. In addition, Japanese on both the Left and the Right regarded SCAP's deconcentration, antitrust, and labor laws "not as a necessary condition to the establishment of democratic government, but as a device to weaken Japan, to destroy its ability to give vigorous competition to American and European business."[27]

At this point, it bears asking why MacArthur, scarcely a radical by American standards, pursued policies in Japan that conservative and pro-American Japanese like Yoshida believed endangered the social, political, and economic fabric of their nation. The answer in regard to the *zaibatsu* lies in the differing historical experiences of Japan and

America. The Japanese viewed monopolies and oligopolies favorably because competitive internal markets had proven inefficient. Concentrated economic power, on the other hand, had enabled their country to compete very effectively in international trade. Most Japanese who thought about such matters entertained the Marxian notion that the tendency of business toward bigness was the product of natural law (the "stages of capitalist development"), and that the trend toward concentration was irreversible.[28]

Thus, the Japanese conservatives believed that their society was fundamentally sound, except for the military, whose political power they wished to curb. Yoshida and his allies wanted to dismantle the war industries while retaining the *zaibatsu*, the Emperor, and the prewar agricultural system. By increasing state control over the economy, SCAP seemed to threaten these pillars of Japanese society.[29]

In contrast, MacArthur saw the concentration of production under monopoly capitalism as the root cause of Japanese militarism. In order to help undermine the power of the entrenched business elite, the American conquerors would need to import entrepreneurial values into Japan. As one U.S. official put it in January 1946, "The job of planning is not primarily statistical but of masterminding the transition of this feudal oligarchy to economic democracy." As an heir, witting or unwitting, to Wilsonian Progressivism, MacArthur viewed the *zaibatsu* and rural landlordism as inimical to individualism and democracy. Although the presence of numerous New Dealers within the American bureaucracy partly explains SCAP's penchant for experimentation, MacArthur hardly fits this mold. His ideals harked back to a mythical American past, when the frontier supposedly nurtured self-reliance and representative government.[30]

SCAP and the Japanese conservatives shared two bases of agreement. First, they were united in their opposition to Communism. SCAP found that anti-Communism proved an effective rallying cry to win the support of conservative Japanese who otherwise mistrusted reform. Second, the Yoshida conservatives believed that Japan was a basically Western society and that she should seek an alliance with America against Russia. These shared principles ensured that the Japanese government would usually cooperate with the occupying authorities.[31]

Still, SCAP's commitment to democratization was genuine, and it liberalized political and economic life with an uncompromising zeal, even if the Japanese economy deteriorated in the process. By the end of

1947, Japanese industrial production had reached only 45 percent, exports 10 percent, and imports 30 percent of the 1930–1934 average. The disruption of foreign trade stemmed the inflow of raw materials, the lifeblood of the Japanese economy. Although the United States expended $400 million in occupation costs during 1947 alone, Japanese real per capita income remained at only one-half of the 1934–1936 average level.[32] SCAP's policies created a climate of uncertainty that discouraged investment, crippled exports, and indirectly raised occupation expenses.

In addition, SCAP did little before the end of 1947 to integrate Japan into the world economy. From the start, SCAP had imposed strict controls on the Japanese domestic economy, and the regime of foreign trade that SCAP established was no exception. Rather than ease wartime Japanese regulations on trade, SCAP added "its own direct controls, which at the international level were more comprehensive and more categorical than any that had been employed in Japan up to that time." Along with low Japanese productivity and discrimination by foreign customers, SCAP's cumbersome methods contributed to an extremely slow recovery in Japanese foreign commerce.[33]

SCAP's efforts to restructure the domestic economy also failed. The breakup of the huge industrial combines into smaller, more competitive units was never achieved. Delays in the industrial deconcentration and reparations programs—the former due to conflict among U.S. policymakers, the latter to both internal strife and disagreement among FEC members—left Japanese economic policy in almost total confusion.[34]

Japanese Reparations and Level of Industry, 1945–1947

The U.S. reparations program in Japan was designed to serve the demilitarization and deconcentration policies. As in Germany, the United States sought to strip Japan of surplus production (especially military-related capacity) and redistribute plant and equipment to victims of Japanese aggression, helping to redress the imbalance in Asian industrial development. According to a mission of American officials in Japan led by Edwin W. Pauley (who also headed the German reparations group) in December 1945, "Militaristic Japanese economic planning deliberately held back the normal industrial development of adjacent areas in Asia." As in Germany, too, the amount of Japanese reparations deliveries was closely linked to the permitted level of industry, for the production ceiling that SCAP set for Japan would determine the amount of surplus capacity available for reparations.[35]

Yet from the beginning, the various parties involved in the reparations question—the Pauley mission, the State Department, SCAP, the FEC, and the Japanese themselves—disagreed bitterly over the definition of Japan's "minimum peacetime economy." On the one hand, some American officials, such as China specialist Owen Lattimore, believed that the United States and the allies should exact heavy indemnities, hold down Japanese production and living standards, and raise those of neighboring countries to ensure that "Japan does not again jump ahead of the development of the rest of Asia too fast and too far." The premise of Lattimore and other members of the Pauley group, which delivered its comprehensive report in April 1946, was that Japan needed only enough industrial plant to satisfy domestic civilian consumption, and that anything above that level was military-related and suitable for reparations.[36] The flaw in this line of reasoning, critics in SCAP and the War Department pointed out, was that Japan required excess *export* capacity in order to pay for vital imports of raw materials and food. The loss of industrial and other assets worth approximately $3 billion in Korea, Formosa, Manchuria, and elsewhere had accentuated Japan's dependence upon foreign trade after the war.[37]

Japan already required heavy American subsidies to survive. As in Germany, U.S. officials treated imports of basic needs as a "first charge" against Japanese assets, including those theoretically available as reparations. If the United States stripped Japan's heavy industries, Japan might lack the export capacity to pay for essential imports, raising occupation costs. Restricting Japanese penetration of foreign markets would also delay the integration of Japan into an open and free-trading world economy, with all of its supposed political advantages over Japan's earlier bilateralist, discriminatory system.[38]

A poorly conceived reparations program could also undermine U.S. political goals within Japan. Without assurances as to which plants or industries SCAP would order dismantled, Japanese industrialists would not resume production and rehire workers. As one American official warned Pauley in January 1946, "We stand to lose the good will of liberal Japanese without whose backing an eventual pro-American nation cannot develop and to create the conditions under which totalitarianism will thrive."[39]

Conflict between the "hard" and "soft" factions of the American government frustrated the realization of coherent policies on reparations and the level of industry. The State Department, considering it imperative that any economic policy for Japan meet the approval of the Far Eastern Commission (FEC), favored a more punitive policy toward Japan than did SCAP, which like OMGUS in Germany was more conscious of occupation costs and local suffering. But the FEC was unable to agree on how to divide the spoils in Japan, as war-damaged countries like the Philippines and China each demanded special treatment. As a result, the Pauley reparations program was never implemented.[40] In early 1947, the State Department devised a tentative compromise. As the American representative informed the FEC in February 1947, Washington would base reparations policy upon the first-charge principle and the Japanese standard of living during the years 1930–1934, a formula that favored Japanese reconstruction. At the same time, the United States would offer speeded-up, "advance" deliveries of reparations to some FEC countries, until the FEC reached final agreement on how to allocate the Japanese indemnity.[41]

The War Department and SCAP generally ignored this interim accord, however. In Japan as in Germany, the Army occupation authorities held most of the cards, and there was little that the State Department could do about it. In January 1947, the War Department had hired a private consulting group headed by Clifford Strike, an engineer with experience in Germany who opposed reparations in principle. The American businessmen and engineers in Strike's group deplored the underutilization of plant and equipment amid the want and misery they witnessed in Japan. The commission concluded in April 1947 that Japan could not meet 1930–1934 standards of living and deliver large amounts of reparations at the same time. Consequently, the War Department encouraged SCAP to delay even the meager deliveries under the interim "advance" program. In June 1947, a War Department official claimed, to the impotent rage of his counterpart in the State Department, that SCAP had authority to take "unilateral action respecting not only reparations and economic recovery programs but also for peace treaty provisions favorable to our avowed intention to assist in world economic stabilization and prevention of political unrest."[42]

Japanese reparations deliveries were miniscule, even if compared with the removals recommended by the Strike mission. By late 1948, only about 20,000 machine tools, some laboratory equipment, and a few power plants had been distributed. To the dismay of America's allies in the Pacific War, the United States called a total halt to deliveries in May 1949.[43]

Japan's reparations, like Germany's, served neither to redistribute economic power within the region nor to eliminate Japan's war potential. Victims of Japanese aggression also did not gain meaningful compensation through industrial removals from Japan proper although the expropriation of overseas Japanese properties was substantial. Reparations in any case were an anachronistic method of redressing the balance of political and economic power in East Asia. Japan had little to offer in movable industrial assets after the war, and nothing short of a permanent occupation could have prevented a postwar revival of its industry.

Aside from the impracticality of reparations, the deadlock in the FEC over the division of interim reparations in 1946 may have irreparably damaged the prospects for a successful resolution of the problem, for that was probably the last year in which substantial removals were politically acceptable to Washington, SCAP, and the Japanese. The Soviet seizure of $1–2 billion worth of Japanese "war booty" in Manchuria also complicated the allocation of reparations and strengthened the hand of SCAP in delaying deliveries.[44] The shift in American reparations policy, however, reflected a broader policy reorientation in Washington, centering around the growing recognition that Japanese reconstruction was necessary for the stabilization of East Asia and the containment of Communism in that region.

The Reverse Course, 1948–1950

When historians refer to the "reverse course," they mean the American decision to bring a halt to experimentation and reform in Japan and to consolidate U.S. strategic interests in East Asia, first and foremost by reconstructing the Japanese economy. Any number of factors explains the shift in American policy: the Army's concern over occupation costs, the clamor of U.S. businessmen against the "socialization" of Japan, SCAP's desire to avoid a Japanese backlash against American reforms, fear of a Communist takeover in Japan, and the growing strategic importance of Japan in East Asia after the fall of China. Upon examination, the reverse course appears to have been many courses at once, each the product of differing policy recommendations by different branches of the U.S. government, and each implemented at various times, not necessarily in tandem with one another.[45]

The pressures for new policies in Japan rose markedly during 1947. In March, MacArthur called for the conclusion of a peace treaty with Japan within a year. SCAP was confident that with its reforms intact, Japan enjoyed all the institutional prerequisites of a democracy. A prolonged occupation would increase Japanese resentment against the conquerors and obstruct recovery. Without a peace treaty, Japan could not trade with other countries on an equal basis or rejoin the family of nations. In July 1947, SCAP began relaxing restrictions on Japanese foreign trade, but exports grew very slowly.[46]

Meanwhile, opposition to SCAP's policies back in the United States was mounting. Criticism centered around FEC 230, the main document concerning the dissolution of the *zaibatsu*. FEC 230 had originated as a SWNCC document adopted in May 1947, when sentiment in Washington for economic deconcentration in Japan was already waning. The seeming trustbusting, pro-labor slant of FEC 230 repelled American businessmen with prewar ties to Japanese industry. They mistakenly believed that FEC 230 was a product of anti-capitalist influence in the FEC or SCAP itself, and they resolved to rally American opinion against the document.

This "Japan Lobby" had an effective mouthpiece in Harry Kern, the foreign affairs editor of *Newsweek* magazine and a strident critic of SCAP's reforms. *Newsweek* singled out for special criticism SCAP's supposed "economic purge" of 25,000 to 30,000 Japanese businessmen and financiers. The actual number was closer to 1,500, and MacArthur was quick to counterattack by observing that the economic purge was a key part of the allied effort to remove militarists from positions of economic power in postwar Japan.

Nonetheless, reports from discontented American businessmen returning from Japan alarmed Secretary of Defense James V. Forrestal and Under Secretary of the Army William H. Draper. Forrestal feared that the breakup of the *zaibatsu* would hinder recovery, encourage the socialization of industry, and obstruct the integration of Japan into the U.S. orbit. Following a visit to Japan in September 1947, Draper, who as an economic deputy to General Lucius Clay had been a leading critic of German reparations, became convinced that FEC 230 posed a dire threat to Japanese recovery and U.S. interests in that country.[47]

The focus of the opposition to SCAP lay in George F. Kennan's Policy Planning Staff (PPS). Aghast at State Department drafts of a peace treaty first circulated in August 1947, Kennan's group in October saw "great risks in an early relinquishment of Allied control over Japan." The former enemy state lacked the political and economic maturity to resist "communist penetration," partly because MacArthur had purged so many of its leading conservatives, who were quite often the Japanese most friendly to the United States. In order to strengthen pro-American forces in Japan, the PPS reasoned that the United States should cease reparations deliveries and decartelize industry only to the extent necessary to prevent a revival of Japanese militarism.[48]

Despite growing criticism from American, as well as Japanese, quarters, MacArthur could not afford to back down after having openly endorsed deconcentration. Against the better judgment of the State Department, MacArthur pushed the Deconcentration Law through the Japanese Diet in the fall of 1947. Although SCAP, the Army, and the PPS all favored Japanese economic recovery, their priorities differed. For SCAP, reconstruction offered an opportunity to implant democracy and Western principles (including Christianity) in Japan. Economic revival and democratic reform would also demonstrate the superiority of the American way.[49] The Army was more concerned with the reduction of occupation costs and was willing to scrap some of SCAP's reforms (especially *zaibatsu* dissolution) to appease the Congress and to achieve U.S. security objectives.[50]

The PPS, in contrast, was more concerned about the possibility of a Communist revolution in Japan. Like the Japanese conservatives, the State Department officials favored a liberalization of Japan's *external* economic relations—through freer trade and integration into an open multilateral system—but opposed the transformation of Japan's *internal* economic institutions.

Kennan's perspective is best understood in terms of his containment strategy, which prescribed the creation of positions of strength in Western Europe and Japan to curb Soviet and Communist influence. American occupation policies had succeeded in disarming and demilitarizing Japan, the PPS noted in November 1947, but "they have not produced . . . the political and economic stability which Japanese society will require if it is to withstand communist pressures after we have gone." To base American policies in the Far East upon sentimental and "unreal objectives such as human rights, the raising of living standards, and democratization," Kennan argued in February 1948, was dangerously naive, for "our influence in the coming period is going to be primarily military and economic." Given Communist gains in China, the United States had to reorder its strategic priorities in the Far East. "It is my own guess . . . ," Kennan wrote, "that Japan and the Philippines will be found to be the corner-stones of such a Pacific security system and that if we can contrive to retain effective control over these areas there can be no serious threat to our security from the East within our time."[51]

Beginning in the fall of 1947, Kennan led efforts within the Truman administration to consolidate the U.S. position in Japan. The PPS chief persuaded Forrestal that a premature peace treaty could leave Japan in a state of economic distress and "near anarchy, which would be precisely what the Communists would want." SCAP's trustbusting, half-hearted as it was, struck Kennan as "eminently agreeable to anyone interested in the future communization of Japan." In November 1947, Forrestal directed Army Secretary Kenneth Royall to study the security implications of Japan's economic condition, and, in February 1948, the Defense Secretary ordered an examination of the limited rearmament of Germany and Japan as well. "The discussion of rearming Japan," a Japanese scholar has observed, "began less than a year after the promulgation of the Japanese Constitution with its renunciation-of-war clause." In March 1948, the State Department signaled a shift in deconcentration policy by withdrawing support from FEC 230 and by dispatching Kennan on a fact-finding mission in Tokyo.[52]

Kennan later likened his conversations with General MacArthur in Tokyo to "opening up communications and arranging the establishment of diplomatic relations with a hostile and suspicious foreign government." Yet the Supreme Commander, perhaps sensing the new mood in Washington, seemed quite amenable to changes in SCAP's policies. MacArthur convinced Kennan that the United States should retain Okinawa as a naval and air base in order to protect Japan and the Philippines. The PPS head, in turn, persuaded the General that Japanese reparations obstructed recovery without significantly benefiting the recipient countries. SCAP's top priority should be Japanese reconstruction, Kennan told MacArthur, and the American commander should feel free to ignore the FEC. Overlooking the obstructionist roles played by the British, Australians, and Chinese in the FEC, Kennan complained that the Soviets had used the multinational body to interfere with the U.S. rebuilding of Japan. (MacArthur himself did not stress the Soviet threat and told Kennan that the "Japanese Communists were no menace.")[53]

Whatever the local circumstances, the State Department's principal aim in Japan was to bring SCAP in line with the containment policy. Following his return to Washington in late March, Kennan recommended that the United States delay conclusion of a peace treaty with Japan. In the meantime, SCAP should relax its controls over Japanese economic and political life, cease reparations deliveries and deconcentration, and strengthen the Japanese national police. American troops, Kennan added, should remain in Japan proper and the surrounding islands for an indefinite period of time. Eventually, the State Department should replace SCAP as the instrument of U.S. occupation policy in Japan. "Economic recovery," Kennan concluded, "should be made the prime objective of United States policy in Japan for the coming period." On October 9, 1948, the National Security Council (NSC) adopted Kennan's main recommendations in NSC 13/2.[54]

SCAP implemented only part of the NSC's new policy. On the one hand, the deconcentration program was sharply decelerated after the demise of FEC 230 in March 1948.[55] Yet SCAP resisted many other measures recommended by Washington, including strict monetary and fiscal reforms, rehabilitation of Japanese "purgees," creation of a strong Japanese national police, and transfer of occupation duties to the State Department. Interestingly, MacArthur did not crack down on the Japanese Communist Party until June 1950, when the JCP adopted a strongly pro-Soviet, anti-American line for the first time. MacArthur's implementation of NSC 13 fell short of Kennan's chief objective: a politically stable, prosperous, and viable Japan before the commencement of peace talks. As one Japanese scholar has concluded, only the "Korean War finally made GHQ, SCAP completely focus on the containment policy as it affected Japan."[56]

The "reverse course" symbolized by NSC 13/2 did not so much reverse, as reorient, U.S. priorities in Japan. For the most part, SCAP's political and social reforms remained intact. The occupation officials shifted gears somewhat on economic issues. To help compensate for Japan's lost markets in China and Korea, American officials encouraged the opening of Japanese trade with Southeast Asia, the "rice bowl of the Orient" and a rich source of raw materials.[57] Yet even before the arrival of containment in Asia, SCAP was taking steps, however clumsily and tentatively, toward the rehabilitation of the Japanese economy—to appease American businessmen, cut occupation costs, reduce domestic unrest, and prepare Japan for self-government.

Insofar as a reverse course did take place, it largely concerned Japan's strategic relationship with the United States. Following Kennan's trip, Japan was increasingly seen as a potential arsenal and an ally in regional defense. When a Japanese delegation headed by Yoshida Shigeru signed a peace treaty in San Francisco with forty-eight nations in September 1951, it also concluded a bilateral security pact with the United States that incorporated Japan into the U.S. defense perimeter.[58]

Significantly, Japan's military realignment took place *before* the United States had fully integrated Japan into the multilateral world economy. Despite the importance of a strong Japan to a restored balance of power in Asia, Japan did not begin a sustained recovery until the Korean War gave it an artificial boost. Belying the American commitment to an open, nondiscriminatory order, SCAP never completely removed the "regime of comprehensive international economic controls" that it had imposed upon Japan. And despite U.S. backing, Japan, unlike Germany, did not win equal status as a trading partner (under the General Agreement on Tariffs and Trade) from most of the former Allies until the late 1950s.[59] By then, Japan had finally emerged as a regional economic power wedded to the U.S.–sponsored multilateralist system.

The Fall of China, 1947–1950

If U.S. economic diplomacy in Japan was only a partial success, in China it was an abysmal failure. As the Chinese Communist offensives gained momentum in the spring and summer of 1947, the attention of the Truman administration remained squarely focused upon Europe. Repeated appeals by the Nationalist Chinese during the spring of 1947 for a special $1 billion loan modeled on the British loan went unheeded. The Congress had allocated $500 million in Eximbank credits to China, but the White House refused to release the funds.[60] To uphold its commitment to Chiang and appease Republican friends of the KMT whose support was needed for the Marshall Plan, the administration gave limited stocks of military equipment to the KMT and lifted the arms embargo in May 1947. In October 1947, the Nationalist regime also received post-UNRRA relief and Interim Aid, thanks in part to the efforts of the China bloc in Congress.[61]

Republican pressure similarly forced the Truman administration to append a provision for aid to China to the European Recovery Program bill in early 1948. In the final version reached in April 1948, the China Aid Act of 1948 provided $463 million for the KMT over one year, with $125 million allocated for military aid. Yet the Congress granted the administration the option to withhold economic aid if the Nationalist government did not implement internal reforms.[62]

Washington's efforts to reform the KMT were to no avail. As Ambassador John Leighton Stuart noted in May 1948, the United States had forfeited all bargaining power with the signing of the aid act. In any event, the Nationalist government could not undertake bold action at this late date. While American leaders debated how much aid to give China, the Chinese Communists launched huge offensives from December 1947 to March 1948 that crushed Nationalist forces in the North and decisively turned the tide of the civil war in the Communists' favor.[63]

The Truman administration now faced a dilemma that it could no longer ignore: while it was determined to avoid U.S. military involvement there, it was equally unwilling to abandon the Nationalists to their fate. Despite its shortcomings, the KMT had been a loyal ally, and Washington could not desert the Nationalists, then the only viable alternative to the Communists, while it was in the process of forging an alliance against Communism in Europe. Moreover, U.S. officials hoped that moderates within or outside the KMT might replace Chiang as the head of the anti-Communist forces in China. Most American officials also underestimated the CCP's strength and did not realize that a Communist victory was imminent. Another obstacle to abandoning Chiang was the Congress, where Republican supporters of the Generalissimo held key committee posts and could impede the Marshall Plan if sufficiently aroused over China. "A battle over China," William Stueck observes, "would have exacerbated national divisions on foreign policy and destroyed the atmosphere of bipartisan cooperation."[64]

Still, the Truman administration rejected the option of stepped-up aid deliveries to the Kuomintang in 1948, let alone direct military intervention in the civil war. The KMT had so far made very poor use of American matériel, and budgetary constraints reinforced the feeling in Washington that Chiang did not deserve more assistance. American military forces were already stretched thin by the Berlin crisis and expanding commitments in Europe and the Middle East, and Congress was threatening to cut the defense budget.[65]

Yet even with the virtual defeat of the KMT in late 1948, U.S. military and economic aid under the China Aid Act continued to reach the Nationalists, albeit in a trickle. (Only $10 million of the $125 million in military aid under the 1948 act had reached China by November 1948.) These circumstances put the United States in the worst possible position, Tang Tsou has pointed out:

> The United States thus continued to be entangled in China. Her immobilized position at the center not only deprived her of freedom of action but also incurred for her the liabilities of both a policy of active intervention and a program of prompt withdrawal. The American policy lent color to the Communists' distorted views of the United States, while failing to impress on them American strength and determination. It discarded the Nationalists while intensifying the hostilities of the Communists.[66]

When Dean Acheson replaced George Marshall as Secretary of State in January 1949, he inherited an almost hopeless situation in China. Acheson sought an accommodation with the Chinese Communists that would minimize Soviet influence on the CCP and permit the United States to maintain a foothold in China. To achieve these ends, Acheson followed three policies: the curtailment of aid to Communist-dominated areas on the mainland, a hands-off policy toward Taiwan, and the use of trade as a bargaining lever with the Communists.

In the fall of 1948, U.S. diplomats in China (with the notable exception of Ambassador Stuart) and officials of the Economic Cooperation Administration, which was charged with administering China aid, had considered the possibility of continuing aid in Communist-controlled areas in order to establish ties with the CCP. O. Edmund Clubb, the Consul General in Peking, argued that the withdrawal of ECA from North China (by then controlled by the CCP) wouldunderscore U.S. support for the Nationalists and eliminate a usefulnegotiating point with the Communists. ECA officials, including Administrator Paul G. Hoffman, also believed that the United States should continue distributing aid in Communist areas to demonstrate the nonpolitical nature of the program. Yet authorities in the State Department, including George Kennan, Under Secretary of State Robert A. Lovett, and Director of the Office of Far Eastern Affairs W. Walton Butterworth, contended that Congress and the American public would object to aid of any kind to the Communists. Butterworth himself favored a compromise in December 1948 whereby ECA stocks on hand in Communist-held territories would be distributed, but any ECA shipments en route would be turned back.[67]

The problem of aid to Communist areas came to a head in January 1949, and the hard-liners prevailed. In a meeting in Lovett's office on January 9, Hoffman strongly urged continuation of aid in hopes of minimizing Soviet influence in China. Lovett and Butterworth responded that this course would not only violate the terms of the China Aid Act, but give the wrong signal to the Communists as well:

> Butterworth generally adopted the line that the Communists were going to be beset with economic troubles as soon as they assumed the responsibility of governing important seacoast areas of China. These areas inevitably look toward the West since they depend for their life on external trade. In his opinion, we should make it just as difficult for the Communists as possible, in order to force orientation toward the West. Mr. Hoffman, agreeing that these areas were forced . . . to have contact and trade with the West, emphasized that the best way to take advantage of this favorable factor was to conduct economic operations within China to the extent that the Communists will allow it.
>
> Toward the end of the meeting, Mr. Hoffman summarized the disagreement between the two agencies in the following terms: "You want to walk out of China," he said to Mr. Lovett; "but if we are going to be out of China, I want to be thrown out."[68]

The question of ECA's role on the mainland was closely related to two other issues: aid to Taiwan and the extension of the China Aid Act. During the fall of 1948, the Joint Chiefs of Staff had appraised the State Department of the strategic significance of the island and had recommended economic and diplomatic efforts to prevent its capture by the Communists. In late February 1949, Acheson explored the possibility of detaching Taiwan from the mainland by recognizing an indigenous independence movement. That failing, Acheson avoided any overt action in support of Taiwanese separatism because he did not wish to alienate the Chinese Communists, who were as devoted as the Nationalists to the reincorporation of Taiwan into China.[69]

Acheson recognized that the United States could not significantly influence events in China. Yet he did not consider China to be critical to U.S. security and doubted that the Soviets would be able to control the Chinese Communists. Anticipating the fall of the mainland to the Communists, Acheson supported just enough aid to Chiang's regime so that the United States would not appear responsible for its collapse. At the same time, the Secretary of State wanted to build an offshore U.S. defense perimeter in the Far East with Japan, the Philippines, and perhaps Taiwan (should a non-Communist regime survive) as the core elements.[70]

Meanwhile, the White House sought extension of the China Aid Act, which was scheduled to expire in April 1949. In carrying over the measure to February 1950, the Congress restricted the expenditure of unobligated funds to those "areas in China . . . not under Communist domination," by which the legislators meant to prohibit aid to a coalition government that included the CCP. On the other hand, the White House could assist Taiwan if a non-Communist regime proved viable there.[71]

Perhaps the best opportunity for the opening of ties with the Chinese Communists came in May and June 1949, when an individual claiming to represent the moderate wing of the CCP under Chou En-lai made overtures to Edmund Clubb for U.S. trade. Officials in Washington were wary. From their perspective, the drift of the CCP into the Soviet sphere appeared to be well advanced, if not irreversible. By the spring of 1949, the White House believed that it would be extremely difficult to win Congressional and public support for the normalization of relations with the CCP. In order to authenticate Chou's supposed démarche, the State Department drafted a message for personal delivery to him. When Chou did not come forward, Washington dropped the matter.[72]

The Truman administration probably miscalculated the extent of the CCP's dependence upon Western aid and trade, and hence, its susceptibility to pressure. In late February 1949, the National Security Council (in NSC 41) recommended the use of economic sanctions to win concessions from the Communists. Although U.S. investment in, and trade with, mainland China was insignificant, the NSC reasoned that the new China would need Western and Japanese commerce, capital, and technical aid in order to develop its industry since indigenous (and Soviet) sources of capital were inadequate. In practice, the United States did not restrict the export of military and strategic industrial goods to China before the Korean War as strictly as it did in the case of the Soviet Union and Eastern Europe. SCAP actually promoted Sino-Japanese trade to boost Japanese production. The main goals of the NSC's policy were to slow the movement of the CCP into the Soviet camp and to prevent transshipment of strategic items from China to the Soviet bloc.[73]

As in Europe, the United States could not easily bring its allies into line with its Asian trade controls policy. The British were the chief obstacle to a unified front against Communist China. Given their considerable interests in Hong Kong, Shanghai, and China as a whole (including an estimated 300 million pounds' investment in 1941), the British were understandably reluctant to provoke the new Chinese regime. London wanted foreign banks, utilities, trading and shipping concerns "to keep their foot in the door in China as long as possible." The British also doubted that it was possible to restrict transshipments to the Soviet bloc as long as other Western countries, such as France and the Netherlands, did not cooperate.[74]

The U.S. government was more successful in enlisting private concerns in the service of its policy toward the CCP. While U.S. firms at first suffered from violent labor strikes under the new regime, American businessmen were pleasantly surprised to find that Communist authorities soon restored order and welcomed the continued operation of foreign enterprise in their country, albeit with numerous restrictions. Compared with Chiang's regime, the new China at least offered the possibility of stable economic development and, hence, larger markets for Western entrepreneurs. Big corporations, such as General Electric and Bank of America, favored U.S. recognition of Red China in hopes of fatter profits. As late as 1950, U.S. business still held $180 million (down from $250 million in 1936) in assets on the Chinese mainland. Nevertheless, American businessmen generally followed State Department guidelines and cooperated with its program of economic sanctions against the CCP. When Acheson asked U.S. oil companies to cut shipments to Shanghai in early 1949, for instance, they readily complied despite their concern that strict controls might encourage Chinese dependence upon Soviet imports and hasten the development of a CCP-government monopoly.[75]

The Truman administration also tried to use the prospect of increased Japanese trade as a bargaining lever with the Chinese Communists, notably to win the release of American diplomats held under house arrest in Mukden. (SCAP wished to revive this trade for a more pragmatic reason: to cut occupation costs.) Since Sino-Japanese trade remained extremely depressed compared with prewar levels, however, its utility as a political weapon was not great.[76]

American trade policy toward Communist China did not change markedly before the Korean War. The American officials sought to prohibit trade in strategic items (the "1A" list) while maintaining commerce in civilian items (the "1B" list). As late as December 1949, the NSC reaffirmed the relatively lenient standards of NSC 41 for trade with mainland China. Acheson consistently favored a higher level of trade with the CCP than did other senior U.S. officials because he believed that commerce could help prevent complete Soviet economic domination of the new China.[77]

In hopes of avoiding a complete break with the Chinese Communists, Acheson also pursued a policy of benign neglect toward Taiwan despite pressures from MacArthur, the China Lobby, the JCS, and top defense officials in Washington. Following the Communist takeover of the mainland in the fall of 1949, the Truman administration opposed a Communist conquest of the island and continued to supply the KMT with aid short of heavy military equipment. But the NSC, siding with Acheson against Defense Secretary Johnson, MacArthur, and other military officials, determined in NSC 48/2 (December 1949) that the United States would not militarily defend Taiwan against a CCP attack.[78]

Truman affirmed Acheson's policy in a public statement on January 5, 1950. The United States, he stated, recognized the island as part of China and had no desire to establish military bases on Taiwan "at this time." While Washington would continue to extend nonmilitary aid to the Kuomintang forces on the island, it would avoid direct involvement in the civil war. Truman was less enthusiastic than his Secretary of State about accommodating the Chinese Communists, but he agreed to adopt a wait-and-see attitude toward Taiwan in order to avoid pushing the CCP into a hard and fast alliance with the Soviet Union.[79]

Acheson and his China advisers believed that the ongoing negotiation of a thirty-year, Sino-Soviet Treaty of Friendship, Alliance, and Mutual Assistance (concluded in February 1950) would force the nascent Sino-Soviet rift into the open. In this they were gravely mistaken. Although the protracted and difficult negotiations in Moscow indeed may have sown the seeds of later Sino-Soviet mistrust and conflict, the treaty in the short term tightened the bond between the two countries.[80]

Acheson never lost faith in his ability to drive a wedge between the Chinese and Russians and continued, almost alone in the administration, to oppose a U.S. military commitment to the Nationalist regime on Taiwan. Acheson was fortified in his conviction by estimates from the CIA and other sources during the spring of 1950 that the fall of Taiwan to the Communists was imminent. (One estimate predicted a CCP invasion between mid-June and late July 1950.) Due to his efforts, the United States extricated itself from the Chinese civil war during the first half of 1950.[81]

Conclusion

In a speech before the National Press Club on January 12, 1950, Secretary of State Acheson identified two factors in modern Asia with which the United States would have to contend: "a revulsion against the acceptance of misery and poverty as the normal condition of life," and "the revulsion against foreign domination." To those who sought a deeper U.S. commitment to reverse the tide of Communism in China, Acheson cited the imperialist example of the Soviet Union, which he claimed was about to detach four provinces from China. "We must not undertake to deflect from the Russians to ourselves the righteous anger, and the wrath, and the hatred of the Chinese people which must develop," Acheson stated. After defining the boundaries of the U.S. defense perimeter in the Far East (which included Japan and the Philippines but excluded South Korea, Formosa, and Southeast Asia), Acheson argued that the American ability to influence events in Asia was limited. The United States, he declared, "can not furnish determination, it can not furnish the will, and it can not furnish the loyalty of a people to its government."[82]

Most commentators on Acheson's Press Club speech have focused on the question of whether it prompted the Korean invasion of June 1950. Clearly, the Secretary of State, by deemphasizing the U.S. military commitment to certain countries in the Far East (notably South Korea), sent the wrong signal to the Communist powers in Asia. But since Acheson's intended audience was the American public, he understandably devoted most of his remarks to an explanation of the American failure in China. His main point was an obvious one: U.S. strategic and economic interests in China were insufficient to justify a greater investment of limited national resources. The United States could not sustain commitments in every part of the world.

The problem was that the logic of containment, especially as expressed in the Truman Doctrine, appeared to commit the United States to just such a quest. Stung by defeat in the 1948 elections and frustrated from playing the loyal opposition on European issues, the Republican Party could not resist the political opportunities offered by American setbacks in Asia. Military officials were equally tempted by the expanded military missions and expenditures that a larger U.S. presence in the Far East promised.

While in retrospect the Truman administration might have been more sensitive to the dangers of coupling globalist rhetoric with a policy of limited intervention in East Asia, its policies before the Korean War were on the whole sophisticated. U.S. officials focused their efforts on the countries where American interests, and the prospects for success, were the greatest, that is to say, Japan and the Philippines. And although Kennan's appreciation for the subtleties of Japanese politics left much to be desired, his containment policy did provide a rationale for the eventual reconstruction and integration of Japan into a multilateral world economy. Despite the ambiguity of Acheson's defense perimeter concept, the United States established an offshore defense and economic network in the Far East that would prove remarkably resilient in subsequent years, sometimes in the face of tremendous pressures.

Economic security considerations played a lesser role in East Asia during the 1945–1950 period than they did in Europe. In part, this was due to the smaller U.S. stakes in Asia. The Truman administration was not about to commit aid on the scale of the Marshall Plan to unstable Asian countries where the potential returns were small at best.

The one exception was Japan, but even here, the decision to reconstruct the Japanese economy lagged behind the adoption of the containment doctrine by about two years. At first, Japanese recovery did not appear as vital to U.S. national security as did the eradication of Japanese militarism. Only after Washington policymakers determined that a strong and pro-Western Japan was essential for the containment of Communism in Asia did the rehabilitation of Japan become an important objective of American foreign policy. With her production restored, her raw material supplies assured, and her economy integrated into an interdependent global structure, Japan could both compete peacefully in the world marketplace and act as a bulwark against Communist influence in Asia.

The Truman administration was less successful in China. Despite billions of dollars' worth of aid, the United States failed to maintain the Kuomintang in power. American economic might was also ineffective in influencing the successor regime. As in Eastern Europe, the American policy of progressively severing economic ties failed to win political concessions from the new government. The U.S. inability to prevent an alliance betwen China and Russia, along with the Russian explosion of an atomic device in 1949 and the Korean invasion in 1950, would help undermine the forces in Washington that favored primary reliance upon economic, rather than military, instruments of containment.

CHAPTER NINE

NATURAL RESOURCES AND NATIONAL SECURITY: U.S. POLICY IN THE DEVELOPING WORLD, 1945–1950

AMERICA APPEARED to have become a "have-not" nation in 1945, its self-sufficiency in natural resources at an end. The war had depleted the most accessible reserves of numerous minerals, and many experts concluded that the United States would require increasing raw material imports to survive militarily and economically. Another widely shared view was that the interwar scramble for raw materials had helped to drive the powers (especially the Axis) to war. During the 1930s, the erection of closed spheres in the Third World by Japan and Britain in particular had exacerbated the already tense relations among the powers. An interdependent, multilateralist regime providing for free access to the world's natural resources was thus a key aim of U.S. policy.

A related, and increasingly important, American goal was to protect developing areas from Soviet and Communist encroachment. By promoting development in Third World countries, the Truman administration hoped to immunize pro-Western governments against the "virus" of Communism. Both the Cold War and the raw material imperatives often worked to the advantage of American business concerns as the U.S. government helped them to exploit foreign sources of natural resources. In the Middle East especially, the interests of Washington and Wall Street closely paralleled one another. By expanding abroad, American corporations helped to contain Communism and to meet U.S. commodity needs. Yet the Truman administration, for all of its concern about resource scarcity, did not act decisively to secure its goals in the Third World. While American officials readily disbursed billions in aid to reconstruct the war-torn industrialized countries, they adopted an almost lackadaisical attitude toward the needs of the developing countries and never formulated a coherent energy or materials policy.

America and Mineral "Dependency"

Ironically, the postwar alarm over resource scarcity was partly the result of U.S. abundance. The United States had traditionally enjoyed virtual self-sufficiency in raw materials. Indeed, America became the world's greatest industrial power early in the twentieth century when it was still one of the main producers and exporters of raw materials. In 1913, the United States ranked first in the extraction of lead (30 percent of world production), coal (40 percent), iron (40 percent), copper (55 percent), oil (60 percent), and other minerals.[1]

The First World War demonstrated the importance of ready access to the world's resources and encouraged the major powers, including the United States, to enter into a postwar competition for assured overseas supplies of raw materials. Most of the powers during the interwar period sought either to develop domestic reserves and substitutes (especially Germany) or to stake out exclusive claims to overseas sources of minerals (Britain in the Commonwealth countries, and Britain and France in the Middle East). Others tried to control, exclude, or nationalize foreign investment in domestic resources (Mexico).

The United States opposed the interwar trend. Foreseeing eventual U.S. dependence upon overseas supplies, American minerals experts favored the development of foreign resources on a free-trading, Open Door basis, both to ensure the availability of foreign resources and to avoid the exhaustion of domestic reserves. Washington successfully attacked numerous commodity-control schemes and cartels during the 1920s, and private American investment in foreign minerals grew rapidly during the decade.[2]

American penetration of overseas raw material markets had an important strategic dimension. While per capita U.S consumption of minerals multiplied fifteen times from 1891 to 1931, demand never exceeded supply for most minerals. And during the interwar period, the United States and Great Britain controlled, commercially or militarily, an estimated 48 percent of the world's iron reserves, 53 percent of coal, 74 percent of zinc, 76 percent of petroleum, 79 percent of copper, and 81 percent of lead. Anglo-American naval dominance enabled the Allies to deny overseas supplies of these critical materials to Germany and Japan during the Second World War. Despite serious bottlenecks and shortages early in the war, the United States experienced few lasting supply problems due to the ready availability of Western Hemisphere (including domestic) resources, Allied control of sea routes, and technical advances, such as the development of synthetic rubber.[3]

Why, then, did American officials and minerals experts speak of a "have-not" America after the war? In the first place, the war effort had used up much of the high-grade deposits of domestic minerals. The United States, for example, had supplied about 80 percent of the petroleum products that the Allies consumed from December 1941 to August 1945. American mines had produced three billion tons of coal, 500 million tons of iron ore, five million tons of copper, and 14 million tons of bauxite during the conflict. The quantity of minerals extracted in 1943, the Army-Navy Munitions Board reported, was 57 percent higher than the 1918 level of output and 23 percent higher than the 1929 level. Meanwhile, wartime demand forced the United States to import large quantities of metals for the first time—for example, a fourth of copper consumption and a third of lead and zinc.[4]

Underestimates of current mineral reserves and overestimates of future consumption levels also contributed to the perception of imminent scarcity by some experts and officials, notably conservationist Gifford Pinchot, Interior Secretary Harold Ickes, War Production Board administrator William L. Batt, and Bureau of Mines economist Elmer Pehrson. They pointed out that American industry, especially in the high-technology and armaments fields, depended to an unprecedented extent upon rare, imported minerals. And of the sixty minerals that the United States imported in 1945, twenty-seven were solely available abroad. For countries like Great Britain and Germany, dependence on foreign imports was a familiar fact of life; for the United States, it generated grave concern. As the World Trade Foundation of America, a lobby representing export-import interests, warned in January 1946, "There is no question that we could exist and even have full employment in the United States without imports [of raw materials]. But our standard of living would collapse."[5]

Actually, the American raw materials situation, as the mining industry and the U.S. Geological Survey argued at the end of the war, was not as serious as the pessimists claimed. New technological developments, allowing for more efficient use of, and substitution for, many raw materials (e.g., aluminum for steel), the development of new domestic and foreign supplies (e.g., Middle Eastern oil), and the lifting of wartime price controls that had inhibited production rapidly eased shortages of most materials. Except for a few minerals, the United States faced few absolute deficiencies; rather, cheap foreign imports had partially or wholly displaced domestic production. For instance, this country possessed abundant reserves of bauxite, but aluminum companies could more cheaply mine Jamaican (and other foreign) bauxite than the American deposits. By developing numerous foreign sources of these "scarce" materials, multinational corporations reduced the possibility that the cutoff of any one source could disrupt a key industrial sector in the United States. Indeed, the postwar rise of raw material imports was partly the result of deliberate U.S. efforts to liberalize trade, protect domestic reserves from exhaustion, and boost the income of developing countries.[6]

The strategic implications of the minerals issue were addressed in postwar debates over a national stockpiling program. To spur domestic mineral production, officials from the Interior Department and the Army-Navy Munitions Board lobbied before Congress in 1945 for continued subsidies to domestic mines and for the storage of mass quantities of critical minerals. These steps, they argued, would protect the United States from raw material shortages in a national emergency. The State Department, however, claimed that the government should instead fill the stockpile with lower-cost *imported* minerals in order to conserve domestic reserves, boost overseas production, and stabilize foreign governments.

The State Department ultimately prevailed, and the July 1946 stockpiling law forbade domestic subsidies when cheaper foreign sources of raw materials were available. "We should not hesitate to purchase abroad ample supplies of any materials," Interior Secretary Julius Krug, who had replaced Ickes in March 1946, told crestfallen members of the American Mining Congress in the fall of 1946. "We should encourage American industry to extend its operations in foreign fields as a means of assuring the United States adequate supplies of materials in which we are deficient." Yet the 1946 law did not deliver the comprehensive minerals policy that its proponents had promised. The Congress appropriated far too little in the following years ($100 million in FY 1947 and $175 million in FY 1948) to meet the ambitious stockpiling goals ($360 million annually over five years) set by the Munitions Board.[7]

Minerals and the Cold War, 1947–1948

The Cold War renewed anxieties about scarcities. Commodity prices skyrocketed following the Congressional dismantling of most wartime price controls programs in 1946, and in 1948 the United States became a net importer of oil for the first time. The growing tensions between the Soviet Union and the United States, moreover, closed off some traditional sources of raw materials. At the end of the war, the USSR supplied the United States with one-third of its manganese, half of its chromite, and over half of its platinum. When the West curtailed machinery exports to the Eastern bloc, the Soviet Union retaliated by slashing sales of chromite and manganese in late 1948. The high prices for these materials, however, soon stimulated increased production from alternate foreign and domestic sources.[8]

Washington's response to minerals problems generally developed on an ad hoc basis. But in broad outline, U.S. initatives before Point IV consisted of efforts to protect existing foreign resources against sabotage or nationalization, to develop new overseas sources of raw materials, and to build a larger national stockpile through the use of ECA counterpart funds. American policymakers feared that the Soviets, through control of Communist parties or labor movements in developing countries, could deprive the United States of vital raw materials. A report by the Central Intelligence Agency in November 1947 on Soviet aims in Latin America foresaw little or no possibility of Communist takeovers anywhere in the region. But Communist infiltration of ostensibly nonpolitical groups, such as labor unions, had "already proceeded so far and so effectively that in the event of war with the US, the USSR can, by merely giving the necessary orders, paralyze the economies of Chile and Cuba and thus deny to the US, at least temporarily, the copper and sugar that they would otherwise contribute to the US war effort."[9]

Beginning in 1948, the CIA studied the danger of sabotage to foreign primary producers. In Venezuela, for instance, the American embassy quietly consulted with the Caracas government on steps to protect the oil fields from Communist guerrillas, and U.S. anti-sabotage experts first arrived in that country in October 1948. Although the CIA probably exaggerated the danger, American officials remained deeply concerned about the problem through the 1950s until the national stockpiling program reduced U.S. vulnerability to external pressures.[10]

The Truman administration also tried to use the Marshall Plan as a vehicle to relieve the presumed materials shortage. Anxious about the budgetary and inflationary impact of the European program, many Congressmen demanded, as Senator William F. Knowland (R-Calif.) wrote in the fall of 1947, "a quid pro quo for the American taxpayer and the American economy" before approving the Marshall Plan. Knowland preferred raw materials from the European dependencies as the medium of exchange because "tremendous drains have been made upon the natural resources of this nation as the result of two world wars." Surplus raw materials accumulated in a national stockpile could provide "the difference between victory and defeat . . . in a war wherein we were cut off from world supplies." The Marshall Plan legislation called for the direct transfer of strategic materials from the European Recovery Program (ERP) countries to the United States for stockpiling purposes. American administrators could also use Economic Cooperation Administration (ECA) funds, including counterpart, to purchase materials from, and to expand production in, European dependencies. Finally, the United States won nominal Open Door treatment for American firms operating in participating countries and their dependencies.[11]

The seemingly straightforward language of the ERP act did not offer a simple mandate for the ECA. While the Marshall Plan countries were to spur raw material production, they were not allowed to apply ERP dollars directly to colonial development, especially to prop up their overseas empires. The State Department, for example, prohibited the French from diverting ERP funds to their war in Indochina, although everyone recognized that the Marshall Plan indirectly provided Paris with additional resources to prosecute that conflict.[12]

If the need for certain raw materials were sufficiently acute, the ECA cast aside all pretense of opposing colonial development. American diplomats overlooked the Portuguese diversion of ERP funds to its colonies when Lisbon agreed to keep open rail and port facilities in Mozambique that were critical to trade with Southern Rhodesia, where the ECA hoped to purchase chromite. In order to gain access to Southern Rhodesia's rich raw materials, the ECA also offered loans on very favorable terms for improving roads and railways in the British colony.[13]

The developmental and stockpiling programs of ECA fell far short of expectations. ECA officials found it difficult to supervise production in faraway European colonies, and they hesitated to starve Europe of materials necessary for recovery. Consequently, the aid agency spent little of the counterpart funds to purchase scarce materials.[14]

U.S. Aid and Trade Policies Toward the Developing Countries, 1945–1948

Despite its desire for new sources of raw materials, the Truman administration did not offer the developing countries a Marshall Plan of their own. True, the ECA administered aid programs in certain Asian countries (mainland China until late 1949, South Korea, Burma, Indochina, Thailand, and the Philippines). But these were very small, technical aid projects that were designed to complement military aid and "defense support" programs, rather than comprehensive development packages.[15]

American officials claimed that the recovery of the European industrial states (traditionally very important customers of the less developed countries, or "LDCs") would quickly restore lagging exports and production in the Third World. From Washington's perspective, the developing countries needed to create a more favorable investment climate for private enterprise and to expand exports by liberalizing trade. The LDCs, however, were less concerned about expanding the volume of exports (though that was important) than with stabilizing commodity prices and substituting native products for imports through industrialization. At the Havana Conference (November 1947 to March 1948), which was convened to consider the formation of an International Trade Organization, the LDCs demanded the right to protect "infant industries" against foreign (especially U.S.) imports. The Latin American officials also questioned American claims that the Marshall Plan, with its promise of $2.6 billion in offshore purchases for their countries, obviated the need for national economic planning and industrial self-sufficiency. The United States, in turn, attacked its southern neighbors at Havana for discriminating against American business and joining in restrictive commodity agreements.[16]

The State Department also sought to negotiate new bilateral treaties of Friendship, Commerce, and Navigation (FCNs) and conventions against double taxation with the LDCs. The primary purpose of these devices was to promote U.S. business investment in those countries by insuring that American firms received the same treatment as local enterprises. (The State Department also assured American businessmen that Point IV and other U.S. aid programs would in no way "crowd out" private investment in the LDCs.) The FCNs were a resounding flop: only eight countries—Ethiopia, Greece, Iran, Israel, Korea, Muscat and Oman, Nicaragua, and Pakistan—had ratified the treaties by 1963.[17]

Foreign aid was not a major feature of the Truman administration's plan for economic development. American officials believed that the LDCs should develop indigenous capital, labor, and natural resources before coming hat-in-hand to Washington. Presumably, trade liberalization would raise export income, which in turn would pay for imports of manufactured goods. (The United States would reciprocate by lowering barriers to imports from the LDCs.) If they improved the climate for foreign investment, U.S. diplomats argued, the emerging nations could also expect an influx of capital from the IBRD, the U.S. government, and private sources.[18]

Neither the World Bank nor private investors met the expectations or needs of the LDCs. To begin with, the limited public capital that Washington channeled through the IBRD and the Eximbank consisted largely of "hard" loans tied to specific projects with fairly strict conditions attached. The Bank of the 1940s adopted a tough stance toward the LDCs because it could not raise funds on Wall Street, then virtually the only source of venture capital, until it established itself as a hard-headed, profit-minded institution. With New York lawyer John J. McCloy as its president and financier Eugene R. Black as its U.S. director, the IBRD offered loans only to countries that were solid credit risks. And although the Bank's charter prohibited "political" loans, politics inevitably influenced its policies. To American bankers, the "creditworthiness" of an applicant often depended upon its stability and receptivity to capitalist modernization. To counter the restrictive practices of many LDCs, the IBRD of the late 1940s adopted a policy of "strategic nonlending," the denial of loans to LDCs that did not welcome private investment and trade. In an August 1948 statement of U.S. foreign credit and investment policy, for instance, the State Department and the National Advisory Council—which controlled U.S. policies in the Bank—declared that Washington would favor private investment and IBRD loans over U.S. governmental loans to promote development. Before extending foreign loans, the United States would carefully scrutinize a country's external debt, its treatment of American property (especially nationalized assets), and its policy toward state enterprises.[19]

The response of private investors was also less than enthusiastic. Total U.S. direct investment abroad grew very little during the war, and in 1946, it dropped to 3.4 percent as a proportion of GNP, its lowest point during this century. In this climate, the lion's share of new U.S. investment in the LDCs went toward the development of petroleum reserves, where the returns were the highest. American investment in LDC manufacturing enterprises rose more slowly.[20]

Thanks to the U.S. Congress, a final disappointment lay in store for the LDCs. American tariffs dropped sharply during the initial postwar years, but since they had been extraordinarily high during the 1930s (an average of 30 percent and up *ad valorem*), the U.S barriers were still steep enough to exclude many imports (especially finished goods) from the developing countries. The LDCs had counted on income from exports to the United States to help finance imports of machinery and other goods; increased dollar earnings would have also strengthened their ability to service foreign debt, and thus attract foreign investors. By retaining substantial trade barriers against the LDCs and by scuttling the International Trade Organization, Congress undermined the Truman administration's already modest development program for the Third World.[21]

Point IV

The one great exception to this pattern was supposed to be Point IV, so named because it was the fourth of four new proposals to achieve "peace and freedom" in President Truman's Inaugural Address of January 21, 1949. Point IV sprang from a mixture of motives: to provide the LDCs with technology and management, stem Communism in the Third World, safeguard U.S. foreign investment, and increase production of strategic materials. (The new program was also a security measure. Congressmen "opposing the Program were those always trying for economy," Truman once told the NSC, "but . . . this would be false economy since the Point IV Program would save us tremendous war expenditures in the long run.")

The President believed that the history of the United States offered valuable clues to how the LDCs could escape poverty and backwardness. In the first place, Truman argued, the developing countries needed to attract foreign capital, just as the United States had during the nineteenth century. As Truman later explained to an aide, the "specific origin of Point 4" was his conviction that the LDCs could never start up the slope of development unless they were willing "to guarantee they would not confiscate risk capital invested in those countries." "All they need is the knowhow and the proper incentives for private investment," he concluded. Truman told his Cabinet that

This country would seek of the foreign country assurances of a stable government and support for the plan and the work would be largely through private enterprise. The private concerns would be required to give assurances that they would not exploit the foreign country into which they went but would operate to the benefit of that country. He said that this is already being done to a degree in Arabia where the oil companies are being called upon to give more for the benefit of the people.[22]

Point IV would not displace private U.S. investment in the developing countries. Anticipating complaints from the private sector about the program, a State Department official observed in December 1948 that in "the long run, it has been our experience that scientific and technical assistance has opened the way for U.S. private activity, has created demands for U.S. products, and has resulted in contracts for additional assistance from private firms."[23]

As was often the case with foreign aid programs, translating ideas into practice proved very difficult. The Point IV program had caught Dean Acheson, who had returned to the State Department to replace George C. Marshall as Secretary of State, completely by surprise. The first Acheson heard of Point IV was when he "came on the platform in front of the Capitol listening to the President expound it in his inaugural address." An internal State Department memo in January 1949 argued that the "expanded scale and emphasis" of the new program called for "immediate, broad scale action" with a "substantial increase" of technical aid to the LDCs. Yet Acheson was notably unenthusiastic about the program in his first press conference as Secretary.[24]

The program soon became "bogged down in a mire of words," according to White House aide David D. Lloyd. An interdepartmental committee that Acheson set up in February 1949 to examine Point IV spent months wrangling over the nature, size, and administration of the program. The fact that more than two dozen U.S. governmental and

UN agencies already administered various forms of technical and educational aid complicated the committee's task. For his part, Acheson argued in a March 1949 memo to the President that technical aid would spur development only if the LDCs were willing to help themselves and encourage foreign investment:

> The introduction of new techniques can advance economic development most if capital investment is taking place at the same time. Most of this capital, however, must come from domestic [LDC] sources, and measures will be needed to foster domestic capital formation as well as to attract private capital from abroad. . . . Activities under the Point IV Program should not be allowed to give an impression that this Government has thereby obligated itself to supply the funds needed to finance development.[25]

Point IV evolved during the spring of 1949 into an instrument primarily, if not wholly, for the benefit of U.S. business in the underdeveloped world. Groups such as the National Association of Manufacturers and the U.S. Associates of the International Chamber of Commerce pressed the administration to safeguard American investment in the LDCs. The National Advisory Council agreed that a U.S. guaranty program and FCN treaties were necessary to encourage additional private investment in those countries. In his message to Congress in June 1949 recommending Point IV legislation, Truman asked for $45 million in U.S. aid and for Eximbank guarantees of any private projects designed to advance development in the Third World.[26]

Despite valiant efforts by Under Secretary of State Willard Thorp and others, Point IV "remained the Cinderella of the foreign aid family," in Acheson's words. Organizational and jurisdictional problems—within the State Department, between the State and Commerce Departments, and among other agencies—had plagued the program from the start. The Congress was reluctant to approve Point IV, for the nation's legislators believed that private companies should supply most technical expertise to developing countries. The U.S. government, it followed, should furnish technical aid only in those rare cases where, through no fault of the recipient government, private investment was absolutely unavailable. Consequently, the Congress authorized only $34.5 million for Point IV during its first year of operation and did not vote appropriations until September 1950.[27]

Point IV and the American plan for economic development fell far short of expectations. In the first place, the Truman administration did not recognize the special needs of individual LDCs and attempted to impose the U.S. model of economic growth upon countries with vastly different resources and institutions. In particular, foreign investment did not always distribute jobs and income throughout the host countries as promised. Foreign-owned industries tended to remain isolated outposts within the LDC economies, with much of their production reserved for exports and their profits repatriated to the United States (or other developed countries). In extreme cases, such as the "banana republics" of Central America, developing countries became locked into the production of a few cash crops, with almost the entire market controlled by U.S.-based companies. Moreover, the terms of trade had turned heavily against the LDCs. As an American economist observed in May 1950, "The industrialized countries have had the best of both worlds, both as consumers of primary commodities and as producers of manufactured articles, whereas the underdeveloped countries have had the worst of both worlds, as consumers of manufactures and as producers of raw materials."[28]

The Truman administration's plan for development rested upon fragile political assumptions as well, notably the belief that foreign investment and economic expansion would promote world peace and democracy. In remarks before the American Society of Civil Engineers in November 1949, for instance, President Truman speculated that if technical aid helped to raise the LDCs' standard of living by just 2 percent,

> our factories and our businesses never could catch up with the demand that would be on them. Just think of that! That's all we need to do. . . . There are resources in this great world that never have been touched. . . . And if those resources produce things for the welfare of the people of the world, to keep the world from being hungry, then no one would have any idea of carrying on a destructive war for the purpose of obtaining something that didn't belong to them. That's what the cause of wars has been. It has been the idea of grasping something that the other fellow has.[29]

Truman was reiterating the familiar notion that economic nationalism and depression caused wars. Growth along capitalist and free-trading lines, he believed, would produce stable, democratic governments that shared U.S. interests. In the context of the Cold War, this meant that the developing countries would help contain Communism.

Yet for these ambitious objectives, the administration asked for only $45 million in Point IV aid (and received only $34.5 million). As Robert

Packenham notes, there was "thus a huge gap between the goals of the program—both the strictly economic goals and the more grandiose political developmental goals—and the potential of the instrument of technical assistance for achieving them." Neither the administration nor the Congress ever seriously examined whether foreign aid truly promoted democracy, or whether, for that matter, capitalist growth necessarily fostered peace-loving and stable governments in the developing world.[30]

By the late 1940s, Packenham observes, U.S. aid policy in the Third World was characterized by two tendencies. The economic approach stressed the importance of American assistance in stimulating growth, for prosperous countries were presumed to be stable and peaceful. The Cold War approach complemented the economic one, but stressed the short-term dividends of foreign aid, notably the containment of Communism. In the latter view, the United States should expect to receive concrete *quid pro quos* from its aid programs, such as military base rights and a reliable supply of strategic raw materials.[31] Cold War aims would increasingly dominate the Truman administration's agenda in Latin America and the Middle East.

U.S. Economic Diplomacy in Latin America, 1945–1950

Latin America emerged from the war more dependent upon U.S. trade, capital, and military assistance than ever before.[32] Cut off from their traditional European customers during the war, the Latin American countries had had no choice but to turn to the United States for manufactured goods. The war, however, preempted much of the machinery that Latin America wished to import from Europe and the United States for industrialization purposes. For its part, the United States needed only a few of the commodities—tin, oil, coffee, among others—that its southern neighbors had to offer. Wartime U.S. contracts and subsidies helped concentrate Latin American production in a few sectors. Critics claimed that the U.S. policy on commodity purchases followed a double standard. During the war, Washington policymakers had engaged in state-trading in order to buy raw materials from Latin America at below-market prices. But after the Allied victory, these same American officials had insisted upon restoring the free market in commodities. The result was disastrous for Latin America. Raw material prices plunged while the cost of manufactured imports soared, forcing countries like Bolivia to the edge of bankruptcy. The $3.4

billion trade surplus that Latin American countries had earned during the war quickly evaporated. No wonder, then, that Washington's periodic pronouncements on the virtues of free trade encountered much cynicism in Latin American capitals.[33]

U.S. direct investment south of the border climbed steadily from 1940 ($2.8 billion) to 1950 ($4.4 billion), but it was concentrated in a few industries, notably oil, rayon, rubber, iron and steel, whose impact on overall growth was limited. The rise of American investment, moreover, was partially offset by the rapid decline of the European economic presence in the region. British public and private investment in Latin America shrank from $636 million in late 1945 to $244 million in late 1951.[34]

Unwilling to offer major aid programs, Washington advertised private channels of trade and investment as the solution to Latin America's problems. In drafting an agreement on regional economic cooperation at the Bogota Conference in 1948, for example, Washington sought to bind the Latin Americans to Open Door principles. The Latin American representatives, however, affirmed the right of their governments to smooth out "dislocations" in the raw materials trade and to discriminate against imports from "other countries" (i.e., the United States). While the U.S. delegates promised to increase Eximbank loans to Latin America, the Truman administration rejected the call for sweeping reforms, and the Bogota Economic Agreement went unratified.[35]

The exigencies of the Cold War, rather than developmental or other economic aims, would increasingly dictate U.S. policies toward Latin America. After the war, Pentagon planners looked for means to preserve the region's strategic resources for use by the United States and its allies in wartime. In the Rio Treaty of September 1947, the United States pledged to use force, if necessary, to prevent "external" interference in the region. Local, U.S.-trained forces would provide internal security. The Bogota Conference, establishing the Organization of American States (OAS), appeared to curb U.S. prerogatives. Article 15 of the OAS Charter expressly prohibited any state from intervening militarily or otherwise "for any reason whatever, in the internal or external affairs of any other State." Yet the charter also permitted undefined "measures" to maintain "peace and security in accordance with existing treaties," a loophole that the United States would later cite when it militarily intervened in certain Caribbean and Central American countries.[36]

In South America, Washington mostly relied upon political and economic, rather than military, instruments to achieve its ends. U.S. relations with Argentina are a case in point. Reviled for its cooperation with the Axis during World War II, the Argentine junta did not break relations with Germany and Japan until early 1944, and the reluctance of Buenos Aires to declare war on the Axis at that time prompted Washington to withdraw its ambassador and impose economic sanctions against Argentina. The ties between the two countries were finally restored when Argentina belatedly declared war on Germany and Japan in March 1945, and for a brief interval, relations appeared to be on the mend.[37]

Yet Argentina would remain a thorn in America's side. In part, the problem was due to the perception in Washington that the Buenos Aires junta and its elected successor, the government of President Juan Domingo Peron (1946–1955), had fascist tendencies—seen in its tight controls over the press and the Axis sympathizers within its ranks. Less justifiably, U.S. diplomats, notably Spruille Braden, the U.S. Ambassador to Argentina (April–August 1945) and the Assistant Secretary of State for Latin American Affairs (October 1945–June 1947), charged that Peron's economic reforms threatened American merchants and investors.

It is true that the Peronists were pledged to economic independence, notably the end of foreign domination of public transportation, utilities, and other key sectors of the economy. Yet the roots of Argentina's economic nationalism lay in her severe balance-of-payments problems rather than a deep-seated antipathy toward foreign business. Peron's highly ambitious, $1.5 billion, Five-Year Plan (announced in October 1946) called for rapid industrialization and expanded social welfare programs. Since so much of her foreign reserves consisted of British sterling and other inconvertible currencies, Argentina could not readily buy the machinery and equipment that it sorely needed from the United States. Increasing exports would not necessarily solve the problem, for the United States had little use for the meat and cereals that Argentina had to offer. To conserve dollars, the Peron government was forced to discriminate against U.S. imports. Thus, Washington's repeated calls for the liberalization of trade fell on deaf ears.[38]

U.S. relations with Argentina sharply deteriorated in 1947, when Peron, seeking to boost oil workers' wages, raised the specter of expropriation against U.S. petroleum companies. Buenos Aires also retaliated against alleged U.S. curbs on agricultural machinery sales by refusing to cooperate in international relief efforts to supply grain to

Europe. In a skillful exploitation of Americans' Cold War fears, the Argentines hinted that they might trade their grain for Soviet equipment.[39]

The Marshall Plan aggravated the situation by diverting scarce U.S. capital goods to Europe. The Argentines at first had hoped that ECA purchases of their farm products would help solve their dollar problem. Yet the House Select Committee on Foreign Aid (Herter Committee) specifically prohibited the use of ERP funds to assist Latin America. And by tying ERP funds to procurement in the United States and Europe, Washington undercut Argentine trade with Europe, helping precipitate a foreign exchange and debt crisis beginning in mid-1948. In December 1948, the ECA finally promised Buenos Aires $100 million in offshore purchases. Yet U.S. officials had overestimated ECA procurement levels, and in February 1949, the American ambassador informed the Peron government that it would be June 1950 before ECA expenditures would reach even $8 million. What little Marshall Plan money reached Argentina had to be used to pay for its debts to the United States.[40]

The turning point in U.S. relations with Peron came in early 1949, when Argentina, unable to meet payments on the $300 million that it owed U.S. banks, plunged into a severe financial crisis.[41] Peron hinted that he might expropriate certain American properties, including meat-packing plants, if Washington did not offer him financial aid. U.S. officials, notably Secretary of State Dean Acheson, bristled at the Argentine president's implicit blackmail, but they feared that an economic collapse might bring to power someone even worse than Peron.[42]

U.S. diplomats, in fact, had long sought a reconciliation with Peron because he appeared to be a relative moderate among Argentine nationalists and an important ally against Communism in Latin America. More than once, Peron had encouraged this image of himself by telling U.S. representatives that he detested Communism and would closely align his country with the United States in any conflict with the Soviet Union. His public railing against Yankee imperialism, he explained, was a mere propaganda ploy to appease the hard-liners within his own party.[43]

Cold War realities and economic necessity finally drove the two countries together. George F. Kennan laid down the new line to the U.S. ambassadors in South America during a visit to Rio in March 1950. "It is better to have a strong regime in power," he stated, "than a liberal government if it is indulgent and relaxed and penetrated by Communists." For their part, Peron and his ministers apparently recognized that they themselves were largely responsible for their country's woes, and that U.S. trade policy was only a contributing cause. From October 1949 to October 1950, the United States and Argentina concluded a series of agreements. In return for American aid, the Argentines agreed to cease discrimination against U.S. imports and to withdraw the threat of nationalization against U.S. property. Following the Eximbank's offer of a $125 million loan, Buenos Aires ratified the Rio Treaty in June 1950. While the two countries had by no means resolved all of their differences, the United States had at least succeeded in integrating Argentina into a loose multilateral association of American states.[44]

Washington's tempestuous relations with Buenos Aires were exceptional in at least one respect: the Truman administration's approach to Latin America was more often characterized by benign neglect than active intervention. U.S. governmental grants and credits to the twenty Latin American republics from 1945 to 1950 totalled only $400 *million*, compared with $19 *billion* to Western Europe during the same period. From 1948 to 1957, Latin America received only 2.4 percent of all U.S. aid, less than any other region.[45]

U.S. Development of Oil in the Middle East, 1945–1950

In contrast, Washington took bold and far-reaching action in the Middle East. More than any other resource, petroleum symbolized the nexus of foreign economic and national security concerns. Oil was the essential resource of modern warfare, and the Allies' ability to control the bulk of world reserves and production was a crucial factor in their victory over the Axis. Yet the war had also stimulated widespread concern in the U.S. government and the petroleum industry over the early exhaustion of reserves in the Western Hemisphere, notably the United States and Venezuela. Indeed, while the United States had produced about 60 percent of world oil during the 1930s, it held only about 15 percent of global reserves, and they were shrinking rapidly. This country had supplied six billion out of the seven billion barrels of oil that the Allies had consumed during the war. With discoveries of new domestic reserves declining, American planners correctly predicted that the United States would soon become a net importer.[46]

America's emerging energy dependency led U.S. officials to look toward the Middle East, repository of the world's largest untapped reserves of oil. An increased flow of oil from this source, they reasoned, would boost West European recovery after the war and reduce the drain on Western Hemisphere reserves. Fortunately, American oil men had already won important concessions in the Persian Gulf. In May 1933, the Standard Oil Company of California (Socal) had gained exclusive rights from the Saudi king, Ibn Saud ('Abd al-'Aziz), to develop petroleum in an area larger than Texas in return for a few hundred thousand dollars cash and a royalty rate of about ten cents per barrel. Socal enlisted the oil marketing giant, the Texas Company (later Texaco), into its Saudi venture in 1936, and by 1940, their subsidiary was producing a modest five million barrels annually, compared with almost 1.5 billion barrels by U.S. wells in that year.[47]

The war cut Saudi exports and precipitated a financial crisis in the Arab kingdom. Rather than risk an isolationist backlash by offering Lend-Lease to Saudi Arabia (hardly a "democratic" nation) in 1941, President Roosevelt asked the British to assume 90 percent of Ibn Saud's budget for the duration of the war. Since London was a Lend-Lease recipient, it was widely understood that the help came from Washington.[48]

The United States quickened its efforts to improve ties with Saudi Arabia as the war underscored the strategic importance of that country's huge oil reserves. In February 1943, President Roosevelt declared Saudi Arabia eligible for Lend-Lease. Three months later, the U.S. Navy estimated that the Middle East held at least 56 billion barrels of oil, and that Saudi Arabia alone contained more oil (22 billion barrels) than America (20 billion). "In Saudi Arabia," the State Department's Chief of the Division of Near Eastern Affairs informed his superiors at the end of the war, "the oil resources constitute a stupendous source of strategic power, and one of the greatest material prizes in world history."[49]

The most ambitious effort to secure U.S. interests in Saudi Arabia was led by Harold L. Ickes, the Secretary of the Interior. As early as 1941, Ickes had recognized the importance of expanding overseas oil production to supplement declining U.S. reserves. The government, he believed, should undertake Arabian oil development because the oil companies would not expand production swiftly enough to meet post-war European demand, let alone U.S. needs in another war. In 1943, Ickes won Roosevelt's support for a Petroleum Reserves Corporation (PRC) that was authorized to buy out the Socal-Texas interests in Saudi Arabia, as well as the substantial holdings by U.S. companies in

Bahrain and Kuwait. The government came very near to closing a deal
with Socal and Texas, but other major oil companies, notably the Standard Oil Company (New Jersey) and the Socony-Vacuum Oil Company
(later Mobil), mobilized sufficient support in the Congress to kill the
measure.[50]

The Anglo-American Oil Agreements of 1944–45 fared little better.
The immediate objective of the talks, a State Department memo reveals, was "to improve . . . relations with the British . . . so that petroleum resources controlled by United States nationals could be
produced on a larger scale without restrictions and interferences." In
the longer term, Washington wished to shift "the geographic pattern of
production" to conserve Western Hemisphere resources. Another aim,
less often verbalized, was to avoid unrestrained production and cut-
throat competition, such as might occur in a pure free-market environment. In the end, the Anglo-American Oil Agreements, as well as the
administration's proposal in 1944 for a trans-Arabian pipeline, foundered on the shoals of the independent U.S. oil companies, the antitrust
philosophy of the Justice Department, and the State Department's policy of not favoring one corporate interest over another. Nonetheless, the
wartime talks laid the basis for the informal division of the Middle East
into postwar spheres of influence—the British predominant in Iran and
Iraq, the United States predominant in the rest of the Gulf—and for
later Anglo-American cooperation to contain the Soviets in the region.[51]

With the failure of the PRC and the Anglo-American agreements,
U.S. policy decisively shifted. Washington still wanted to boost Mideastern production and to retain the Saudi concession in American
hands, Irvine H. Anderson has demonstrated, but the means had
changed. The United States returned to its traditional Open Door,
privatist approach to investment and trade in the Middle East: the oil
companies, rather than the government, were expected to act as the
vanguard of U.S. interests in the Middle East. As Secretary of the Navy
James V. Forrestal wrote in May 1945, he did not "care which American
company or companies develop the Arabian reserves" as long as they
were "*American.*"[52]

In critical instances, the State Department helped the petroleum
corporations consolidate their position in the Persian Gulf. To promote
more rapid exploitation of Saudi reserves and to satisfy Ibn Saud's
desire for greater revenues, State and Navy officials in the spring of
1945 privately encouraged the Socal-Texas subsidiary, by then called

the Arabian-American Oil Company or Aramco, to seek a partnership with Socony-Vacuum and Standard Oil (New Jersey). "Not only was the government in favor of broadening participation in the concession," Anderson comments, "but it was on the verge of serving as a marriage broker." Socony and Jersey, it was hoped, could provide the much-needed capital and marketing outlets that Aramco needed to exploit the Saudi bonanza. Equally important, the Aramco partners, by controlling Gulf production, could prevent cheap Mideastern oil from flooding world markets; at about 90 cents per barrel, Arabian crude easily undersold oil from Latin American or U.S. wells ($1.28).

The Justice, War, and Interior Departments gave their blessings to the Aramco merger in December 1946. (By coincidence, Jersey and Socony concluded the Aramco agreement on March 12, 1947, the very day of the Truman Doctrine speech. The actual merger was consummated in December 1948.) Socal, Texas, and Jersey each took a 30 percent share in the consortium, while Socony—whose president feared that investment in Mideastern oil "was not absolutely safe"—settled for 10 percent.

In 1947, Aramco began construction on a trans-Arabian pipeline connecting Persian Gulf oil fields with port facilities in Sidon, Lebanon. At a cost of $201 million, the 1,068-mile pipeline, capable of moving 300,000 barrels per day, was completed in September 1950. The first tanker was loaded three months later.[53]

In at least one other instance of governmental-corporate cooperation, U.S. officials in 1950 worked behind the scenes to strengthen the ties between the oil companies and the Saudi king. Even with the vastly increased royalties from the Aramco oil fields—production grew over four hundred times between 1938 and 1950 to 200 million barrels annually—Ibn Saud's hunger for higher revenues did not abate. Like the Venezuelans, who had negotiated a new agreement with U.S. oil companies in 1948, the Saudis sought a share of Aramco's overall profits, rather than royalties determined by a rate on each barrel of oil sold. In November 1950, amid the tensions of the Korean War, George C. McGhee, the Assistant Secretary of State for Near Eastern, South Asian, and African Affairs, met with representatives of Aramco's parent companies and strongly urged them to accept the Venezuelan formula. Recalling the Mexican expropriation of the 1920s, McGhee feared that a tougher negotiating position by the oil companies might arouse Arab ultra-nationalists and open the region to Soviet influence. (For similar reasons, Secretary of State George C. Marshall and Under

Secretary Robert A. Lovett had opposed President Truman's hasty recognition of Israel in May 1948.) In late December, Aramco and Saudi officials agreed that the oil group would pay a 50 percent tax on its net operating income. The "fifty-fifty agreement of 1950" ensured harmonious relations between the United States and the Arab kingdom for many years to come. The wisdom of this course can be best appreciated by contrasting the American experience in Saudi Arabia with the British one in Iran, where the Anglo-Iranian Oil Company's unwillingness to compromise with Iranian nationalists helped spark a violent, xenophobic revolution in the early 1950s.[54]

Historians still hotly debate whether or not the cartel-like practices of the majors violated U.S. antitrust laws. The least that can be said is that the Truman administration (and later, the Eisenhower administration) did not press the matter. Aramco, for instance, wrote off the taxes that it paid Saudi Arabia against its U.S. tax liability. The Truman White House apparently did not, as critics have charged, pressure the Internal Revenue Service on behalf of the oil companies; the IRS did not approve Aramco's procedure until 1955. But State Department officials did not object when oil company representatives brought up the idea of a tax break in the fall of 1950. The Truman administration probably accepted the practice because Aramco's tax payments made it possible to bolster the Saudi regime without having to ask the Congress for new foreign aid appropriations.[55]

Indeed, while the Truman administration had privately done much to improve ties with Saudi Arabia, it had great difficulty finding a politically acceptable way to funnel official aid to the desert nation. President Truman extended Lend-Lease to Saudi Arabia into early 1946 and diverted War Department funds toward the construction of an airfield at Dhahran. After long and tortuous negotiations, the Eximbank also offered a $10 million credit to Saudi Arabia in August 1946 and approved another $15 million for the development of Saudi transportation in October 1946. Yet Washington turned down further requests for economic aid and arms, urging the Saudi government to rely upon private investment for its income.[56]

Even more remarkable was the virtual absence of U.S. military forces in the Persian Gulf. As usual, the Truman administration was more willing to undertake new commitments abroad than to provide the funding to protect them. In early 1948, for instance, the Navy estimated that it would take at least six divisions to defend the oil fields in the Gulf, but given other U.S. responsibilities abroad, only one reinforced Marine battalion was available for dispatch from Guam to Bahrain at that time. Thus, the National Security Council (in NSC 26) called in that year for preparations to destroy all above-ground facilities in order to deny the Saudi oil fields to the Soviets in the event of war. Significantly, in a conference at Istanbul in November 1949, the U.S. chiefs of mission in the Near East concluded that the United States should not ratify military pacts with Mideastern countries. Washington could best support regional stability, the American diplomats determined, by promoting social and economic development with Point IV and other aid, including modest amounts of military assistance.[57]

To an extraordinary extent, certainly unequalled in any other part of the world, private individuals and firms acted as the agents of U.S. policy in the Middle East. The government supported corporate interests because they were serving U.S. national security. In building the Arabian pipeline, American oil companies enhanced U.S. prestige and security at minimal cost to the government. The pipeline also brought revenues to pro-Western regimes in the Middle East and supplied oil to fuel West European recovery. (Mideastern oil grew in importance as European industry converted from coal to oil.) The drain on Western Hemisphere reserves also was slowed. In 1938, the Eastern Hemisphere had provided only 11.5 percent of the non-Communist world's crude oil needs, compared with 88.5 percent by the Western Hemisphere. By 1965, the East, largely the Persian Gulf, was producing 46.4 percent, and the West 53.6 percent of the total.[58] Working together, American diplomats and oil men had secured vital U.S. strategic interests.

Failure to Develop a Coherent Energy and Materials Policy

While the monumental oil deals of American companies brilliantly served U.S. aims in the Middle East, they carried a price. "As national interests thus became more and more interwoven with the interests of private enterprise," Michael Stoff argues, "the wartime effort to define and to carry out a coherent foreign oil policy fell to pieces." The traditional American aversion to governmental planning and control over the economy strongly reasserted itself after the war. As the multinational corporations gained autonomy, they would impede the formulation and implementation of a comprehensive U.S. energy policy.[59]

The case of oil imports during the late 1940s illustrates the problem. The quantities in question (160 million barrels in 1947 and 310 million barrels in 1950, offset in part by U.S. oil exports) were a mere trickle compared with the deluge that would follow. Yet U.S. officials recognized that American dependence upon foreign oil would inexorably grow, eventually posing the danger that U.S. energy supplies could be cut off in wartime.

The plethora of interests involved in energy issues obstructed planning. The main coal- and oil-producing states, the independent (U.S.-based) oil companies, and the coal industry strongly opposed oil imports. Oil distributors, on the other hand, favored unlimited purchases of foreign oil, the better to crush their gas and coal competitors. The major oil companies producing abroad, notably the Aramco partners, held a middle position. They desired *limited* imports—enough to pay for their heavy overseas investment, but not enough to cause a precipitous drop in crude prices and a subsequent displacement of their domestic production.

The national debate over oil imports was carried on in governmental agencies as well. The State Department, as usual the champion of multilateralism, favored heavier importation of foreign crude because it would stimulate world trade, lower prices, and promote conservation of Western Hemisphere reserves. In terms of national security, however, the argument cut both ways. As the Interior Department concluded in the summer of 1950, oil imports might preserve U.S. holdings, but they might also discourage domestic production and increase U.S. dependence on overseas supplies. The Korean War intervened before President Truman could reach a decision on the issue, but interest-group pressure and the multitude of governmental agencies responsible for oil policy probably would have precluded the formulation of a coherent policy.[60]

The pattern of limited national planning extended to other areas as well. The American synthetic fuels industry died in its infancy due to market forces (the glut of cheap oil and natural gas), Congressional hostility, and the competing demands of rearmament following the Korean invasion. Until the Korean War, national stockpiling also proceeded slowly.[61]

The President's Materials Policy Commission (PMPC), or "Paley Commission" as it was popularly known, marked the most serious effort by the Truman administration to devise a comprehensive materials policy. Prompted by commodity shortages during the Korean War, President Truman established the PMPC in January 1951 to investigate America's long-term requirements in raw materials. The Paley Commission recognized the strategic dimensions of resource problems. "A strong economy is in itself our greatest security asset," a PMPC staff member observed in the early stages of the commission's work. But "to the extent the United States turns increasingly abroad for supplies of important industrial materials we are confronted increasingly with security problems in event of war."[62]

The Paley Commission forecast a geometrical growth in U.S. consumption of materials coupled with rising dependence on imported commodities. Generally, the PMPC opposed extensive governmental intervention in the marketplace. While the commission's experts forecast a doubling of energy requirements by 1975, they assumed that technical advances and substitutability among fuels would safeguard America's energy future.

To spur development of foreign materials, the PMPC favored greater U.S. private investment in the developing countries. Specifically, the commission recommended that Washington conclude FCN treaties and taxation conventions with the LDCs, offer technical aid to resource-rich countries, and create a permanent U.S foreign materials agency. (The PMPC also supported international agreements to stabilize commodity prices, a step that would have met a key demand of the LDCs.) Finally, the Paley Commission strongly advocated obtaining materials from least-cost sources. In effect, it rejected national self-sufficiency and endorsed free trade and interdependence in raw materials.

The PMPC recognized that private capital could not always fulfill the investment needs of the developing countries and that U.S. governmental aid was necessary to boost overseas mineral production. Reflecting the infighting within the Truman administration over Point IV, the Paley Commission failed to reach a consensus on the relative importance of the public and private sectors in foreign development. It was also symptomatic of the administration's policy toward materials questions as a whole that the PMPC's report was released too late (June 1952) for the White House to implement any of its major recommendations.[63]

Conclusion

The Second World War highlighted the strategic importance of minerals and the growing dependence of the United States upon foreign sources of them. Given its immense economic and military power, the United States probably could have met its raw material needs through a combination of various subsidies and protectionist measures to spur domestic production and the erection of exclusive U.S. spheres of influence in important materials-producing regions. With the exception of oil, however, the Truman administration took few decisive steps to achieve security in the minerals field. Instead, Washington officials generally promoted the Open Door in the Third World in order to accelerate the development of raw materials and to preclude another global struggle for natural resources by the powers. A plentiful and accessible supply of raw materials would promote the prosperity and stability of the Western industrial democracies and Japan while foreign trade and investment, especially from private sources, would stimulate economic and political development in the Third World.[64]

Political and strategic factors, especially with the advent of the Cold War, usually determined U.S. policies in developing countries. In Washington's dealings with Buenos Aires, for instance, the need for hemispheric unity took precedence over the quest for economic multilateralism. Postwar U.S. security and economic interests neatly coincided in the Persian Gulf. But in instances where U.S. strategic and business interests were in potential conflict, as in the 1950 readjustment of Saudi oil revenues, the State Department ensured that the oil companies acted in the national interest.

Ultimately, the developing countries lay at the periphery of U.S. concerns. Due to America's relative wealth in natural resources, East-West and West-West issues almost completely eclipsed North-South ones in Truman's foreign policy. By default, private interests became the main agents of the United States in the Third World.

CHAPTER TEN

THE WANING OF ECONOMIC CONTAINMENT: NATO, MILITARY AID, AND NSC 68, 1948–1950

UNTIL THE KOREAN WAR, the growth of the American military establishment did not keep pace with the postwar expansion of U.S. commitments overseas. Defense budgets remained limited primarily because Truman administration officials believed that economic instruments could adequately safeguard U.S. security interests around the world. Their confidence in this strategy appeared well-founded as the United States achieved its most important foreign policy aims without resorting to full-scale rearmament: the reconstruction of Western Europe, Germany, and Japan, their integration into a multilateral system under American auspices, and the containment of Soviet power.

By late 1949, however, three developments had forced a reevaluation of American policy. With the formation of the North Atlantic Treaty Organization (NATO), the United States felt compelled to offer increasing amounts of military aid (and later, ground troops) to its European allies in order to provide solid evidence of the American commitment to their security. The Soviet explosion of an atomic bomb in August 1949 persuaded most American policymakers that they had underestimated Soviet military and technical capabilities while overestimating the ability of economic leverage to protect vital U.S. interests against what was now generally perceived as a military threat. And finally, Mao's victory in mainland China, coming at a time of rising anti-Communist sentiment in the United States, led the Truman administration to give greater support to "democratic" forces in Asia as well as Europe.

These factors alone, however, would not have forced the Truman administration to implement the massive rearmament program outlined in NSC 68. Until June 1950, the economic security strategy still dominated American thinking, and Truman's fiscal conservatism stood in the way of sharply higher defense budgets. This is contrary to the thesis, expounded by Daniel Yergin among others, that the Truman administration had created by late 1947 a "national security state" organized "for perpetual confrontation and for war" with the Soviet Union, and that NSC 68 was the culmination of that crisis mentality.[1]

The Korean War was the true watershed in Truman's defense policy. The invasion of South Korea appeared to refute the central concept of economic containment, namely that Communist political penetration of war-disrupted societies posed a greater danger to Western security than did Communist military aggression. In the face of the enhanced Sino-Soviet military capabilities and the aggression in Korea, economic aid seemed a frail deterrent indeed. After the Korean invasion, American policymakers no longer regarded economic power and multilateral institutions as the first line of defense in the Cold War.

Origins of NATO and Military Aid, 1948–1949

American participation in a North Atlantic alliance was by no means an inevitable outgrowth of the Marshall Plan. Indeed, the European Recovery Program (ERP) was designed in part as a substitute for the rearmament of Western Europe and for a permanent U.S. military presence on the continent. Even after the Truman administration endorsed the Brussels Pact in March 1948, American officials believed that the United States should provide political leadership and matériel to its allies without assuming a major military role in the defense of Western Europe.

Historians have offered widely differing explanations for the U.S. decision to join the "entangling alliance." The conventional explanation is that the United States rearmed and joined NATO in response to a distinctly more menacing posture by the Soviet Union after the Czech coup and the Berlin blockade.[2] The problem with this thesis, as we shall see, is that many top U.S. officials did not perceive a marked shift in Moscow's policies and that Washington in any case moved very slowly to meet the Soviet threat before the Korean War. Alternatively, revisionist historians have argued that NATO marked the culmination of a gradual militarization of American foreign policy (and society) that had its roots in wartime planning but only became official policy following the March 1948 war scare. Still other scholars, stressing the "aggressive tendencies" of U.S. capitalism, regard NATO as an American invention designed to impose political discipline upon the European allies. According to this view, economic nationalism and political radicalism in Western Europe endangered U.S. interests more seriously than did the Red Army. These historians also suggest that the Truman administration adopted a program of massive rearmament along the lines of NSC 68 specifically in order to combat the 1949 recession.[3]

In fact, the Truman administration did just the opposite: the White House responded to recession by adopting austere fiscal policies to hold down the deficit. Keynesianism was still not widely accepted in Washington. Indeed, one of the most effective arguments mobilized by opponents of rearmament was that it could bankrupt the country. The tight defense budgets of the Truman administration before the Korean War also contradict the case for the emergence of a "national security state" before 1950.

The main impetus for a Western defense organization came from the European allies themselves, rather than from the United States. The Brussels Pact countries, particularly France and Britain, insisted that defense planning and coordination could not go forward without a firm American commitment to European security. Membership in NATO was also part of the price that Washington had to pay for French acceptance of the reconstruction of the West German state and economy— and eventual German rearmament. (The other American inducement to Paris was the Marshall Plan.) The British and the French had no illusions about Moscow's intentions and feared Communist encroachment upon a united, but neutralized Germany. In January 1948, British Foreign Minister Ernest Bevin proposed the formation of a "Western Union" of European states in association with the United States. "The plain truth," the British Ambassador informed Under Secretary of State Robert A. Lovett, "is that Western Europe cannot yet stand on its own feet without assurance of support."[4]

American policymakers at first gave only lukewarm encouragement to the Europeans. "Some form of political, military and economic union in Western Europe will be necessary," the Policy Planning Staff (PPS) concluded in a major review of U.S. foreign policy in February

1948, "if the free nations of Europe are to hold their own against the people of the east united under Moscow rule." But PPS Director George F. Kennan believed that the Marshall Plan countries should consolidate their economic and political gains before proceeding to a military pact, and argued that the United States should avoid a close association with any European security organization. Others, like Director of the Office of European Affairs John D. Hickerson, looked more favorably upon an Atlantic pact, but demanded European initiative and self-help (as in ERP) before the United States participated.[5]

The Czech coup and the ensuing war scare of February-March 1948 catalyzed official opinion behind the Western alliance. Secretary of State Marshall on March 12 told the British that the United States was "prepared to proceed at once in the joint discussions on the establishment of an Atlantic security system." On March 17, President Truman applauded the signing of the Brussels Pact (by Britain, France, and the Benelux) on that day, and just three days later the NSC called for "a world-wide counter-offensive" against the Soviet bloc, including U.S. military aid to the Western Union. Secret consultations with the British and Canadians began at the Pentagon shortly thereafter.[6]

The Americans were still not enthusiastic about an open-ended security commitment to Western Europe, however. The Joint Chiefs of Staff were wary of assuming commitments beyond U.S. military capabilities and concerned about the virtual exhaustion of World War II stocks. (Due to the JCS' pressure, the military aid legislation would specifically prohibit the depletion of matériel needed by U.S. forces.) The Congress also disapproved of extensive military aid, let alone a hard-and-fast alliance with Western Europe, while Marshall Plan legislation was still pending. "The general feeling of Congress," Under Secretary of State Robert A. Lovett reported to the National Security Council (NSC) in May 1948, "is that we should not formalize our participation in Western Union military talks but that we should merely send observers."[7]

Senator Arthur H. Vandenberg (R-Mich.), a barometer of bipartisan opinion, finally drafted a Senate resolution (approved in June 1948) that opened the way to American membership in NATO. The Vandenberg Resolution stated that U.S. participation in any collective security agreement did not automatically commit the United States to go to war in case of aggression against another member country. Congressional approval, in other words, was still necessary. Moreover, the European countries, as in the ERP, would have to provide reciprocal aid. In July 1948, the NSC approved military assistance to Western Europe on this basis.[8]

During the same month, amid the Berlin crisis, exploratory talks on Western defense began in Washington. The Europeans demanded concrete assurances of U.S. military support, Special Representative to Europe W. Averell Harriman told Marshall and Forrestal. Economic assistance "aids in meeting the threat of internal aggression, but it is military support which strengthens the will to resist external aggression."

At this point, U.S. officials favored shipping matériel in lieu of troops to the European allies. Part of their reticence was due to the lingering isolationism of the American public. In July 1948, for instance, Secretary Marshall at first hesitated to send U.S. B-29s to England to demonstrate Western resolve in Berlin because he feared a popular backlash against any apparent provocation of the Soviets. But aside from domestic constraints, senior policymakers did not believe that a major U.S. military presence in Europe was necessary. State Department Counselor Charles E. Bohlen, for example, doubted the Soviets would attack Western Europe and valued the new alliance primarily for its "psychological" impact, especially upon French morale. Thus, when the Washington talks concluded in September 1948, the U.S. role in the proposed Atlantic security pact was mostly confined to political and material support. As Marshall told Defense Secretary James A. Forrestal in November, "We should not, at this stage, proceed to build up U.S. ground forces for the express purpose of employing them in Western Europe." In testimony before the Senate Foreign Relations Committee in July 1949, the new Secretary of State, Dean Acheson, affirmed that the treaty did not require the United States either to provide military aid or to send additional troops to Europe. On July 21, 1949, the Senate approved the North Atlantic treaty by an 82 to 13 margin.[9]

Yet as the French never tired of pointing out, NATO remained no more than a paper treaty until Congress approved a military aid program (MAP) to help rearm Western Europe. European anxiety was understandable: about ten U.S. and West European divisions, for the most part ill-equipped and poorly trained, faced over thirty Soviet divisions in Eastern and Central Europe alone. Interestingly, however, economic considerations played a prominent role even in Washington's planning for MAP. Policymakers above all wished to ensure that European rearmament did not undercut the Marshall Plan. As the Foreign Assistance Correlation Committee, an interdepartmental committee on military aid, stated in February 1949,

> Economic recovery must not be sacrificed to rearmament and must continue to be given a clear priority. . . . rearmament expenditures and manpower diversion should not be permitted to bring about any serious reduction in the allotment of European resources to the recovery effort. Of basic importance is recognition of the limits of U.S. financial and economic aid available.[10]

Striking a balance between rearmament and recovery was no simple matter. "Rearmament," Lawrence Kaplan states, "signified to Western Europe a diversion of men and materials from the manufacture of dollar-earning products to economically unprofitable war goods." But if the Western Union countries did not increase their defense budgets, Paul Nitze noted after visiting Europe in January 1949, "the additional cost of the rearmament program would fall entirely on the U.S. taxpayer." In its presentation of MAP legislation before the Congress, the

> Administration found itself in a dilemma: It had to admit that Europe's will to resist would be seriously injured by the failure to follow up the Atlantic Treaty with an aid bill, and at the same time it could not counter the claim that the limited aid program anticipated for that year would be insufficient to stop Russian aggression and could possibly have harmful effects upon the recovery program.[11]

Congress significantly revised the MAP legislation for FY 1950, tightly restricting executive discretion to disburse funds. The military aid initially available to NATO countries was cut to $100 million, and as of April 1950, a mere $42 million of the total $1 billion in MAP funds authorized for NATO had been obligated, with only token shipments reaching European shores. Nonetheless, the administration had provided a major boost to European morale and unity at a time of military weakness and insecurity.[12]

The State Department, rather than the Defense Department, administered MAP because the program's main purpose was, like the ERP, to buttress the political and economic stability of Western Europe, rather than to build a war machine capable of fighting the Red Army. The Mutual Defense Assistance Act of 1949 explicitly stated this principle:

> The Congress recognizes that economic recovery is essential to international peace and security and must be given clear pri-

ority. The Congress also recognizes that the increased confidence of free peoples in the ability to resist direct and indirect aggression and to maintain internal security will advance such recovery and political stability.[13]

Unfortunately, this concept of NATO as a politico-military adjunct to the Marshall Plan reinforced the European propensity to defer both rearmament and the formulation of an integrated defense plan. Wary of endorsing a strategy that could entail a prolonged and destructive "liberation" of the continent from Soviet occupation, many Europeans persuaded themselves that the mere existence of a political alliance with the United States was a sufficient deterrent against Soviet aggression. Yet until the assignment of U.S. ground troops to NATO in 1951, Timothy Ireland observes, "none of the American policies for Europe . . . implied permanent American involvement in continental affairs." Indeed, the Marshall Plan and the military aid program had been specifically designed to restore the balance of power in Europe so that direct U.S. military intervention would be unnecessary.[14]

Defense Budgets before Korea, 1948–1950

The internal debate over U.S. defense budgets from 1948 to 1950 most clearly illustrates the primacy of economic containment before the Korean War. Truman's near obsession with fiscal prudence permeated almost every layer of the administration's foreign policy and national security apparatus. As Robert J. Donovan has noted, the President "was more attentive to the advice of his fiscal advisers than he was to the strategic concerns of the military leaders."[15]

The battle of the budget was a central feature of the decisive debate over defense policy in 1948. In his March 1948 address asking for prompt Congressional approval of the Marshall Plan, the President had also sought authorization of a Universal Military Training (UMT) program that would have required virtually all young men to undergo basic military instruction. In addition, he asked Congress to restore the draft for five years in order to expand the regular armed forces. These conventional forces, the administration believed, would provide an inexpensive substitute for large standing forces and offer a more flexible deterrent against Soviet aggression than did atomic weapons. Yet the Republican-controlled Congress, in effect opting for a strategy based on atomic weapons, soundly defeated UMT, cut back the President's proposed Selective-Service measure from five to two years, and voted start-up funding for a 70-group Air Force, as opposed to Truman's request for 55 groups.

While U.S atomic capabilities had greatly improved by the fall of 1948, the bomb was still regarded as a weapon of last resort. "Through 1950, the nuclear stockpile was . . . too small and the weapons too large and unwieldy to be used against true tactical targets, such as troops and transportation bottlenecks." The United States, in short, lacked a credible deterrent in Europe.[16] The quarrels within the U.S. government over military strategy should not obscure the similarity in approach by the various parties to the budgetary issue: everyone was looking for a cheap alternative to forces-in-being.

Truman himself was instrumental in curbing the Pentagon's appetite for a bigger piece of the fiscal pie. As Truman explained to Forrestal in May 1948, "Military strength is dependent on a strong economic system and a strong industrial and productive capacity." Before considering higher defense budgets, "the effect on our national economy must be weighed." Increased military expenditures could bring runaway inflation, taxes, and deficit spending, Truman warned Forrestal, and "unless world conditions deteriorate and tensions increase," the President planned to *cut* the Pentagon budget.[17]

The battle over the FY '50 defense budget revealed the Commander-in-Chief at his most stubborn. In the wake of the Czech and Berlin crises, Truman had boosted the FY '49 defense budget from $9.8 billion to $13 billion, but U.S. rearmament then levelled off. By capping the defense budget for FY '50 at $14.4 billion (exclusive of $600 million for stockpiling), the President effectively ordered the military services to adapt their programs to prescribed budgetary limits, rather than to what the world situation seemed to require. Actual, calendar-year defense outlays tended to be even smaller than the budgetary figures suggested (see appendix, table A.3 and graph 3). Forrestal, responding to strong JCS pressure for more funds, sought to outflank Truman's economic advisers by soliciting the support of the Secretary of State in November 1948, but Marshall told Forrestal that "we must expect for the current fiscal year a [world] situation which is neither better nor worse than that which we have found in 1948 insofar as it affects the ceiling of our military establishment." Bohlen added that the main deterrents to Soviet aggression remained strategic air power and the "productive potential of the United States. "Following Forrestal's departure in early 1949, Truman actually sought to clip another $1 billion off the Pentagon's $14.4 billion budget. And when the Congress added $600 million to the Air Force's budget for FY '50, Truman and his new Defense Secretary Louis Johnson responded by impounding the supplementary funds.[18]

Even in the face of greatly expanded U.S. commitments in Western Europe, Truman sought to keep defense budgets below $15 billion. In fact, at precisely the same moment that the administration was pressing for final passage of the North Atlantic Treaty (and was about to introduce MAP legislation), the President instructed the NSC to explore new ways to reduce spending in FY '51 (NSC 52). With the onset of a recession, Truman argued in July 1949, the combination of declining revenues and rising expenditures had brought about "such a serious fiscal and economic problem that a complete reevaluation of current and proposed programs is required." Domestic expenditures, in Truman's estimation, had already been cut to the bone, so he instructed the NSC to look for fat in military and international programs. (He expected European recovery to reduce the need for extensive foreign aid programs.)[19]

The Bureau of the Budget (BOB) sought to meet Truman's objectives by cutting the defense budget from $14.4 billion in FY '50 to $13 billion in FY '51. It also sliced ECA, military aid, and other international programs roughly in half. By the BOB's calculations in July 1949, military and international programs should have cost about $5 billion less in FY '51 ($17.8 billion) than they did in FY '50 ($23 billion).[20]

In late September 1949—as the Communists were sweeping to victory in mainland China, and as the Truman administration was discovering that the Soviets had exploded an atomic device—the NSC determined that the Defense Department "can, under the $13 billion ceiling allocated to it in NSC 52/1, maintain substantially the same degree of military strength, readiness and posture during FY 1951 which it will maintain in FY 1950." The Council of Economic Advisors (CEA) did not foresee a continuation of the recession into 1950, and CEA Chairman Edwin Nourse made a strong pitch for austerity. "The strains on our economy of increasing the deficit with its attendant problems," notably higher inflation, would pose "no less a risk than our military and diplomatic risks," Nourse argued. "Any jeopardy to our domestic industry had also to be considered as jeopardy to our national security." The Treasury Department, too, pleaded for spending cuts to combat the widening federal deficits. With the CEA, Budget Bureau, Treasury, and even Defense Secretary Johnson squarely lined up against them, the JCS and other proponents of rearmament were fighting a losing battle.

In the fall, the President, despairing of the chances for an agreement on the international control of atomic energy, reluctantly approved the substantial increase in nuclear weapons production that the JCS had requested in response to the May 1949 Harmon Report. But Truman was determined to hold down other defense programs. In his annual budget message on January 9, 1950, the Chief Executive asked for $13.5 billion for the FY '51 defense budget, more than a 6 percent cut from the previous year. (In May 1950, the House of Representatives went even further, voting only $12.9 billion for the Pentagon.) As one historian has noted,

> For the Department of Defense the President's budget suggested the onset of a new era of austerity. Although subsequent developments—the drafting of NSC 68 and the outbreak of the Korean War—would radically alter Truman's plans, it seemed clear in January [1950] that his efforts to clamp a lid on military spending were on the verge of complete success.

The result was a partial demobilization of the armed forces from 1,617,000 in July 1949 to 1,460,000 on the eve of the Korean War (see appendix, graph 1).[21]

The rationale behind the Truman administration's position on defense spending was the widely shared conviction that the Soviets would not launch a general war in the near future, but that they hoped to bankrupt the United States in a costly arms race. Economic and military assistance was still regarded as the most effective means of supporting the Atlantic alliance, but as Europe recovered, U.S. foreign aid programs could be scaled down. Surprisingly, this viewpoint prevailed even as some key officials, notably Secretary of State Dean Acheson, became increasingly alarmed by the Soviet threat. In April 1950, with projected deficits of $4 billion to $8 billion looming for each of the fiscal years 1950 to 1953, Budget Director Frederick J. Lawton contemplated holding the defense budget ceiling at $13 billion while cutting foreign aid by $3 billion in FY '53. This evidence, incidentally, directly contradicts the view that Truman sought to fight the 1949 recession with rearmament.[22]

Defense Secretary Johnson has suffered more criticism for the inadequacy of U.S. defense programs on the eve of the Korean War than have Truman and his economic advisers—Nourse, Treasury Secretary John Snyder, and the successive Budget Directors, James E. Webb

(1946–1949), Frank Pace, Jr. (1949–1950), and Lawton (1950–1953). Despite his deservedly poor reputation among contemporaries and historians for other reasons, Johnson probably has been unfairly maligned for his position on the defense budget, for he was simply following his chief's orders. If anyone deserved credit or blame for the military posture that the United States adopted before June 1950, it was Harry S. Truman, the military services' main foe in the battle of the budget.[23]

Business and Rearmament

One might suppose that military leaders would have been able to recruit powerful backing for rearmament in the corporate boardrooms of America. After all, it was commonly acknowledged that the fat government contracts during the war had ended the Great Depression and generated record profits for U.S. business. Yet interestingly, business opinion was overwhelmingly opposed to both Keynesian fiscal policies and a large peacetime military establishment. "Business leaders recognized that the economic recovery brought about by World War II had provided them with a final chance to build a prosperous peacetime economy under private direction," William S. Hill, Jr., has found in his study of businessmen and national defense. Corporate leaders generally supported an end to governmental controls and the reduction of federal spending and taxes. Truman's decision to slash military expenditures at the end of the war met with applause on Wall Street, and most businessmen heartily approved of the President's decision in mid-1948 to cap the defense budget at $14.4 billion. Even during the 1949 recession, organizations such as the Chamber of Commerce of the United States and the Committee for Economic Development (CED) continued to demand cuts in federal outlays, including military expenditures, in order to balance the budget.[24]

It is true that some private groups, such as the National Planning Association, favored governmental intervention to assure high levels of postwar employment and production. Yet most entrepreneurs, even the progressive members of the CED, preferred private expansion over governmental pump priming. By 1945, businessmen no longer feared demobilization because the massive accumulated savings of consumers during the war promised strong postwar demand. While many government analysts were predicting a postwar depression, manufacturers were generally confident that they could quickly reconvert to civilian output and find markets. Indeed, just a year later, inflation clearly posed a greater danger to the U.S. economy than did unemployment. The Chamber of Commerce and the National Association of Manufacturers (NAM) probably spoke for most businessmen in calling for an end to deficit spending, which they associated with excess demand and high prices. Hoping to spur private investment, these groups helped persuade the Congress to reduce tax rates and to decontrol production, prices, and wages. Thanks in part to lobbying by the NAM and the CED, the Employment Act of 1946 was also watered down so that Washington would not be required to guarantee full employment.[25]

Demobilization affected different industries in different ways. In August 1946, just one year after the war had ended, munitions procurement fell to less than 10 percent of wartime levels. Aircraft manufacturers and shipbuilders were especially hard hit and clamored for federal relief. Output of military airplanes fell from 96,000 in 1944 to 1,800 in 1947, and civilian demand came nowhere close to filling the gap. The aviation industry finally revived after the March 1948 war scare, as the Congress more than doubled the budget for the Air Force and naval air in FY '49 compared with FY '48. Airpower advocates, notably the President's own Air Policy (Finletter) Commission, prompted the Congress to appropriate even more money for air procurement than Truman desired, while subsidies to the Merchant Marine helped to sustain beleaguered shipbuilders.[26]

The aircraft and shipbuilding industries were exceptions to the rule, however. Steel and automobile manufacturers, for instance, easily reconverted to civilian production and had little or no desire for military business—which in any case suffered from the boom-and-bust syndrome—when they were struggling to meet consumer demand. Steel shipments to the government for military purposes from 1946 to 1950 amounted to less than 2 percent of total industry output. Electronics companies like Raytheon, RCA, and General Electric were more willing to accept postwar military contracts, especially to promote research, development, and preparedness. Yet with the rapid growth of the television and radio market after the war, the industry did not need military contracts to survive, and factory sales reached a peacetime record in 1949. Similarly, the machine tool industry by 1949 had given up on government contracts and was looking forward to new orders from the automobile industry (then retooling for automatic transmissions) to revive it. And needless to say, the postwar boom in housing more than compensated for the drop in military base construction.[27]

Business sentiment on fiscal policy, let alone the defense budget, did not markedly shift even with the onset of the first postwar recession beginning in late 1948. Congress had already targeted the Pentagon for cuts in the FY '50 budget. When the economy took a turn for the worse, the CED, NAM, and Chamber of Commerce called for further decreases in defense spending in order to offset declining revenues. Secretary of Commerce Charles Sawyer reported that "business leaders everywhere expressed enthusiastic approval of reductions in the military budget." Even the aircraft industry was fairly acquiescent; by 1949, it was operating at high capacity and had a backlog of orders totalling over $2 billion. Like the White House, Congressional appropriation committees set the budget according to fiscal, rather than strategic, criteria, and spent a good deal of their time searching for hidden inefficiencies in Pentagon programs. Due to the long lag between approval and actual production and delivery of equipment, it is doubtful that either the White House or the Congress conceived of the military assistance program of 1949 as an anti-recession measure.[28]

On most issues, the business community was divided into innumerable factions: large and small producers, internationally and domestically oriented sectors, New Dealers and laissez-faire enthusiasts. But it is probably safe to say that private groups on the whole acted to restrain U.S. rearmament before the Korean War. The corporate leaders sternly shunned what was later called "military Keynesianism," the notion that defense spending was necessary to sustain production and employment. Even during and immediately after the Korean War, "they clung stubbornly to the idea that businessmen, not government, should be responsible for economic growth."[29]

NSC 68 and the Debate over Containment

What finally shifted the momentum toward rearmament was a subtle change in official thinking about the Sino-Soviet threat in late 1949. While the President tried to put on a brave face in announcing the detection of a Soviet atomic explosion in September 1949, Truman and his key aides were privately apprehensive about the American vulnerability to a devastating atomic attack. The Soviet bomb also eroded the deterrent effect of U.S. strategic air power against a Red Army attack on Western Europe. And Mao's triumph in China, once regarded as a sideshow in the Cold War, suddenly appeared to be part of a renewed Communist offensive masterminded by the Kremlin. With Moscow's growing capacity for aggression, many of Truman's top advisers became persuaded that economic containment alone could no longer guarantee vital U.S. interests abroad, and that an expansion of military programs was necessary.[30]

The year preceding the Korean invasion thus witnessed the erosion of the consensus built around economic containment and the rise of a new one centered around military containment. The declining influence of George F. Kennan during late 1949 reflected the evolution of official thinking. Kennan thought that a number of the administration's policies from 1948 to 1950—the creation of NATO and the West German state, the decision to retain U.S. troops in post-occupation Japan, and the development of the H-bomb—all were certain to freeze the division of Europe and Asia into existing spheres of influence. Without conciliatory, positive efforts to bring the Russians to the negotiating table, the United States would confirm Soviet hard-liners' worst fears about American intentions and provoke an uncontrollable arms race. In an October 1949 meeting of the PPS with Acheson in attendance, Kennan criticized the "acceptance throughout the Government of the infallibility of the Joint Chiefs of Staff," who he believed tended to draw their conclusions from improbable, worst-case scenarios. Given Moscow's new atomic capability, the PPS chief argued, the United States could not respond to a Red Army attack on Western Europe with strategic air strikes against the Soviet Union. Yet Kennan continued to oppose a major rearmament of NATO's conventional forces.[31]

Acheson countered that an agreement with the Russians on atomic energy was unattainable "and made the point that to agree with the Russians not to use atomic bombs in warfare was to deprive yourself of the effect on the enemy of the fear of retaliation by atomic bombing against orthodox aggression."[32] The Secretary of State also dismissed Kennan's argument that West European recovery was all that was needed to contain Soviet power and influence. As Acheson later wrote, "The threat to Western Europe seemed to me singularly like that which Islam had posed centuries before, with its combination of ideological zeal and fighting power." Acheson regarded MAP and the atomic bomb as essential deterrents to Soviet aggression and believed the Pentagon "was not so unresponsive to the idea that our war preparations are designed to keep us out of war." His real fear, however, was probably not a Soviet invasion, but the "drift of Western Europe toward neutralism, prompted by the lack of credibility" of the U.S. deterrent.[33]

Like Acheson, Paul H. Nitze, who succeeded Kennan as PPS Director on New Year's Day, 1950, believed that a meaningful settlement with Moscow was possible only if the United States approached negotiations from a position of military superiority. On January 31, 1950, a special NSC advisory committee chaired by Nitze recommended accelerated development of atomic weapons, including the hydrogen bomb, and a thorough review of U.S. national security policies. Truman approved both proposals, and work immediately began on the strategic review that would culminate in NSC 68.

On the same day, the Defense Department and CIA forwarded new and higher estimates of Soviet atomic capabilities (predicted to reach a stockpile of about 100 fission bombs by 1953). Nitze shortly thereafter warned that the "danger of war . . . seemed considerably greater than last fall." Citing Moscow's recognition of Ho Chi Minh and lesser evidence of a shift in the Kremlin's tactics, Nitze postulated that

> recent Soviet moves reflect not only a mounting militancy but suggest a boldness that is essentially new—and borders on recklessness. . . . Nothing about the moves indicate that Moscow is preparing to launch in the near future an all-out military attack on the West. They do, however, suggest a greater willingness than in the past to undertake a course of action, including a possible use of force in local areas, which might lead to an accidental outbreak of general military conflict. Thus the chance of war through miscalculation is increased.[34]

Just before he left the Foreign Service, Kennan, then Counselor of the State Department, sought to counteract the growing alarm in Washington. "There is little justification," he wrote Acheson in February 1950, "for the impression that the 'cold war,' by virtue of events outside of our control, has suddenly taken some drastic turn to our disadvantage." The fall of China, Kennan argued, was the product of long-term trends that neither Washington nor Moscow controlled. The Soviet explosion of an atomic device likewise had not changed the strategic equation, he contended, and the Americans, not the Russians, were starting the race to build the hydrogen bomb. Kennan charged that the inauguration of NATO and MAP had led to a harmful "tendency to view the Russian threat as just a military problem rather than as a part of a broad political offensive." The Counselor recommended less dependence upon atomic weapons and greater reliance upon economic initiatives to contain the Soviets.[35]

One of the few other remaining advocates of economic containment in the administration was Willard L. Thorp, the Assistant Secretary of State for Economic Affairs. In an April 1950 memo to Acheson, Thorp charged the Nitze group with exaggerating the Soviet threat. While Soviet defense spending as a proportion of GNP was higher than that of the United States, total U.S. military expenditures were still roughly double the Soviet total. With the continued expansion of the American economy, the U.S. advantage would grow. The focus of the Nitze report was misplaced, Thorp claimed, for the true measure of a country's power was its industrial productivity, defense mobilization capability, and technology, all areas in which America had a big edge. Rearmament was a drain on the Western economies and a poor investment in national security, Thorp wrote. The Cold War would be decided in the economic arena:

> On the economic side, I feel that we cannot emphasize enough the disaster which an economic depression would be. This could destroy the entire structure even though we might weather the storm ourselves. The inventory adjustment [recession] in early 1949 did plenty of harm in the international field. This is not only the hope of the Kremlin but the fear of our friends.[36]

Acheson was unimpressed by these arguments. In a March 1950 conversation with Representative Christian Herter (R-Mass.), Acheson scoffed at the Budget Bureau's projections for lower defense and foreign aid obligations in FY '53: "I said that I did not think our position [had] deteriorated between 1948 and 1949, except for the loss of China which was expected, but that during the last six to nine months there had been a trend against us which, if allowed to continue, would lead to a considerable deterioration in our position."[37] Acheson advocated a campaign to mobilize the U.S. public behind the rearmament of NATO, the ultimate aim of which was nothing less than a Soviet military withdrawal from Eastern Europe. Without a Soviet pullback, Acheson believed, Western Europe could never be secure from aggression. (In this sense, the Truman administration set a precedent for the "roll-back" rhetoric of the Eisenhower administration.)[38]

Acheson's line of reasoning reflected the emerging consensus that achieved official status in NSC 68. The State-Defense Policy Review Group that drafted NSC 68 contended that the differences between "free" and "slave" societies were irreconcilable and that the only way to achieve peaceful relations between the two spheres would be a fundamental change in the Soviet system. In contrast with Kennan and many Sovietologists of the day, the authors of NSC 68 portrayed the Kremlin leaders as unequivocally hostile and uncompromising, bent upon "the domination of the Eurasian land mass," and dedicated to the destruction of the United States. Negotiations with the Soviets were out of the question because the United States, despite superior military potential, suffered from "a sharp disparity between our actual military strength and our commitments." Unlike Kennan, who wished to focus U.S. efforts on certain strongpoints in Europe and Asia, Nitze and the other architects of NSC 68 believed that "a defeat of free institutions anywhere is a defeat everywhere" and that the United States should be prepared to defend against Communist aggression wherever it occurred. According to NSC 68, the only effective response to the Communist challenge was a sharp American buildup in both the atomic and the conventional areas, creating what Acheson called situations of strength. "Without superior aggregate military strength, in being and readily mobilizable," the memo stated, "a policy of 'containment'— which is in effect a policy of calculated and gradual coercion—is no more than a policy of bluff."[39]

One of the most important legacies of NSC 68 was a new set of assumptions about the economic foundations of security. Despite its vastly larger industrial capacity, the authors of NSC 68 claimed, the United States spent only one-half what the Soviets did on defense and military-related programs as a proportion of GNP. An American buildup need not entail a reduction in the standard of living, for the U.S. economy contained enough slack in the aftermath of the 1949 recession to permit a substantial expansion of both civilian and military production. The report did not clarify whether stimulatory steps were necessary to expand the economy, for Keynesianism was still frowned upon. In a message clearly directed at the White House, however, the review group stated that "budgetary considerations will need to be subordinated to the stark fact that our very independence as a nation may be at stake." Citing the American experience in World War II, the memo argued that the United States could afford both guns and butter.[40]

The authors of NSC 68 in fact may have deliberately exaggerated the Soviet threat—they estimated 1954 to be the year of greatest danger of an all-out Soviet attack upon the United States—in order to sway the

President and his economic advisers. The State-Defense group focused on the Soviet military danger because West European neutralism—the more immediate object of their fears—was too amorphous a threat to catalyze the government. Truman, after all, had repeatedly stated that only a national emergency could justify a major escalation of U.S. defense spending. As Acheson explains in his memoirs, "The purpose of NSC-68 was to so bludgeon the mass mind of 'top government' that not only could the President make a decision but that the decision could be carried out."[41]

Truman did not fall for this gambit. His response to an early draft of NSC 68 in April 1950 was to call for "a clearer indication of the programs which are envisaged in the Report, including estimates of the probable cost of such programs." He instructed the Bureau of the Budget (BOB), the Treasury Department, the Economic Cooperation Administration, and the Council of Economic Advisers (CEA) to participate in an *ad hoc* committee to review NSC 68. The CEA was confident that the U.S. economy, with the proper fiscal and tax measures, could easily accommodate the rearmament programs outlined in NSC 68 "without serious threat to our standards of living," excessive inflation, or large deficits.

The counterattack against NSC 68 was led by the Budget Bureau, joined to a lesser extent by Defense Secretary Louis Johnson and individuals at State (such as Under Secretary James Webb, the former Budget Director). In addition to questioning the memo's dire portrayal of Soviet military power, the BOB in May 1950 pointed out that the extraordinary productivity that this country had achieved during World War II was irrelevant to a drawn-out Cold War. Massive rearmament in peacetime could disrupt the civilian economy. Even with the 3.5 million unemployed in 1949, the agency argued, inflation remained a danger. In the BOB's view, full-scale rearmament would divert resources from the civilian sector (and thus negate any growth in the defense sector), limit the funds available for foreign aid, and require higher taxes and deeper deficits. The President appeared to agree. "The defense budget next year will be smaller than it is this year," he stated at a press conference in early May 1950, "and we are continually cutting it by economies." As late as June 5, Louis Johnson told Acheson that "he doubted that the over-all US defense budget would be increased."[42]

Even though the administration clearly accepted the general premises and conclusions of NSC 68, many senior officials balked at full implementation of its recommendations. There is no way of knowing for certain what the President would have done if the Korean War had not intervened. Truman did not approve NSC 68 as U.S. policy until late September 1950, *after* the Korean War had radically altered Western perceptions of the Soviet danger. Initial cost estimates of all the programs recommended in the report were around $50 billion annually, but without Korea, spending on defense and international programs probably would have risen by only a few billion dollars annually, if at all. As it was, defense outlays for FY '50 (ending June 30, 1950) totalled only $13.5 billion; deducting occupation costs, Army civil expenditures, and Greek-Turkish military aid, the Pentagon spent only $11.9 billion. "The real significance of NSC 68," Samuel F. Wells, Jr., observes, "was its timing—the tocsin sounded just before the fire."[43]

Decline of the Multilateralist Approach, 1949–1950

The 1945–1949 period had witnessed great creativity in American foreign economic policy. In forging durable multilateral institutions governing world currencies, trade, and finance, the United States had helped to integrate the Western industrial economies and encourage political cooperation among nation-states. To be sure, the Soviet bloc countries had elected not to join the U.S.-led system, but their self-exclusion did not threaten the viability of the system. The Truman administration successfully contained Soviet power and influence through economic aid and political support to certain "strongpoints" in Europe and Asia—Germany, France, Britain, and Japan.

NSC 68 challenged the notion that economic security eliminated the need for rearmament. In one of a series of meetings convened to discuss the implementation of the document, the *ad hoc* committee on NSC 68 in May 1950 reached a

> consensus of opinion that NSC 68 had emphasized the inseparability of the military build-up from other weapons of the cold war, and that the one without the other would fail to achieve the objectives of the United States. There was also general agreement on the serious risks of war involved in proceeding with more aggressive political, economic, and psychological measures in the absence of an adequate military shield.[44]

The Korean invasion on June 25 finally turned the tide in favor of rearmament. The new mood in the administration was reflected in an NSC meeting of late November 1950 called to discuss NSC 68 and the FY 1951–52 defense budgets. Dean Acheson emerged as the main spokesman for accelerated rearmament. The Secretary of State argued that the United States must be prepared simultaneously for a long war in Korea and additional military responsibilities in Western Europe, as well as a possible Soviet atomic attack as early as 1952, the year, in his estimation, of "the greatest danger."

The national emergency also made it easier to accept big deficits. In the November 1950 NSC meeting, CEA Chairman Leon Keyserling made "no judgment regarding Defense needs," but argued that "the economy could stand the job required by NSC 68 and . . . no reduction of effort was necessary." In an annex to NSC 68/3 dated December 8, 1950, Keyserling further argued that the country could easily meet the report's mobilization aims. "These programs . . . ," he wrote, "fall about half way between 'business as usual' and a really large-scale dedication of our enormous economic resources . . . , even when defining this large-scale dedication as something far short of an all-out . . . mobilization for war purposes." Following the massive Chinese intervention in Korea during late November-early December, Truman and the NSC moved up the target date for the completion of the military buildup from 1954 to June 30, 1952. The President and his top advisers probably had not become sudden converts to Keynesianism; rather, the Korean crisis had encouraged them to discount the economic costs of rearmament. As Acheson put it in a December 1950 NSC meeting, "It would not be too much if we had all the troops that the military want . . . [and] all of the things that our European allies want. . . . The danger couldn't be greater than it is."[45]

The Truman administration's declining faith in the ability of economic instruments to contain Communism is reflected in statistics on U.S. foreign assistance. While U.S. military aid totalled only $69 million in 1946 and $97 million in 1947, it more than quintupled to $523 million in 1950. By 1952, 80 percent of American assistance to Western Europe consisted of military matériel, and for the first time in the postwar era, U.S. military aid world-wide ($2.7 billion) exceeded economic aid ($2 billion), setting a pattern for the rest of the decade (see appendix, graphs 2 and 3).[46] Economic aid had become an adjunct to military programs, a reward for good behavior rather than a vital instrument in the renovation of an integrated and stable Western economy.

The ascendancy of military containment fostered sterility in official thinking on economic diplomacy. U.S. export control policy, for instance, became frozen into a futile punitive exercise. Originally designed as a temporary measure to ease shortages in Marshall Plan countries and prevent transfer of strategic items to the Soviet Union, trade restrictions became a litmus test of Cold War orthodoxy within the Western alliance. The United States very quickly lost all economic contact with, and leverage over, the Soviet bloc and Red China. Of course, the process of economically isolating the Sino-Soviet bloc was well under way before NSC 68 and the Korean invasion, but after the spring of 1950, export controls became a permanent and immutable feature of U.S. policy—one that has irritated relations among the allies ever since.[47]

Nevertheless, one of the most remarkable features of U.S. foreign policy before the Korean War was the durability of the economic security strategy. Officials in the Truman administration remained confident that American economic power, backed by the deterrent power of atomic weapons, could almost single-handedly stabilize vital regions and countries against Communist encroachment. Changing perceptions of the Soviet threat did not substantially affect U.S. defense budgets before June 1950. The national security state, such as it was, emerged only with the outbreak of the Korean War.

CHAPTER ELEVEN

CONCLUSION

T HE EXTRAORDINARY GLOBAL recessions of the past decade have seriously weakened the international economic structure established by the Truman administration. Slow growth and rising unemployment have left Western governments at odds over economic policy and susceptible to internal protectionist pressures. The U.S. economy, which until the 1970s was almost immune to external developments, is increasingly vulnerable to volatile world commodity prices and to fluctuations in international interest and exchange rates. Foreign competition has badly hurt U.S. manufacturing. The global interdependence eagerly anticipated by American leaders in 1945 is nearly realized, but more and more Americans are now asking if the costs exceed the benefits.

Americans are not alone in questioning the value of the multilateralist system. Faced with financial collapse, many developing countries are clamoring for major reforms of the world trading system, notably the indexing of commodity prices to stabilize exporters' incomes. As the champion of the free market system, the United States is the principal target of Third World criticism.

American policies have also come under sharp attack from our closest allies. At one time, West European critics commonly charged that the open economic system was a Trojan horse for the invasion of their markets by American corporations. During the 1970s, the Japanese replaced the Americans as the main competitive threat, and European penetration of U.S. domestic markets proceeded at a brisk pace. Now it is more fashionable to complain about American protectionism and high interest rates. With some justice, the NATO allies also contend that Washington's effort to impose harsh controls on East-West trade has unnecessarily exacerbated Cold War tensions and strained the alliance.

Goals and Motives of U.S. Economic Diplomacy

In light of these developments, it is worth reexamining the motives and designs behind the creation of the postwar multilateralist system. The key element of U.S. foreign policy after World War II was economic security, the reliance upon economic power to achieve strategic aims. The United States would use its enormous industrial might to restore international stability, deferring rearmament as long as the Soviet Union (its only potential adversary) did not start a war. As Defense Secretary James Forrestal wrote in December 1947:

> At the present time we are keeping our military expenditures below the levels which our military leaders . . . estimate as the minimum which would in themselves ensure national security. By so doing we are able to increase our expenditures to assist in European recovery. In other words, we are taking a calculated risk in order to follow a course which offers a prospect of eventually achieving national security and also long-term world stability.

American economic strength and the atomic monopoly made this possible:

> As long as we can outproduce the world, can control the sea and can strike inland with the atomic bomb, we can assume certain risks otherwise unacceptable in an effort to restore world trade, to restore the balance of power—military power— and to eliminate some of the conditions which breed war.
>
> The years before any possible power can achieve the capability effectively to attack us with weapons of mass destruction are our years of opportunity.[1]

This study has challenged the revisionist characterization of Truman's foreign economic policy as coercive, "haughty, expansionist, and uncompromising."[2] The original impulse behind American multilateralism was neither anti-Communism nor a need to sustain world capitalism. Instead, American officials backed the Open Door largely because they were determined to prevent a revival of the closed autarkic systems that had contributed to world depression and split the world into competing blocs before the war. "Sound and healthy trade, conducted on equitable and non-discriminatory principles," President Truman wrote in October 1946, "is a keystone in the structure of world peace and security."[3]

Insofar as they could influence the behavior of other countries, American policymakers generally encouraged local policies that were aimed at improving productivity and output rather than redistributing income. Based on their New Deal and war experiences, U.S. leaders had concluded that economic growth, accompanied by a wide distribution of wealth, would do more to ameliorate social ills than would radical reforms or open class conflict, which discouraged investment and disrupted normal economic activity. In numerous cases, from Germany to Argentina to Japan, American policymakers preferred growth over socialistic reform.

Of course, economic considerations were not the only influence upon U.S. foreign policy. The exigencies of the Cold War forced major changes in the multilateral programs. In order to isolate the Soviet-bloc economies, the Truman administration restricted the flow of trade and credits to the Eastern countries. The Eximbank and other governmental agencies also extended "political" loans to help stabilize U.S. allies, such as Italy, Greece, and Turkey.

Domestic factors also played an important part in American decision making, although Truman faced fewer constraints in economic diplomacy than did his successors. Fears of a domestic depression at first seemed to underline the need to promote U.S. exports. But beginning in 1946, in the face of huge export surpluses and double-digit inflation, these anxieties subsided, and the administration instead sought to keep domestic prices down and increase imports. The Congress also curtailed some executive programs, slowing the liberalization of trade and trimming foreign aid.

All things considered, the Truman administration was remarkably adept at forging a Cold War consensus and at winning over Congressional leaders and elite opinion makers. With the possible exception of the Korean War period, the President usually had a clear sense of what limits the economy and the public would bear in the way of overseas commitments. Thus, executive skill, rather than the absence of domestic constraints, may best explain the relative ease with which White House-sponsored legislation made its way through Congress during these years.

It is also fairly clear that corporate and financial interests rarely exerted a direct influence upon American foreign policy. The concerns of specific firms and industries were almost always subordinated to larger economic, political, and strategic objectives. In spite of spirited opposition from such private groups as the National Association of

Manufacturers, for example, the Truman administration liberalized trade and currency exchange in the British loan agreements of 1945, the Marshall Plan, and the GATT negotiations.

The Truman administration did respond to what it saw as the long-term need of American business for an open worldwide economic environment. Washington officials recognized that foreign trade enhanced domestic prosperity and that U.S. corporations needed access to cheap overseas raw materials in order to remain competitive. Business, in turn, served as a spearhead for American influence in other countries. A clear case in point is the role that U.S. petroleum companies played in the Middle East. By supplying the capital and technology to develop the area's underground wealth, the oil corporations provided Western Europe with an essential resource, stabilized friendly Mideastern regimes, and set the stage for closer Arab ties with the United States.

The multilateral system, then, helped serve a number of political, strategic, and economic purposes. By definition, multilateralism implied a mutuality of interests among participating countries and a rejection of economic nationalism. It implied, too, an American willingness to accept responsibility for world economic problems. Policymakers realized, for instance, that the worldwide dollar shortage of the late 1940s and early 1950s required a reduction of U.S. commercial barriers, for ultimately, exports of American goods and services could grow only in tandem with imports. The fact that the Truman administration did not always live up to multilateralist ideals is less important than the fact that it accomplished as much as it did.

Interestingly, the expansion of American management of the world economy occurred when foreign trade played a smaller role in the U.S. economy than it had twenty years earlier. As a percentage of GNP, American exports during the 1945–1950 period ranged from a high of 6.5 percent in 1947 to a low of 3.6 percent in 1950. The corresponding figures for the 1920s were higher, and yet Washington took a far less active role in international affairs in that decade than it did in the decade following World War II.[4]

The explanation for the postwar activism of the United States in the world economy has much more to do with official perceptions and strategic goals than the needs of private enterprise. The interwar period, in which the United States had largely abjured its responsibilities as a great power, had left a deep impression upon the generation of Americans who became national policymakers after the war. Rather than rely primarily upon private institutions, U.S. leaders were determined to make extensive use of governmental and multilateral agencies to reshape world commercial, monetary, and financial systems. America's unrivalled economic power offered the most cost-effective means of securing political ends in the postwar period. As President Truman put it, "Which is better for the country, to spend twenty or thirty billion dollars [on foreign aid] to keep the peace or to do as we did in 1920 and then have to spend 100 billion dollars for four years to fight a war?"[5]

Evaluating Truman's Foreign Economic Policy, 1945–1950

It should come as no surprise that the Truman administration fell short of its bold objectives. During the years 1945 and 1946, Washington did not mobilize U.S. economic might effectively. Planners had overestimated the ability of multilateral institutions (such as the IMF and IBRD) and limited relief programs (Lend-Lease, UNRRA, and Eximbank loans) to restore prewar patterns of production, trade, and finance.

A major source of difficulty was the failure to anticipate the postwar confrontation with the Soviet Union. American officials had assumed that the Soviets would continue to cooperate with the United States after the war in order to gain reconstruction aid. As it turned out, Moscow was willing to suffer extraordinary hardship to exclude Western influence from Eastern Europe. The American application of economic sanctions was uneven and ineffective, possibly causing the Soviets to crack down on autonomous political movements in the satellite countries harder and sooner than they otherwise would have. In retrospect, Washington's partial embargo was probably a mistake. It eroded U.S. political influence in the region while inflicting minimal economic damage upon the Soviet Union.

Still, it must be remembered that Stalin and his cohorts were themselves mostly responsible for the isolation of the Soviet bloc from the world economy. The persistent American effort to win Soviet participation in the Bretton Woods system belies the revisionist charge that U.S. economic policy toward the Soviet Union was invariably coercive. Washington's multilateralist principles and practices were not incompatible with postwar Soviet security needs. Agreements with Moscow on Eastern Europe, a reconstruction loan, and Lend-Lease were all possible before the Soviet crackdown in Poland. Soviet-American tensions arose more from security considerations and competition over the political future of Europe than from disputes over trade and aid. The

American quest for multilateralism—the Open Door—was *not* the central cause of the Cold War.

U.S. economic policy in Western Europe was far more successful. Planners correctly foresaw that conflict among the West European powers—Britain, Germany, and France—would be reduced if their economies were inseparably linked. Consequently, the United States vigorously opposed trade barriers, currency restrictions, and state control of local economies. The unhappiness of American diplomats with European socialism arose less from any antagonism toward social reform than from a determination to prevent the revival of prewar economic nationalism. In Lend-Lease and other early postwar negotiations, the Truman administration applied heavy pressure to make Britain and other European countries remove obstacles to world commerce. Still, the Truman administration frequently bent the rules of the "pure" multilateralist approach to accommodate European needs. In the British loan negotiations of 1945, for instance, London won numerous exemptions and extensions to its obligation to dismantle the Commonwealth preference and sterling systems.

The war had damaged the European economies far more than anyone had realized, and the piecemeal U.S. aid programs did not provide the breathing space needed to rebuild a balanced trading relationship within and outside the continent. The largest stumbling block to European stability was Germany. Western Europe could not recover until the blast furnaces of the Ruhr were at work again. Yet since Washington did not wish to alienate the French, it initially settled for a policy of indefinite stagnation in Germany.

Kennan's containment doctrine had provided the analytical framework for a more activist policy in Europe, but the Truman administration lacked the public and Congressional support necessary to sustain an expensive new reconstruction program. The President's evocation of the Communist danger in the Truman Doctrine finally supplied the rationale for a greater U.S. role in Western Europe. Despite its universalist rhetoric, the Truman Doctrine was primarily intended to reduce American inhibitions about establishing a sphere of influence in Western Europe to counterbalance the Red Army's presence in Eastern Europe.

The Marshall Plan proved to be a brilliant mechanism for achieving several related aims in postwar Europe: the dismantling of trade barriers, German reconstruction, and political stabilization. While progress on economic integration was disappointing, the European Recovery Program created the preconditions for the remarkable resurgence of Western Europe in the 1950s. The revival of morale that accompanied European reconstruction laid the basis for mutual defense arrangements as well. The Marshall Plan also helped to solve the German problem by making possible a lasting rapprochement between West Germany and France, an objective that had eluded diplomats for three generations. With the integration of West Germany into new regional institutions, Western Europe was restored to viability in world politics.

The Far East commanded considerably less attention in Washington because U.S. interests in that area were more limited. American aid programs, moreover, could do little to affect the outcome of the civil war in China, the country that had been expected to play the leading role in postwar Asia. Until 1948, American efforts in Japan were focused upon demilitarization. General MacArthur did not promote Japanese recovery until Washington policymakers determined that a strong and pro-Western Japan, acting as the hub of trade in East Asia, was essential to the containment of Communism in Asia. By integrating Japan into an open multilateral system, the United States offered Tokyo access to world markets and raw materials on the basis of peaceful economic competition.

The legacy of the Truman era in the underdeveloped world was mixed. Few of the developing countries achieved the balanced growth and political maturity that American officials had promised would come in the wake of increased private investment. On the other hand, the United States captured, for itself and its allies, control over the most important sources of strategic minerals in the non-Communist world. In particular, the vast expansion of cheap overseas oil supplies helped to sustain postwar economic expansion and to promote Western security. From a short-term perspective, American diplomacy in the Third World succeeded in achieving key economic and strategic aims.

The same can be said for American foreign economic policy as a whole. During the five years from Roosevelt's death to the Korean invasion, the Truman administration built an open world order that helped integrate the Western economies and reduce conflict in the non-Communist world. The United States, of course, was acting in its own interest by facilitating world trade and recovery. Yet one has only to remember the interwar experience to appreciate why leaders of the industrialized democracies welcomed American leadership of the international economy after World War II.

Legacy and Lessons of the Truman Era

The economic cooperation of the main non-Communist powers after World War II profoundly enhanced the prospects for a political and military partnership. The fact that West Germany and France, for instance, could count on American assistance to facilitate reconstruction and rearmament made it easier for these traditional enemies to work together, first in industrial projects, and then in NATO. Other formal and informal arrangements—the IMF's stabilization of exchange rates, the GATT's reduction of trade barriers, and central bankers' resolution of multinational currency crises—offered further proof that multilateral cooperation yielded rich political and economic dividends.

By the same token, economic friction, if unchecked, could irreparably damage the alliance. Mutual recriminations between the United States and its allies over economic sanctions against the Soviet Union, coupled with discord over Western trade and financial issues, have more than once endangered the unity of NATO. One of the main lessons of the Truman era is that punitive commercial tactics are not likely to work in an open system. The fact that Washington was unable to win political concessions from the Soviet-bloc countries during the late 1940s, when American economic leverage was at its peak, should give pause to later generations of U.S. policymakers entertaining the thought of sanctions. And the growing inability of Washington to exercise control over U.S.-based multinational corporations further erodes the usefulness of this economic weapon.[6]

Despite its many shortcomings, the system created at Bretton Woods was bold, creative, even visionary. The real alternative was not a socialist commonwealth, but a return to the protectionist, discriminatory system of the prewar years. The reduction of commercial barriers and the establishment of stable exchange rates, based upon a strong dollar, were prerequisites to the recovery of world trade while U.S. and World Bank loans were an important element in European reconstruction.

The United States also acted as a responsible creditor nation during Truman's presidency. In contrast with its behavior after the First World War, the United States forgave war debts, widely distributed aid, and opened its markets to imports, gradually restoring world equilibrium. Both the Truman and the Eisenhower administrations closely balanced American resources with domestic and international commitments. As a result, they successfully restrained governmental spending, budget deficits, and inflation. The U.S. record during the forties and fifties

seems especially impressive when compared with the economic mis-
management of the last two decades.[7]

Despite some lapses, the Truman presidency was probably more successful than any other postwar administration in planning and execut-
ing foreign economic policy. The consensus among postwar American
leaders on the need for international economic reform clearly facilitated
policy implementation, as did the extremely close consultation that top
officials maintained with the nation's legislators. William Clayton,
George Kennan, and Dean Acheson played an indispensable role in
defining the link between foreign economic and strategic goals. But
perhaps most importantly, President Truman's personal interest in a
more open world economy helped mobilize the U.S. government and
public behind liberal policies. The contrast with recent Presidents
could not be starker: even in the face of dire energy and monetary
crises, successive administrations have dealt with foreign economic issues in an *ad hoc*, offhand manner, making virtually no attempt to take
a comprehensive approach.

President Truman perhaps can be faulted for his preoccupation with
balanced budgets. To many contemporaries, the Korean invasion and
the subsequent Chinese entry into the war exposed the lack of U.S.
military preparedness and the folly of Truman's ceiling on defense
expenditures. There is no doubt that the proliferation of U.S. global
commitments after the war stretched U.S. armed forces to the limit,
and that the neglect of conventional forces encouraged an over-reliance
upon atomic weapons in military strategy.

In retrospect, however, the Truman administration's dependence
upon economic power (and the bomb) before Korea is understandable.
The demise in the Congress of the President's limited proposal for
Universal Military Training indicates the depth of popular resistance to
the notion of a large military. The increments in the Pentagon budget
that Congressional defense advocates desired were heavily oriented toward air and atomic power and would not have significantly relieved the
shortage of ground forces that military leaders faced in June 1950. In
the final analysis, the economic security strategy worked: the GATT
did promote world trade; the Marshall Plan did restore European production and facilitate Franco-German cooperation; and Western economic growth did make possible an enduring and powerful alliance
between America, Japan, and most of Europe. The United States
achieved all this with a defense budget that never exceeded 5.7 percent
of GNP during the fiscal years 1947 to 1950, compared with 9–10 per-

cent during the late fifties (see appendix, graph 2).[8] President Truman, in short, did not succumb to the temptations of what his successor would label the "military-industrial complex."

In recent years, the "free-trade" system begun at Bretton Woods has come under increasing attack. Critics have pointed out that free trade has always been more a slogan than a reality: even in the 1980s, about 75 percent of world commerce remains protected by tariffs, quotas, export subsidies, and other barriers. World steel, among other major industries, is organized into cartels (U.S., European, and Japanese) that coordinate production and prices.

The economic benefits of multilateralism, moreover, are no longer as clearcut as they were during the Truman presidency. The United States and Western Europe have lost their monopoly in advanced technology and manufacturing, and Japan and the developing countries command an increasing share of world trade. (Since 1980, U.S. trade with the "Pacific Rim" countries—Japan, South Korea, China, Taiwan, Hongkong, and Singapore—has exceeded that with Western Europe.) Many emerging nations have adopted a "state-centered capitalism" in which the government controls and subsidizes export-oriented firms. The danger, the pessimists warn, is that as U.S. industries struggle to compete with these newcomers under an open trading regime, wages may sink to Third World levels. Alternatively, if the developed countries allow "old" manufacturing industries, such as steel and automobiles, to perish, the outlook is for chronically high unemployment since newer industries, such as computers, are unlikely to generate many jobs. The solution would seem to lie in more "market-sharing" and protectionism.[9]

The critics may have overstated the costs and underestimated the benefits of multilateralism. The worldwide availability of state-of-the-art capital equipment does not by itself ensure the flight of heavy industry to Third World countries with large pools of cheap labor. Managerial competence, worker productivity, national infrastructure, savings levels, governmental incentives, and many other factors can compensate for the labor differential enjoyed by the developing countries. Protectionism, as the steel and automobile companies have found, provides only a temporary respite from foreign competition, unless, that is, the country is willing to withdraw from world trade altogether. Advocates of a new industrial policy have not explained how to identify the economic sectors that the government should support. The American political process is so weighted in favor of established interest groups that a national planning program might end up sub-sidizing inefficient industries.[10]

There is no turning back to economic isolationalism. "The Ricardian principle of comparative advantage has been learned, and few . . . would question the proposition that free as opposed to less free trade means greater prosperity."[11] Radical critics of the Open Door should also consider the unenviable state of the East European economies—let alone their political systems—before belittling the benefits of competi-tion, minimal state intervention in national economies, and a multi-lateralist order.

Aside from the economic costs or benefits of the *status quo*, the United States probably cannot abandon the present system without forfeiting many of its political advantages. The Open Door was de-signed to open both ways. American credibility would be severely damaged if the United States, suffering now from competition in the world marketplace, were to withdraw from the very system that it imposed upon its major allies after the war. This does not mean that Washington must sit idly by as foreign competitors dump their prod-ucts on U.S. shores or otherwise engage in unfair trading practices. But the main causes of the U.S. economic malaise are probably internal, a product of fiscal irresponsibility and managerial complacency. "To put its affairs in order," David Calleo comments, "the United States will have to sacrifice more at home to pay for its international position, or it will have to scale down its world commitments."[12]

Participation in an open economic order bound together the Western countries in the most potent alliance in the world. Economic coopera-tion yielded unprecedented prosperity, which in turn provided the basis for political and military partnership. In this sense, the Truman administration leaders were correct: the foundation of American se-curity was a healthy and interdependent world economy. The Western alliance now faces its greatest challenge not from the Soviet military threat but from its own economic ills. The crisis comes at a time when the resources, will, and determination of America and its partners may no longer be sufficient to sustain the alliance.

Appendix

Table A.1. Military Personnel on Active Duty, 1945–1953

YEAR	TOTAL[a]	ARMY	AIR FORCE[b]	NAVY	MARINES	NAVY + MARINES
1945	12,123,455	8,267,958	—	3,380,817	474,680	3,855,497
1946	3,030,088	1,891,011	—	983,398	155,679	1,139,077
1947	1,528,999	991,285	—	498,661	93,053	591,714
1948	1,445,910	554,030	387,730	419,162	84,988	504,150
1949	1,615,360	660,473	419,347	449,575	85,965	535,540
1950	1,460,261	593,167	411,277	381,538	74,279	455,817
1951	3,249,455	1,531,774	788,381	736,680	192,620	929,300
1952	3,635,912	1,596,419	983,261	824,265	231,967	1,056,232
1953	3,555,067	1,533,815	977,593	794,440	249,219	1,043,659

Source: United States Department of Commerce, Bureau of the Census. *Historical Statistics of the United States, Colonial Times to 1970*, 2:1141. Washington, D.C.: GPO, 1975.
[a] Does not include the Coast Guard.
[b] Before 1948, Army figures include air personnel.

Graph 1
Military Personnel on Active Duty, 1945-1953

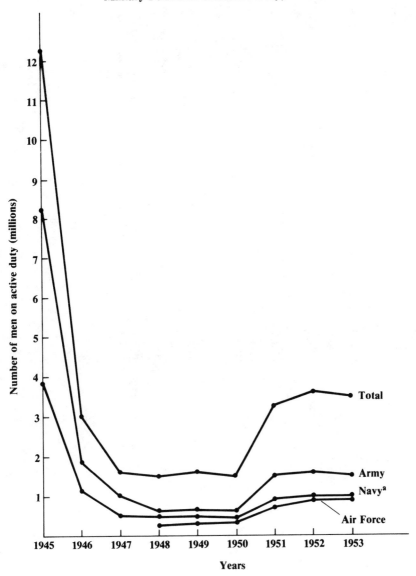

ªIncludes Marines.

Source: see Table A.1.

Table A.2. Government Outlays As a Percentage of G.N.P., 1945–1953

YEAR	G.N.P. ($ million)	FEDERAL BUDGET ($ million)	FEDERAL BUDGET/G.N.P. (percentage)
1945	213,558	95,184	44.6%
1946	209,246	61,738	29.5%
1947	232,228	36,931	15.9%
1948	257,325	36,493	14.2%
1949	257,301	40,570	15.8%
1950	285,067	43,147	15.1%
1951	328,232	45,797	14.0%
1952	345,229	67,962	19.7%
1953	364,520	76,769	21.1%

YEAR	INTERNATIONAL ($ million)	INTERNATIONAL/G.N.P. (percentage)	DEFENSE ($ million)	DEFENSE/G.N.P. (percentage)
1945	83,568	39.1%	81,585	38.2%
1946	50,124	24.0%	44,731	21.4%
1947	18,822	8.1%	13,059	5.6%
1948	18,495	7.2%	13,015	5.1%
1949	18,770	7.3%	13,097	5.1%
1950	17,299	6.1%	13,119	4.6%
1951	27,165	8.3%	22,544	6.9%
1952	49,059	14.2%	44,015	12.8%
1953	56,757	15.6%	50,413	13.8%

YEAR	FOREIGN MIL. AID ($ million)	FOR. MIL./G.N.P. (net new grants)	FOREIGN ECON. AID ($ million)	FOR. ECON./G.N.P. (net new grants and credits)
1945	610	.3%	1,377	.6%
1946	69	—	5,324	2.5%
1947	97	—	5,666	2.4%
1948	473	.2%	5,007	2.0%
1949	213	.1%	5,460	2.1%
1950	519	.2%	3,661	1.3%
1951	1,440	.4%	3,181	1.0%
1952	2,656	.8%	2,388	.7%
1953	4,266	1.2%	2,078	.6%

Sources: U.S. Department of Commerce, Bureau of the Census. *Historical Statistics of the United States, Colonial Times to 1970,* 2:874 and 1116. Washington, D.C.: GPO, 1975; U.S. Department of Commerce, Bureau of the Census. *Statistical Abstract of the United States, 1956,* p. 202. Washington, D.C.: GPO, 1956.

Graph 2
Government Outlays as a Percentage of G.N.P., 1945-1953

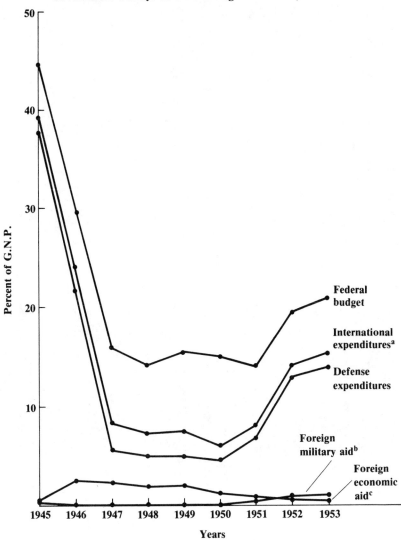

ᵃIncludes Defense and Foreign Aid.
ᵇNet new grants.
ᶜNet new grants and credits.

Source: see Table A.2.

Table A.3. Outlays of the Federal Government, 1945–1953

YEAR	TOTAL GOVERNMENT OUTLAYS ($ million)	NATIONAL DEFENSE ($ million)
1945	95,184	81,585
1946	61,738	44,731
1947	36,931	13,059
1948	36,493	13,015
1949	40,570	13,097
1950	43,147	13,119
1951	45,797	22,544
1952	67,962	44,015
1953	76,769	50,413

Foreign Military and Economic Aid, Grants and Credits, 1945–1953

YEAR	NET NEW MILITARY GRANTS ($ million)	NET NEW ECONOMIC GRANTS AND CREDITS ($ million)
1945	610	1,377
1946	69	5,324
1947	97	5,666
1948	473	5,007
1949	213	5,460
1950	519	3,661
1951	1,440	3,181
1952	2,656	2,388
1953	4,266	2,078

Source: U.S. Department of Commerce, Bureau of the Census. *Historical Statistics of the United States, Colonial Times to 1970.* 2:874 *and* 1116. (Washington, D.C.: GPO, 1975).

Graph 3
Outlays of the Federal Government, 1945-1953

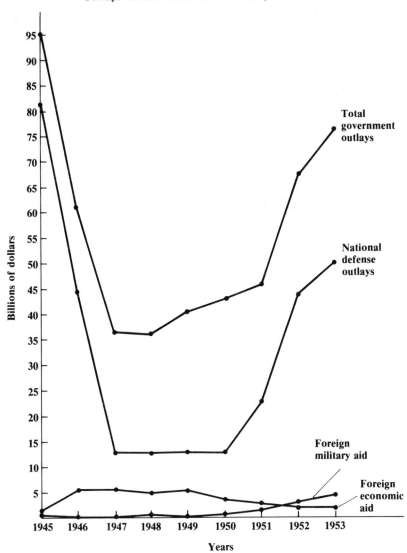

Source: see Table A.3.

Notes

1. The Political Economy of Postwar America

1. C. Fred Bergsten, "International Economic Relations," p. 2. For trade during 1930s, see U.S. Department of Commerce, Bureau of the Census, *Historical Statistics of the United States: Colonial Times to 1970, Part 2*, p. 887. Hereafter cited as "Commerce, *HSUS*."

2. Quotations from William L. Clayton, "The Foreign Economic Policy of the State Department," Address before Economic Club of Detroit, May 21, 1945, in *Department of State Bulletin* (May 27, 1945), 12: 979, 981, 982. Hereafter cited as "*DSB*."

3. The most important revisionist works for the purpose of this study are Fred L. Block, *The Origins of International Economic Disorder: A Study of United States International Monetary Policy from World War II to the Present;* Thomas G. Paterson, *Soviet-American Confrontation: Postwar Reconstruction and the Origins of the Cold War;* and Joyce and Gabriel Kolko, *The Limits of Power: The World and United States Foreign Policy, 1945–1954.* Two other general revisionist studies also deserve mention here: William Appleman Williams, *The Tragedy of American Diplomacy,* and Walter LaFeber, *America, Russia, and the Cold War, 1945–1975.* The reader will find reference to numerous revisionist works on specific topics in subsequent chapters. For useful discussions of revisionist interpretations of the Cold War, see Charles S. Maier, "Revisionism and the Interpretation of Cold War Origins," and Michael Leigh, "Is There a Revisionist Thesis on the Origins of the Cold War?" For a critique of Marxian theories on the economic causes of U.S. imperialism, see Robert B. Zevin, "An Interpretation of American Imperialism."

4. Probably the most popular and representative "orthodox" work currently is John Spanier, *American Foreign Policy Since World War II.* Also see Martin F. Herz, *Beginnings of the Cold War* (Bloomington: Indiana University Press, 1966); Louis J. Halle, *The Cold War as History.* The most important "post-revisionist" works are John Lewis Gaddis, *The United States and the Origins of the Cold War, 1941–1947,* and Daniel Yergin, *Shattered Peace: The Origins of the Cold War and the National Security State.* On post-revisionist literature, see John Lewis Gaddis, "The Emerging Post-Revisionist Synthesis on the Origins of the Cold War."

5. Kolko, *Limits*, pp. 1–6, quotation on p. 2.

6. Quotation from Gaddis, "Post-Revisionist Synthesis," p. 174.

7. Kolko, *Limits*, p. 11, also see p. 709.

8. E.g., see *ibid.*, p. 2; Paterson, *Confrontation*, p. 13.

9. In each case, economic policymakers faced two basic problems: first, "how to reconcile national self-determination with the widely understood advantages of international economic collaboration," and second, how to adjust trade and payment mechanisms without either discouraging the free movement of trade and capital or disturbing domestic prices and employment. See Alfred E. Eckes, Jr., *A Search for Solvency: Bretton Woods and the International Monetary System, 1944–1971*, p. 2.

10. On the gold standard, see Harold Van B. Cleveland, "The International Monetary System in the Interwar Period," in Benjamin M. Rowland, ed., *Balance of Power or Hegemony: The Interwar Monetary System*, pp. 12–18, 25–26; Robert J. A. Skidelsky, "Retreat from Leadership: The Evolution of British Economic Foreign Policy, 1870–1939," in Rowland, pp. 150–51, 157–60. Historians and economists differ over the degree to which the Bank of England or market forces (the "Hidden Hand") acted as coordinator of the prewar international monetary system. Both Cleveland and Skidelsky stress that an imperial manager is necessary to uphold international monetary stability (Britain in the prewar system, America after 1945), while David P. Calleo argues that sterling was "a bloc within the world system rather than the world system itself" and that economic order can survive in a pluralist system ("The Historiography of the Interwar Period: Reconsiderations," in Rowland, p. 240). Similarly, W. H. Bruce Brittain believes that the relationship between international political and international economic order is weak; "while political hegemony . . . *may* lead to economic order," he states, "economic order may also exist in its absence" ("The Relevance of Political Leadership to Economic Order: Evidence from the Interwar Period," in Rowland, p. 64).

11. Charles P. Kindleberger, "U.S. Foreign Economic Policy 1776–1976," p. 399.

12. On British decline and weakness of "gold-exchange" system of 1920s, see Skidelsky, "Retreat," pp. 163–75. On American privatism, see Eckes, *Search*, pp. 8–10, 14–15; Michael J. Hogan, *Informal Entente: The Private Structure of Cooperation in Anglo-American Economic Diplomacy, 1918–1928*, p. 103. Hogan adds that despite the tough public line taken by the Harding and Coolidge administrations, the United States had reached agreements with 13 nations by 1927 that effectively cancelled 50 percent of total Allied war indebtedness (p. 52).

13. Hogan, *Entente*, pp. 215–18.

14. *Ibid.*, pp. 102–03; Kindleberger, "U.S. Policy," pp. 399–402; Eckes, *Search*, pp. 6–19; Block, *Economic Disorder*, pp. 17–22. For a monetarist explanation of the European crisis, see Cleveland, "Monetary System," pp. 45–49.

15. Eckes, *Search*, pp. 19–21; Cleveland, "Monetary System," pp. 48–49.

16. Quotation cited in Eckes, *Search*, p. 22, also see pp. 19–31; and Kindleberger, "U.S. Policy," pp. 404–05; Block, *Economic Disorder*, pp. 22-30. On German manipulation of its economic bloc in Eastern Europe for political pur-

poses, see David E. Kaiser, *Economic Diplomacy and the Origins of the Second World War: Germany, Britain, France, and Eastern Europe, 1930–1939*, pp. 316–18.

17. Acheson quotation from Dean Acheson,"Bretton Woods: A Monetary Basis for Trade," Address before Economic Club of New York, April 16, 1945, in *DSB* (April 22, 1945), 12:738. Wallace quotation cited in Eckes, *Search*, p. 34. White quotation cited in Armand Van Dormael, *Bretton Woods: Birth of a Monetary System*, p. 45. For books by contemporary economists propounding these "lessons," see Albert O. Hirschman, *National Power and the Structure of Foreign Trade* (Berkeley: University of California Press, 1945; expanded ed., 1980), pp. 3–81; Herbert Feis, *The Changing Patterns of International Economic Affairs* (New York: Harper, 1940), passim; Jacob Viner, *International Trade and Economic Development* (Glencoe, Ill.: Free Press, 1952), pp. 97–98. Also see Block, *Economic Disorder*, pp. 30–31; Thomas G. Paterson, *On Every Front: The Making of the Cold War*, pp. 74–75; Lloyd C. Gardner, *Economic Aspects of New Deal Diplomacy* (Madison: University of Wisconsin Press, 1964), passim.

18. Quotation from Irvine H. Anderson, *Aramco, the United States, and Saudi Arabia: A Study of the Dynamics of Foreign Oil Policy, 1933–1950*, p. 16.

19. Charles S. Maier, "The Politics of Productivity: Foundations of American International Economic Policy after World War II," pp. 611–14.

2. Planning for the Peace

1. Gaddis, *Cold War*, p. 23.

2. Eckes, *Search*, p. 38. On Hull, see William R. White, "Cordell Hull and the Defense of the Trade Agreements Program, 1934–1940," in Alexander De-Conde, ed., *Isolation and Security*, pp. 114, 121, 127.

3. Eckes, *Search*, pp. 39–40; Gaddis, *Cold War*, pp. 18–20.

4. Hull quotations cited in Dormael, *Bretton Woods*, p. 25, Hawkins quotation on p. 26; on distinction between protectionism and discrimination, see pp. 24–25.

5. On White's role in early wartime planning, see Eckes, *Search*, pp. 42, 46–57; on the Soviet issue, see pp. 50, 103–05; and Dean Acheson, *Present at the Creation: My Years in the State Department*, pp. 122–23.

6. White quotation cited in Eckes, *Search*, p. 52. For State quotation, see Leddy Memo, Feb. 16, 1944, forwarded by Catudal to Pasvolsky on Feb. 22, 1944, Office Files of Leo Pasvolsky, File "Feb.–March 1944," RG 59, National Archives, Washington, D.C. Pasvolsky office files hereafter cited as "Pasvolsky Papers." All further references to RG 59 files hereafter cited as "NA." For a similar memo, see Emilio G. Collado to Secretary of State, (hereafter abbreviated as "SecState"), "International Financial Program," March 20, 1944.

7. Roosevelt and Morgenthau quotations from *The New York Times*, July 2, 1944, hereafter cited as "NYT." Also see Richard N. Gardner, "The Political Setting," in A. L. K. Acheson, J. F. Chant, and M. F. J. Prachowny, eds., *Bretton Woods Revisited*, p. 22.

8. Gardner, "Political Setting," pp. 24–26; *NYT,* July 3, 4, 13, 19, 1944; Eckes, *Search,* p. 149; Richard M. Cooper, *The Economics of Interdependence: Economic Policy in the Atlantic Community,* pp. 27–34.

9. Raymond F. Mikesell, "Negotiating at Bretton Woods, 1944," in Raymond Dennett and Joseph E. Johnson, eds., *Negotiating with the Russians,* pp. 101–12. The British, too, appreciated the political importance of giving the Soviets a prominent role in Bretton Woods. See Dormael, *Bretton Woods,* pp. 71, 215; quotation on p. 191.

10. Mikesell, "Negotiating," p. 109; Dormael, *Bretton Woods,* pp. 191–96, 216–17; *NYT,* July 7, 13, 20, 22, 23, 24, 1944.

11. James T. Patterson, *Mr. Republican: A Biography of Robert A. Taft,* pp. 292–93.

12. Another option to Bretton Woods was the bilateral trading practices that some European countries adopted out of necessity after the war, but the European participants did not seriously propose this as an alternative "system." On U.S. Chamber of Commerce and Wall Street, see *NYT,* June 25, July 4, 13, Sept. 16, 1944; Dormael, *Bretton Woods,* pp. 245–48. The bankers in the August 1944 meeting, including members of the Federal Reserve System of New York, expressed less opposition to the World Bank. But the State Department official present complained that their dislike of both the IMF and the Bank was based upon "a very superficial knowledge of the contents of the Bretton Woods documents." See Emilio G. Collado, "Attitude of New York Bankers with Respect to the International Monetary Fund and Bank Proposals," Aug. 15, 1944, Records of Dean Acheson, File "Stabilization Fund: No. 3 from 7/24/44," NA. For a critical interpretation of the key currency plan and its proponents, see Block, *Economic Disorder,* pp. 52–53.

13. Byrnes' quotation from *NYT,* Jan. 2, 1945; also see July 13, 1944.

14. Morgenthau's sounding of the economic security theme was based partly upon conviction, partly upon opportunism. Since few professional economists, let alone Congressmen, could agree on how Bretton Woods would work, Harry White told his staff in March 1945, the Treasury's campaign should avoid technicalities and instead stress that "economic security and political security are inseparable." White quotation cited in Dormael, *Bretton Woods,* p. 244; Morgenthau's testimony cited on p. 252. "Power politics" quotation from Henry Morgenthau, Jr., "Bretton Woods and International Cooperation," *Foreign Affairs* (January 1945), 23:184, 191; also H. D. White, "The Monetary Fund: Some Criticisms Examined," on pp. 195–210; and William A. Fowler Speech, "Commercial Policy Objectives," *DSB* (Sept. 24, 1944), 11:317–18.

15. Richard N. Gardner, *Sterling-Dollar Diplomacy: The Origins and Prospects of Our International Economic Order,* pp. 139–42; Block, *Economic Disorder,* p. 52.

16. The House approved Bretton Woods by 345–18 in June 1945; the Senate followed suit in July by 61–16. The Roosevelt and Truman administrations engaged in a major public relations campaign to pass the bill; see *NYT,* Feb. 19, March 4, 20, May 4, 1945; on concessions to critics, Feb. 16, 1945; on Congressional debate, June 8, and July 13, 17, 18, 19, 20, 1945. On NAC, see Gardner, *Sterling-Dollar,* p. 134; Block, *Economic Disorder,* p. 54.

17. *NYT,* Dec. 6, 1945, Jan. 3, 6, 10, 1946.

18. Lloyd C. Gardner, *Architects of Illusion: Men and Ideas in American Foreign*

Policy, 1941–1949, p. 120; *Paterson, Confrontation*, p. 147; Gabriel Kolko, *The Politics of War: The World and United States Foreign Policy, 1943–1945*, pp. 256–58. For a similar argument, see Michael Hudson, *Super Imperialism: The Economic Strategy of American Empire* (New York: Holt, Rinehart & Winston, 1968), pp. 83–88.

19. Besides, revisionists assume that multilateralism—the "Open Door"—was inferior to other commercial arrangements, whereas in the context of the times, the only alternatives were either closed national economies tied to bilateral trading blocs—the very antithesis of international cooperation—or the "key currency" approach advocated by Wall Street bankers. See Mikesell, "Negotiating," pp. 109–16; Alfred E. Eckes, Jr., "Open Door Expansionism Reconsidered: The World War II Experience," p. 920. Purely ideological or economic considerations, moreover, did not necessarily compel Stalin to adopt autarkic practices in the Soviet sphere after the war, for Stalin's successors eagerly pursued trade with the West. See Jerry Pubrantz, "Marxism-Leninism and Soviet-American Economic Relations Since Stalin," pp. 538–42.

20. Gaddis, *Cold War*, p. 23.

21. Robert J. Donovan, *Conflict and Crisis: The Presidency of Harry S Truman, 1945–1948*, p. xiv; Eben A. Ayers' Diary May 25, 1945, Papers of Eben A. Ayers, File "January 1, 1945, to December 31, 1945," Harry S Truman Library. Hereafter cited as "Ayers Diary (date), Ayers Papers . . ." and as "HSTL." Also see Paterson, *Front*, pp. 100–01.

22. Significantly, the main "soft-liners" on the Soviet Union in the early Truman Cabinet—Stimson, Morgenthau, and Secretary of Commerce Henry A. Wallace—all resigned or were fired during 1945–46. Stimson quotation of April 12, 1945, cited in Donovan, *Conflict and Crisis*, p. 13; also see pp. 22–23.

23. On background to Molotov meeting and on nature of Truman's advisers, see Harry S. Truman, *Memoirs: Year of Decisions*, pp. 70–82; Yergin, *Shattered Peace*, pp. 73–83; Donovan, *Conflict and Crisis*, pp. 36–42; Paterson, *Front*, pp. 101–04; Walter Millis, ed., *The Forrestal Diaries*, pp. 48–51.

24. Historians have greatly exaggerated the importance of Truman's confrontation with Molotov, perhaps because the dramatic, symbolic nature of the incident offers a convenient introduction to what followed. For a review of the debate, see Leigh, "Revisionist Thesis," pp. 106–08. Yergin feels the incident marked a major shift in American attitudes toward the Soviets; see *Shattered Peace*, pp. 73, 80–86; also Paterson, *Front*, pp. 98–99, 112.

25. Donovan, *Conflict and Crisis*, p. 25.

26. Not surprisingly, the pressure of events sometimes overwhelmed the new President, who was embarrassed by a number of well-publicized gaffes during his first year as President. Eben Ayers, the assistant White House press secretary under Truman and an unofficial chronicler of the administration, notes in a diary entry of October 1945 that Truman resolved to cut drastically his personal appointments and to delegate more authority to his staff in order to alleviate the confusion and pressure in the White House. See Ayers Diary, Oct. 19, 1945, File "January 1, 1945 to December 31, 1945," HSTL.

27. Selig Adler, *The Isolationist Impulse: Its Twentieth Century Reaction*, pp. 291–93.

28. *Ibid.*, pp. 296–300, 316–20, 324–25.

29. Quotation from Millis, *Forrestal Diaries*, p. 129; also see Donovan, *Conflict and Crisis*, p. 128; Gaddis, *Cold War*, pp. 261–62; James F. Schnabel, *The Joint Chiefs of Staff and National Policy, 1945–1947*, volume 1 of *The History of the Joint Chiefs of Staff*, pp. 195-226.

30. Donovan, *Conflict and Crisis*, pp. 129, 165, 285; Gaddis, *Cold War*, p. 262; H. Bradford Westerfield, *Foreign Policy and Party Politics: Pearl Harbor to Korea*, pp. 197–99. On across-the-board demobilization, Schnabel notes: "Less than two months after Japan's capitulation, millions of Americans remained in uniform but the combat effectiveness of most units had declined from 50 to 75 percent although their authorized strength had declined by only a small percentage" (*JCS*, p. 212).

31. Donovan, *Conflict and Crisis*, p. 200; Gaddis, *Cold War*, p. 262. On the administration's commitment to UMT, see War Department [unsigned], "Notes on Universal Military Training," n.d. [Sept. 1945], Papers of Harry S. Truman, President's Secretary's File, Subject File, File "Agencies: Military Training," HSTL; and Stimson statement before Cabinet meeting, Sept. 7, 1945. Hereafter cited as "Papers of HST-PSF-Subject File." On link between failure of UMT and atomic program, see Lynn Eden, "Capitalist Conflict and the State: The Making of United States Military Policy," in Charles Bright and Susan Harding, eds., *Statemaking and Social Movements: Essays in History and Theory*, passim.

32. On strategic planning, see Schnabel, *JCS*, pp. 136–37; David MacIsaac, "The Air Force and Strategic Thought."

33. Alan Sweezy, "The Keynesians and Government Policy, 1933–1939," pp. 116–24; Byrd L. Jones, "The Role of Keynesians in Wartime Policy and Postwar Planning, 1940–1946," pp. 129–32; Herbert Stein, *The Fiscal Revolution in America*, pp. 169–75; Robert M. Collins, *The Business Response to Keynes, 1929–1964*, pp. 77–141; Donovan, *Conflict and Crisis*, p. 285. Ayers also notes Treasury Secretary John W. Snyder's skepticism toward Navy and Army Air Force plans for defending "all the world," at an annual price tag of $10–12 billion. See Ayers Diary, Aug. 24, 1945, Ayers Papers, File "January 1, 1945 to December 31, 1945," HSTL.

34. In contrast, Michael Sherry and Daniel Yergin argue that by early 1946, key American military officials reached a strategic consensus. The American national security "ideology" allegedly called for the permanent maintenance of a vast military establishment and the assumption of almost limitless commitments abroad to contain the Soviet Union, which military planners early identified as the only serious threat to the United States. Given American scientific and technological superiority, as well as budgetary considerations, strategic air power and the atomic bomb emerged as the main instruments of U.S. military policy. See Michael S. Sherry, *Preparing for the Next War: American Plans for Postwar Defense, 1941–45*, passim; Yergin, *Shattered Peace*, passim; and Melvyn P. Leffler, "The American Conception of National Security and the Beginnings of the Cold War, 1945–1948," passim.

35. Quotation from J. Weldon Jones, "Policies for Postwar Full Employment," Oct. 10, 1944, Papers of Edwin G. Nourse, File "Employment Act of 1946, Origins of," HSTL. Hereafter cited as "Nourse Papers." Congress in February 1946 passed a watered-down Employment Act that affirmed the

federal government's responsibility to maintain production and employment. The act also established the Council of Economic Advisers (CEA). See Donovan, *Conflict and Crisis*, pp. 169–70. On exports, see LaFeber, *Cold War*, pp. 10–11.

36. Donovan, *Conflict and Crisis*, pp. 107–08, 110–11, 113, 119, 121–22, 167–68, 198–99; Patterson, *Mr. Republican*, pp. 302–04.

37. During the war, what unity there was on domestic issues usually "came from Democrats bending to Republican strength" as the New Deal underwent a formidable assault. Truman's own Cabinet reflected the split among Democrats over whether to extend or to consolidate the New Deal. Liberal spokesmen blamed the President for the decline of reform and the disunity within the Democratic Party. Donald R. McCoy, "Republican Opposition during Wartime, 1941-1945," p. 180; Donovan, *Conflict and Crisis*, pp. 109–13; Alonzo B. Hamby, "The Liberals, Truman and FDR as Symbol and Myth," pp. 859–61, 863–65.

38. On State Department, see Acheson to Dunn, Aug. 4, 1944, Acheson Papers, File "Stabilization Fund: No. 3 from 7/24/44," NA. Rostow's analysis is contained in an essay, "Economic Emergency Measures for the Transition Period," which he enclosed in a letter to Pasvolsky. See Rostow to Pasvolsky, Oct. 3, 1944, Pasvolsky Papers, File "July-December 1944," NA.

39. Cooper, *Interdependence*, pp. 27–28; quotation from Gardner, "Political Setting," p. 23.

40. Paterson, *Confrontation*, pp. 76–77.

41. On UNRRA in Poland, see Durbrow to Gilpatric, Jan. 16, 1945, U.S. Department of State, *Foreign Relations of the United States (FRUS 1945)*, 2:959; Kennan to SecState, July 27, 1945, 998–99; Lane to SecState, Sept. 24, 1945, 1,029–31. On Czechoslovakia, see Steinhardt to SecState, Sept. 12, 1945, pp. 1,028–29; Steinhardt to SecState, Oct. 2, 1945, pp. 1,031–32; Steinhardt to SecState, Oct. 31, 1945, pp. 1,036–37; Steinhardt to SecState, Nov. 28, 1945, pp. 1,043–44. On Yugoslavia, see Thorp to Clayton, July 19, 1945, pp. 994–97; Grew to Winant, July 30, 1945, pp. 999–1,000; Matthews to SecState, Oct. 22, 1945, pp. 1,032–34; Patterson to SecState, Dec. 26, 1945, pp. 1,056–57.

42. Harriman to SecState, June 30, 1945, *FRUS 1945*, 2:988–89; Wilcox to Dort, Aug. 23, 1945, pp. 1,020–21; Paterson, *Confrontation*, pp. 77–86, 89–91.

43. On Soviet issue, see Acheson to Harriman, Sept. 8, 1945, *FRUS 1945*, 2:1,025–27; for Byrnes' order, see Byrnes to Smith, Dec. 8, 1945, pp. 1,050–52. Also see Paterson, *Confrontation*, pp. 82–85. On food issue, see Donovan, *Conflict and Crisis*, p. 203; Paterson, *Confrontation*, pp. 91–94.

44. Paterson, *Confrontation*, pp. 84–89.

45. Gaddis, *Cold War*, pp. 81–83; George C. Herring, Jr., "Lend-Lease to Russia and the Origins of the Cold War, 1944–1945," pp. 94–99. For the authoritative account of Lend-Lease, see Herring, *Aid to Russia, 1941–1946: Strategy, Diplomacy, the Origins of the Cold War* (New York: Columbia University Press, 1973).

46. Crowley to Stettinius, Jan. 13, 1945, *FRUS 1945*, 5:951–52; Stettinius to Harriman, March 16, 1945, p. 988; Harriman to Stettinius, March 20, 1945, pp. 988–89.

47. Crowley and Grew to Roosevelt, March 23, 1945, *FRUS 1945*, 2:991;

State Department to Soviet Embassy, March 24, 1945, pp. 991–93. Quotation from Herring, "Lend-Lease," p. 114.

48. Herring, "Lend-Lease," pp. 101–05, 108–13; Donovan, *Conflict and Crisis*, p. 53. For Truman's views on Lend-Lease, see Truman, *Year of Decisions*, p. 46.

49. In secret communications with Washington, Harriman had urged the overt use of Lend-Lease for political purposes. On Truman's blunder, see Crowley to Truman, May 11, 1945, *FRUS 1945*, 5:999–1,000; Truman to Crowley, May 11, 1945, p. 1,000; Herring, "Lend-Lease," pp. 108–14. On Soviet reaction and Harriman's rejoinder, see Novikov to Grew, May 16, 1945, p. 1,003; Page Memo, June 11, 1945, pp. 1,018–21; W. Averell Harriman and Elie Abel, *Special Envoy to Churchill and Stalin, 1941–1946*, pp. 465–67.

50. Herring, "Lend-Lease," pp. 108–14; Hazard to McCabe, Nov. 29, 1945, *FRUS 1945*, 5:1,047–48.

51. Quotations from Robert S. Rendell, "Export Financing and the Role of the Export-Import Bank of the United States," p. 94; and Herbert Feis, "Political Aspects of Foreign Loans," p. 610. Feis made the case for a large postwar loan to Russia on the grounds that Russia had the ability to repay, had yet to interfere in any other country's "sphere of security," and would not modify its policies in Eastern Europe in the face of American economic pressures (p. 612). Also see statement of Hawthorne Arey, "History of Operations and Policies of the Export-Import Bank of Washington," in U.S. Congress, Senate, *Study of Export-Import Bank and World Bank*, p. 121.

52. Cox and Angell to Crowley, "Export-Import Bank Legislation," May 31, 1945, Papers of Samuel I. Rosenman, File "Subject File 1945: Export-Import Bank," HSTL. Cox and Angell estimated that the Soviet Union required $2–3 billion, compared with $4–5 billion for all the rest of liberated Europe, during the year beginning Sept. 1, 1945. In this memo as elsewhere, total Russian needs were estimated at $6 billion.

53. On State Department views, see Collado to Acheson, July 7, 1945, *FRUS 1946*, 1:1,395–96. On Congress, see Gaddis, *Cold War*, pp. 222–23. On extension of lending authority, see Senate Committee on Banking and Currency, *Eximbank*, pp. 103–05.

54. Byrnes to Crowley, n.d. [drafted Sept. 3, 1945], *FRUS 1946*, 1:1,402–03. NAC membership included the Secretaries of the Treasury (who served as Chairman) and Commerce, the Chairman of the Eximbank, the Chairman of the Federal Reserve Board, and interested State Department officials like Clayton and Collado. Also see Senate Committee on Banking and Currency, *Eximbank*, p. 115.

55. NAC-37, Jan. 8, 1946, *FRUS 1946*, 1:1,413.

3. Cold War in the Soviet Sphere

1. For representative orthodox works, see Lynn Davis, *The Cold War Begins: Soviet-American Conflict over Eastern Europe*, and George F. Kennan, *Russia and the West under Lenin and Stalin* (Boston: Little, Brown, 1961), chs. 23–25. For

revisionist works, see Paterson, *Confrontation*, ch. 5, and Kolko, *Limits*, ch. 7. For a post-revisionist account, see William Taubman, *Stalin's American Policy: From Entente to Detente to Cold War*, chs. 3–6.

2. Bohlen cited in Eduard Mark, "American Policy Toward Eastern Europe and the Origins of the Cold War," p. 336. The Roosevelt and Truman administrations accepted the Soviet right to an "open" sphere of influence in Eastern Europe, whereby Moscow would provide foreign policy guidance to client states without intervening extensively in their financial affairs. The United States objected to an "exclusive" or "closed" Soviet sphere, whereby the Soviet Union controlled the domestic affairs of subject states and prohibited them from engaging in normal diplomatic and economic relations with other states. On distinction between spheres of influence, see Paterson, *Front*, p. 42; Geir Lundestad, *The American Non-Policy Towards Eastern Europe, 1943–1947: Universalism in an Area Not of Essential Interest to the United States*, pp. 92–98.

3. Vojtech Mastny, *Russia's Road to the Cold War: Diplomacy, Warfare, and the Politics of Communism, 1941–1945*, p. 212. On Roosevelt's vacillation, see Lundestad, *Non-Policy*, p. 94; Gaddis, *Cold War*, pp. 12–17. On Roosevelt's position on the Anglo-Soviet percentages agreements, see Davis, *Cold War Begins*, pp. 144–50, 164–70; Albert Resis, "The Churchill-Stalin Secret 'Percentages' Agreement on the Balkans, Moscow, October 1944," pp. 386–87.

4. Litvinov quotation cited in Taubman, *Stalin's American Policy*, p. 133. On Roosevelt and the American public, see Davis, *Cold War Begins*, pp. 197–98, 375, 382–83; Lundestad, *Non-Policy*, pp. 56–59; Gaddis, *Cold War*, pp. 134, 138–39, 157–60. For the view that public opinion rarely influenced policy, see Paterson, *Front*, pp. 127–29.

5. Quotation from Nikolai Mikhailov, "The Soviet Peacetime Economy," p. 635. Also see Alec Nove, *An Economic History of the U.S.S.R.*, pp. 284–92.

6. Commentators on international trade observed that both Nazi Germany and the Soviet Union "used trade for political purposes and . . . imposed harsh commercial treaties on Eastern European countries. Germany and Russia thus forced weaker nations to buy goods at exorbitant prices and to sell products to them at reduced rates." See Les K. Adler and Thomas G. Paterson, "Red Fascism: The Merger of Nazi Germany and Soviet Russia in the American Image of Totalitarianism, 1930's–1950's," p. 1,059. Under the peace treaties of 1947, Rumania and Hungary each pledged to pay $200 million in reparations to the Soviet Union. Finland owed $300 million. In 1948, however, the Soviets cut these figures in half. The Soviets also seized 200 firms in Hungary alone. See Paterson, *Confrontation*, pp. 102–05, 105n., 118n., 118–19, 138; K. R. S., "Economic Planning in Eastern Europe," pp. 432–34. The Soviets had commanded only about 1 percent of Eastern European trade during the 1930s, when Germany controlled the market there. Also, Stalin's notion of "socialism in one country" meant that the Soviet Union's share of world trade during the 1930s dropped to about 1 percent, compared with 4 percent in 1913. See K. R. S., "Planning," pp. 433–34; Alexander Baykov, *Soviet Foreign Trade*, pp. 64–65, Appendices: Table 7; Harry Schwartz, *Russia's Soviet Economy*, pp. 588–614; Nove, *Economic History*, pp. 312–13; Edward Ames, "International Trade Without Markets—The Soviet Bloc Case," pp. 791–807.

7. Barbara Ward, "Europe Debates Nationalization," pp. 44–55; Kolko,

Limits, pp. 215–16; Paterson, *Confrontation*, pp. 116–19; Isaac Deutscher, *Stalin: A Political Biography*, pp. 529–32, 536–37; Mastny, *Russia's Road*, pp. 60–71, 85–97, 167–82, 212–18.

8. Yalta conversation cited in Davis, *Cold War Begins*, pp. 178–79. Also see Deutscher, *Stalin*, pp. 529–32; Adam B. Ulam, *Expansion and Coexistence: Soviet Foreign Policy, 1917–1973*, p. 429.

9. Mark, "Eastern Europe," pp. 313–14, quotation on p. 336. Bohlen quotation cited in John Lewis Gaddis, "The United States and the Question of a Sphere of Influence in Europe, 1945–1949."

10. Khrushchev released the figures on the Soviet armed forces in 1960; see Ulam, *Expansion*, pp. 403–04. At the London Council of Foreign Ministers in September 1945, the Soviets made it clear that the American bomb would not frighten them into concessions. See Yergin, *Shattered Peace*, pp. 123, 137; Robert L. Messer, *The End of an Alliance: James F. Byrnes, Roosevelt, Truman, and the Origins of the Cold War*, pp. 90, 132, 139–42; Gregg Herken, *The Winning Weapon: The Atomic Bomb in the Cold War, 1945–1950*, chs. 1–4. Soviet work on the atomic bomb began in early 1943. "Stalin can hardly have thought that a Soviet bomb could be built in time to affect the outcome of the war," David Holloway notes. Probably "the decision should be seen as a hedge against uncertainty" (*The Soviet Union and the Arms Race*, pp. 18–19). For the classic revisionist statement of the atomic diplomacy thesis, see Gar Alperovitz, *Atomic Diplomacy: Hiroshima and Potsdam* (New York: Vintage Books, 1967).

11. These observations were derived from a seminar presentation by Jean L. Laloy on "Stalin and Europe: Policy Objectives at the End of World War II."

12. Quotation from Schwartz, *Soviet Economy*, p. 592. Also see Pubrantz, "Economic Relations," pp. 535, 538–42.

13. For Molotov request, see Harriman to SecState, Jan. 4, 1945, *FRUS 1945*, 5:942. The Soviets later rationalized that American aid and trade were unnecessary because their planned economy would ensure rapid recovery; see Mikhailov, "Peacetime Economy," p. 636. Varga formally recanted in 1949 after being stripped of his privileges; see Evsey D. Domar, "The Varga Controversy," pp. 143–51. On rivalry, see E. Varga, "Anglo-American Rivalry and Partnership: A Marxist View," pp. 583–95. "Dependence" quotation from Mastny, *Russia's Road*, p. 215.

14. On sychophants, see Milovan Djilas, *Conversations with Stalin*, pp. 105–07. Quotation from Vojtech Mastny, "The Cassandra in the Foreign Commissariat: Maxim Litvinov and the Cold War," p. 372. Regarding Stalin's advisers, George F. Kennan complained that "there is no limit to the extent to which these people can fill his mind with misinformation and misinterpretation about us and our policies, and all this without our knowledge." See Kennan to SecState, March 20, 1946, *FRUS 1946*, 6:722.

15. Italics in original. Werth interviewed Litvinov in February 1947. Litvinov quotation from Alexander Werth, *Russia at War, 1941–1945*, p. 850. Also see Mastny, "Cassandra," pp. 374–76; Paterson, *Front*, pp. 161–65.

16. Stalin quotation from Djilas, *Conversations*, p. 114. Other quotation from Holloway, *Arms Race*, p. 27. Also see Mastny, *Russia's Road*, pp. 306, 309–10; Taubman, *Stalin's American Policy*, p. 74.

17. Ulam, *Expansion*, pp. 400–03; William O. McCagg, Jr., *Stalin Embattled 1943–1948*, passim.

18. Paterson, *Confrontation*, pp. 101–02. Revisionist historians generally recognize that Washington sought more than the protection of business profits in Eastern Europe, but they fail to integrate Open Door ideology into the larger scheme of U.S. security aims (see e.g., pp. 99–119; also Kolko, *Limits*, pp. 176–217; Williams, *Tragedy*, pp. 202–59).

19. Paterson, *Confrontation*, pp. 101–04, 107. Also see Memo of Conversation, "Petroleum Chemistry Technology for USSR-Hungary," April 18, 1946, Clayton-Thorp Papers, File "Memoranda of conversation (folder 1)," HSTL.

20. George C. McGhee, "Conditions in Rumania Affecting Operations of Standard Oil Company of New Jersey," July 16, 1946, Clayton Papers, File "871.6363/7-1746," NA. Similarly, the State Department told Socony representatives that it could do nothing about Soviet seizure of an oil refinery in the Soviet zone of Austria. See Francis T. Williamson, "Soviet Seizure of Socony-Vacuum Property in Austria," Aug. 14, 1947, Records of the Office of European Affairs, 1934–1947: Files of John Hickerson, File "Memoranda of Conversation 1947–48," NA. Hereafter cited as "Matthews-Hickerson Papers."

21. U.S. diplomats stationed in Eastern Europe tried to protect American properties, but economic considerations played a small role in overall U.S. relations with those countries. See Thomas T. Hammond, "Conclusions," in Hammond, *Witnesses to the Origins of the Cold War*, p. 308. In order to attain a German reparations agreement excluding Soviet influence from the Western zones, support the position of Mikolajczyk and the London Poles, and increase the chances for free elections, Byrnes also devised a package deal at Potsdam that gave tacit consent to Polish annexation of German territory. See Lundestad, *Non-Policy*, pp. 189–90, 195–96, 200–07.

22. Lundestad, *Non-Policy*, pp. 207–08.

23. On Eximbank policy, see Acheson to Lane, Sept. 21, 1945, *FRUS 1945*, 5:374-75; quotations from Durbrow Memcon, Nov. 8, 1945, p. 403. Lane had earlier compared Soviet-Polish barter trade with "Nazi and Fascist commercial policy." Lane to Byrnes, Aug. 22, 1945, p. 365. On November aid decisions, see Byrnes to Lane, Nov. 24, 1945, p. 419; Durbrow Memcon, Dec. 5, 1945, p. 428.

24. Brant to Truman, Jan. 14, 1946, Papers of HST-PSF-Subject File: Foreign Affairs, File "Poland," HSTL. Also see Lundestad, *Non-Policy*, pp. 210–12.

25. The Warsaw government did not make a firm pledge to hold free elections. On aid negotiations, see Lundestad, *Non-Policy*, pp. 210, 212–13; Paterson, *Confrontation*, p. 133; Acheson to Byrnes, Jan. 22, 1946, *FRUS 1946*, 6:382–84; and Byrnes to Lane, April 22, 1946, pp. 432–33. On American offer, see McCabe to Polish Ambassador, April 22, 1946, pp. 433–35; Acheson Memcon, April 24, 1946, pp. 435–36.

26. Lane quotation from Lane to SecState, April 16, 1946, *FRUS 1946*, 6:428. Byrnes' message pertained specifically to Czechoslovakia, but generally to Eastern Europe. For quotation, see Byrnes to Acheson, Aug. 30, 1946, pp. 216–17. Byrnes had suspended the Eximbank and surplus credits in May. The surplus credits were finally approved on June 25, 1946. See Byrnes to Acheson, May 6, 1946, pp. 448–49; Acheson Memcon, May 8, 1946, pp. 451–52; Thomp-

son Memcon, June 25, 1946, pp. 466–67. The Eximbank loan was finally approved on Oct. 2, 1946. See Lane to SecState, Aug. 5, 1946, pp. 489–90, 490n.; Paterson, *Confrontation*, pp. 134–35; Lundestad, *Non-Policy*, p. 214. Byrnes' Stuttgart speech, Lane reported, aroused anti-American sentiment among all Polish factions; Lane to SecState, Sept. 17, 1946, pp. 494–95; Lundestad, *Non-Policy*, pp. 214–15. Lane reiterated this view to Secretary of State George C. Marshall; Lane to Marshall, April 29, 1947, *FRUS 1947*, 4:425–27; Marshall Memcon, May 9, 1947, pp. 427–29.

27. Acheson Memcon, Dec. 11, 1946, *FRUS 1947*, 6:526–29; Hooker Memcon, Dec. 13, 1946, pp. 529–34; Thompson Memcon, Dec. 14, 1946, pp. 534–36.

28. Acheson Memcon, Dec. 18, 1946, *FRUS 1946*, 6:542. From Warsaw, Lane reported that Poland had already committed most of its coal exports to the Soviet Union. But Lane for once sympathized with the Poles. He recommended a loan to increase coal production since Western Europe needed the coal, and coal revenues were the only way Poland could compensate American property owners. Furthermore, such aid constituted the last American lever in Poland. Lane to SecState, Dec. 22, 1946, pp. 546–48.

29. Moderate and Communist ministers alike sought to retain ties with the West and only abstained from the Marshall Plan due to Soviet pressure. But American officials no longer tolerated neutralism in the Cold War. E.g., see Lane to SecState, Feb. 17, 1947, *FRUS 1947*, 4:419; Thompson Memcon, April 3, 1947, pp. 421–22; Clayton to Lovett, July 29, 1947, pp. 435–38; Marshall Memcon, Aug. 6, 1947, pp. 438–41; Marshall Memcon, Sept. 26, 1947, pp. 446–52; Lundestad, *Non-Policy*, p. 221. On post-UNRRA relief, see Truman Message to Congress, Feb. 21, 1947, *FRUS 1947*, 1:1,034–35; Thorp to Eaton, April 23, 1947, pp. 1,036–38. On agricultural mission, see Lovett Memcon, June 24, 1947, *FRUS 1947*, 4:433–34; Editorial Note, pp. 434–35. The agronomist was Professor Noble Clark of the University of Wisconsin. See Thompson, "FAO Mission to Poland," Oct. 9, 1947, Clayton-Thorp Papers, File "Memoranda of conversation-copies of, July 1-Dec. 31, 1947," HSTL.

30. Ambassador Lane, in his farewell call of February 1947, told Polish officials in Warsaw that "good faith or lack of good faith" would influence the Bank's evaluation of a country's creditworthiness. See Lane to SecState, Feb. 24, 1947, *FRUS 1947*, 4:420–21. On initial U.S. reaction to Polish aid request, see Clayton to SecState, Oct. 5, 1946, *FRUS 1946*, 6:504–06. On October 4, 1946, Byrnes had cabled that the U.S. would not aid the Polish coal industry "without absolute guarantees that a reasonable proportion of coal exports will be allocated to countries west of the iron curtain" (p. 504n). Quotation on Bank's position from Collado to Snyder, Nov. 29, 1946, with attached memo, "Special Considerations Relating to Loans in Eastern Europe and Elsewhere," Papers of John W. Snyder, File "Int'l Monetary Fund, 1946–51," HSTL. Hereafter cited as "Snyder Papers." In December 1946, Clayton told the Poles that the Eximbank no longer handled long-term reconstruction loans, and that its resources were in any case fully committed. See Hooker Memcon, Dec. 13, 1946, *FRUS 1946*, 6:530.

31. Clayton to Lovett, July 29, 1947, *FRUS 1947*, 4:435–38; Thompson Memcon, Sept. 30, 1947, with attached Garner memo, Sept. 30, 1947, pp.

452-55; Southard to Snyder, "International Bank Loan to Poland," Nov. 25, 1947, Snyder Papers, File "Int'l Monetary Fund and Bank: Legislation 1946–1951 Folder #2," HSTL. Also see Lundestad, *Non-Policy*, pp. 221–22.

32. On crackdown, see Paterson, *Confrontation*, pp. 135–36. On Mikolajczyk, see Andrews Memo, Nov. 17, 1947, *FRUS 1947*, 4:460–64.

33. Lundestad, *Non-Policy*, pp. 153–61.

34. Lundestad estimates American properties at $30–50 million (pp. 160–61), while Paterson estimates them at $109 million (*Confrontation*, p. 122). Also see Steinhardt to SecState, Feb. 26, 1946, *FRUS 1946*, 6:185.

35. The Eximbank had tentatively approved a $50 million loan on May 8, 1946. Quotation from Steinhardt to SecState, Feb. 26, 1946, *FRUS 1946*, 6:187. Also see Byrnes to Steinhardt, Feb. 7, 1946, pp. 182–83; Byrnes to Steinhardt, Feb. 19, 1946, pp. 184–85; Steinhardt to SecState, May 3, 1946, p. 195; Acheson to Steinhardt, May 9, 1946, pp. 196–97; Steinhardt to SecState, May 11, 1946, p. 197n.

36. On Steinhardt's satisfaction with the May elections and the Gottwald government, see Steinhardt to SecState, May 27, 1946, *FRUS 1946*, 6:199–200; Steinhardt to SecState, July 3, 1946, pp. 204–05. On surplus and cotton credits, see McCabe to Hurban, May 28, 1946, pp. 200–03; Eximbank press release, May 31, 1946, pp. 203–04. For Byrnes' quotation, see Byrnes to Steinhardt, July 19, 1946, p. 206. Also see Lundestad, *Non-Policy*, pp. 164–65. On the surplus dispute, see *FRUS 1946*, 6:212–15; on compensation, see pp. 209–10, 215–16.

37. The Czechs had expended only $9 million of their surplus credits at the time of Byrnes' suspension. Byrnes to Acheson, Aug. 30, 1946, *FRUS 1946*, 6:216–17; Byrnes to Acheson, Sept. 17, 1946, p. 220. Will Clayton felt uneasy about the Eximbank loan. The Czechs, he argued, had submitted a satisfactory draft note on the compensation question. Given the NAC's approval of the loan, the United States had a "moral commitment" to extend Eximbank credits. Nevertheless, the department soon informed the Czechoslovak Embassy that since their country had impugned the generosity of American aid policy and had yet to compensate American investors, the Eximbank loan was indefinitely suspended. Quotation from Clayton to SecState, Sept. 21, 1946, p. 224. Also see Department of State to Czech Embassy, Sept. 28, 1946, p. 229; Paterson, *Confrontation*, pp. 123–24.

38. Quotation from Steinhardt to SecState, Oct. 11, 1946, *FRUS 1946*, 6:230. Also see Steinhardt to SecState, Oct. 7, 1946, pp. 229–30.

39. Steinhardt to SecState, Oct. 7, 1946, *FRUS 1946*, 6:231; Riddleberger Memcon, Dec. 3, 1946, pp. 237–38; Steinhardt to SecState, Dec. 23, 1946, pp. 238–41. On Czech request for cotton credit, see Slavik to Martin, Feb. 19, 1947, *FRUS 1947*, 4:196; Steinhardt to SecState, Nov. 13, 1947, p. 242. On Czech participation in, and withdrawal from, Paris Conference, see Marshall (Thorp) to Caffery (Clayton), July 9, 1947, pp. 218–19; Riddleberger Memcon, July 10, 1947, pp. 219–21; Steinhardt to SecState, July 15, 1947, pp. 221–23; Steinhardt to SecState, July 7, 1947, *FRUS 1947*, 3:313–14; Steinhardt to SecState, July 10, 1947, pp. 318–19; Steinhardt to SecState, July 10, 1947, pp. 319–20. On Czech attempt to salvage an economic agreement with the U.S., see Beam Memcon,

Nov. 14, 1947, *FRUS 1947*, 4:242–44; Steinhardt to SecState, Nov. 20, 1947, pp. 246–47, Steinhardt to SecState, Nov. 24, 1947, pp. 247–48; Steinhardt to SecState, Nov. 24, 1947, pp. 248–50. Also see Paterson, *Confrontation*, pp. 125–30; Lundestad, *Non-Policy*, pp. 172–80; Kolko, *Limits*, pp. 189–92, 208–12.

40. Instead of reciprocating Gottwald's gesture, Steinhardt and Byrnes decided to withhold aid until the Czechs provided more evidence of their independence and friendship. Although the United States and Czechoslovakia reached an interim agreement on commercial policy and compensation in November 1946, the Eximbank soon committed funds earmarked for Czechoslovakia elsewhere. Steinhardt to SecState, Oct. 11, 1946, *FRUS 1946*, 6:231; Byrnes to Steinhardt, Oct. 14, 1946, p. 233; Steinhardt to SecState, Oct. 25, 1946, pp. 233–34; Editorial Note, p. 236; Acheson to Steinhardt, Nov. 27, 1946, pp. 236–37.

41. During the first half of 1947, some American officials, including Steinhardt upon occasion, had second thoughts and considered small credits to orient Czech trade to the West. In July, however, the State Department rejected Clayton's recommendation that the U.S. reopen negotiations on the $50 million Eximbank loan to encourage Czech participation in the Marshall Plan. See Bruins to SecState, March 3, 1947, *FRUS 1947*, 4:197–98; Acheson to Murphy, March 25, 1947, pp. 198–200; Acheson to Steinhardt, April 24, 1947, pp. 203–04; Steinhardt to SecState, June 19, 1947, p. 215 and p. 215n. On Marshall Plan and aid, see Clayton to Thorp, July 9, 1947, p. 218n.; Thorp to Clayton, July 9, 1947, pp. 218–19; Riddleberger Memcon, July 10, 1947, pp. 219–21; Steinhardt to SecState, July 7, 1947, *FRUS 1947*, 3:313–14. "Irrefutable" quotation from Steinhardt to SecState, July 22, 1947, *FRUS 1947*, 4:223, and see pp. 224–26. Following U.S. rejection of the Czech overtures, the Soviet Union concluded a commercial agreement with Czechoslovakia under which the Soviets began large grain deliveries in December 1947. See Steinhardt to SecState, Nov. 20, 1947, pp. 246–47; Bruins to SecState, Dec. 19, 1947, pp. 250–51, 251n. Also see Yergin, *Shattered Peace*, pp. 344–46.

42. Brynes quoted in Acheson to Steinhardt, Nov. 7, 1946, *FRUS 1946*, 6:236.

43. Harriman statement in Minutes of SecState's Staff Committee, April 20, 1945, *FRUS 1945*, 5:841. On State Department officials, see Hugh de Santis, "Conflicting Images of the USSR: American Career Diplomats and the Balkans, 1944–1946," pp. 483–90. Truman statement from Ayers Diary, Aug. 7, 1945, Ayers Papers, File "January 1, 1945 to December 31, 1945," HSTL.

44. For explication of American fears concerning economic warfare, see, e.g., Fred M. Vinson, "After the Savannah Conference," p. 622; Herbert Feis, "The Conflict over Trade Ideologies," pp. 218–20.

45. Harriman to SecState, Jan. 6, 1945, *FRUS 1945*, 5:946. On Molotov's "unconventional request," see Harriman and Abel, *Envoy*, pp. 384–87.

46. Collado Memo, Jan. 4, 1945, *FRUS 1945*, 5:938–40; Morgenthau to Roosevelt, Jan. 10, 1945, pp. 948–49; State Department Memcon, Jan. 17, 1945, pp. 961–63.

47. Collado Memo, Jan. 4, 1945, *FRUS 1945*, 5:940; Collado Memo, Jan. 17, 1945, pp. 956–60; Clayton to SecState, Jan. 20, 1945, pp. 965–66; Mason to

Clayton, Feb. 7, 1945, pp. 973–75; Harriman to SecState, April 11, 1945, pp. 994–96; Collado Memo, April 19, 1945, pp. 997–98, 997n.

48. In a letter to a colleague concerning a speech on the British loan, Clayton advised: "I believe that it would be better if you avoided any mention of the Russian credit which has been mentioned from time to time in the press. This matter is not now being actively considered by the two governments." William L. Clayton to Charles P. Taft, Nov. 1, 1945, Clayton-Thorp Papers, File "T," HSTL. After the summer of 1946, the Eximbank no longer extended direct loans for economic reconstruction; the IBRD was to assume this function thereafter. See Editorial Note, *FRUS 1946*, 1:1,435–36. Also see Minutes of 10th meeting of NAC, Jan. 29, 1946, pp. 1,417–19; Minutes of 11th Meeting of NAC, Feb. 7, 1946, pp. 1,420–24; Minutes of 22nd Meeting of NAC, April 25, 1946, pp. 1,430–31; Minutes of 24th Meeting of NAC, May 6, 1946, pp. 1,432–33.

49. Quotation from Mikhailov, "Peacetime Economy," p. 636. The Russians did not directly bring up the loan question at either Yalta or Potsdam. In August 1945, a mid-level Soviet bureaucrat made a perfunctory request for a loan at rates lower than the Eximbank charged other countries. As late as January 1946, Harriman noted, the Russians apparently had yet to make up their minds on the loan. The Soviets finally officially inquired about the loan in March and May 1946. See Rudenko to Crowley, Aug. 28, 1945, *FRUS 1945*, 5:1,034–36; Byrnes (Crowley) to Harriman, Aug. 31, 1945, pp. 1,036–37; Harriman and Abel, *Envoy*, pp. 387, 533–34; Laloy, "Stalin." Also Paterson, *Confrontation*, pp. 33–56; Taubman, *Stalin's American Policy*, pp. 86–87.

50. Quotation from Paterson, *Froni*, p. 165. Of the $11 billion furnished to the Soviets under Lend-Lease, the Americans primarily sought compensation for the $2.3 billion in nonmilitary items, including over $225 million in postwar pipeline shipments as of February 1947. The United States offered the Soviets terms virtually identical with those which the Western allies accepted in settlement of their Lend-Lease accounts. See Clayton (Truesdell) Memo, Feb. 26, 1947, *FRUS 1947*, 4:658–64. Apparently, no one in particular in the Soviet bureaucracy had exclusive responsibility for the Lend-Lease negotiations. American officials went through a bureaucratic maze just to recover naval vessels furnished under the wartime aid program. Soviet officials sometimes came unprepared for meetings, or did not answer American proposals for months. See *FRUS 1945*, 5:999–1,048; *FRUS 1946*, 6:818–66; *FRUS 1947*, 4:653–717; *FRUS 1948*, 4:950–1,023. It is noteworthy, however, that many Americans overestimated the contribution of Lend–Lease to the Soviet war effort. "If it hadn't been for our supply line," Truman told his staff, "they'd all have been licked." Ayers Diary, Dec. 19, 1945, Ayers Papers, File "January 1, 1945 to December 31, 1945," HSTL.

51. The ITO never materialized, but the ITO negotiations led to a growing suspicion of Soviet intentions among American policymakers. On ITO, see Kolko, *Limits*, pp. 82–89. On Soviet-American trade, see Paterson, *Confrontation*, pp. 57–74.

52. "Fictitious" quotation from Harriman to SecState, Oct. 19, 1945, *FRUS 1945*, 2:1,339; MFN suggestion from Acheson to Harriman, Dec. 12, 1945, pp. 1,348–49; "unrealistic" from Harriman to SecState, Dec. 15, 1945, p. 1,350.

Acheson later explained that the department would for the time being overrule Harriman and seek Soviet participation in the ITO. Acheson to Harriman, Dec. 28, 1945, pp. 1,355–58. Kennan shared Harriman's skepticism; see George F. Kennan, *Memoirs: 1925–1950*, pp. 267–70; Kennan to SecState, Jan. 16, 1946, *FRUS 1946*, 1:1,274–75. Frustrated by the uncoordinated, *ad hoc* character of American policies in Europe, Harriman complained in December 1945 that "certain decisions are being made in the economic field without relating them to our over-all policy. . . . Since Soviet political policy appears to be influenced by economic objectives it would seem that we should give at this time greater attention to the concerting of our economic policy with our political policy towards the Soviet Union." Harriman to SecState, Dec. 11, 1945, *FRUS 1945*, 5:1,049. Harriman reiterated this point in January 1946; Harriman to SecState, Jan. 19, 1946, *FRUS 1946*, 6:820. Also Durbrow to Acheson, Jan. 21, 1946, p. 821. Acheson agreed that American eagerness to dispose of overseas surplus property undermined U.S. bargaining strength. Acheson to SecState, Jan. 22, 1946, pp. 821–22.

53. The Kremlin apparently regarded the ITO as an instrument of U.S. economic blackmail. Quotation from Horace H. Smith, "Statement on Russian Economic Policy Presented to Conference of Economic Counselors and Advisers," and Thomas Whitney, "Russia's view on the trade and employment conference," Jan. 31, 1946, Papers of Thomas C. Blaisdell, Jr., File "Miscellaneous Documents from the London Conference, 1945–46," HSTL. Hereafter cited as "Blaisdell Papers." Harriman later advised that the administration should seek legislation giving the executive authority to negotiate bilateral commercial agreements with state-trading nations. Harriman to SecState, April 23, 1946, *FRUS 1946*, 1:1,313–17.

54. Collado to Clayton, Feb. 4, 1946, *FRUS 1946*, 6:823–25; Byrnes to Orekov, Feb. 21, 1946, pp. 828–29; Byrnes to Novikov, April 18, 1946, pp. 834–37; Luthringer to Clayton, May 23, 1946, pp. 842–43; Byrnes to Novikov, June 13, 1946, pp. 844–46; Novikov to Byrnes, March 15, 1946, pp. 829–30; Novikov to Acheson, May 17, 1946, pp. 841–42; Acheson (Durbrow) Memcon, May 14, 1946, pp. 838–39; Editorial Note, pp. 839–40; U.S., President, *Public Papers of the Presidents of the United States*, Harry S. Truman, 1945, June 14, July 18, Aug. 2, 1946, pp. 301, 381, 382–83. Hereafter cited as *"Public Papers, Truman, (year)."* Once it became clear that the phantom loan had failed to induce a change in Soviet policy, the State Department tried a new approach. Clayton told the Soviets in September 1946 that Soviet purchase or restoration of merchant vessels furnished under Lend-Lease would help break up the diplomatic logjam. Despite repeated entreaties during the following months, the Soviets did not bother to reply. See Matlock to Ness, Sept. 3, 1946, *FRUS 1946*, 6:853; Clayton to SecState, Sept. 11, 1946, pp. 853–54; Clayton to Orekhov, Sept. 14, 1946, pp. 854–55; Aide-Memoire to Soviet Embassy, Oct. 31, 1946, pp. 855–56; Clayton to SecState, Dec. 3, 1946, pp. 858–59; Byrnes (Clayton) to Smith, Dec. 23, 1946, pp. 860–62; Smith to Molotov, Dec. 31, 1946, p. 865; Smith to SecState, Jan. 2, 1947, pp. 865–66.

55. E.g., see Smith to SecState, Nov. 23, 1946, *FRUS 1946*, 1:1,355–56.

56. Even so, American policies toward Eastern Europe continued to vacillate until late 1946 because American officials never systematically defined U.S. goals and interests there. See Davis, *Cold War Begins*, pp. 22–23, 70–75, 160. Lundestad adds, "The main point of this study is that Washington was never able to develop any consistent policy towards Eastern Europe" (*Non-Policy*, p. 429). In addition, bureaucratic momentum, or what Hugh de Santis terms "the image of ideological cooperation," discouraged American diplomats from responding aggressively against the Soviets in the early postwar period. From late 1943 to late 1945, most American diplomats, especially those based in Washington, were predisposed to minimize disturbing reports from representatives in Eastern Europe because the primary goal of U.S. foreign policy was the maintenance of great power unity. When evidence of Soviet oppression in Eastern Europe became overwhelming, American officials over-rationalized all Soviet behavior to fit their revised view. These sudden swings in the ideological pendulum not surprisingly fostered Soviet suspicions about the trustworthiness, and British doubts about the competence, of American foreign policy. De Santis' argument challenges Yergin's thesis concerning the "Riga axioms." Compare de Santis, "Images," pp. 475–94, with Yergin, *Shattered Peace*, pp. 17–41.

57. Kennan, *Memoirs*, p. 256.

58. Quotation from *ibid.*, p. 293. A close reading of Stalin's speech reveals that it was mostly for internal consumption. Stalin stressed the need to increase Party power in the postwar period. See *NYT*, Feb. 10, 1946. Kennan's initial analysis of the speech, incidentally, was by no means alarmist. See Kennan to SecState, Feb. 12, 1946, *FRUS 1946*, 6:694–96. Also see McCagg, *Stalin Embattled*, pp. 217–37; Yergin, *Shattered Peace*, pp. 166–67. Interestingly, Kennan mistakenly recalls in his memoirs that the long telegram was inspired by a query originating in the Treasury Department—which for Kennan symbolized the forces of appeasement—on why the Soviets had abstained from Bretton Woods: "Now, at long last, with the incomprehensible unwillingness of Moscow to adhere to the Bank and the Fund, the dream seemed to be shattered, and the Department of State passed on to the embassy, in tones of bland innocence, the anguished cry of bewilderment that had floated over the roof of the White House from the Treasury Department on the other side" (*Memoirs*, p. 293). Also see fn. 44, *FRUS 1946*, 6:696n.

59. Kennan to SecState, Feb. 22, 1946, *FRUS 1946*, 6:697–99; quotation from p. 699.

60. *Ibid.*, pp. 700–01.

61. *Ibid.*, p. 706.

62. *Ibid.*, pp. 706–09; quotation from p. 708.

63. In addition, Kennan's argument was ambiguous in that it identified, with varying degrees of emphasis, three major sources of Soviet conduct: traditional Russian imperialism; Marxist-Leninist (or Stalinist) ideology; and the insecurity of the Kremlin rulers due to the fragility of their internal power base. Kennan apparently believed the last point was the most important. As he explained a month after the long telegram: "Official Soviet thesis that outside world is hostile and menacing to Soviet peoples is . . . an *a priori* tactical posi-

tion deliberately taken and hotly advanced by dominant elements in the Soviet political system for impelling selfish reasons of a domestic political nature. . . . A hostile international environment is the breath of life for prevailing internal system in this country. . . . Thus we are faced with a tremendous vested interest dedicated to proposition that Russia is a country walking a dangerous path among implacable enemies" (Kennan to SecState, March 20, 1946, pp. 721–22). Also see X, "The Sources of Soviet Conduct," pp. 566–82; C. Ben Wright, "Mr. 'X' and Containment," pp. 7–9, 15–16, 28–31; Daniel F. Harrington, "Kennan, Bohlen, and the Riga Axioms," pp. 425–27.

64. Acheson quotation from Acheson, *Present*, p. 209. On Forrestal, see Yergin, *Shattered Peace*, pp. 170–71; Millis, *Forrestal Diaries*, pp. 136, 140; Wright, "Mr. 'X'," pp. 12–16. For examples of a "militarist" interpretation of Kennan's telegram, see Matthews to SWNCC, April 1, 1946, *FRUS 1946*, 1:1,167–71; JCS Memo, March 27, 1946, pp. 1,160–65; McFarlane for JCS to SecState, March 29, 1946, pp. 1,165–66.

65. Quotation from Robert P. Patterson to the President, July 27, 1946, Papers of George M. Elsey, File "Russia," HSTL. Hereafter cited as "Elsey Papers." Also see Yergin, *Shattered Peace*, p. 243.

66. "Hot" quotation cited in Richard M. Freeland, *The Truman Doctrine and the Origins of McCarthyism: Foreign Policy, Domestic Politics, and Internal Security, 1946–48*, p. 67. Also see Yergin, *Shattered Peace*, p. 245; Donovan, *Conflict and Crisis*, p. 222. Truman had also backed down from publicizing the rift with the Soviet Union when Churchill delivered his "Iron Curtain" speech in March 1946 (*ibid.*, pp. 190–92). "Loose talk" quotation from Truman to Garner, Sept. 21, 1946, Papers of HST-PSF-Subject File: Foreign Affairs, File "Russia 1945–48," HSTL.

67. For Leahy's warning, see Leahy to Truman, March 12, 1946, Papers of HST-PSF-Subject File: Agencies, File "Military-Army-Navy unification," HSTL. Truman was commenting on a report by Drew Pearson about American stationing of atomic bombs in Germany or England, a story the President branded a "lie." See Ayers Diary, Oct. 14, 1946, Ayers Papers, File "Diary (Ayers) 1946," HSTL; and Schnabel, *JCS*, p. 294. On size and readiness of U.S. atomic arsenal, see David Alan Rosenberg, "U.S. Nuclear Stockpile, 1945 to 1950," p. 261.

68. On Forrestal, see Millis, *Forrestal Diaries*, pp. 198, 236, 239–40. On constraints on military programs, see Donovan, *Conflict and Crisis*, pp. 138–40, 172, 200–02, 222, 265. CEA Chairman Nourse told Truman that a $3–5 billion "budget surplus is urgently called for" in this period. See Nourse to Truman, "Budget Estimate of Expenditures," Dec. 13, 1946, Nourse Papers, File "Daily Diary 1946–7 Memorandum of contacts with President and the White House Staff December 3–28," HSTL. Truman endorsed the JCS' view in January 1947 that UMT was necessary until scientists perfected "the so-called 'push-button' type of warfare." Truman to Karl T. Compton, Jan. 17, 1947, Papers of HST-PSF-Subject File: Agencies, File "Military Training," HSTL.

69. Schoenfeld to SecState, Feb. 15, 1946, *FRUS 1946*, 6:260.

70. Mastny, *Russia's Road*, p. 283, and pp. 109–10, 265–66, 306, 309–10. Charles Maier adds, "To follow a policy of abnegation might indeed have al-

lowed more openness in Eastern Europe; on the other hand, the Stalinist tendencies toward repression might well have followed their own Moscow-determined momentum" ("Revisionism," p. 319).

4. Recovery and Crisis in Western Europe, 1945–1947

1. See Gaddis, "Sphere of Influence"; Geir Lundestad, "Empire by Invitation? The United States and Western Europe, 1945–1952," passim; Yergin, *Shattered Peace*, pp. 304–05.

2. All figures are rounded off. Unless otherwise specified, figures reflect current, rather than constant, dollars. In some cases, the statistics for "Western Europe" exclude minor recipients of American aid, such as Greece before 1947. Statistics from U.S. Department of Commerce, Bureau of Foreign and Domestic Commerce, Office of International Trade, *Foreign Trade of the United States 1936–49* (hereafter cited as "Commerce, *Trade*"), pp. 44, 46; United Nations, Economic and Social Council, Economic Commission for Europe, Research and Planning Division, *A Survey of the Economic Situation and Prospects of Europe* (hereafter cited as "ECOSOC, *Survey*"), p. 42.

3. ECOSOC, *Survey*, pp. 40, 42; Commerce, *Trade*, p. 46; Commerce, *HSUS*, pp. 903, 905.

4. Exports constituted only about 6 percent of U.S. GNP in 1946–47; imports about 2.5 percent. See ECOSOC, *Survey*, p. 63. Job estimate from Clayton to Johnston, April 4, 1945, Clayton-Thorp Papers, File "Copies of Correspondence Drafted by other Offices for WLC's Signature," HSTL. On value of imports and need for trade equilibrium, see Percy W. Bidwell, "Imports in the American Economy," pp. 86–87. On American import dependence, see World Trade Foundation of America, "Selected Industries and Products Dependent upon Imported Materials," Jan. 24, 1946, Clayton-Thorp Papers, File "W," HSTL.

5. While the latter set of figures includes investment by non-West European countries in the U.S., East and Central European investment in the U.S. was minimal during this period. Commerce, *HSUS*, pp. 870–71.

6. F. L. Hopkinson before Senate Small Business and Foreign Trade Subcommittee, May 19, 1945, *NYT*.

7. Culbertson quotation from William S. Culbertson, "Concerning the Recommendations of the 'Corporation,'" Dec. 11, 1944; for a summary of the mission's activities and recommendations, see Gilpatric to Taft and Clayton, Jan. 24, 1945, Clayton-Thorp Papers, File "D," HSTL. For State Department reaction, see John D. Hickerson, "Assistance by the American Government to American Property Interests Abroad," Oct. 23, 1944, Matthews-Hickerson Papers, File "Memoranda 1944," NA; Charles P. Taft to R. R. Townshend, "Culbertson Report," June 14, 1945, and "Private enterprise" quotation from R. R. Townshend to Clayton and Haley, "Culbertson Mission recommendations . . . ," June 21, 1945, Clayton-Thorp Papers, File "D," HSTL.

8. On NFTC meeting, see George C. McGhee, "National Foreign Trade Council," April 8, 1946, Clayton-Thorp Papers, File "Memoranda of conversation (folder 1)," HSTL.

9. Truman to SecState, July 25, 1945, Confidential Decimal File 1945–49, File [Unnumbered, first folder, Box C-529], NA. On premises of U.S. foreign economic policy, see Raymond F. Mikesell, "The Role of the International Monetary Agreements in a World of Planned Economies," pp. 498–99.

10. E. H. Armstrong and H. N. Sandifer, "Comments on United States Proposal to Establish a European Economic Council," April 26, 1946, Confidential Decimal File 1945–49, File "840.50/1–46," NA.

11. Commerce, *HSUS*, p. 874.

12. ECOSOC, *Survey*, pp. 95–96. On general causes of European crisis, see Yergin, *Shattered Peace*, pp. 306–07.

13. ECOSOC, *Survey*, pp. 17, 35, 44–47, 55–60; quotation from p. 55.

14. By mid-1946, Italian wholesale prices had increased twenty-six times over prewar levels. French prices had increased nine times over prewar by mid-1947. United Nations, Department of Economic Affairs, *Economic Report: Salient Features of the World Economic Structure, 1945–47*, p. 164. Also see John M. Cassels, "Anglo-American Economic Relations," in Seymour E. Harris, ed., *Foreign Economic Policy of the United States*, p. 65; ECOSOC, *Survey*, pp. 78–92.

15. On labor productivity, see UN, *Economic Report*, p. 128. On European destruction, see Richard Mayne, *The Recovery of Europe: From Devastation to Unity*, pp. 29–32.

16. The fifteen countries include three in Eastern Europe: Poland, Czechoslovakia, and Yugoslavia. Postwar production figures are measured against constant 1938 levels expressed in dollars; i.e., 1938 = 100. ECOSOC, *Survey*, pp. 1, 3, 16.

17. *Ibid.*, p. 2.

18. *Ibid.*, pp. 102–10; William Diebold, Jr., *Trade and Payments in Western Europe: A Study in Economic Cooperation, 1947–51*, pp. 19–20; quotation from p. 156.

19. Mayne, *Recovery*, pp. 66–67.

20. E. F. Penrose, *Economic Planning for the Peace*, pp. 348–54; Gardner, *Sterling-Dollar*, pp. 179–84.

21. Kolko, *Limits*, pp. 59–69, 162–66.

22. Robert M. Hathaway, *Ambiguous Partnership: Britain and America, 1944–1947*, pp. 313–14.

23. Paterson, *Confrontation*, p. 161. Also see n. 25 below.

24. Quotation from Winant to SecState, Jan. 19, 1944, *FRUS 1944*, 2:6. Also see Winant to SecState, Feb. 12, 1944, p. 11; Winant to SecState, Sept. 8, 1944, p. 73; Gardner, *Sterling-Dollar*, pp. 154–58; Henry Clay, "Britain's Declining Role in World Trade," pp. 418–19; Herbert Feis, "The Future of British Imperial Preferences," p. 672.

25. On British wartime losses, see Winant to SecState, Sept. 8, 1944, *FRUS 1944*, 2:74–75; unsigned Memcon (Keynes-Clayton), Aug. 3, 1945, *FRUS 1945*, 6:80–84; Gardner, *Sterling-Dollar*, pp. 178–79. For British position on state trading, see Winant to SecState, Feb. 6, 1944, *FRUS 1944*, 2:7–10; Winant to SecState, July 20, 1944, pp. 62–63; Winant to SecState, Dec. 15, 1944, pp. 102–03. Hull rejected the British argument on state trading. See Hull to Winant, July 12, 1944, pp. 54–55; Hull to Winant, Sept. 19, 1944, pp. 77–79.

26. For representative British views, see Winant to SecState, Aug. 11, 1944, *FRUS 1944*, 2:68–69; Winant to SecState, Jan. 12, 1945, *FRUS 1945*, 6:8–10; Winant to SecState, Jan. 24, 1945, pp. 15–17; Winant to SecState, Feb. 8, 1945, pp. 19–21. Also see Gardner, *Sterling-Dollar*, p. 150.

27. On efforts by Winant and others, see Winant Memo, n.d. [Feb. 1945], *FRUS 1945*, 6:22–24; SecState's Staff Committee Memo, March 5, 1945, pp. 25–27; Winant to SecState, March 12, 1945, pp. 29–30; Executive Committee on Economic Foreign Policy Memo, July 21, 1945, pp. 74–76. On Congressional opposition, see Grew to Winant, March 5, 1945, pp. 27–28; Clayton to Hawkins, April 28, 1945, pp. 45–46; Leddy Memcon July 9, 1945, pp. 61–62; Leddy Memcon, n.d. [July 1945], pp. 68–69; Executive Committee on Economic Foreign Policy Memo, July 21, 1945, p. 75; Brown Memcon, Aug. 2, 1945, p. 78; Gardner, *Sterling-Dollar*, pp. 192–95. On Vinson, see *ibid.*, pp. 193–95; and David S. McLellan, *Dean Acheson: The State Department Years*, p. 71.

28. Under the American "multilateral-bilateral" approach, a nuclear group of several countries would first negotiate bilateral agreements among themselves for selective tariff reductions, and then proceed to broader multilateral negotiations by incorporating more participating countries. See Gardner, *Sterling-Dollar*, p. 151; Clayton to Hawkins, April 28, 1945, *FRUS 1945*, 6:45–46; Leddy Memcon, July 9, 1945, p. 62; Leddy Memcon, n.d. [July 1945], pp. 68–73; Executive Committee on Economic Foreign Policy Memo, July 21, 1945, pp. 74–76, 75n; Byrnes to Winant, Aug. 9, 1945, pp. 88–90. On British and Canadian objections, see Winant to SecState, June 28, 1945, pp. 56–60; Leddy Memcon, July 9, 1945, pp. 62–64; Leddy Memcon, n.d. [July 1945], pp. 67–69, 74; Brown Memcon, Aug. 2, 1945, p. 78. On Canadian-American economic relations in this period, see R. D. Cuff and J. L. Granatstein, *American Dollars— Canadian Prosperity: Canadian-American Economic Relations 1945–1950*, pp. 21–37; Robert B. Bruce, "Some Aspects of Canadian Economic Relations with the United States," in Harris, ed., *Policy of U.S.*, pp. 134–54.

29. Winant (Clayton and Collado) to SecState, Aug. 17, 1945, *FRUS 1945*, 6:100.

30. *Ibid.*, p. 101.

31. On Lend-Lease cancellation and British surprise over it, see Byrnes (Phelps and Maxwell) to Winant (Clayton and Collado), Aug. 18, 1945, *FRUS 1945*, 6:102–03; Brown Memcon, Aug. 19, 1945, pp. 105–06; George C. Herring, Jr., "The United States and British Bankruptcy: Responsibilities Deferred," pp. 276–77; Gardner, *Sterling-Dollar*, p. 185; Paterson, *Confrontation*, pp. 160–61; Gardner, *Architects*, p. 123. Quotation from Attlee to Truman, Sept. 1, 1945, *FRUS 1945*, 6:115.

32. Concerning Roosevelt's wartime commitments on postwar Lend-Lease, see Herring, "Bankruptcy." For Truman's reply to Attlee, see Truman to Attlee, Sept. 6, 1945, *FRUS 1945*, 6:117.

33. Until the very end of the Anglo-American talks, British negotiators continued to press for the separation of the commercial and financial issues, but American officials held steadfast. The agreements were signed on December 5, 1945. On the negotiations, see Acheson (Clayton) to Winant (Hawkins), Sept. 6, 1945, *FRUS 1945*, 6:116–17; Executive Committee on Economic Foreign Policy

Memo, Sept. 7, 1945, pp. 120–21; Winant to SecState, Sept. 24, 1945, pp. 134–36; Minutes of Meeting of U.S. Financial Committee, Oct. 11, 1945, pp. 145–49; Minutes of Meeting of U.S. Top Committee, Nov. 7, 1945, pp. 157–62; Minutes of Meeting of U.S.-U.K. Finance Committee, Nov. 19, 1945, pp. 162–67; Minutes of Special Meeting of U.S.-U.K. Combined Top Committee, Nov. 24, 1945, pp. 168–73; U.S. Draft Memo, Nov. 30, 1945, pp. 173–77; Minutes of Meeting of U.S.-U.K. Committee on Commercial Policy, Dec. 1, 1945, pp. 178–84; Minutes of Meeting of U.S.-U.K. Combined Finance Committee, Dec. 5, 1945, pp. 193–94. Attlee specifically complained that Britain had to relinquish the five-year transitional period and scarce currency clauses won at Bretton Woods. See Winant to SecState, Dec. 3, 1945, pp. 188–89. Also see Gardner, *Sterling-Dollar*, pp. 188–207, 213–21; Judd Polk and Gardner Patterson, "The British Loan," pp. 429–40.

34. British officials, members of Parliament, and the public expressed considerable dissatisfaction over the American failure to extend a grant instead of a loan, or at least an interest-free loan. But given the climate of opinion in the U.S., Keynes and others realized that the loan agreed upon was the best that the Truman administration could offer. Repayment was stretched out over fifty years. With a five-year grace period, interest charges came to only 1.6 percent. Incidentally, Canada also pledged $1.25 billion in aid to Britain. Gardner, *Sterling-Dollar*, pp. 208, 210–13, 225–36.

35. The Kolkos, for instance, argue that the U.S. pressured the U.K. into taking the loan with strings attached so that the U.S. could capture the lion's share of Britain's far-flung trading Empire. See *Limits*, pp. 60–63. For a similar interpretation, see Block, *Origins of Disorder*, pp. 56–68. For more balanced interpretations of the British loan, see Paterson, *Confrontation*, pp. 159–73; Gardner, *Architects*, pp. 123–29; Yergin, *Shattered Peace*, pp. 177–78. Quotation cited in LaFeber, *Cold War*, p. 12. On Baruch's opposition to the loan, see Gardner, *Architects*, p. 125.

36. For a contemporary British official's over-optimistic assessment of the Commonwealth's prospects, see H. Duncan Hall, "The British Commonwealth as a Great Power," pp. 594–608. Quotation from Paterson, *Confrontation*, p. 164. Clayton emphasized the first two points in instructions to a colleague who was about to speak on the loan before Ohio bankers in November 1945: "Recent informal discussions with business leaders indicate that the public does not yet appreciate the advantages which would accrue to the United States as the result of a substantial credit to the United Kingdom. . . . the primary advantage of the loan to us would be the effects it would have in making possible a great expansion in world trade on a multilateral basis. . . . If the British must pursue a course of increased sterling area controls, it will be difficult to avoid a situation of dollar or sterling blocs or spheres which would be an open invitation to dangerous forms of political and economic rivalry." Clayton to Charles P. Taft, Nov. 1, 1945, Clayton-Thorp Papers, File "T," HSTL.

37. Paterson, *Confrontation*, pp. 164–71; Kolko, *Limits*, pp. 65–67; Gardner, *Sterling-Dollar*, pp. 236–48.

38. Herter and Clayton quotations cited in Gardner, *Sterling-Dollar*, p. 250. The Senate approved the loan on May 10, 1946, by a 46 to 34 margin; the House

on July 13 by 219 to 155. On the Soviet factor in the passage of the loan agreement, see *ibid.*, pp. 248–52; McLellan, *Acheson*, pp. 94–95; Paterson, *Confrontation*, pp. 168–69, 171–72; Hathaway, *Partnership*, pp. 244–46; Kolko, *Limits*, pp. 65–69. Incidentally, Yergin incorrectly claims that Churchill's Fulton speech in March 1946 bolstered American support for the loan (*Shattered Peace*, pp. 177–78). For the correct story, see Gardner, *Sterling-Dollar*, pp. 238–39; Hathaway, *Partnership*, pp. 241–42.

39. Hathaway, *Partnership*, pp. 249–75.

40. Quotation from *ibid.*, p. 263, also see pp. 260–72; and Schnabel, *JCS*, pp. 140–64.

41. American neglect of Britain cannot be adequately explained by a desire to support the UN or to avoid power politics, for by mid-1946, American faith and interest in the UN was waning. See Hathaway, *Partnership*, pp. 272–75.

42. Gardner, *Sterling-Dollar*, pp. 242–48, 306–47; Paterson, *Confrontation*, p. 168; Cassels, "Anglo-American Relations," p. 59.

43. On political roles of France and Italy in American planning, see Charles S. Maier, "'You People in Europe': Regional Concepts and National Roles Within the Marshall Plan."

44. I am indebted to the Italian scholar Massimo Salvadori for these insights.

45. Figures on trade and deficits derived from Commerce, *Trade*, pp. 42, 50; Commerce, *HSUS*, pp. 903–05.

46. On the postwar French standard of living, see Alexander Werth, *France 1940–1955*, pp. 236–38, 298–300, 313, 319–21; on Lend-Lease, p. 279. Total Eximbank aid to Europe totalled $900 million in 1945. On the Eximbank loan to France, see NAC-37, Jan. 8, 1946, *FRUS 1946*, 1:1,412. On French obligations, see Quirin Memcon, July 30, 1945, *FRUS 1945*, 4:762–65; Quirin Memcon, Aug. 1, 1945, pp. 765–67; Caffery to SecState, Sept. 19, 1945, pp. 767–68.

47. "Recognition" quotation from Caffery to SecState, Nov. 14, 1945, *FRUS 1945*, 4:772. For a further example of Caffery's tough tactics with the French in this period, see Caffery to SecState, Nov. 25, 1945, pp. 773–74. Also see Caffery to SecState, Nov. 8, 1945, pp. 768–69; Lacoste to SecState, Nov. 8, 1945, pp. 770–71. "British loan" quotation from Byrnes to Caffery, Feb. 4, 1946, *FRUS 1946*, 5:410. Also see Clayton to SecState, Feb. 22, 1946, pp. 415–16; Byrnes to Caffery, April 9, 1946, p. 425.

48. Quotation from Werth, *France*, p. 257, and see p. 258.

49. On De Gaulle resignation, see *ibid.*, pp. 275–83; Caffery to SecState, Jan. 18, 1946, *FRUS 1946*, 5:400–01; Caffery to SecState, Jan. 20, 1946, pp. 401–02; Caffery to SecState, Feb. 9, 1946, p. 413. Also see Caffery to SecState, Jan. 27, 1946, p. 407; Caffery to SecState, April 4, 1946, pp. 421–22.

50. The NAC did not formally announce cancellation of the Russian loan because it would have complicated a request for $1.25 billion in additional Eximbank lending authority about to go before Congress. See Minutes of 22nd NAC Meeting, April 25, 1946, *FRUS 1946*, 1:1,430–31. Once the Russian loan was formally shelved, the legislation was dropped (Editorial Note, p. 1,435). On the French loan discussions, see Minutes of 22nd NAC Meeting, April 25, 1946, *FRUS 1946*, 5:432–34; Yergin, *Shattered Peace*, p. 236. On Blum visit, see Werth, *France*, pp. 314–16. Also see Kolko, *Limits*, pp. 153–57.

51. No such coup was attempted. For War Department order, see Patterson to Acheson, May 3, 1946, with attached War Department to McNarney, May 3, 1946, *FRUS 1946*, 5:435–36. Interestingly, Caffery at first judged the probability of a coup as "very unlikely"; see Caffery to SecState, May 2, 1946, p. 435. But Caffery later decided to hedge his bets; see Caffery to SecState, May 6, 1946, pp. 438–40. Acheson tried to make Truman rescind the order, but failed. See Hickerson Memo, May 6, 1946, pp. 436–38; Millis, *Forrestal Diaries*, pp. 157–58.

52. Minutes of 24th NAC Meeting, May 6, 1946, *FRUS 1946*, 5:440–46; Eccles quotation on p. 442.

53. Clayton quotation from Minutes of 24th NAC Meeting, May 6, 1946, *FRUS 1946*, 5:443, 445, respectively. The State Department denied press stories that the French loan was "political"; see Acheson to Caffery, May 8, 1946, p. 450. The French loan marked the last major Eximbank loan that was designated strictly for reconstruction of a war-ravaged country (Editorial Note, *FRUS 1946*, 1:1,435). On Franco-American agreements, see Minutes of 29th NAC Meeting, May 24, 1946, *FRUS 1946*, 5:453–58; Minutes of 30th NAC Meeting (with attachments), May 28, 1946, pp. 459–64; for French multilateral pledges, see pp. 462–63.

54. Quotation from Caffery to SecState, May 8, 1946, *FRUS 1946*, 5:450. Caffery reported that after Communist setbacks in the May constitutional referendum, Molotov advised the French Communist Party to adopt a less militant posture. Caffery to SecState, May 25, 1946, p. 459. The Kolkos accuse the French Communists of collaborating, at the Kremlin's instigation, with bourgeois reformers (*Limits*, pp. 151–60). Also see Werth, *France*, pp. 244–45, 268–70, 275.

55. Quotation from Caffery to SecState, Feb. 19, 1947, *FRUS 1947*, 3:690–91. On November 1946 elections, see Werth, *France*, pp. 323–25. On Caffery's fears, see Caffery to SecState, Oct. 29, 1946, *FRUS 1946*, 5:468–70; Caffery to Matthews, Nov. 26, 1946, with attached Chipman Memo, Nov. 23, 1946, pp. 471–77; Caffery to SecState, Jan. 23, 1947, *FRUS 1947*, 3:688–89; Caffery to SecState, Jan. 28, 1947, p. 689.

56. Commerce, *HSUS*, p. 874.

57. Quotation from H. Stuart Hughes, *The United States and Italy*, p. 174. Statistics from Massimo L. Salvadori, *Storia Dell'eta Contemporanea: Dalla Restaurionze All'Eurocommunismo* (Turin: Loescher, 1976), pp. 959–60. On Italian distress, see also Tarchiani to Phillips, May 28, 1945, *FRUS 1945*, 4:1,257; Kirk to SecState, June 14, 1945, p. 1,265; Italian Embassy to Department of State, Aug. 14, 1945, pp. 1,280, 1283–84.

58. "Low priority" from Kirk to SecState, June 14, 1945, *FRUS 1945*, 4:1,264. British quotation from British Embassy to Department of State, Sept. 18, 1945, p. 1,287. Byrnes on private trade from Byrnes to Kirk, Oct. 12, 1945, pp. 1,290–92. UNRRA aid to Italy from Paterson, *Confrontation*, p. 77. On Italian import and foreign credit needs, see Sergio Fenoaltea, "Italy at Work: Achievements and Needs," pp. 715–22.

59. On Eximbank loan, see Fetter Memcon, Feb. 14, 1946, *FRUS 1946*, 5:891–92; Hamilton Memcon, March 29, 1946, p. 901; Hamilton Memcon, May

16, 1946, p. 914; Italian Embassy to Eximbank, May 18, 1946, p. 916. Quotation from Minutes of 15th NAC Meeting, March 4, 1946, p. 896. The Treasury aid took the form of dollar transfers to cover U.S. military procurement in Italy. See Minutes of 21st NAC Meeting, April 19, 1946, pp. 902–06. Also, see Key (Tasca) to SecState (Treasury), March 27, 1946, p. 900.

60. The ostensible grounds for the NAC's refusal to help Italy were rather technical: Britain and France had yet to cancel their reparation claims against Italy. See Minutes of 26th NAC Meeting, May 9, 1946, *FRUS 1946*, 5:907–10.

61. On Congressional opposition to Treasury aid, see Memo of Vinson-Clayton Meeting with Subcommittee of House Appropriations Committee, May 10, 1946, *FRUS 1946*, 5:911–12; Minutes of 27th NAC Meeting, May 14, 1946, p. 913. On Clayton-Snyder Meeting (July 25, 1946) with Congressmen, see Clayton Memcon, Dec. 10, 1946, pp. 926–27. On actual extension of Treasury aid, see Caffery (Brynes) to Key (De Gasperi), Oct. 10, 1946, p. 937. On cotton credit, see Acheson to Key, April 1, 1946, pp. 901–02. On September 1946 surplus property credits (worth $368 million), see Editorial Note, pp. 932–33. On October 1946 ship sales, see Editorial Note, p. 941.

62. Reasons for the administration's reluctance to start the Eximbank talks included shortages of funds and Congressional opposition, Italian incompetence in preparing an application for a loan, and an over-optimistic view of Italy's prospects for recovery. On the latter points, see Hart to Wood, July 9, 1946, *FRUS 1946*, 5:922–25; Key (Livengood) to SecState, Aug. 9, 1946, pp. 928–29; Hughes, *U.S. and Italy*, p. 175. On the belated recognition of Italy's plight, see Key to SecState, Sept. 5, 1946, *FRUS 1946*, 5:930–32; Key (Tasca) to SecState, Sept. 15, 1946, pp. 934–36; Key to SecState, Oct. 17, 1946, pp. 940–41; Key to SecState, Nov. 26, 1946, p. 946; Hickerson to Acheson and Clayton, Dec. 2, 1946, p. 948. "Urgent" quotation from NAC Staff Committee Memo, Nov. 15, 1946, p. 945. "Intimation" quotation from Hughes, *U.S. and Italy*, p. 145. The NAC finally approved a $100 million Eximbank loan in January 1947; see Minutes of 50th NAC Meeting, Jan. 13, 1947, *FRUS 1947*, 3:859–60. On De Gasperi's visit, see pp. 835–61.

63. Italy received $136 million in U.S. grants and credits during 1945, and $500 million during 1946. See Commerce, *HSUS*, p. 874.

64. On the ITO and GATT, see Gardner, *Sterling-Dollar*, pp. 269–86, 348–80; *FRUS 1945*, 6:1–204 passim; *FRUS 1946*, 1:1,263–1,366 passim; *FRUS 1947*, 1:909–1,025.

65. Gardner, *Sterling-Dollar*, pp. 291–93; on the disappointing performance of the Bretton Woods institutions in this period, see pp. 287–305.

66. Quotations from ECOSOC, *Survey*, pp. 17, 35, respectively.

5. Indecision in Germany, 1945–1947

1. Indeed, wartime planners in the Pentagon often assumed that Germany, rather than the Soviet Union, would again be the main enemy in a future war. But distrust of Russia, as reflected in secret American war plans, mounted toward the war's end. See Sherry, *Next War*, pp. 159–61.

2. Germany absorbed only 3.8 percent of American exports during the period 1936–1938, as compared with Britain's 16.8 percent of American exports. Imports from Germany, meanwhile, averaged only about one-half of U.S. exports to Germany during the interwar years (1920–1938). Throughout the interwar years, hefty U.S. trade surpluses with most European countries encouraged the very autarkic practices that Cordell Hull and other free traders deplored. In this respect, German foreign economic practices differed only in degree from other European countries. On U.S. trade with Germany, see Commerce, *HSUS*, pp. 903, 905–06; Commerce, *Trade*, p. 46.

3. German exports to the U.S. rose to only $32 and $45 million in 1948 and 1949, respectively. See Commerce, *HSUS*, pp. 874, 903, 905.

4. The IT&T vice-president was Mark Sunstrom. Quotation from Clayton to Hilldring, June 23, 1945, Clayton-Thorp Papers, File "Correspondence Drafted by other Offices for WLC's Signature," HSTL.

5. Behn hoped "to build up a big domestic company." Quotation cited in Yergin, *Shattered Peace*, p. 304. On IT&T's troubles, see W. P. Pitkin (vice-president and general attorney of IT&T) to SecState, Jan. 4, 1946, Clayton-Thorp Papers, File "P," HSTL; Pitkin to Clayton, March 14, 1946, and Pitkin to Hilldring, April 26, 1946, Papers of the Pauley Reparations Mission, European Mission Subject File, File "German Report-Bennett," NA. Hereafter cited as "Pauley Papers—Eur. Mission."

6. ECOSOC, *Survey*, pp. 35, 44–46, 66–77, 92. "It is only in the case of manufactured goods," the report stated, "that any considerable substitution of European production for products hitherto imported would appear to be feasible" (p. 75).

7. On the agrarian tradition in American political thought, see Richard Hofstadter, *The Age of Reform: From Bryan to F. D. R.* (New York: Vintage Books, 1955), pp. 23–59.

8. "Transplant" quotation from Morgenthau conversation with Roosevelt on Sept. 2, 1944. See John Morton Blum, *From the Morgenthau Diaries, Years of War, 1941–1945*, 3:353; "destroying" quotation from Morgenthau conversation with White et al. on Sept. 4, 1944, pp. 354–55; on Morgenthau Plan and wartime planning on Germany, pp. 327–420 passim; see also Paterson, *Confrontation*, pp. 236–37.

9. The Treasury Department favored U.S. loans over German reparations to meet Allied reconstruction needs. Quotations from unsigned Treasury Memo, "Long Range Program for Germany," Jan. 19, 1945, James F. Byrnes Papers, File "613/(1): Morgenthau Plan-Germany," Robert Muldrow Cooper Library, Clemson, South Carolina. Hereafter cited as "Byrnes Papers, . . . Clemson." The Treasury delivered a similar memo to the President as a briefing paper for the Yalta Conference; see Blum, *Morgenthau Diaries*, 3:394, 396. Bruce Kuklick argues that Morgenthau opposed reparations to Russia in order to make Russia dependent upon American aid and trade. This interpretation is inconsistent with other evidence on Morgenthau's motivation regarding German reparations and the loan to Russia. See Bruce Kuklick, "The Division of Germany and American Policy on Reparations," pp. 288–90. Morgenthau claimed in 1946 that his critics had distorted his plan and that Roosevelt, in any case, had fully

endorsed it. See Henry Morgenthau, Jr., "Postwar Treatment of Germany," pp. 125–29. For critiques of the Morgenthau Plan, see M. J. Bonn, "The Economics of Fear," pp. 130–42; Penrose, *Planning*, pp. 245–48.

10. On FDR's indecision on the German question, see Blum, *Morgenthau Diaries*, 3:363; Gaddis, *Cold War*, pp. 96–97. On interdepartmental disputes over German policy, see Walter L. Dorn, "The Debate over American Occupation Policy in Germany in 1944–1945," pp. 481–501; Paterson, *Confrontation*, pp. 237–40. On Quebec Agreement and its aftermath, see *ibid.*, p. 237; Blum, *Morgenthau Diaries*, 3:377–79; Gaddis, *Cold War*, pp. 120–21. On JCS 1067, see *ibid.*, pp. 122–25, 129–31; Paterson, *Confrontation*, pp. 238–40.

11. Clay to McCloy, June 16, 1945, in Jean Edward Smith, ed., *The Papers of General Lucius D. Clay, Germany 1945–1949*, 1:23.

12. For Truman's views on the Morgenthau Plan, see Truman, *Year of Decisions*, pp. 235–36, 327, quotation on p. 309. On shift within Truman administration against Morgenthau before Potsdam, see Gaddis, *Cold War*, pp. 236–38. Immediately after Roosevelt's death, Leo Crowley of the FEA began sniping at the Morgenthau Plan, which he unfairly characterized as a program to eliminate *all* heavy industry in Germany. See Fowler to Crowley, May 22, 1947, with attached Crowley to Stettinius, April 15, 1945, Byrnes Papers, File "71(1): Not to be used [in book? 1943–1947]," Clemson.

13. Cited in Gaddis, *Cold War*, p. 127.

14. Hull quotation from Blum, *Morgenthau Diaries*, 3:328. Reparations quotation from "U.S. Proposal with Regard to Questions of Reparations," n.d. [Oct. 1943], *FRUS 1943*, 1:740. Harriman quotation from Harriman to Roosevelt, Nov. 5, 1943, *FRUS 1943*, 3:591.

15. The United States, Roosevelt added, would not countenance a peace that left Germany starving. While the U.S. hoped to help restore devastated areas of Europe, he said, reparations were an insufficient and improper means to achieve reconstruction. See Minutes to Second Plenary Meeting, Feb. 5, 1945, *FRUS: Malta and Yalta*, pp. 621–22 (Bohlen Minutes), p. 632 (Matthews Minutes).

16. Geoffrey Warner, "The Division of Germany 1946–1948," p. 65. Cf. Kuklick, "Reparations," pp. 277–80.

17. John Gimbel, *The American Occupation of Germany: Politics and the Military, 1945–1949*, pp. 13–14. The administration failed to reach a consensus on Germany before the Big Three met at Potsdam. Truman's hasty preparations aboard the U.S.S. *Augusta* on the way to Potsdam suggested "the way of a man who habitually sought simple versions from which he could arrive at quick decisions." See Herbert Feis, *Between War and Peace: The Potsdam Conference*, p. 160. For a more favorable appraisal of Truman at Potsdam, see Charles E. Bohlen, *Witness to History 1929–1969*, pp. 225–30, 239.

18. In addition to being dubbed "Assistant President for the homefront" by the press while serving as Roosevelt's Director of the Office of War Mobilization, Byrnes won an exaggerated reputation as a foreign policy expert following service at the Yalta Conference. Bitterly disappointed over his failure to win Roosevelt's endorsement as vice-presidential nominee in 1944, Byrnes told Truman before becoming Secretary of State in July 1945 that he would not accept the job unless he could exercise more authority over foreign policy than had

Hull under Roosevelt. Indeed, Byrnes' tenure as Secretary of State—like those of Marshall and Acheson after him—was marked by exceptional autonomy in foreign policy decision-making. Byrnes' personal style, however, offended Truman, while Marshall and Acheson asserted themselves more subtly. See Robert L. Messer, *The End of an Alliance: James F. Byrnes, Roosevelt, Truman, and the Origins of the Cold War,* pp. 78–79.

19. Minutes, Sixth Foreign Ministers' Meeting, July 23, 1945, *FRUS: The Conference at Potsdam,* 2:279–80.

20. The Soviets had to pay for 15 percent of western zonal reparations with shipments of raw materials; the other 10 percent was free. See Gaddis, *Cold War,* pp. 240–41; Bohlen, *Witness,* pp. 232–33; B. U. Ratchford and William D. Ross, *Berlin Reparations Assignment: Round One of the German Peace Settlement,* pp. 42–45; R. Harrison Wagner, "The Decision to Divide Germany and the Origins of the Cold War," p. 179; Kuklick, "Reparations," pp. 282–85.

21. Kuklick charges that Byrnes designed the zonal reparations plan to exclude the Soviets from Ruhr production and to influence Soviet policies in Eastern Europe. The Americans acted, he states, in full awareness that such policies, in the event of a Soviet refusal to back down, would divide Germany and Europe ("Reparations," pp. 282–90). Cf. Wagner, "Decision to Divide Germany," p. 189. Also see Paul Y. Hammond, "Directives for the Occupation of Germany: The Washington Controversy," in Harold Stein, ed., *American Civil-Military Decisions: A Book of Case Studies,* pp. 436–37.

22. Mayne, *Recovery,* pp. 30–35; Gordon Wright, *The Ordeal of Total War, 1939–1945,* pp. 263–64.

23. Quotation and biographical sketch of Clay from unsigned [Robert Stephens], "Profile—General Clay," *The Observer* [London], Feb. 22, 1948.

24. On JCS 1067, see Lucius D. Clay, *Decision in Germany,* pp. 6–7. "Bare minimum" quotation from Clay to Byrnes, April 20, 1945, in Smith, *Clay Papers,* 1:6; "ray" quotation from Clay to McCloy, June 16, 1945, p. 24; on German destruction, see Clay to McCloy, April 26, 1945, p. 8; Clay to Hilldring, May 7, 1945, p. 12; Clay, *Decision,* pp. 15–16, 21, 31–32.

25. Quotation from Ratchford and Ross, *Reparations,* p. 69. Another visitor to Germany in May 1945 observed "the instinctive constructive bent of officers faced with machines not running, railroads idle, people unemployed. They find it unnatural and painful not to put things right and not to try to raise the level of performance of the area or activity for which they are responsible. Our limited observation leads us to feel that it is important not to minimize the capacity that local officers have for finding ways around the obstacles that high policy may set in their way." See Moses Abramovitz to Isidor Lubin, May 14, 1945, Clayton-Thorp Papers, File "Germany," HSTL. For another participant's view of the German question, see Penrose, *Planning,* pp. 216–309 passim.

26. One American official had predicted before the war ended: "Although the Army's civilian responsibilities have been reduced to a minimum, i.e., prevention of disease and safety of the armed forces, hungry mouths are hard to control and it will not make a pretty picture if our armies must shoot rioting women and children. The present political policy has been dominated by the desire of maintaining a tough attitude towards Germany. There is a possibility of

this position resolving itself into short-sightedness." Cook to Clayton, Feb. 2, 1945, and J. B. K., "Economic Implications for Germany of Proposed Territorial and Population Transfers in Eastern Europe," Jan. 24, 1945, Clayton-Thorp Papers, File "Germany," HSTL. Pauley's staff also recognized that occupation costs and reparations were inseparable. Unsigned memo, May 28, 1945, and George Luthringer, "Occupation Costs," June 18, 1945, Pauley Papers-Eur. Mission, File "Occupation Costs," NA.

27. John Gimbel, *The Origins of the Marshall Plan*, p. 27.

28. Deutscher, *Stalin*, pp. 537–38; Ulam, *Expansion and Coexistence*, pp. 440–47.

29. Stalin's paranoid behavior during the Berne incident of March 1945 demonstrated the depths of his feelings on this point. For tactical reasons, notably the desire to hasten the collapse of the Axis powers, the Soviets had offered relatively mild surrender terms to the Germans in the early stages of the war. The Soviets had also initially shown ambivalence toward the principle of unconditional surrender even though it should have allayed their fears of a separate peace. See Mastny, *Russia's Road*, pp. 145–56.

30. *Ibid.*, pp. 292–306; Laloy, "Stalin and Europe."

31. Quotation from Barbara Ann Chotiner and John W. Atwell, "Soviet Occupation Policy Toward Germany, 1945–1949," in Hans A. Schmitt, ed., *U.S. Occupation in Europe after World War II*, p. 50; also see pp. 48–49, 60–61; and Laloy, "Stalin and Europe"; Ulam, *Expansion and Coexistence*, p. 442.

32. On Soviet expediency in eastern Germany, see Kolko, *Limits*, pp. 131–37. On Soviets and French Communist Party, see e.g., Caffery to SecState, July 11, 1946, *FRUS 1946*, 5:576–77. George Kennan differed from most American policymakers in that from the beginning he argued that the Soviets sought to reduce Germany to a Communist satellite. He advocated repudiation of the Oder-Neisse line and the Potsdam agreements in order to free the United States to exploit the differences between the Polish and German Communists, embarass the Soviets, and remove a commonly cited precedent for French territorial demands in western Germany. See Kennan to Carmel Office, May 10, 1946, pp. 555–56.

33. On early Soviet dismantling and economic policies in the eastern zone, see Vladimir Alexandrov, "The Dismantling of German Industry," in Robert Slusser, ed., *Soviet Economic Policy in Postwar Germany: A Collection of Papers by Former Soviet Officials*, pp. 14–17; Clay, *Decision*, p. 124; Chotiner and Atwell, "Soviet Occupation Policy," pp. 53–54.

34. One faction in the Soviet government, identified with Central Committee Secretary G. M. Malenkov, favored a policy of "economic disarmament" that would have dismantled much of German industry for shipment to the Soviet Union. The other faction, identified with Minister for Foreign Trade A. I. Mikoyan, wished to build up the economy of eastern Germany and to rely upon industrial deliveries rather than plant removals for Soviet reconstruction needs. Mikoyan's group won, and in the summer of 1946 the Soviets adopted a strategy of reparations from current production. See Chotiner and Atwell, "Soviet Occupation Policy," pp. 54–55; Vladimir Rudolph, "The Execution of Policy," in Slusser, ed., *Soviet Economic Policy*, pp. 47–56; Yergin, *Shattered Peace*, pp.

95–97, 227; Bruce Kuklick, *American Policy and the Division of Germany: The Clash with Russia over Reparations*, pp. 69–72, 218–19; Millis, *Forrestal Diaries*, p. 266; Caffery to SecState, Aug. 24, 1946, *FRUS 1946*, 5:593–94; Durbrow to SecState, Sept. 6, 1946, pp. 602–03.

35. Kolko, *Limits*, p. 134; Chotiner and Atwell, "Soviet Occupation Policy," pp. 55–58.

36. By September 1945, Robert D. Murphy, U.S. political adviser for Germany, was warning that a heavy German reparations settlement could impair general European recovery as well. For Truman's views on reparations, see Truman's letters to his wife, July 20 and 31, 1945, in Robert H. Ferrell, *Dear Bess: The Letters of Harry to Bess Truman, 1910–1959*, pp. 520, 522–23; Truman, *Year of Decisions*, p. 308; Clay, *Decisions*, p. 38. For Pauley's instructions on reparations, see Instructions for Pauley, May 18, 1945, *FRUS 1945*, 3:1,222–27. On White House aide's instructions to Pauley, see Justin M. Wolf Memo, Aug. 23, 1945, Pauley Papers-Eur. Mission, File "Cables: General," NA. On Murphy, see Murphy to SecState, Sept. 30, 1945, *FRUS 1945*, 3:1,320–21.

37. On American suspicions regarding Soviets, see Harriman to SecState, April 3, 1945, *FRUS 1945*, 3:1,186; Harriman to SecState, April 6, 1945, pp. 1,190–92; Kennan to SecState, April 27, 1945, p. 1,200; Kennan to SecState, May 3, 1945, pp. 1,203–05; Kennan to SecState (Harriman), May 14, 1945, pp. 1,211–13; Byrnes to Pauley, Aug. 13, 1945, pp. 1,255–56.

38. See Clayton to SecState, April 22, 1946, *FRUS 1946*, 5:541–42; Murphy to SecState, May 2, 1946, pp. 545–47.

39. Certain historians, such as Bruce Kuklick, believe that the Americans tried to use reparations, like Lend-Lease and the Russian loan, as a lever by which to influence Soviet policies in Eastern Europe and Germany. To Kuklick, American policies were primarily responsible for the division of Germany and Europe. Yet the anti-Communist consensus within the Truman administration, let alone the country, did not crystallize until later in 1946. Furthermore, Byrnes and Clay, the key American actors in Germany, did not share the same suspicion of Soviet motives in Germany as did certain officials in the State Department. Kuklick also argues that the principle of zonal autonomy, promoted by Byrnes at Potsdam, eliminated the possibility of treating Germany as an economic unit. The Soviets, however, had championed the very same principle in the sole paper they put before the European Advisory Commission in 1944. Indeed, zonal autonomy worked greatly to the Soviet advantage, for eastern Germany was more economically balanced, and recovered more quickly after the war, than the other zones. Thus, the Soviets had less reason to treat Germany as an economic unit than the Americans. In any case, the chaotic system of zonal autonomy that developed in Germany after the war reflected, rather than caused, the partition of that country. On anti-Soviet motive, see Acheson and Hilldring to SecState, May 9, 1946, *FRUS 1946*, 5:549; Acheson to SecState, May 9, 1946, pp. 550–55. For revisionist argument, see Kuklick, *American Policy*, pp. 156–72, 214–15. Cf. Richard Hiscocks, "Divided Germany," in Edgar McInnis et al., eds., *The Shaping of Postwar Germany*, p. 70; Clay to Baruch, April 22, 1946, in Smith, *Clay Papers*, 1:202.

40. Quotation from Warner, "Germany 1946–48," p. 63; also see p. 63n; and Byrnes (Clayton) to Murphy, Oct. 12, 1945, *FRUS 1945*, 3:1,341–43; Clay to

Eisenhower, May 26, 1946, in Smith, *Clay Papers*, 1:214; Yergin, *Shattered Peace*, pp. 228–29; Kuklick, *American Policy*, p. 234.

41. Ratchford and Ross, *Reparations*, pp. 79, 82–83, 124–25; Penrose, *Economic Planning*, p. 288.

42. On steel negotiations, see Murphy to SecState, Dec. 22, 1945, *FRUS 1945*, 3:1,484–86; Murphy to SecState, Dec. 31, 1945, pp. 1,499–1,502; Murphy to SecState, Jan. 11, 1946, *FRUS 1946*, 5:484–86; Murphy to SecState, Jan. 18, 1946, pp. 486–88; unsigned Memcon (Byrnes-Halifax), Jan. 28, 1946, pp. 493–94; Murphy (Clay) to SecState, Jan. 31, 1946, pp. 494–96.

43. John Gimbel has shown that American and British taxpayers actually did foot the bill for the massive "hidden reparations" that the French, Belgians, Dutch, and others received in the form of subsidized German coal, timber, and shipping services. Only part of U.S.-U.K. occupation expenses, then, benefited Germans and the German economy. See Gimbel, *Marshall Plan*, pp. 154–75. "Piecemeal" quotation from Clay to Echols, April 8, 1946, in Smith, *Clay Papers*, 1:188. Two percent figure from Murphy to Clayton, Oct. 23, 1945, *FRUS 1945*, 3:1,536. "Scenic" and central organs references from Murphy to SecState, May 2, 1946, *FRUS 1946*, 5:546; also see Clay, *Decision*, p. 121. "Postwar level" quotation from Clay to Eisenhower, May 26, 1946, *FRUS 1946*, 5:213–14.

44. Luther Gulick, "Germany—A Single Economic Unit," Aug. 17, 1945, Pauley Papers-Eur. Mission, File "Claims and Procedures," NA.

45. Patterson observation from Patterson to Pauley, July 24, 1946, *ibid.*, File "Incoming Correspondence; April 1946," NA. On nationalization, see Murphy to SecState, Sept. 1, 1946, File "Memos to Mr. Bennett-May 1946 Cables and Daily Summary Information," NA. Lt. General Hoyt S. Vandenberg, Director of the Central Intelligence Group, rather excitedly argued that the Soviets had seized German industries in order to circumvent the Potsdam prohibition against war production in German-owned plants. See Vandenberg to Truman, Oct. 4, 1946, Papers of HST-PSF-Intelligence Files, File "Central Intelligence—Memoranda 1945–1948," HSTL.

46. Clay to McNarney, July 23, 1946, in Smith, *Clay Papers*, 1:243–44; cf. Clay, *Decision*, pp. x, 124, 131. Patterson, in the memo cited in n.45 above, directly quoted from Clay's report, but interpreted the evidence quite differently.

47. W. Stuart Symington, "Interview with General Clay, July 25, 29, 30," n.d. [July 1946], Papers of HST-PSF-Subject File: Cabinet, File "Air Force, Dept. of—Secy. of War for Air—W. Stuart Symington," HSTL. Symington's trip followed close on the heels of another around-the-world trip by Secretary of the Navy Forrestal, who gained much the same impression of Clay's views after interviewing him. See July 16, 1946, entry in Millis, *Forrestal Diaries*, p. 182.

48. E.g., see Acheson to SecState, May 9, 1946, *FRUS 1946*, 5:550–55. For further exposition of this thesis, see Gimbel, *Occupation*, pp. 57–61; and John Gimbel, "Cold War Historians and the Occupation of Germany," in Schmitt, ed., *U.S. Occupation*, pp. 89–91.

49. On Clay's distaste for socialism, see Kolko, *Limits*, ch. 5, pp. 111–45; Warner, "Germany 1946–1948," p. 64. On Adenauer and the CDU, see Konrad Adenauer, *Memoirs 1945–1953*, pp. 51, 123.

50. Warner, "Germany 1946–1948," p. 66; Murphy (Angell) to Acheson, Jan. 21, 1946, *FRUS 1946*, 5:490–91; Murphy to SecState, Feb. 24, 1946, pp. 505–07; Murphy to SecState, March 19, 1946, pp. 527–28.

51. Wagner, "Decision to Divide Germany," p. 189. Kuklick in particular contends that American hostility and intransigence on the reparations issue "were responsible for the partition of Germany and perhaps for the rigid division of Europe" (*American Policy*, p. 2).

52. For an exposition of this thesis, see Gimbel, *Occupation*, passim; and Robert Cecil, "Potsdam and its Legends," pp. 460–61. Also see Clay to War Department, Sept. 24, 1945, in Smith, *Clay Papers*, 1:84–85; Clay to War Department [not sent], Oct. 4, 1945, pp. 90–91; Clay to Russell, Dec. 15, 1945, p. 137; Murphy to SecState, Sept. 23, 1945, *FRUS 1945*, 3:871–73; Byrnes to Caffery (Bidault), Feb. 1, 1946, *FRUS 1946*, 5:496–98; Murphy to SecState, Feb. 24, 1946, pp. 505–07; Murphy to SecState, April 4, 1946, pp. 536–37; Murphy to SecState, Aug. 11, 1946, pp. 590–92; Murphy to SecState, Aug. 17, 1946, pp. 592–93; Murphy to SecState, Oct. 25, 1946, pp. 629–30.

53. E.g., see Jean Edward Smith, "The View from USFET: General Clay's and Washington's Interpretations of Soviet Intentions in Germany, 1945–1948," in Schmidt, ed., *U.S. Occupation*, pp. 64–85; Gimbel, "Historians and Occupation," in Schmidt, pp. 86–102; Gimbel, *Occupation*, passim.

54. Bidault to Byrnes, March 2, 1946, *FRUS 1946*, 5:512–15. State Department officials toyed with the idea of approving French annexation of the Saar in exchange for French cooperation on the administrative issue. As it turned out, the French gained American consent to economic merger of the Saar without giving in on the administrative issue for several months. On the Saar issue, see, e.g., Matthews to SecState, Feb. 28, 1946, pp. 507–08; Acheson (Hilldring) to SecState, May 13, 1946, pp. 778–79. On French goals and policies in this period, see André Fontaine, "Potsdam: A French View," pp. 466–69.

55. Caffery to SecState, June 11, 1946, *FRUS 1946*, 5:566–67; Caffery to SecState, Aug. 30, 1946, p. 596; Matthews Memcon (Byrnes-Bidault), Sept. 24, 1946, pp. 607–10. French obstructionism, however, alarmed Robert Murphy and State Department officials insofar as it appeared to further Communist infiltration of the western zones. Through their intransigence, Robert Murphy argued, the French not only curtailed German (and European) recovery, but "played directly into the hands of the Soviet Union." By exploiting Western differences, Murphy feared, the Soviet Union could emerge as "the champion of a united Reich whose only salvation lies in close affiliation with Moscow." Central agencies, on the other hand, could break down zonal boundaries and challenge the Soviets' exclusive control over eastern Germany. Until the United States took a firm stand against the French, Murphy warned, the German people would believe that the Americans favored the French at the expense of German reunification. Murphy to SecState, Feb. 24, 1946, p. 506. Other important decision makers agreed; see Matthews to SecState, Feb. 28, 1946, p. 508; Byrnes to Murphy, March 12, 1946, pp. 524–25.

56. Clay had first suggested the idea in May 1946. See Clay to Anderson, April 11, 1946, *FRUS 1946*, 5:540, 540n.; Heath (Mayer) to SecState, Dec. 9, 1946, pp. 649–50; Byrnes to Murphy (Mayer), Dec. 18, 1946, pp. 653–54. The

U.S. also threatened to cut off restitution deliveries in retaliation for unilateral French reparation removals from Germany. See Acheson to Byrnes (and Clay), June 20, 1946, pp. 570–71.

57. In 1947, the deficit for the American zone was an estimated $200 million, and that for the British zone $400 million. After protracted and difficult negotiations, the Americans agreed in December 1947 to assume 50 percent of the occupation costs of the merged zones. Hathaway argues that the Americans favored the bizonal merger solely in order to bolster their own interests in Germany and Europe, and not to bail out the British (*Partnership*, pp. 258–60). On Anglo-American relations in Germany, see Paterson, *Confrontation*, pp. 256–57; Kolko, *Limits*, pp. 137–39, 167–75; Kuklick, *American Policy*, pp. 202–03; Gimbel, *Marshall Plan*, pp. 159–60, 181–83, 201–03, 208–19; J. K. Snowden, *The German Question 1945–1973: Continuity in Change*, pp. 111–16.

58. Caffery to SecState, Sept. 18, 1946, *FRUS 1946*, 5:605.

59. Quotation from Warner, "Germany 1946–1948," p. 66. For Saar incident, see Brynes to Bidault, Oct. 14, 1946, *FRUS 1946*, 5:621, Brynes to Clay, Dec. 24, 1946, pp. 655–56; Murphy (Clay) to Byrnes, Dec. 27, 1946, pp. 656–57; Byrnes to Clay, Dec. 30, 1946, pp. 657–58.

60. Since Clay's definition of economic unity entailed the opening of the four zones to free commercial intercourse, the equitable distribution of resources, and a uniform financial system, he could not have held much hope for its early realization. In the meantime, Clay favored the establishment of decentralized German councils that would oversee economic affairs in the American zone. He opposed the formation of a strong German central government in the near future. Clay to Echols, July 19, 1946, in Smith, *Clay Papers*, 1:236–43.

61. *Ibid.*, p. 243. A year earlier, Acheson had drawn a parallel between American treatment of Germany and modern penology. The object of American policy, Acheson stated, was the rehabilitation of Germany and its reintegration into the community of nations. See Minutes of 140th Meeting of Secretary's Staff Committee, July 16, 1945, Byrnes Papers, File "589: SC Minutes [Secretary's]," Clemson.

62. See editorial comments in Smith, *Clay Papers*, 1:253–55; on Clay's outrage at Washington's initial reaction to his policy statement, see Clay to Hilldring, Aug. 13, 1946, p. 251; Clay to Hilldring, Aug. 15, 1946, pp. 252–53; Clay to Hilldring, Aug. 16, 1946, ibid., p. 254.

63. Quotation from Byrnes to Snyder, Sept. 9, 1946, Snyder Papers, File "Germany-general, 1946–51," HSTL. Also see John Gimbel, "On the Implementation of the Potsdam Agreement: An Essay on U.S. Postwar German Policy," pp. 242–63; Gimbel, *Occupation*, pp. 85–87. On the French reaction to Byrnes' speech, see also Kindleberger Memcon, Sept. 9, 1946, *FRUS 1946*, 5:603–04.

64. On the origins of the Bizone, see Gimbel, "Historians and Occupation," pp. 91–92. "Political integration" quotation from Murphy to SecState, Aug. 2, 1946, *FRUS 1946*, 5:587; Byrnes' comments from Matthews Memcon, Sept. 24, 1946, p. 609. Also see Murphy to SecState, Oct. 11, 1946, pp. 613–21; Clay's Draft Memo [not sent], Feb. 26, 1947, in Smith, *Clay Papers*, 1:320. On "economic magnet" thesis, see Gimbel, *Occupation*, p. 112. Quotation from Avi

Shlaim, *The United States and the Berlin Blockade, 1948–1949: A Study in Crisis Decision-Making*, p. 25.

65. Unsigned Memo, "Excerpts from Telephone Conversation between Honorable James Forrestal, Secretary of the Navy, and Mr. James Reston of the New York Times," March 13, 1947, Papers of Joseph M. Jones, File "Drafts of the Truman Doctrine," HSTL. Hereafter cited as "Jones Papers."

66. Quotation from Truman, *Year of Decisions*, p. 308. For a critical appraisal of Pauley, see Kuklick, "Reparations," pp. 279–80. On Pauley's background, see Donovan, *Conflict and Crisis*, pp. 78, 178.

67. Quotation from Pauley to W. H. Grimes (editor of *Wall Street Journal*), Dec. 20, 1946, Pauley Papers-Eur. Mission, File "Outgoing Correspondence January 1946," NA. In a press conference, Pauley warned that "the Allies will be successfully courting World War III if they embrace any proposal for raising the level of German industry as the price of economic unification of that country." Ostensibly, Pauley's remarks were meant to answer a Soviet offer to support the economic unification of Germany in exchange for reparations from current production in the western zones. But from the context and the date, it is clear that Pauley was also issuing a warning to the Western Allies, the State Department, OMGUS, and the American public. See Press Release, Oct. 30, 1946, Pauley Papers, File "Press Release 10-30-46," NA. Months later, following his retirement as U.S. reparations representative, Pauley also forcefully attacked the March 1947 (Herbert) Hoover Report, which recommended a higher level of industry for Germany. See Pauley to Truman, April 15, 1947, File "U.S. Reparations Mission—Chronological File—April 9, 1946–," NA; Pauley to Truman, May 27, 1947, File "Outgoing Correspondence January 1946," NA; Pauley to Truman, June 9, 1947, *FRUS 1947*, 2:1,106–08. John R. Steelman, Truman's main adviser on domestic policy at the time, sided with Pauley against Hoover, but to no avail. See Steelman to Truman, "Hoover and Pauley Recommendations on Germany," n.d. [stamped, "Noted May 21 1947"], Snyder Papers, File "Germany-general, 1946–51," HSTL.

68. On Pauley's relations with OMGUS and the State Department, see Grew to Truman, May 7, 1945, *FRUS 1945*, 3:1,206–08; Pauley to Clay, Aug. 4, 1945, pp. 1,240–43; Truman to Pauley, Aug. 20, 1945, pp. 1,261–62; Byrnes to Angell, Oct. 24, 1945, p. 1,357. On Truman's abortive appointment of Pauley as Secretary of the Navy, see Donovan, *Conflict and Crisis*, pp. 178–83. Truman quotation from Connelly Minutes of Cabinet Meeting, Feb. 7, 1947, Connelly Papers, File "Notes on Cabinet Meetings-White House File (Set I): January 3–December 19, 1947," HSTL. Pauley's resignation is mentioned in Truman to Marshall, March 7, 1947, *FRUS 1947*, 2:1,104–05. Pauley continued in the administration as a special assistant to the Secretary of War, but he was forced to resign from that post in January 1948 following public revelations of his commodity speculation. See Donovan, *Conflict and Crisis*, p. 350.

69. Byrnes to Snyder, Sept. 9, 1946, and Snyder to Byrnes, Sept. 26, 1946, Snyder Papers, File "Germany-general, 1946–51," HSTL.

70. In the interim, before large-scale American aid could resuscitate the German economy, OMGUS blocked the infiltration of the Soviet-backed Socialist Unity Party (SED) into the western zones. By moving ahead with upwardly

revised levels of industry in the Bizone, the British and the Americans forced the French to take the first hesitant steps toward trizonal fusion, economic integration, and the creation of a West German state. On alleged Communist (KPD and SED) infiltration into the western zones, see *FRUS 1947*, 2:856–67; on revised level of industry, Bizone, and France, see pp. 977–1,072.

71. Bohlen, *Witness*, p. 263.

72. For explication of this argument, see Wagner, "Decision to Divide Germany," pp. 162–73. France associated herself with the Potsdam agreements in August 1945, but expressed reservations on the establishment of a central authority for Germany. French reservations cast into doubt whether or not France was party to Potsdam. In practice, French authorities acted as if she were not. See Fontaine, "Potsdam," p. 466; Cecil, "Potsdam Legends," p. 461.

73. Quotation from Gimbel, *Marshall Plan*, p. 60. Also see Walter C. Clemens, Jr., "The Soviet World Faces West, 1945–1970," p. 476; Fontaine, "Potsdam," p. 471.

6. The Truman Doctrine

1. Quotation cited in Lawrence S. Wittner, *American Intervention in Greece, 1943–1949*, p. 18. Saudi oil statistics from Bruce Robellet Kuniholm, *The Origins of the Cold War in the Near East: Great Power Conflict and Diplomacy in Iran, Turkey, and Greece*, p. 180n.

2. Cited in John R. Oneal, *Foreign Policy Making in Times of Crisis*, p. 81.

3. Hathaway, *Partnership*, pp. 297–98, 301.

4. See Oneal, *Crisis*, p. 93; Gary R. Hess, "The Iranian Crisis of 1945–46 and the Cold War," pp. 117–46; Richard Pfau, "Containment in Iran, 1946: The Shift to an Active Policy," pp. 359–72; and Kuniholm, *Near East*, pp. 188, 203–05, 298–302, 304–50.

5. Kuniholm, *Near East*, p. 201.

6. *Ibid.*, pp. 145–46; Oneal, *Crisis*, pp. 78–80.

7. Kuniholm, *Near East*, pp. 192–94, 199.

8. *Ibid.*, pp. 278–82; Oneal, *Crisis*, pp. 86–89.

9. Oneal, *Crisis*, p. 88.

10. Cited in Kuniholm, *Near East*, p. 297. Truman probably did not state his position in quite these terms before Byrnes, but the quotation accurately reflects his feelings on Soviet policy (see p. 298, also Oneal, *Crisis*, p. 91).

11. Oneal, *Crisis*, pp. 93, 100.

12. Churchill was dismayed that the Americans went no further. The *Missouri*, escorted by a cruiser, arrived in Istanbul on April 6, 1946. The original U.S. plans had called for a full naval task force. On March 10, 1946, Forrestal meeting with Churchill, see Millis, *Forrestal Diaries*, pp. 144–45.

13. Oneal, *Crisis*, pp. 104, 115.

14. On March 13, 1946, JCS Memo to Byrnes, see Schnabel, *JCS*, pp. 109–11. On the Straits crises and the American commitment to Turkey before the Truman Doctrine, see Kuniholm, *Near East*, pp. 59–72; Paterson, *Confrontation*, pp. 190–93.

15. Acheson to SecState, Aug. 15, 1946, *FRUS 1946*, 7:840–41. Also see Kuniholm, *Near East*, pp. 355–76.

16. Quotation from Forrestal diary entry of Aug. 15, 1946, in Millis, *Forrestal Diaries*, p. 192. Acheson note in Acheson to Orekhov, Aug. 19, 1946, *FRUS 1946*, 7:847–48. On naval force, see Paterson, *Confrontation*, p. 189. On U.S. military restraint, see Jonathon Knight, "American Statecraft and the 1946 Black Sea Straits Controversy," pp. 453–59, 470–75.

17. Kuniholm, *Near East*, pp. 344–50.

18. *Ibid.*, pp. 389–95.

19. Quotation from Memo of Conversation, "Entrance of SONJ Officials into Iran," Jan. 28, 1947, Hickerson Papers, File "Memoranda of Conversation 1947–49," NA; Allen to SecState, Oct. 3, 1947, *FRUS 1947*, 5:965–66; Jernegan to Allen, Dec. 9, 1947, pp. 992–93; Kuniholm, *Near East*, pp. 383–98; Paterson, *Confrontation*, pp. 177–83.

20. Quotation from Oneal, *Crisis*, p. 93. Truman's reaction from Truman, *Memoirs: Years of Trial and Hope*, p. 97. Quotation on Acheson from McLellan, *Acheson*, p. 111.

21. On Greek wartime losses, see Paterson, *Confrontation*, p. 183.

22. On EAM-ELAS, see Library of Congress, European Affairs Division, *War and Postwar Greece: An Analysis Based on Greek Writings*, pp. 49–50, 57; and John O. Iatrides, *Revolt in Athens: The Greek Communist "Second Round," 1944–45*, pp. 20–24; Wittner, *Intervention*, pp. 2–3. On the governments-in-exile and associated groups, see Wittner, pp. 3–4; Iatrides, *Revolt*, 31–41.

23. On the First Round, see Iatrides, *Revolt*, pp. 41–43, and the Second Round, pp. 200–255. Also on the Second Round, Wittner, *Intervention*, pp. 22–29; Oneal, *Crisis*, pp. 146–48.

24. Quotation from Iatrides, *Revolt*, p. 283, also see pp. 284–85; and Oneal, *Crisis*, p. 148.

25. Oneal, *Crisis*, pp. 148–49; Iatrides, *Revolt*, pp. 210–20, 286–87; Wittner, *Intervention*, pp. 10–17, 23–26.

26. Quotation from William Hardy McNeill, *The Greek Dilemma: War and Aftermath*, p. 145. Also see Library of Congress, *War and Postwar Greece*, pp. 72, 77; Iatrides, *Revolt*, pp. 221–24; Oneal, *Crisis*, pp. 146, 149; Wittner, *Intervention*, pp. 6–9, 26–27. For the standard Greek viewpoint, which claims that the Kremlin controlled the EAM-ELAS, as well as the KKE, virtually from the beginning of the war, see Stephen G. Xydis, *Greece and the Great Powers: Prelude to the "Truman Doctrine"* (Thessaloniki: Institute for Balkan Studies, 1963), passim.

27. Quotation from Bohlen, *Witness*, p. 261. Also see Iatrides, *Revolt*, p. 279; Yergin, *Shattered Peace*, p. 245; McLellan, *Acheson*, pp. 109–10; Acheson, *Present*, p. 290. Cf. Wittner, *Intervention*, pp. 310–11.

28. On U.S. aid to Greece before the Truman Doctrine, see Paterson, *Confrontation*, pp. 183–90. In January 1946, MacVeagh told Washington that a big package of Anglo-American aid was necessary to avert political chaos and famine in Greece. See MacVeagh to SecState, Jan. 11, 1946, *FRUS 1946*, 7:91–92. On Byrnes' policy, see Byrnes to Tsouderos, Jan. 15, 1946, pp. 95–96. On Greek request for $6 billion in aid, see Unger to SecState, July 5, 1946, pp.

175–77; Matthews Memcon, July 5, 1946, pp. 177–79. On Acheson's reluctance to extend aid to Greece, see Acheson to Rankin, June 14, 1946, p. 170; Acheson to Harriman, July 13, 1946, pp. 181–82. Quotations from Acheson to Truman, Aug. 7, 1946, *FRUS 1946*, 7:187–88. Also, see Acheson to MacVeagh, Aug. 14, 1946, pp. 190–92; Acheson to MacVeagh, Sept. 7, 1946, pp. 201–02. On Porter mission, see Wittner, *Intervention*, pp. 168–69.

29. For Clayton on military aid, see Clayton to SecState, Sept. 12, 1946, *FRUS 1946*, 7:209–13. Byrnes quotation from Byrnes to Clayton, Sept. 24, 1946, pp. 223. Also see Wittner, *Intervention*, pp. 55–56.

30. Quotation from Acheson to MacVeagh, Oct. 15, 1946, *FRUS 1946*, 7:232–36. On U.S. policy changes, see Clayton to Byrnes, Sept. 25, 1946, pp. 225–26.

31. Henderson to Byrnes and Acheson, Oct. 21, 1946, with attached NEA Memo, Oct. 21, 1946, *FRUS 1946*, 7:240–45.

32. On Greek-American talks on aid, see Baxter to Henderson, Oct. 29, 1946, *FRUS 1946*, 7:247–49; State Department Memo, Oct. 29, 1946, pp. 250–54. On "extravagant hopes," see Byrnes to MacVeagh, Oct. 31, 1946, p. 257. Acheson on economic and military aid in Acheson to MacVeagh, Nov. 8, 1946, pp. 262–63. On Congressional delay of aid, see Acheson to MacVeagh, Dec. 28, 1946, pp. 285–86.

33. Byrnes quotation on Tsaldaris in Byrnes to MacVeagh, Jan. 3, 1947, *FRUS 1946*, 7:287. Acheson's portrayal of Tsaldaris in Acheson, *Present*, p. 268. Tsaldaris irritated Byrnes by publicly announcing that the Secretary had promised him additional aid; in fact, Byrnes had said that an Eximbank or special, Congressionally approved loan was highly unlikely. See Byrnes Memcon, Jan. 4, 1947, *FRUS 1947*, 5:1–2. Possible cancellation of Eximbank loan discussed in Ness Memcon, Jan. 22, 1947, pp. 11–12.

34. Paterson quotation from Paterson, *Confrontation*, p. 194. On Porter mission, see Porter to Clayton, Feb. 17, 1947, *FRUS 1947*, 5:17–22; Porter to SecState, Feb. 19, 1947, p. 26. Ethridge quotation from Ethridge to SecState and Austin, Feb. 17, 1947, p. 24. Marshall quotation from Marshall to MacVeagh, Feb. 18, 1947, p. 25.

35. *Times* cited in Joseph M. Jones, *The Fifteen Weeks: February 21–June 5, 1947*, p. 81, also see pp. 78–82, and Freeland, *Truman Doctrine*, pp. 70–73.

36. Acheson to SecState, Feb. 21, 1947, *FRUS 1947*, 5:31. Acheson's memo was based upon a memo from Henderson to Acheson on Feb. 20, 1947, see p. 29n. Wittner quotation from Wittner, *Intervention*, p. 66. Still, Wittner surely exaggerates when he claims that American policymakers "exhibited a definite eagerness to assume the 'burdens of power'" (pp. 66, 68–69).

37. I have found no documentary evidence to substantiate Jones' claim that Marshall sent a memo to Acheson to this effect; it is possible that Jones mistook the memo by Acheson (see n.36 above) for the one by Marshall. See Jones, *Fifteen Weeks*, p. 131.

38. On Acheson's Feb. 21, 1947, initiatives and his coordination of interdepartmental planning on the Truman Doctrine, see Acheson, *Present*, p. 291; Truman, *Trial and Hope*, pp. 104–05; Oneal, *Crisis*, p. 162.

39. Paterson, *Confrontation*, pp. 265, 266. Paterson takes Congressional op-

position to administration programs just before the Truman Doctrine more seriously (see p. 196). Joyce and Gabriel Kolko argue that Democrats and Republicans differed only marginally over foreign policy questions in early 1947. Richard Freeland does not entirely dismiss Republican opposition, but agrees with the Kolkos that the administration manufactured the crisis over Greece and Turkey in order to break the legislative logjam. See Kolko, *Limits*, pp. 334–36; Freeland, *Truman Doctrine*, pp. 88–95.

40. In a speech at Baylor University on March 6, 1947, the President sought to counteract neo-isolationist tendencies by pleading for bipartisan support against the rising protectionist tide in the country. As "the giant of the economic world," Truman stated, the United States could not escape responsibility for the postwar international economic order. Truman added, "The world is waiting and watching to see what we shall do." See Harry S. Truman, "Address on Foreign Economic Policy, Delivered at Baylor University," March 6, 1947, *Public Papers, Truman, 1947*, p. 168. Jones quotation from Jones, *Fifteen Weeks*, p. 91. On the 80th Congress' budget-cutting and protectionism, see Jones, pp. 90–99; Gaddis, *Cold War*, pp. 344–46; Patterson, *Mr. Republican*, pp. 373–75; Acheson, *Present*, p. 296. On the battle over RTA, see Susan M. Hartmann, *Truman and the 80th Congress*, pp. 49–53.

41. Forrestal quotation from Forrestal to Charles Thomas, Feb. 24, 1947, in Millis, *Forrestal Diaries*, p. 240. Truman quotation from Forrestal diary entry, Feb. 24, 1947, p. 246.

42. Joseph Jones to William Benton, Feb. 26, 1947, Jones Papers, File "Truman Doctrine—'Important Relevant Papers,'" HSTL.

43. Acheson, *Present*, p. 293. Also see Jones, *Fifteen Weeks*, pp. 142–43; Marshall to Truman, Feb. 27, 1947, *FRUS 1947*, 5:60–62.

44. Jones later recounted: "The President had been concerned from the beginning not so much about the decision he had to make regarding Greece and Turkey as about the extent to which Congress and the American people could be convinced that a program of aid was necessary. . . . the President, Marshall, Acheson, and Vandenberg, and the Cabinet as a whole had emphasized the central importance of the public approach." Jones, "The Drafting of the President's Message of March 12, 1947: *Chronology*," n.d., Jones Papers, File "Drafts of the Truman Doctrine," HSTL. Vandenberg quotation from Acheson, *Present*, p. 293. Clifford cited in Gaddis, *Cold War*, p. 350, also see p. 351, and McLellan, *Acheson*, pp. 115, 118–19.

45. "Sweeping globalism" from Hathaway, *Partnership*, p. 303. All other quotations from SWNCC Minutes, "Subcommittee on Foreign Policy Information Meeting," Feb. 28, 1947, Jones Papers, File "Truman Doctrine: 'Important Relevant Papers,'" HSTL. Also see Jones, *Fifteen Weeks*, pp. 150–51. In the Truman Doctrine speech and other statements of policy, White House assistant press secretary Eben Ayers noted in May 1947, the administration generally preferred use of the term "totalitarian" to "Communist." "This leaves the Soviets no room for complaint," Ayers observed appreciatively, "for if they charge that the reference is to them the reply could be that they admit they are totalitarian." Thus, the SWNCC subcommittee's draft on March 3 of the President's speech did not entirely rule out the possibility of Soviet-American cooperation:

"There is, at the present point in world history, a conflict between two ways of life. . . . the major issue that is posed for the world is not one of objectives, not one between socialism or free enterprise, not one of progress or reaction, not one of left versus right. The issue is one of methods: between dictatorship and freedom; between servitude of the majority to a minority and freedom to seek progress." See Ayers Diary, May 22, 1947, Ayers Papers, File "Diary (Ayers) 1947," HSTL; SWNCC Subcommittee on Foreign Policy Information, "Informational Objectives and Main Themes," n.d. [March 3, 1947], *FRUS 1947*, 5:76–77.

46. Quotation from Kennan, *Memoirs*, p. 317, also see pp. 315–16, and Jones, *Fifteen Weeks*, pp. 154–55.

47. Elsey quotations from Elsey to Clifford, March 8, 1947, Elsey Papers, File "March 12, 'Truman Doctrine' Speech," HSTL. "Flamboyant" quotation from Bohlen, *Witness*, p. 261.

48. Truman quotation from Matthew Connelly, Minutes of Cabinet Meeting, March 7, 1947, Connelly Papers, File "Notes on Cabinet Meetings—White House File (Set I): January 3-December 19, 1947," HSTL.

49. Quotations from Truman Doctrine speech in "Special Message to the Congress on Greece and Turkey: The Truman Doctrine," March 12, 1947, *Public Papers, Truman, 1947*, pp. 177–80. On economic component of aid, see Paterson, *Confrontation*, p. 202.

50. The administration was anxious to silence liberal critics. When the White House received a few hundred telegrams attacking the Truman Doctrine, assistant press secretary Eben Ayers publicly charged on March 14 that many were inspired by "Communist or 'fellow traveler' organizations." The presidential party on vacation in Key West informed Ayers a few days later that "the feeling there was that I had handled it perfectly." See Ayers Diary, March 14 and 19, 1947, Ayers Papers, File "Diary (Ayers) 1947," HSTL. Also see entry for March 15, 1947. Acheson quotation from Acheson, *Present*, p. 298. State Department survey of public attitudes from Shepard Jones to J. M. Jones, "Evaluation of the Current Opinion Situation on Greek-Turkish Problem," March 27, 1947, Jones Papers, File "Greece: Newspaper Clippings," HSTL.

51. Vinson quotation cited in Donovan, *Conflict and Crisis*, p. 286. Also see Paterson, *Confrontation*, pp. 200–02. Lippmann quotation cited in Ronald Steel, *Walter Lippmann and the American Century*, p. 439.

52. Reston quotation from "Excerpts from Telephone Conversation . . . ," March 13, 1947, Jones Papers, File "Drafts of the Truman Doctrine," HSTL.

53. Acheson testimony in U.S., Congress, Senate, Committee on Foreign Relations, *Assistance to Greece and Turkey, Hearings on S. 938*, pp. 1–2, 6–9, 13, 19–20, 24, 28, 39, 41 passim. Also see Freeland, *Truman Doctrine*, pp. 102–04.

54. On strategic importance of Turkey, see Jones, *Fifteen Weeks*, p. 164. Mac-Veagh statement of March 28, 1947, from U.S., Congress, Senate, Committee on Foreign Relations, *Legislative Origins of the Truman Doctrine: Historical Series, Assistance to Greece and Turkey, Hearings on S. 938*, p. 66; Vandenberg quotation on April 2, 1947, p. 128; Acheson exchange with Lodge on April 1, 1947, p. 84; also pp. 141, 160.

55. LaFeber quotation from LaFeber, *America, Russia, and Cold War*, p. 57.

Vandenberg statement on March 28, 1947, from U.S., Congress, *Legislative Origins of Truman Doctrine*, p. 46; White statement on April 2, 1947, p. 131; also see pp. 142–43.

56. Paterson, *Confrontation*, p. 201. On the Congressional debate on the Truman Doctrine, see pp. 199–203; and Hartman, *80th Congress*, pp. 60–64.

57. Acheson quotation from Acheson, *Present*, p. 285. Also see McLellan, *Acheson*, pp. 33, 58–59, 97. "The change was felt from top to bottom," Joseph Jones recalls, "and called forth a great surge of ideas and constructive effort" (*Fifteen Weeks*, p. 107).

58. Truman quotation from Ayers Diary, April 14, 1952, Ayers Papers, File "Diary (Ayers) 1952," HSTL. Quotation on "self-assured leader" from Hartmann, *80th Congress*, p. 29. Jones quotation from Jones, "Memo for the File," March 12, 1947, Jones Papers, File "Drafts of the Truman Doctrine," HSTL. On the administration's unity, see Jones, *Fifteen Weeks*, pp. 117–18, 148.

59. On decision to concentrate on Greece and Turkey, see Jones, *Fifteen Weeks*, p. 137; Acheson, *Present*, p. 293. Acheson quotation from Acheson to Patterson, March 5, 1947, *FRUS 1947*, 5:94. For SWNCC report, see Report of the Ad Hoc Committee of SWNCC, April 21, 1947, *FRUS 1947*, 3:204–19.

60. For Kennan's views, see Kennan, *Memoirs*, pp. 318–19. On Acheson, see Freeland, *Truman Doctrine*, p. 83, also see pp. 88–109; Kolko, *Limits*, pp. 336–41; McLellan, *Acheson*, p. 115.

61. "Excerpts from Telephone Conversation . . . ," March 13, 1947, Jones Papers, File "Drafts of the Truman Doctrine," HSTL.

62. Quotation from Eisenhower (for JCS) to Patterson and Forrestal, March 13, 1947, *FRUS 1947*, 5:114. Also see Schnabel, *JCS*, p. 131.

63. On British troop withdrawal, see Wittner, *Intervention*, pp. 228–30; Balfour to SecState, July 30, 1947, *FRUS 1947*, 5:268. For Marshall quotation, see Marshall to Lovett, Aug. 25, 1947, p. 313. Also see Marshall to Bevin, Aug. 1, 1947, pp. 273–74; Marshall to Douglas, Aug. 1, 1947, pp. 274–75. For Royall-Forrestal quotation, see Royall and Forrestal to SecState, Sept. 5, 1947, pp. 327–29; also see Royall to SecState, Sept. 11, 1947, pp. 335–36. On Marshall's meeting with Senate committee, see Henderson to Rankin, March 25, 1948, *FRUS 1948*, 4:64–65. On American consideration of sending troops to Greece, see Oneal, *Crisis*, pp. 178–83; Wittner, *Intervention*, pp. 237–39; Wilds Memcon, Oct. 15, 1947, *FRUS 1947*, 5:367–68; Keeley to SecState, Dec. 8, 1947, with attached Dec. 6, 1947, Memo, pp. 438–49; Henderson Draft memo [not sent], Dec. 22, 1947, pp. 458–61; Jernegan Memcon, Dec. 26, 1947, pp. 466–69; Souers to NSC (NSC 5), Jan. 6, 1948, *FRUS 1948*, 4:2–7; Henderson to SecState, Jan. 9, 1948, pp. 9–14; Thompson to Henderson, Jan. 9, 1948, p. 15; PPS/18, Jan. 10, 1948, pp. 21–24; NSC Draft Report, Jan. 10, 1948, pp. 24–26; Marshall to American Mission in Greece, Jan. 12, 1948, pp. 26–27; Kennan Memo, Jan. 13, 1948, pp. 27–28; Griswold to SecState, Jan. 14, 1948, pp. 28–29; Editorial Note, pp. 39–41; NSC to Truman (NSC 5/2), Feb. 12, 1948, pp. 46–51; Henderson to Rankin, March 25, 1948, pp. 64–65; Souers to NSC (NSC 5/3), May 25, 1948, pp. 93–95; Hickerson to Lovett, June 1, 1948, pp. 98–99; Editorial Note, p. 101.

64. For Bevin quotation, see Douglas to SecState (Lovett), Sept. 1, 1947,

FRUS 1947, 5:323. For Marshall's acceptance of Bevin's invitation, see Marshall to Douglas, Sept. 8, 1947, pp. 330–32. For the general U.S. position at the Pentagon talks, see State Department Memo, n.d., pp. 575–76. Truman signed this paper in November 1947; see Lovett to Truman, Nov. 24, 1947, pp. 623–24, 623n. On the Anglo-American division of responsibilities, see, e.g., State Department Memo, n.d., pp. 511–21; Hare Memo, Nov. 5, 1947, p. 579. On military bases, see statements by U.S. and U.K. Groups, n.d., pp. 584–86, 586–88, 688–90.

65. On the Greek civil war, see Oneal, *Crisis*, pp. 169–87; on the international dimension of the civil war, see pp. 193–95; and D. George Kousoulas, "The Truman Doctrine and the Stalin-Tito Rift: A Reappraisal," pp. 429–37; Wittner, *Intervention*, pp. 254–82. On NSC decision, see discussion of NSC 18/1, "Economic Relations between the United States and Yugoslavia," Feb. 17, 1949, Papers of HST-PSF-NSC Meetings, File "N.S.C. Meeting No. 34 2–17–49," HSTL.

66. On American "lessons" of the Greek experience, see Paterson, *Confrontation*, p. 205; Wittner, *Intervention*, pp. 254, 265, 281, 307–09.

67. On the military solution, see Wittner, *Intervention*, pp. 223–53; on U.S. economic aid program, pp. 167–91.

68. On the link between the Truman Doctrine and domestic anti-Communism, see Freeland, *Truman Doctrine*, pp. 115–50.

69. John Lewis Gaddis, "Was the Truman Doctrine a Real Turning Point?" pp. 386–92. In contrast, Thomas Paterson states, "The vaguely defined containment doctrine served as the rationale for American intervention on a global scale thereafter" (*Confrontation*, p. 206). Bruce Kuniholm also sees the Truman Doctrine as an important *psychological* turning point (*Near East*, pp. 420–25). For various revisionist viewpoints, see Freeland, *Truman Doctrine*, pp. 99–102; Kolko, *Limits*, pp. 336–45; Richard J. Barnet, *Roots of War* (Baltimore: Penguin Books, Pelican Books, 1973), pp. 161–62.

70. On Moscow CFM, see Yergin, *Shattered Peace*, pp. 296–302; Jones, *Fifteen Weeks*, pp. 214–23, Marshall quotation on p. 223.

71. Report of Ad Hoc Committee of SWNCC, April 21, 1947, *FRUS 1947*, 3:210–11.

7. The Marshall Plan

1. Statistic on CEEC countries' deficit with U.S. from Imanuel Wexler, *The Marshall Plan Revisited: The European Recovery Program in Economic Perspective*, p. 15. On the origins of the Marshall Plan, see Jones, *Fifteen Weeks*, pp. 206–13, 239–56; Paterson, *Confrontation*, pp. 207–13; Kennan, *Memoirs*, pp. 325–43; Gimbel, *Marshall Plan*, passim; Harry Bayard Price, *The Marshall Plan and its Meaning*, pp. 21–26; Hadley Arkes, *Bureaucracy, the Marshall Plan, and the National Interest*, pp. 19–58; Scott Jackson, "Prologue to the Marshall Plan: The Origins of the American Commitment for a European Recovery Program," pp. 1,043–68.

2. For SWNCC subcommittee report, see SWNCC Ad Hoc Committee Report, April 21, 1947, *FRUS 1947*, 3:204–19. Also see Paterson, *Confrontation*, pp. 208–09. Statistics from Cleveland to Jones, "U.S. Foreign Financing," May 2, 1947, Jones Papers, File "Truman Doctrine—'Important Relevant Papers,'" HSTL. Jones referred to the McCloy speech (delivered on April 18, 1947) in a memo advising Acheson to emphasize, in his own Delta Council speech of May 8, the inability of the World Bank and private institutions to replace the U.S. government as the main instrument of aid to Europe (Jones to Acheson, May 1, 1947).

3. On formation of PPS, see Kennan, *Memoirs*, pp. 325–29. Marshall quotation from diary entry, April 21, 1947, in Millis, *Forrestal Diaries*, p. 267. On PPS report, see Kennan to Acheson, with attached PPS Report, May 23, 1947, *FRUS 1947*, 3:223–30; quotation from p. 228; also see Kennan, *Memoirs*, pp. 335–41. Speechwriter Joseph Jones wrote in regard to the drafting of the Marshall Plan speech, "We have a great deal to gain by convincing the world that we have something positive and attractive to offer, and not just anti-Communism." Jones to Havlik et al., May 20, 1947, Jones Papers, File "Marshall Plan Speech," HSTL.

4. Acheson quotations from Dean Acheson, "The Requirements of Reconstruction," speech delivered May 8, 1947, in *DSB* (May 18, 1947), 16:993–94. Also see Jones, *Fifteen Weeks*, pp. 206–13.

5. Clayton Memo (to Acheson), n.d. (May 27, 1947), *FRUS 1947*, 3:230–32, quotation from p. 232.

6. For Marshall Plan speech on June 5, 1947, see *FRUS 1947*, 3:237–39. On the background to the speech, see Gimbel, *Marshall Plan*, pp. 6–16. Compared with its performance during the Truman Doctrine episode, Jones notes, the administration's planning for the Marshall Plan was quite disorganized (*Fifteen Weeks*, p. 241).

7. On Clayton's meetings with British officials, see Peterson Memcon, June 24, 1947, *FRUS 1947*, 3:268–73; Peterson Memcon, June 24, 1947, pp. 274–76; Peterson Memcon, June 25, 1947, pp. 276–83; Block, *Economic Disorder*, p. 88; Paterson, *Confrontation*, pp. 213–15.

8. Kennan quotation from Kennan, *Memoirs*, p. 342; also see Acheson, *Present*, p. 309. Other quotation from Allen, "Summary of Discussion," May 29, 1947, *FRUS 1947*, 3:235. Clayton later made the case against Soviet participation in a letter to Marshall. In addition to the opposition of the U.S. public to aid to the Soviet Union, Clayton cited Russia's supposedly strong foreign reserve and financial position. See Clayton to Marshall, June 19, 1947, 840.50 Recovery Series, File "840.50 Recovery/6–3047," (hereafter cited as "Recovery Series"), NA. Also see Peterson Memcom, June 26, 1947, *FRUS 1947*, 3:291.

9. Forrestal quotation from diary entry, June 23, 1947, in Millis, *Forrestal Diaries*, p. 279.

10. On Bevin and Bidault views, see Paterson, *Confrontation*, p. 214; also pp. 215–18. Molotov also opposed German (and Italian) participation in a recovery program, but his British and French counterparts insisted that European recovery was impossible without German coal. On Soviet suspicions, see e.g., Smith to SecState, June 26, 1947, *FRUS 1947*, 3:294–95; Caffery to SecState, June 27,

1947, p. 296. On Paris conference, see Caffery to SecState, June 28, 1947, pp. 297–99; Caffery to SecState, June 29, 1947, pp. 299–301; Caffery to SecState, July 1, 1947, pp. 301–03; Caffery to SecState, July 2, 1947, pp. 305–06; Douglas to SecState, July 3, 1947, pp. 306–07. For Couve de Murville quotation, see Caffery to SecState, June 29, 1947, p. 300. For Bevin on "blank check," see Caffery to SecState, July 1, 1947, p. 302.

11. Paterson, *Confrontation*, p. 218; also Yergin, *Shattered Peace*, p. 324; Kolko, *Limits*, p. 363; Freeland, *Truman Doctrine*, pp. 169–70.

12. See Paterson, *Confrontation*, pp. 100–02, 116–18, 217–19; K. R. S., "Economic Planning in Eastern Europe," pp. 434, 437; Schwartz, *Russia's Soviet Economy*, pp. 592–93; Alexander Baykov, *Soviet Foreign Trade*, pp. 64–65, Table VII (Appendix).

13. The Poles and Czechoslovaks finally withdrew from the Marshall Plan on July 9–10, 1947, a week after Molotov left Paris. See Steinhardt to SecState, July 10, 1947, *FRUS 1947*, 3:318–19; Steinhardt to SecState, July 10, 1947, pp. 319–20; Griffis to SecState, July 10, 1947, pp. 320–22; Ulam, *Expansion and Coexistence*, pp. 403–04, 436–39; Deutscher, *Stalin*, pp. 584–85.

14. Quotation from Michael Kaser, *Comecon: Integration Problems of the Planned Economies*, p. 19; also see pp. 16–21. On the reversal of Soviet-bloc commercial policies after Stalin's death, see Pubrantz, "Economic Relations," pp. 538–42.

15. John Gimbel, in an otherwise learned study, overemphasizes the role of the German issue in the origins of the Marshall Plan. For a summary of his argument, see Gimbel, *Marshall Plan*, pp. 3–16, 267–80. For a more eclectic interpretation, see Jackson, "Prologue," pp. 1,043–68.

16. On State Department views on Germany and France, see Gimbel, *Marshall Plan*, pp. 35–36, 203–06; Yergin, *Shattered Peace*, pp. 319–20.

17. Hoover Commission quotation cited in Paterson, *Confrontation*, p. 244. Hoover's report supported the position of OMGUS and the War Department in their dispute with State. A State Department memo retorted months later that the United States had never sought to curb German peaceful industrial capacity, and the March 1946 level-of-industry agreement did not in fact limit such production. See unsigned "Memorandum on Mr. Hoover's Third Report . . . ," n.d. (June 1947), RG 59, Decimal File 1945–49, Recovery Series, File "840.50 Recovery/6–2147—6–3047," NA. On March 1946 level-of-industry agreement, see Gimbel, *Marshall Plan*, pp. 78–80.

18. General Lucius Clay and the War Department believed that the socialization and centralization of German industry, especially coal, would distort free market mechanisms, curtail German recovery, raise American occupation costs, and ultimately facilitate Soviet political penetration of the Western zones. The State Department, while not in principle opposed to socialization, feared that public ownership of the coal mines, as witnessed by the British failure to boost production in their zone, would hold coal production and exports below the level necessary to sustain European industry. On the German coal and socialization issues, see Gimbel, *Marshall Plan*, pp. 207–19; *FRUS 1947*, 2:909–76. On the final negotiations leading to a revised Bizonal level of industry, see Murphy to SecState, June 30, 1947, pp. 977–82; British Embassy to SecState, July 15,

1947, pp. 986–87; Murphy to SecState, July 16, 1947, pp. 988–90. For text of JCS/1779 (July 11, 1947), see *DSB* (July 27, 1947), 17:186–93. Also see Paterson, *Confrontation*, p. 245; Gimbel, *Marshall Plan*, pp. 220–26.

19. On French protests over Bizonal level-of-industry plan, see Bidault to SecState, July 17, 1947, *FRUS 1947*, 2:991–92; Bidault Communication, July 17, 1947, *FRUS 1947*, 2:991–92; Bidault Communication, July 17, 1947, pp. 992–93; Caffery to SecState, July 18, 1947, pp. 993–96; Marshall to Bevin, n.d. (July 19, 1947), p. 997; Caffery to SecState, July 20, 1947, pp. 997–99; Reber Memcon, Aug. 5, 1947, pp. 1,021–22; Caffery, Douglas, and Clayton to SecState, Aug. 13, 1947, pp. 1,029–31. On delay of announcement, see Marshall to Bidault, July 21, 1947, pp. 1,003–04. Also see Gimbel, *Marshall Plan*, pp. 228–33.

20. Marshall conversation in Marshall Memcon, July 21, 1947, *FRUS 1947*, 2:1,000–03.

21. Clayton on French motives in Clayton to Lovett, July 30, 1947, *FRUS 1947*, 2:1,011–12. Gimbel quotation from Gimbel, *Marshall Plan*, p. 252. On evolution of compromise on Germany engineered by Caffery et al., see Clayton to SecState (and Lovett), Aug. 7, 1947, *FRUS 1947*, 2:1,022–24; Caffery, Douglas, and Clayton to Lovett, Aug. 14, 1947, pp. 1,033–35; Caffery et al. to SecState, Aug. 19, 1947, pp. 1,039–41. On State Department position, see Marshall to Douglas, Aug. 12, 1947, pp. 1,027–29; Lovett to Clayton and Caffery, Aug. 14, 1947, pp. 1,035–37; Caffery et al. to Lovett, Aug. 19, 1947, pp. 1,041–42; Lovett to Douglas, Aug. 27, 1947, pp. 1,063–64. Also see Gimbel, *Marshall Plan*, pp. 252–53.

22. On Clay's threat to resign and the reassurances from Royall and Marshall, see Murphy to SecState, July 25, 1947, *FRUS 1947*, 2:1,008–09; Royall and Marshall to Clay and Murphy, July 26, 1947, pp. 1,009–10; Royall and Marshall to Clay and Murphy, July 28, 1947, pp. 1,010–11.

23. On Royall's flap, the French reaction, and Lovett's misgivings, see Lovett to SecState, Aug. 3, 1947, *FRUS 1947*, 2:1,014–16; Lovett to SecState, Aug. 5, 1947, pp. 1,017–20. On Clay and Army opposition to French proposals (and to State Department tactics), see Murphy to SecState, Aug. 9, 1947, pp. 1,026–27; Hickerson to Lovett, Aug. 23, 1947, pp. 1,050–54; Clay to War Department, Aug. 25, 1947, pp. 1,063–64; Clayton to Saltzman, Sept. 10, 1947, pp. 1,069–71; and Gimbel, *Marshall Plan*, pp. 234–46.

24. Gimbel, *Marshall Plan*, p. 247.

25. "Shopping lists" quotation from Woodruff Wallner, "Call of the French Ambassador . . . ," Aug. 21, 1947, Recovery Series, File "840.50 Recovery/8–1547—8–3147," NA. On primary U.S. aims, see Lovett to Clayton and Caffery, Aug. 14, 1947, *FRUS 1947*, 3:356–60.

26. Quotation from Lovett to Marshall, Aug. 24, 1947, *FRUS 1947*, 3:373, 375n.

27. Lovett to Clayton and Caffery, Aug. 26, 1947, *FRUS 1947*, 3:384, 388. Similarly, in a meeting with the CEEC's Executive Committee on August 30, Clayton and other officials criticized the Europeans' preliminary request for $29.2 billion in aid over four years. The Americans instructed the CEEC to devise a plan providing for European self-support after four years, sharply

increased coal and food production, "the reactivation of the most efficient existing productive facilities," financial and monetary stability, reduction of trade barriers, and a multilateral governing organization. The CEEC did not conform very closely to American guidelines, but the most important aim at this point was the appearance of cooperation in reviving German production. As John Gimbel states, the "State Department's strategy was to dovetail German rehabilitation with the general European recovery program and to present to the United States Congress a single foreign-aid package" (*Marshall Plan*, p. 258; also see pp. 257–66). See Caffery (Clayton) to Marshall and Lovett, Aug. 31, 1947, *FRUS 1947*, 3:392–93. For a review of this session and of general European problems, see Kennan Memo, "Situation with Respect to European Recovery Program," Sept. 4, 1947, pp. 397–405.

28. Yergin, *Shattered Peace*, pp. 329–34.

29. Given the totalitarian mold into which the Soviets were forcing the eastern zone, Marshall added, the Western allies could not but seek to integrate western Germany into Western Europe, first economically, and then perhaps politically as well. German unification remained an important U.S. goal, Marshall added, but not "under conditions which are likely to bring about effective domination of all Germany by Soviets." On French conditions for trizonal fusion, see, e.g., Achilles Memcon, Feb. 13, 1948, *FRUS 1948*, 2:63–65. Marshall quotation from Marshall to Embassy in U.K., Feb. 20, 1948, pp. 71, 72. Also see Marshall to Truman, Feb. 11, 1948, pp. 60–63; Marshall to Embassy in France, Feb. 19, 1948, p. 71.

30. For London discussions on trizonal fusion, German reconstruction, the Ruhr, and security against German aggression, see, e.g., Douglas to SecState, Feb. 25, 1948, *FRUS 1948*, 2:87–89; Douglas to SecState, Feb. 26, 1948, pp. 92–94; Douglas to SecState, Feb. 28, 1948, pp. 98–100; Marshall to Embassy in U.K., Feb. 28, 1948, pp. 101–02; Douglas to SecState, March 2, 1948, pp. 110–11. The Americans had initially responded to French recalcitrance by threatening to withhold ERP aid from the French zone in Germany. See Douglas to Lovett, March 1, 1948, p. 107; Beam Memcon, March 2, 1948, pp. 112–13; Marshall (Lovett) to Douglas, March 2, 1948, p. 113. On U.S. draft for Ruhr organization, see Douglas to SecState, March 4, 1948, pp. 124–26; Marshall to Embassy in U.K., March 5, 1948, p. 131. Douglas assurances and quotation from Douglas to Lovett, March 6, 1948, p. 138. For agreements of first session, see Communique, March 6, 1948, pp. 141–43.

31. Continuously badgered by the French, Marshall privately admitted that he was beginning to understand Army officials who questioned the reliability of French officials. Washington, he wryly concluded, "would be justified in demanding assurances of French, rather than *vice versa*." See Marshall to Embassy in U.K., May 14, 1948, *FRUS 1948*, 2:248. On French demands regarding Germany and the American response, see also Douglas to SecState, May 10, 1948, pp. 230–31; Marshall to Douglas, May 11, 1948, pp. 233–34; Douglas to SecState, May 19, 1948, pp. 256–58; Marshall and Lovett to Douglas, May 24, 1948, pp. 275–76; Marshall to Embassy in France, May 25, 1948, pp. 276–77; Douglas to SecState, May 25, 1948, pp. 279–80. For final agreement on security, see "Report on Security," May 26, 1948, pp. 291–94.

32. For Royall's protest on Ruhr, see Royall to Marshall, May 18, 1948, *FRUS 1948*, 2:251–53; Douglas to Lovett, May 12, 1948, pp. 235–37. On State Department compliance with Royall's request, see Marshall (Saltzman) to Douglas, May 19, 1948, p. 253. For Lovett quotation, see Lovett to Royall, May 25, 1948, p. 282.

33. For agreement on Ruhr, see "International Control of the Ruhr," May 26, 1948, *FRUS 1948*, 2:285–88. For Nitze's instructions, see Lovett (Nitze) to Douglas, Nov. 10, 1948, p. 467.

34. Gimbel, *Marshall Plan*, p. 4.

35. On the administration's desire not to publicize the Marshall Plan speech, see Freeland, *Truman Doctrine*, pp. 183–84. Quotation from State Department Office of Public Affairs, Division of Public Studies, "Press and Radio Reaction to Secretary Marshall's Harvard Address, June 6, 1947," June 13, 1947, Jones Papers, File "Marshall Plan speech," HSTL. Italics in original.

36. Jones to Russell, June 30, 1947, Jones Papers, File "Truman Doctrine—Marshall Plan: 15 Weeks," HSTL. Jones later found that Clark Clifford had persuaded Truman to issue a clarifying statement on the Marshall Plan, so that the President would act as "*the* chief spokesman" on foreign policy. See Jones to Russell, July 2, 1947. On weak public support for Marshall Plan and disagreement within the State Department over publicity, see Freeland, *Truman Doctrine*, pp. 184–87; James Reston columns in *NYT,* Oct. 24, 28, 1947; Gallup poll, Oct. 8, 1947, in George H. Gallup, *The Gallup Poll: Public Opinion, 1935–1971*, 1:677–78.

37. F. H. Russell, Office of Public Affairs, State Department, to General Carter, "Public Opinion Concerning Recovery Plan," Dec. 26, 1947, with attached Memo, "An 'Area' Analysis of U.S. Opinion on Interim Aid and European Recovery Program," Dec. 24, 1947, Recovery Series, File "840.50 Recovery/12–2547—12–3147," NA.

38. Congressmen also feared that the Marshall Plan would bypass the UN, antagonize Russia, entangle America in European affairs, or bankrupt the economy. Others wondered why the U.S. did not offer similar aid to the Nationalist Chinese. On Congressional attitudes toward the Marshall Plan, see *NYT,* July, 20, 23, Sept. 17, 23, 25, Oct. 5, 10, Nov. 2, 1947; Senator Alexander Wiley to Marshall, Oct. 9, 1947, and Lovett to Wiley, Oct. 21, 1947, Recovery Series, File "840.50 Recovery 10–147—10–1647," NA; Vandenberg to Marshall, Oct. 20, 1947, with attached "Memorandum on European Aid," n.d., by Senator Henry Cabot Lodge, Recovery Series, File "840.50 Recovery/10–1747—10–2047," NA; Darrell St. Clair, "European Relief," Oct. 23, 1947; Representative J. Caleb Boggs (Delaware) to Marshall, Oct. 24, 1947, and Lovett to Boggs, Nov. 13, 1947; Norman T. Ness to Carlisle H. Humelsine, "Report of the Subcommittee on Foreign Economic Policy of the (House) Committee on Foreign Affairs entitled, 'Needs, limits, and sources of American aid to foreign countries . . . ,'" July 8, 1947, Recovery Series, File "840.50 Recovery/7–147—7–847," NA; Freeland, *Truman Doctrine*, pp. 246–66. For the argument that the Marshall Plan faced few legislative obstacles, see Paterson, *Confrontation*, pp. 221–27.

39. On Congressional attitudes toward, and influence upon, the administration of the European aid program, see F. B. Lyon to Lovett, "Brief Report of

Observations Made While Accompanying the Herter Committee on Trip Abroad," Oct. 20, 1947, Recovery Series, File "840.50 Recovery/10–1747– 10–2047," NA; Elsey to Clifford, "The Marshall Plan," Sept. 22, 1947, Clark M. Clifford Papers, File "European Recovery Program," HSTL (hereafter cited as "Clifford Papers"); Arkes, *Bureaucracy,* pp. 59–100.

40. On origins of Harriman, Krug, and Nourse committees, see Price, *Marshall Plan,* pp. 39–42. On Committee for Marshall Plan and other interest groups, see Paterson, *Confrontation,* pp. 221–22; Acheson, *Present,* pp. 320–21; Wexler, *Marshall Plan,* pp. 31–35.

41. For an analysis of British problems, see British Embassy Memo to Department of State, "U.K. Financial Position and World Dollar Shortage," n.d. (June 18, 1947), *FRUS 1947,* 3:17–24; Douglas to SecState, July 25, 1947, pp. 43–44; Marshall Memcon, with attached British Aide-Memoire, July 28, 1947, pp. 44–48; Lovett to Marshall, Aug. 19, 1947, pp. 61–62. Quotation on British suspension of convertibility from NAC Staff Subcommittee Memo, Aug. 16, 1947, p. 59.

42. PPS quotation from PPS 6, August 14, 1947, *FRUS 1947,* 3:361. For advocacy of Interim Aid, see also, e.g., Caffery et al. to SecState, Aug. 6, 1947, pp. 344–45; Haraldson Memcon, Aug. 8, 1947, pp. 345–50; Kennan Memo, Sept. 4, 1947, pp. 397–405. On Congressional reaction, see Marshall (Lovett and Wood) to Clayton, Aug. 11, 1947, pp. 350–51; Lovett to Marshall, Aug. 20, 1947, pp. 66–67; Haraldson Memcon, Aug. 8, 1947, pp. 346, 348.

43. On Interim Aid, special session of Congress, and inflation issues, see Editorial Note, *FRUS 1947,* 3:470–71. Truman's announcement on special session in *DSB* (Nov. 2, 1947), 17:852–55. Also see *NYT,* Sept. 30, Oct. 24, 1947; Donovan, *Conflict and Crisis,* pp. 339–41.

44. Truman quotation from Address to Congress, Nov. 17, 1947, *DSB* (Nov. 30, 1947), 17:1022.

45. White quotation from William S. White, "Marshall Plan Faces Undercover Opposition," *NYT,* Nov. 2, 1947. For quotation on Herter Committee, see Lyon, "Brief Report." Krock quotation from *NYT,* Oct. 5, 1947. The Herter Committee blamed Communism for the economic problems of France and Italy in the fall of 1947. See *NYT,* Nov. 14, 1947; Price, *Marshall Plan,* pp. 52–53. On the legislative history of Interim Aid and the role of anti-Communism, see Hartmann, *80th Congress,* pp. 108–20.

46. Quotation from President's Committee on Foreign Aid, *European Recovery and American Aid,* p. 3; also see pp. 3–12, and Price, *Marshall Plan,* pp. 42–46.

47. On the Harriman Committee and inflation, see Price, *Marshall Plan,* p. 45. On CEA report, see Donovan, *Conflict and Crisis,* p. 341. In February 1948, CEA Chairman Edwin G. Nourse recalled that when he had asked the President in March 1947 if the CEA, then preoccupied with inflation, should study the impact of foreign aid upon domestic economic policy, Truman's reply "was completely non-committal. Subsequent events in connection with the Marshall Plan suggest that the Administration had no clear idea as to what the Truman Doctrine would mean in practice." Nourse Memo, Feb. 23, 1948, Nourse Papers, File "Daily Diary *1947–17* Memorandum dictated on February 23/48 deal-

ing with the issues from Mar. 4 through March 19," HSTL. Nourse's original query to Truman was a memo to the President dated March 19, 1947. Nourse's papers document Truman's amateurish understanding of economic questions and the exclusion of Nourse and the CEA from decision-making on major economic questions.

48. "Totalitarian" quotation from Advisory Steering Committee Memo, Sept. 29, 1947, *FRUS 1947*, 3:476.

49. PPS quotation from PPS 13, "Review of World Situation," Nov. 6, 1947, PPS Files, NA. Marshall quoted in Cabinet meetings of Nov. 7, 1947, in Millis, *Forrestal Diaries*, p. 340. Undated (November 1947) Vandenberg letter quoted in Vandenberg, *Vandenberg Papers*, p. 378.

50. For the Senate committee's discussion and amendment of Interim Aid, see U.S., Senate, Committee on Foreign Relations, *Foreign Relief Aid: 1947; Historical Series: Hearings held in Executive Session on H. Res. 153 and S. 1774*, pp. 134, 148–53, 201–10, 229–38. The conference report on Interim Aid passed by voice vote in the Senate and by 313–82 in the House. Congress also appropriated $18 million for China. See Paterson, *Confrontation*, p. 221n.; Price, *Marshall Plan*, pp. 48, 48n.; Donovan, *Conflict and Crisis*, p. 341; Editorial Note, *FRUS 1947*, 3:484. On renewed drawings on British loan, see Editorial Note, pp. 93–94. On Bizonal costs, see Freeland, *Truman Doctrine*, p. 189.

51. On Lovett and Snyder, see diary entries of June 13 and 26, 1947, in Millis, *Forrestal Diaries*, pp. 279, 282 respectively. On Republican reaction to ERP, see Freeland, *Truman Doctrine*, pp. 248–51; Vandenberg, *Vandenberg Papers*, pp. 384–85; James Reston column in *NYT*, Jan. 18, 1948, and Arthur Krock columns Feb. 6, March 5, 1948. On Taft, see Patterson, *Mr. Republican*, pp. 388–89. Vandenberg quotation from diary entry of Nov. 18, 1947, in Vandenberg, *Vandenberg Papers*, pp. 379–80.

52. The 16 CEEC countries were the U.K., France, Italy, Austria, Belgium, Denmark, Greece, Iceland, Ireland, Luxembourg, the Netherlands, Norway, Portugal, Sweden, Switzerland, and Turkey. Portugal did not participate in ERP, but western Germany and Trieste did. On Truman message on ERP, see Harry S. Truman, "Special Message to Congress on Marshall Plan," Dec. 19, 1947, *Public Papers, Truman, 1947*, pp. 515–29. Also see Freeland, *Truman Doctrine*, pp. 246–47. Truman comment on size of ERP funding from Truman, *Trial and Hope*, p. 118.

53. The White House and the State Department, hoping to avoid the mistakes of the Truman Doctrine legislation, began a campaign of personal consultation with Congressional leaders in the late summer of 1947. See Carl Marcy, "Congressional Liaison on the 'Marshall Plan,'" Sept. 2, 1947, Recovery Series, File "840.50 Recovery/9–147—9–1547," NA; Elsey to Clifford, "The Marshall Plan," Sept. 22, 1947, Clifford Papers, File "European Recovery Program," HSTL; Marcy to Bohlen, "Assignments of Responsibility for Congressional Relations in Connection with European Recovery Program," Dec. 31, 1947, Recovery Series, File "840.50 Recovery/12–2547—12–3147," NA. Forrestal wrote Truman that "we should begin now to plan the campaign for ERP in Congress so that everyone in the Cabinet may be able to testify in the same general pattern." See Forrestal to Truman, Dec. 21, 1947, Papers of HST-PSF-

Subject File: General File, File "European Emergency," HSTL. For Vandenberg on businessmen, see Vandenberg to Lovett, Dec. 10, 1947, Recovery Series, File "840.50 Recovery/12–147—12–1047," NA. Lovett accepted Vandenberg's suggestion; see Lovett to Vandenberg, Dec. 11, 1947. On Vandenberg's suggestion regarding ERP legislation, see Vandenberg to Marshall, Dec. 31, 1947, File "840.50 Recovery/12–2547—12–3147," NA; Vandenberg, *Vandenberg Papers*, pp. 383–88.

54. On Marshall's surrender on administrative issue, see Arkes, *Bureaucracy*, pp. 80–82. Vandenberg quotation on ECA from Vandenberg to Marshall, March 24, 1948, Recovery Series, File "840.50 Recovery/3–2348—3–2548," NA.

55. Forrestal to Truman, Dec. 21, 1947, Papers of HST-PSF-Subject File: General File, File "European Emergency," HSTL.

56. For Marshall quotations on Jan. 8, 1948, see U.S., Congress, Senate, Committee on Foreign Relations, *European Recovery Program, Hearings on S. 2202, pt. 1*, pp. 10, 36 respectively. Ambassador to Great Britain Lewis Douglas likewise declared before the Senate Committee that the United States would become an "armed camp" if Western Europe and, subsequently, Africa "should fall under the domination of the police state." Douglas testimony Jan. 9, 1948, pp. 76, 82; Royall testimony, Jan. 14 and 15, 1948, pp. 444–65, 469–72. The administration also stressed the security argument in executive (closed) hearings. See U.S., Congress, Senate, Committee on Foreign Relations, *Foreign Relief Assistance Act of 1948: Historical Series*, passim.

57. Harold L. Hitchens, "Influences on the Congressional Decision to Pass the Marshall Plan," pp. 55–57, 62–64.

58. For examples of the Alsops' articles, see Joseph and Stewart Alsop, "Are We Ready for a Push Button War?" *Saturday Evening Post* (Sept. 6, 1947), 220:18ff.; "If Russia Grabs Europe,"(Dec. 20, 1947), pp. 15 ff.; "Must America Save the World?" (Feb. 21, 1948), pp. 15 ff. Marshall comment on Brussels Pact from George C. Marshall, "Survival of Democracy Dependent on Success of ERP," Feb. 13, 1948, in *DSB* (Feb. 22, 1948), 18:232. Marshall on "reign of terror" from *NYT,* March 11, 1948. The State Department, reflecting the sense of the Senate, also informally served notice on Italy that she would receive no aid if the Communists won the April 1948 elections (*NYT,* March 16, 1948). For Senate vote on ERP, see *NYT,* March 14, 1948. For Clay quotation, see Yergin, *Shattered Peace*, p. 351. It later came out that Clay was exaggerating the Soviet danger in order to boost Congressional appropriations for the Army. See Smith, *Clay Papers*, pp. 568–69.

59. On legislative progress of ERP, see *NYT,* March 18, 20, 25, April 1, 2, 4, June 10, 13, 20, 1948; Freeland, *Truman Doctrine*, pp. 269–76. On total expenditures for ERP, see Wexler, *Marshall Plan*, p. 249; cf. Paterson, *Confrontation*, p. 232.

60. Reston quotation from *NYT,* Jan. 18, 1948. Vandenberg quotation from diary entry of March 1, 1948, in Vandenberg, *Vandenberg Papers*, p. 389.

61. Clifford quotation cited in Freeland, *Truman Doctrine*, p. 192. Truman message to Congress on Nov. 17, 1947, in *Public Papers, Truman, 1947*, pp. 492–98; Truman message to Congress on Dec. 19, 1947, pp. 515–29. Also see Freeland, *Truman Doctrine*, pp. 339–40; Robert A. Divine, "The Cold War and

the Election of 1948," pp. 90–110; Hartmann, *80th Congress*, pp. 128–30, 184–217.

62. Yergin, *Shattered Peace*, p. 350.

63. Truman quotations from Harry S. Truman, "Toward Securing Peace and Preventing War," Speech before Congress, March 17, 1948, *DSB* (March 28, 1948), 18:419, 420. When Truman told his Cabinet that he intended to speak before Congress on national security, Marshall warned him against provoking the Soviets by delivering too emotional a speech. The President replied that "it was better to do that than to be caught, as we were in the last war, without having warned the Congress and the people." See Ayers Diary, March 16, 1948, Ayers Papers, File "Diary 1948-Ayers," HSTL. Marshall on appeasement from George C. Marshall, "Relation of Military Strength to Diplomatic Action," Statement before Senate Armed Services Committee, March 17, 1948, *DSB* (March 28, 1948), 18:421. Marshall on Soviet policy from *NYT*, March 20, 1948.

64. On progress of ERP, UMT, and draft legislation, see Yergin, *Shattered Peace*, p. 357.

65. Forrestal diary entry, Feb. 18, 1948, in Millis, *Forrestal Diaries*, p. 376; also see p. 375.

66. For Truman quotation, see Ayers Diary, March 23, 1948, Ayers Papers, File "Diary 1948-Ayers," HSTL. On interservice rivalry and the supplemental appropriations of spring 1948, see Millis, *Forrestal Diaries*, pp. 435–39; Yergin, *Shattered Peace*, pp. 357–60; Steven L. Rearden, "History of the Office of the Secretary of Defense, Volume 1: The Formative Years, 1947–1950" (hereafter cited as "Rearden, *OSD*") (draft, 1981), chapter 8; Warner R. Schilling, "The Politics of National Defense: Fiscal 1950," in Warner R. Schilling, Paul Y. Hammond, and Glenn H. Snyder, *Strategy, Politics and Defense Budgets*, pp. 1–266 passim.

67. As Truman explained in an off-the-record talk before the American Society of Newspaper Editors on April 17, 1948, he wished to avoid the boom-and-bust cycle during and after the First World War. In light of the rapid obsolescence of aircraft, a sudden expansion of airpower would lead to waste. "The proper way to approach this thing," the President stated, "is to take the construction program on a basis that will keep us lined up all the time, so that we can put these factories to work immediately, if that is necessary." See Ayers transcript of Truman speech before American Society of Newspaper Editors, April 17, 1948, Ayers Papers, File "Foreign Policy: Russian Relations," HSTL. For Truman on Forrestal, see Ayers Diary, April 21, 1948, Ayers Paper, File "Diary 1948-Ayers," HSTL. For Truman on "muttonheads," see Ayers Diary, April 26, 1948.

68. See Millis, *Forrestal Diaries*, pp. 435–38.

69. Howley cited in Yergin, *Shattered Peace*, p. 380; also see pp. 378–79.

70. See chapter 10 and appendix. On FY 1950 defense budget, see Rearden, *OSD*, chapter 9; Yergin, *Shattered Peace*, pp. 398–400. Quotation on NSC 20/4 from Leffler, "American Conception of National Security."

71. For Lodge quotation on Nov. 17, 1947, see Senate Committee on Foreign Relations, *Foreign Relief Aid 1947—Executive Hearings*, pp. 153–54. Senator Walter George (D-Ga.) added, "There isn't any question but what we will run

the whole show." Senators Connally and Hickenlooper agreed that foreign politicians should not be allowed to abuse future American aid as they allegedly had done in the case of UNRRA (see p. 154).

72. Kolko, *Limits*, p. 381.

73. On businessmen and ECA, see *ibid.*, pp. 381–82. On role of business elite in postwar American foreign policymaking, see Thomas Graham Paterson, "The Economic Cold War: American Business and Economic Foreign Policy, 1945–1950," pp. 1–55. On influence of interest groups, see Kolko, *Limits*, pp. 444–47; on raw materials, p. 448; quotation on manipulation of European economies (italics in original), pp. 382–83; also p. 452. For a similar argument, see Block, *Economic Disorder*, pp. 89–92.

74. Charles S. Maier, "The Postwar Eras and the Conditions for Stability in Twentieth-Century Western Europe," pp. 332–47, and "Politics of Productivity," pp. 607–33.

75. Arkes, *Bureaucracy*, pp. 285–86.

76. On multilateral relations between the ERP countries and the United States during 1948 and 1949, see *FRUS 1948*, 3:352–501 passim; *FRUS 1949*, 4:367–468 passim. On the devaluation and trade discrimination issues, see, e.g., Hoffman (Bissel) to Harriman, March 17, 1949, pp. 377–80; Bruce to Harriman, April 29, 1949, p. 388.

77. Under this system, recipient governments matched ECA dollar grants with a reserve of local currencies. Generally, an importer in the ERP country would first place an order for goods with American suppliers, and then deposit an equivalent amount of local currency with his own government. The government would retain the local currency and pay for the goods with ECA dollars. The ECA shared control of these "counterpart" funds. The ECA retained 5 percent of counterpart for administrative costs and for the purchase of raw materials needed in the U.S., while the European governments, subject to ECA approval, could spend 95 percent on further relief programs, reconstruction projects, or debt retirement. See Arkes, *Bureaucracy*, pp. 156–58, 287–93, quotation on p. 293.

78. On U.S. relations with France, see *FRUS 1948*, 3:592–682 passim; *FRUS 1949*, 4:626–90; Wexler, *Marshall Plan*, pp. 103–07. On ECA release of counterpart funds, see, e.g., Bruce to Hoffman, Sept. 14, 1948, *FRUS 1948*, 3:649–51; Foster to ECA Mission in France, Dec. 6, 1949, *FRUS 1949*, 4:682–86. Cf. Kolko, *Limits*, pp. 365–67, 439–42.

79. On U.S. relations with Italy, see *FRUS 1948*, 3:816–90. In particular, see Dunn to SecState, March 22, 1948, pp. 860–65. Cf. Kolko, *Limits*, pp. 370–71, 437–39.

80. On U.S. relations with Great Britain, see *FRUS 1948*, 3:1,066–1,124 passim; *FRUS 1949*, 4:781–852. On the special Anglo-American relationship, see, e.g., Douglas to SecState, Aug. 11, 1948, *FRUS 1948*, 3:1,113–17. On sterling crisis and American reaction, see, e.g., Douglas to SecState, May 18, 1949, *FRUS 1949*, 4:391–94; U.S Embassy Memo, Aug. 18, 1949, pp. 806–20; PPS 62, Sept. 3, 1949, pp. 822–30. Cf. Kolko, *Limits*, pp. 365–67, 442–44; Block, *Economic Disorder*, pp. 93–103.

81. Arkes, *Bureaucracy*, p. 300, also see pp. 294–330. As a prerequisite for

aid, Congress had mandated the nondiscriminatory access of American companies to scarce materials in areas controlled by ERP recipients, the accumulation of such materials by the United States for stockpiling or other purposes, and the promotion of strategic material production in European colonial dependencies through ECA development grants or loans. Yet the ECA hesitated to pressure European recipients to meet the Congressional statutory requirements regarding strategic materials. Not wishing to starve Europe of minerals necessary for recovery, the ECA used little of the 5 percent in counterpart funds reserved for this purpose until the second half of 1949, following a reprimand by a Congressional investigatory committee (Arkes, pp. 279–85). In the end, the United States bought $82 million in strategic minerals with counterpart and invested $105 million in counterpart and $33 million in U.S. funds to promote new raw material supplies, especially in European colonial dependencies. See Alfred C. Eckes, Jr., *The United States and the Global Struggle for Minerals*, pp. 158–60.

82. For the argument that the economic integration of Europe was the central American goal in the Marshall Plan, see Michael J. Hogan, "The Search for a 'Creative Peace': The United States, European Unity, and the Origins of the Marshall Plan," pp. 267–85. On political advantages and economic costs of European economic integration, see Wexler, *Marshall Plan*, pp. 155, 198–201, 218, 231, 239–44; Arkes, *Bureaucracy*, pp. 274–75.

83. Coal exports declined from $276 million in the first quarter of 1949 to just $3 million in the third quarter of that year; thereafter, ECA financed no American coal exports whatsoever. On Congressional mandate, see Wexler, *Marshall Plan*, pp. 42–47; Arkes, *Bureaucracy*, pp. 163–71. On agricultural commodities, coal, shipping, and machine tools cases, and Hoffman's role, see Arkes, pp. 262–69. American oil companies, which charged high (Gulf of Mexico) prices for inexpensive Middle Eastern oil and demanded payment in scarce dollars, prevailed over ECA's efforts to economize. "There exists no public *power* to compel a modification of commercial practices," John A. Loftus of the State Department concluded in the spring of 1948. "The [ECA] Administration has no bargaining capacity since the companies present a solid front and there is no place the Administrator can turn or threaten to turn to obtain the supplies which he must have." On oil, see Arkes, pp. 276–79. Quotation from Martin to Nitze, "Petroleum Prices and the European Recovery Program," May 21, 1948, with attached John A. Loftus, "Memorandum on Petroleum Prices," n.d., Recovery Series, File "840.50 Recovery/5–2048—5–2548," NA.

84. On steel mill, see Thompson, "Supply of Equipment for Steel Mill for Czechoslovakia," Aug. 25, 1947, Hickerson Records, File "Memoranda of Conversation, 1947–48," NA. Also see Thompson Memcon, June 17, 1947; C. Tyler Wood to Robert A. Lovett, "Proposed Soviet Contracts with International General Electric," Oct. 14, 1947, Clayton-Thorp Papers, File "Memoranda . . .," HSTL.

85. On PPS report, see PPS 17, Nov. 26, 1947, *FRUS 1948*, 4:489–507. On Commerce concern about red tape, see Lovett to Harriman, Dec. 8, 1947, pp. 508–09.

86. Souers added that the controls would increase the popularity of the Marshall Plan in the United States, for, presumably, Washington could screen West

European trade with the Soviet bloc as well. On NSC recommendations, see NSC Report, Dec. 17, 1947, *FRUS 1948*, 4:511–12. On "R" procedure and Souers' quotation, see Sidney Souers to Clark Clifford, Dec. 23, 1947, "The 'R' Procedure for Export Control," Clifford Papers, File "European Recovery Program," HSTL. Also see Department of Commerce Memo, n.d. (Jan. 5, 1948), *FRUS 1948*, 4:512–13.

87. For McCloy and Lovett conversation, see Lovett Memcon, Jan. 19, 1948, *FRUS 1948*, 4:514–16.

88. On conversation with Polish Ambassador, see Armour Memcon, Jan. 30, 1948, *FRUS 1948*, 4:516–20. Also see Griffis to SecState, Feb. 25, 1948, pp. 520–21; Griffis to SecState, April 3, 1948, pp. 528–30. On Polish Ambassador's explanation for delay in economic normalization, see Thorp Memcon, April 9, 1948, pp. 531–34. Also see Thompson Memcon, July 30, 1948, pp. 555–56; Paterson, *Confrontation*, pp. 157–58, 157n., 231. Czechoslovakia suffered the same treatment from the World Bank. See Steinhardt to SecState, March 1, 1948, *FRUS 1948*, 4:521–22; Steinhardt to SecState, March 5, 1948, p. 522; Clayton to Vandenberg, April 22, 1948, pp. 534–36; Penfield to SecState, Dec. 16, 1948, pp. 590–91.

89. Charles Bohlen to Representative William A. Dawson (Utah), March 11, 1948, Recovery Series, File "840.50 Recovery/2–1748—2–2048," NA.

90. On Marshall's views, see Marshall Memo, March 26, 1948, *FRUS 1948*, 4:527–28, 527n. For estimate of East-West European trade, see C. Tyler Wood to Paul H. Nitze, April 8, 1948, "ERP and Trade with the Soviet Sphere," Recovery Series, File "840.50 Recovery/4–748—4–848," NA. On importance of strategic materials and other imports from Soviet bloc, see Armstrong to Martin, Dec. 10, 1947, *FRUS 1948*, 4:509–11; Marshall Memo, March 26, 1948, pp. 527–28; Commerce Ad Hoc Subcommittee Report, May 4, 1948, pp. 536–42; Thorp to SecState, May 6, 1948, pp. 542–44; Smith to SecState, Aug. 25, 1948, pp. 563–64; Lovett to Embassy in Soviet Union, Nov. 10, 1948, pp. 580–81; Connelly Minutes of Cabinet Meetings, June 25, 1948, Connelly Papers, "Notes on Cabinet Meetings—WH File (Set I): January 9–December 31, 1948," HSTL. Lovett quotation from Memo to President on 12th Meeting of NSC, June 4, 1948, Papers of HST-PSF-NSC Meetings, File "Memo for President—Meeting Discussions (1948)," HSTL. Also see Memo to President on 13th Meeting of NSC, June 18, 1948.

91. The NAC, e.g., approved a small World Bank loan to Poland and Czechoslovakia in October 1948 in order to increase timber production since it seemed to serve the purposes of West European reconstruction. See Minutes of 109th NAC Meeting, Oct. 26, 1948, *FRUS 1948*, 4:575–78. For ERP countries' resistance to export controls, see Marshall to Douglas, Jan. 14, 1948, *FRUS 1948*, 3:1,066; Douglas to SecState, Aug. 16, 1948, *FRUS 1948*, 4:562; Lovett to Embassy in U.K., Oct. 22, 1948, pp. 574–75; Current Economic Developments #178, Nov. 22, 1948, pp. 585–88.

92. Wexler, *Marshall Plan*, p. 81.

93. Arkes, *Bureaucracy*, pp. 316–20.

94. Wexler, *Marshall Plan*, pp. 5, 19–20, 88–89, 93, 95, 250–52.

95. *Ibid.*, pp. 108–17, 252–53, quotations on pp. 114, 117.

96. *Ibid.*, pp. 121–22, 135, 155, 199–201, 252, quotation on p. 199.
97. *Ibid.*, p. 253.
98. *Ibid.*, pp. 249, 253–54; Paterson, *Confrontation*, pp. 232–34.

8. U.S. Economic Diplomacy in East Asia

1. U.S. exports to Japan during the 1930s averaged almost $200 million annually, compared with an annual average of $60 million in exports to China. U.S. imports from Japan ($170 million average annually) were also almost triple U.S. imports from China ($60 million) during the prewar decade. In 1935, U.S. investment in the Far East was $758 million, 6 percent of the American total. Again, the U.S. investment in Japan ($387 million) vastly exceeded that in China ($132 million). While U.S. exports to China grew substantially in the early postwar years to approximately $360 million annually, 1946–1948, these gains largely reflected U.S. aid shipments. By 1948, U.S. trade with Japan had overtaken that with China. The only accessible, strategic raw materials that China offered in significant quantities, a State Department official found in March 1948, were antimony, tin, and tungsten. See E. W. Pehrson to Karl L. Anderson, March 22, 1948, Recovery Series, File "840.50 Recovery/3–2148— 3–2248," NA. For U.S. trade statistics, see Department of Commerce, *HSUS*, pp. 903, 905–06. On U.S. investment, see A. Whitney Griswold, *The Far Eastern Policy of the United States*, pp. 468–69.

2. Michael Schaller, *The U.S. Crusade in China, 1938–1945*, pp. 17–18.

3. Akira Iriye, "Continuities in U.S.-Japanese Relations, 1941–49," in Yonosuke Nagai and Akira Iriye, eds., *The Origins of the Cold War in Asia*, pp. 400–04; Akira Iriye, *The Cold War in Asia: A Historical Introduction*, pp. 94–96.

4. The Soviets also gained control over northern Korea and China's formal cession of Outer Mongolia. The concessions that the Western allies made to the Soviet Union at Yalta, Iriye adds, demonstrate American and British confidence in Soviet good faith at the end of the war; power realities, rather than ideological considerations, dictated the nature of the peace in postwar Asia. On the agreements at Yalta, see Iriye, *Cold War*, pp. 93–97; on the background to Yalta, pp. 47–93.

5. Schaller, *Crusade*, p. 212. For the story of wartime U.S.-KMT relations and for evidence of KMT corruption and weaknesses, see Barbara W. Tuchman, *Stilwell and the American Experience in China, 1911–45*, pp. 301–531 passim.

6. At the end of the war, Chiang commanded three million troops (compared with 900,000 CCP troops), and his armed forces held a five-to-one advantage in light arms and a near monopoly in heavy arms, in addition to controlling the only air force in China other than the American one. Chiang also exercised at least nominal control over territory several times as large as that controlled by the Communists. See Tang Tsou, *America's Failure in China, 1941–1950*, pp. 401–02; Kolko, *Limits*, pp. 248, 552; William Whitney Stueck, Jr., *The Road to Confrontation: American Policy Toward China and Korea, 1947–1950*, pp. 11–12.

7. By the end of 1945, the United States had landed 113,000 of its troops in northern Chinese ports, ostensibly to accept the surrender of Japanese troops,

but also to block the entry of CCP armies into the region and to facilitate the KMT's occupation of northern China and Manchuria. (By late 1946, however, U.S. forces in China had declined to 12,000.) American planes and ships helped transport about one-half million KMT troops into northern China and Manchuria, even though the KMT had never fully controlled those areas before the war. In addition, the United States handed over substantial stocks of surplus ammunition, weapons, and military equipment to Chiang's armies at nominal cost. By the end of the war, Chiang had accumulated $1 billion in gold and dollars alone, again thanks to the generosity of the United States. See Kolko, *Limits*, pp. 248, 251; Stueck, *Road to Confrontation*, p. 14.

8. China received $518 million in UNRRA relief and $83 million in Eximbank aid during 1945–46. Chiang's cronies, however, siphoned off much of the aid for resale on the black market and stored most of the remainder in warehouses while the population suffered from famine. Chiang's family, friends, and subordinates had also embezzled much of the $500 million in special economic assistance that Congress had appropriated in 1942. Shortages were more the product of a distorted distribution system than of a shortfall of production, for most indexes rose substantially during and immediately after the war. See Kolko, *Limits*, pp. 269–73; Tang Tsou, *America's Failure*, pp. 48–49, 376–77, 380–82, 450–51, 461, 483–84; Paterson, *Confrontation*, p. 77.

9. On Marshall Mission, see Tang Tsou, *America's Failure*, pp. 401–40; Schaller, *Crusade*, pp. 300–02.

10. Warren I. Cohen, "The United States and China Since 1945," in Cohen, ed., *New Frontiers in American-East Asian Relations*, pp. 133–34.

11. Quotation from Marshall Memcon, Feb. 17, 1947, *FRUS 1947*, 7:1,071. Even advocates of aid to the Nationalist government within the Truman administration, such as John Carter Vincent, the director of the State Department's Office of Far Eastern Affairs, and John Leighton Stuart, the U.S. Ambassador to China, had difficulty convincing the Eximbank to extend a loan to the Chinese. Eximbank officials, doubting the ability of the Nationalists to repay and generally opposed to "political" loans, believed that either the Chinese should go to the World Bank or the State Department should ask for a special loan from Congress. For Marshall's views on economic aid to China, see Smyth (Marshall) to SecState, Feb. 25, 1946, *FRUS 1946*, 10:950; Marshall to Gillem (Chiang Kai-Shek), March 28, 1946, pp. 970–72; Stuart (Marshall) to SecState, July 31, 1946, pp. 996–97; Minutes of Meeting between Marshall and Butterworth, Nov. 18, 1946, pp. 1,020–21; Minutes of Meeting between Marshall and Wong, Nov. 18, 1946, pp. 1,022–23; Caughey (Marshall) to Carter, Nov. 30, 1946, p. 1,027. Also see Tang Tsou, *America's Failure*, p. 411. On advocates of aid, see Stuart (Butterworth) to SecState (with enclosures), Jan. 3, 1947, *FRUS 1947*, 7:1,033–41; Stuart to SecState, Feb. 12, 1947, pp. 1,059–60; Stuart to SecState, Feb. 12, 1947, pp. 1,061–63; Vincent to SecState, March 14, 1947, pp. 1,088–89; Stueck, *Road to Confrontation*, p. 41.

12. Among other things, the Americans demanded that the KMT lower tariffs, protect foreign property, allow foreign enterprise free access to Chinese markets, release foreign exchange for private use, stabilize its currency, and settle its debts with the United States. Similarly, the Eximbank blocked a

small cotton credit to the KMT in early 1946 because it would not guarantee that the loan would benefit private, as well as government-owned, mills. The U.S. government also registered numerous complaints against the KMT throughout 1946 on the behalf of American oil firms, which felt the Nationalist regime discriminated in favor of the government-owned oil company. On NAC and Chinese loan request, see *FRUS 1946*, 10:911–53; on the Chinese oil issue, pp. 1,374–94; for evidence of American pressure on the KMT to ease restrictions on U.S. business, specifically the registration of U.S. firms operating in China, pp. 1,296–1,308. On KMT and foreign business, see also Nancy Bernkopf Tucker, *Patterns in the Dust: Chinese-American Relations and the Recognition Controversy, 1949–1950*, pp. 115–16.

13. The CCP hailed the American victories in the Pacific as part of its united front policy against fascism and welcomed Soviet-American cooperation at the Teheran and Yalta conferences as signs that progressive forces in the United States would prevail after the war. From the American viewpoint, the efficiency and order behind the CCP lines in Yenan during the war contrasted sharply with the confusion and decadence in Chungking. The surplus aid agreement with the KMT was reached on August 30, 1946. Mao quotation cited in Tucker, *Patterns*, p. 45; also see pp. 40–47; and Steven M. Goldstein, "Chinese Communist Policy Toward the United States: Opportunities and Constraints, 1944–1950," in Dorothy Borg and Waldo Heinrichs, eds., *Uncertain Years: Chinese-American Relations, 1947–1950*, pp. 238–53; Tang Tsou, *America's Failure*, pp. 208–18.

14. In the late 1930s—well before the exigencies of Big Three diplomacy required friendly gestures toward Chiang—the Soviets had funneled large quantities of weaponry and matériel to the KMT armies for use against Japan while aid to the CCP was almost nil. Although Soviet armies after the war turned over large caches of captured Japanese arms to CCP troops and otherwise facilitated CCP control over North China and Manchuria, the denuded factories in the industrial heartland of Manchuria must have further disillusioned the CCP. Stalin and Mao Tse-Tung also disagreed on tactics in the postwar era. Stalin's efforts to restrain the militant and revolutionary elements of the world Communist movement, of which the CCP was among the most fervent, in order to reach an accommodation with the capitalist West, did not sit well with the CCP, whose experience with the West did not encourage trust and compromise. For this and related questions, see Steven I. Levine, "Notes on Soviet Policy in China and Chinese Communist Perceptions, 1945–1950," in Borg and Heinrichs, eds., *Uncertain Years*, pp. 293–303; Iriye, *Cold War*, pp. 90–93; Tucker, *Patterns*, pp. 27–29.

15. Interestingly, the Japan Crowd's view of Japan—as a Western, capitalist, democratic, and modern society that had only temporarily gone astray during the depression and the war—was shared by Japanese conservatives who wished to retain the main features of prewar Japanese society. On the stages of the U.S. debate concerning policy in postwar Japan, see Ray A. Moore, "Reflections on the Occupation of Japan," pp. 730–33; Eleanor M. Hadley, *Antitrust in Japan*, p. 9. For examples of the Japan Crowd's views, see Grew Memcon, May 28, 1945, *FRUS 1945*, 6:545–47; Grew to Stimson, June 28, 1945, with enclosed Policy Paper, June 22, 1945, pp. 566–80; Grew Memcon, with enclosed Memo, Aug. 4,

1945, pp. 584–87. On Japanese conservatives, see J. W. Dower, *Empire and Aftermath: Yoshida Shigeru and the Japanese Experience, 1878–1954*, pp. 300–01.

16. As Acheson publicly stated in September 1945, "The present economic and social system in Japan which makes for a will to war will be changed so that whatever it takes to carry this out will be used to carry it out." See *DSB* (Sept. 23, 1945), 13:427. Acheson was rebuking General MacArthur for prematurely predicting the early withdrawal of U.S. occupation troops from Japan.

17. Ray Moore defines the end of the second stage as the autumn of 1948, while I define it as the spring of 1948, with the decision to "reverse course." For the former view, see Moore, "Occupation of Japan," pp. 730–33.

18. Dower, *Empire and Aftermath*, p. 293; Kolko, *Limits*, pp. 307–08; Charles E. Neu, *The Troubled Encounter: The United States and Japan*, p. 207; Edwin O. Reischauer, *The United States and Japan*, pp. 207–09.

19. Neu, *Troubled Encounter*, p. 204.

20. Quotation from Neu, p. 204. On FEC, see Russell D. Buhite, *Soviet-American Relations in Asia, 1945–1954*, pp. 120–23.

21. When Secretary of the Navy James V. Forrestal visited MacArthur in Tokyo in July 1946 and asked for his views on the occupation, MacArthur couched his reply in religious terms. See account in Millis, *Forrestal Diaries*, pp. 77–78.

22. Neu, *Troubled Encounter*, pp. 205–10.

23. SCAP's democratization of Japan entailed a remarkably thorough reform of political and social institutions. In its rewriting of the Japanese Constitution and other decrees, SCAP established the principle of popular sovereignty, while the political status of the emperor was irreparably lowered with his renunciation of divinity. The peerage, except for the royal family, was abolished. SCAP eliminated both the armed forces and their role in political life; article nine of the Constitution expressly renounced the use of force in international relations. The Constitution also safeguarded basic human rights and civil liberties and established a Western-style parliament (Diet) as the sole law-making authority of the state. The suffrage was broadened, trade unions and other interest groups (including left-wing parties like the Communists) gained the right to organize, and local government was strengthened. SCAP's land reform program, probably the most successful of the American reforms, dramatically reduced land tenancy. The Americans also instigated a thorough purge of alleged "war criminals," as well as of hundreds of thousands of other individuals whose connection with the old Japan disqualified them from holding jobs (including teaching) in the new Japan. See Neu, pp. 207–08; J. A. A. Stockwin, *Japan: Divided Politics in a Growth Economy*, pp. 39–46.

24. Quotation from Kozo Yamamura, "Zaibatsu, Prewar and Zaibatsu, Postwar," p. 539; also see p. 540. On the history and nature of the *zaibatsu*, see Hadley, *Antitrust*, pp. 20–60.

25. Hadley, *Antitrust*, p. 4; on "Big Four," pp. 118–19.

26. Dower, *Empire and Aftermath*, pp. 277–93.

27. Hadley, *Antitrust*, p. 11.

28. *Ibid.*, pp. 13–19, 64.

29. Dower, *Empire and Aftermath*, pp. 297–301.

30. Quotation from Barnett to Dickover and Martin, Jan. 25, 1946, Pauley Papers, File "Administrative Cables: Japan—Outgoing Nov. 1945–Jan. 1946," NA. Also see Dower, *Empire and Aftermath*, pp. 297–98, 301. SCAP, apprehensive that Japan might follow the Russian example of 1917, sought to initiate a bourgeois phase in Japanese society in order to prevent a leap from the "feudalism" of prewar Japan to socialism or Communism. Interestingly, the Japanese Left welcomed SCAP's intervention as a necessary step on the road to socialism (Dower p. 301).

31. Dower, *Empire and Aftermath*, pp. 302, 307; Reischauer, *U.S. and Japan*, pp. 209–11.

32. Kolko, *Limits*, pp. 518–21.

33. While SCAP delegated implementation of domestic economic controls to the Japanese government, it retained exclusive control over Japanese trade because that was consistent with its mission to deter Japanese aggression (in the world marketplace as well as in the military arena), and because SCAP was responsible for the distribution of American aid, which comprised a large portion of Japanese imports (58 percent from 1945 to 1950). Quotation from Leon Hollerman, "International Economic Controls in Occupied Japan," p. 708; also see pp. 709–18.

34. While SCAP's far-reaching land reform radically restructured rural ownership to the benefit of Japanese peasants, it ironically fostered inefficient small-scale agriculture, the source of later protectionism and an enduring political alliance between farmers and the Yoshida conservatives, under whose auspices the reforms took place. On land reform, see Stockwin, *Japan*, pp. 45–46; Dower, *Empire and Aftermath*, pp. 329–32; on deconcentration, see Dower, pp. 341–46.

35. For quotation, see American Mission on Reparations in Japan (Owen Lattimore et al.) to Pauley, Dec. 26, 1946, Pauley Papers, File "Draft of Comprehensive Report on Reparations-Japan-Volumes I & II," NA. Also see Pauley Statement, "U.S. Reparations Policy for Japan," Oct. 31, 1945, *FRUS 1945*, 6:997–98; Pauley to Truman (and MacArthur), Dec. 6, 1945, pp. 1,004–07; Pauley Press Statement, Dec. 7, 1945, pp. 1,007–09. For a discussion of the Pauley Mission and its recommendations on Japan, see Bruce M. Brenn, "U.S. Reparations Policy for Japan: September 1945 to May 1949," in Richard K. Beardsley, ed., *Studies in Japanese History and Politics*, pp. 75–78.

36. Quotation from Owen Lattimore to H. D. Maxwell, Nov. 12, 1945; also see A. G. Coons to H. D. Maxwell, Dec. 3, 1945, Pauley Papers, File "Reparations—General," NA; Lattimore to Maxwell, Nov. 10, 1945, Pauley Papers, File "7. Finance b. Zaibatsu," NA; Lattimore and Bennett to Pauley and Maxwell, "War Potential," Nov. 15, 1945, Pauley Papers, File "16. Memoranda m. Lattimore," NA. Even within the Pauley Mission, there was vigorous debate over the minimum Japanese standard of living. See "Notes on Staff Meeting," Dec. 4, 1945, Pauley Papers, File "20. Administrative h. Staff Meetings," NA.

37. For critics, see, e.g., Joseph Z. Reday, "Reparations from Japan," p. 145; Reischauer, *U.S. and Japan*, pp. 248–50.

38. For a discussion of the problems posed by reparations and commercial controls, see Coons to Maxwell, Dec. 17, 1945, Pauley Papers, File "Foreign

Trade—General," NA. For a discussion of the conflict among the various parties (especially the FEC) involved in formulating Japanese reparations policy, see Brenn, "Reparations Policy," pp. 79–81.

39. John P. Hurndall to Pauley, "Interim Reparations, Implementing of," Jan. 24, 1946, Pauley Papers, File "16. Memoranda H. Hurndall," NA.

40. In tentatively adopting a version of Pauley's interim reparations program in April 1946, SWNCC defined the first-charge principle on American occupation costs in such a way as to delay reparations deliveries indefinitely. Meanwhile, SCAP refused to make a commitment to a specific Japanese level of industry. For SWNCC report, see SWNCC 236/10, April 30, 1946, *FRUS 1946*, 8:493–504; on delays in implementation, see Pauley to Clayton, April 30, 1946, pp. 506–07; Hilldring to Moseley, April 30, 1946, p. 507. SCAP appeared to favor retention of the *zaibatsu* in their current state under American or international control, rather than assume responsibility itself for dismantling and shipping plant and equipment to other Asian countries. See Lattimore to Maxwell, "Treatment of Zaibatsu in relation to Reparations Policy," Nov. 10, 1945, Pauley Papers, File "7. Finance b. Zaibatsu," NA. In June 1946, the State Department arrived at new interim reparations schedules and, implicitly, production ceilings, but SCAP again ignored the directive. For State Department directive, see JCS to MacArthur, June 15, 1946, *FRUS 1946*, 8:538–39; Reday, "Reparations from Japan," pp. 538–39. On SCAP, see Pauley to SecState, Dec. 28, 1946, *FRUS 1946*, 8:601–04; Martin to Hilldring, March 4, 1947, *FRUS 1947*, 6:370–71.

41. In May 1947, the FEC grudgingly acknowledged the American *fait accompli*. On State Department compromise, see SWNCC Memo, April 7, 1947, *FRUS 1947*, 6:382–83; State Department Memo to McCoy, May 13, 1947, pp. 393–94. On developments leading to the new reparations formula, see JCS to MacArthur, Feb. 12, 1947, pp. 354–55; Hilldring to McCoy, Feb. 19, 1947, pp. 357–59; Hilldring to SWNCC, March 4, 1947, pp. 367–69; JCS to MacArthur, April 4, 1947, pp. 376–80; Marshall to Acheson, May 16, 1947, p. 399; Brenn, "Reparations Policy," pp. 82–83.

42. Petersen Memo of June 19, 1947, quoted in Hilldring to Petersen, July 15, 1947, *FRUS 1947*, 6:413. Hilldring (State Department) was specifically reprimanding Petersen (War Department) for misinterpreting the mandate of the Strike Commission, which had an advisory status only. For Strike's views, see Clifford S. Strike, "Revenge is Expensive," *American Magazine* (Sept. 1947), 144:50–51, 84–85. For a rebuttal to Strike by a member of the Pauley team, see Martin Toscan Bennett, "Japanese Reparations: Fact or Fantasy?," pp. 185-94. Later groups investigating the problem—Overseas Consultants, Inc., which Strike again headed, and the Johnston Mission, both reporting in the spring of 1948—basically agreed with the Strike Commission's conclusions. On the Strike, OCI, and Johnston missions, see Reday, "Reparations from Japan," pp. 148–49. For the different reparations figures recommended by these groups, see Hadley, *Antitrust*, p. 146. The War and State Departments continued to feud over this problem. See Hilldring to Petersen, July 17, 1947, *FRUS 1947*, 6:413–14; Petersen to Hilldring, July 22, 1947, pp. 414–18; Draper to Lovett, Nov. 20, 1947, pp. 441–42; Lovett to Draper, Jan. 13, 1948, *FRUS 1948*,

6:945–46; Saltzman to Draper, Jan. 22, 1948, pp. 946–47; and Brenn, "Reparations Policy," pp. 83–84, 88–95.

43. The Philippine government in particular charged the Americans with bad faith in their reparations policy. The reparations problem proved to be one of the main obstacles in the way of a peace treaty with Japan. Finally, Japan concluded bilateral reparations settlements with several of the claimant nations following the conclusion of the Japanese peace treaty in September 1951. See Memo to President on 22nd Meeting of NSC, Oct. 1, 1948, Papers of HST-PSF-Subject File: NSC Meetings, File "Memo for President—Meeting Discussions (1948)," HSTL; Memo to President on 38th Meeting of NSC, April 21, 1949, File "Memos for President—Meeting Discussions (1949)," HSTL; Reday, "Reparations from Japan," pp. 145, 147–48; Shuzo Inaba, "Reparations and Japan's Economy," pp. 110–13.

44. On the deadlock of the FEC in 1946, see Reday, "Reparations from Japan," p. 147. On the Soviet seizure of Manchurian assets, see Press Release, Dec. 13, 1946, Pauley Papers, File "Press Release-Department of State (Dec. 13, 1946)," NA; Pauley to Acheson, June 22, 1946, *FRUS 1946*, 8:541–42; SWNCC Memo, July 12, 1946, pp. 546–55.

45. For the historiography of the reverse course, see Carol Gluck, "Entangling Illusions—Japanese and American Views of the Occupation," in Cohen, ed., *Frontiers*, pp. 199–207.

46. Takeshi Igarishi, "The Ordeal of the Containment Policy—George Kennan and the Redirection of American Occupation Policy for Japan," pp. 3–4.

47. The Japan Lobby gained further influence and visibility in June 1948 with the formation of the American Council on Japan, a private group of American businessmen and consultants (including Kern) that served as a lobby in the United States for Japanese industry over the next several years. Altogether, 220,000 Japanese were purged. About 180,000 were former military officers, 1,500 business executives, and the rest largely teachers or employees in the mass media industry. See Hadley, *Antitrust*, pp. 92–99, 125, 135–36; Howard Schonberger, "The Japan Lobby in American Diplomacy, 1947–1952," pp. 328–34; "Reversal on Japan," *The Economist* (April 24, 1948), 154:670; Mark Gayn, "Japan: Full Speed Astern," *New Republic* (August 9, 1948), 119:118; Richard J. Barnet, *The Alliance: America, Europe, Japan—Makers of the Postwar World* (New York: Simon & Schuster, 1983), p. 86.

48. Quotations from Kennan Memo, PPS/10, Oct. 14, 1947, *FRUS 1947*, 6:537, 538; also see pp. 541–42; and Igarishi, "Containment Policy," pp. 5–7.

49. On Deconcentration Law, see Schonberger, "Japan Lobby," pp. 334–35; and Hadley, *Antitrust*, pp. 136–37. On SCAP's economic goals, see Igarishi, "Containment Policy," p. 8.

50. Igarishi, "Containment Policy," p. 8. Critics of SCAP's policies greatly exaggerated the magnitude of occupation costs. The Japanese government paid for the costs of maintaining U.S. forces in Japan; during the early postwar years, these costs amounted to about one-third of the Japanese national budget. American occupation expenditures paid for U.S. civilian personnel and for the imports of goods and services necessary to prevent disease and unrest in Japan. While these costs grew from $194 million during the first sixteen months of the occu-

pation (September 1945 to December 1946) to $404 million in 1947, the sums were quite small compared with concurrent U.S. aid to Germany, let alone the cost of the Marshall Plan or of the war in the Pacific. See Hadley, *Antitrust*, pp. 133–34.

51. First quotation from PPS 13, Nov. 6, 1947, *FRUS 1947*, 1:775; other quotations from PPS 23, Feb. 24, 1948, *FRUS 1948*, 1(1):525. Also see Kennan, *Memoirs*, pp. 374–76; Igarishi, "Containment Policy," pp. 8–9.

52. Meanwhile, Kennan was encouraging the Navy Department to press for military basing rights in the Ryukus and the Japanese main islands. "Anarchy" quotation from Millis, *Forrestal Diaries*, p. 328; "rearming" quotation from Igarishi, "Containment Policy," p. 9; "communization" quotation from Kennan, *Memoirs*, p. 388. SCAP's purge of the Japanese leadership, disruption of the Japanese economy, reparations and other policies led Kennan to suspect Communist infiltration of SCAP's ranks. See *Memoirs*, pp. 388–91; Annex 2 to Kennan Report, Explanatory Notes, PPS 28, March 25, 1948, *FRUS 1948*, 6:712–13.

53. Quotation from Kennan, *Memoirs*, p. 382. Also see Annex to Kennan Report, PPS 28, March 25, 1948, *FRUS 1948*, 6:700–02, 705–06. Kennan suggested that since the FEC was charged with the sole task of outlining the terms of the Japanese surrender, and since SCAP had fulfilled those terms, MacArthur should simply ignore it. "The General," Kennan reported in late March, "seemed much impressed with this suggestion and said that he believed that I had found the answer. . . .it was exactly the right line for us to take." See Annex to Kennan Report, PPS 28, March 25, 1948, *FRUS 1948*, 6:704. In his memoirs, Kennan states that MacArthur "slapped his thigh in approval" of this suggestion (*Memoirs*, p. 386). The American occupying forces, Kennan explained, would nonetheless remain until a peace treaty was concluded. Scuttling the FEC, the only real instrument of Allied control in Japan, would then force the Soviets to join in negotiating a peace treaty with Japan, Kennan reasoned. "We would then have them over a barrel; for they would either have to agree to the type of treaty we liked or consent to see us remain indefinitely in Japan with our military forces." See Annex to Kennan Report, PPS 28, March 25, 1948, *FRUS 1948*, 6:704. MacArthur's quotation of March 1, 1948, from Annex 1 to Kennan Report, PPS 28, March 25, 1948, *FRUS 1948*, 6:697.

54. Quotation from Kennan Report, PPS 28, March 25, 1948, *FRUS 1948*, 6:694; for recommendations, see pp. 691–96. For NSC 13/2, see Souers to Truman, Oct. 7, 1948, pp. 857–62; Takeshi Igarishi, "George Kennan and the Redirection of American Occupation Policy for Japan: The Formulation of National Security Council Paper 13/2."

55. SCAP had selected 325 firms for possible reorganization in February 1948, but subsequently scaled down this figure to 131 in May 1948, 100 in July 1948, and 19 in August 1949. (Yet by the end of 1949, 28 out of 82 top holding companies had been dissolved.) SCAP also ended dismantling and reparations deliveries and took some minor steps to increase Japanese foreign trade. See Hadley, *Antitrust*, pp. 166–80; Hadley, "Japan: Competition or Private Collectivism?" pp. 293–94.

56. Quotation from Igarishi, "Containment Policy," p. 25; also see pp. 14–24.

As a result of SCAP's failure to implement monetary and fiscal reform, President Truman was finally forced to order Detroit banker Joseph Dodge to take command over the Japanese economy in 1949. While the exact policies pursued by Dodge need not concern us here, the Dodge Plan, much as MacArthur and his advisors had foreseen, fomented severe deflation, unemployment, and labor strife, with questionable benefits for Japan's long-term economic health. See Kolko, *Limits*, pp. 521–24; William S. Borden, "The Pacific Alliance: The United States and Japanese Trade Recovery, 1947–1954," pp. 112–16, 121–26.

57. Michael Schaller, "Securing the Great Crescent: Occupied Japan and the Origins of Containment in Southeast Asia," pp. 393, 395, 400, 410.

58. Dower, *Empire and Aftermath*, pp. 369–70. On the evolution of the U.S. defense perimeter, see John Lewis Gaddis, "The Strategic Perspective: The Rise and Fall of the 'Defensive Perimeter' Concept, 1947–1951," in Borg and Heinrichs, eds., *Uncertain Years*, pp. 61–118.

59. In this sense, Japan presents something of an anomaly in U.S. policy. In Western Europe, the American commitment to multilateralism—"economic security"—antedated the outbreak of the Cold War. But in Japan, the decision to support reconstruction *followed* the application of containment to Asia. On controls, see Hollerman, "International Controls," p. 719.

60. On Eximbank issue, see Stuart to SecState, May 8, 1947, *FRUS 1947*, 7:1,116–17; Vincent to SecState, May 16, 1947, p. 1,121; Ness Memcon, June 11, 1947, pp. 1,132–34; Ness Memcon, June 17, 1947, pp. 1,136–40; Tang Tsou, *America's Failure*, pp. 452–53.

61. China received $27.7 million in post-UNRRA relief and an authorization of $18 million for Interim Aid. Members of the China bloc included Representatives Joseph W. Martin (R-Mass.), Walter Judd (R-Minn.), and John Vorys (R-Ohio), and Senators Styles Bridges (R-N.H.) and Arthur H. Vandenberg (R-Mich.). On Republican criticism of the Truman administration's China policy, see Tang Tsou, *America's Failure*, pp. 447-51. Most historians now give less credence to the coherence and power of the China Lobby before 1950, but they do not entirely discount its influence on Truman. See Cohen, "U.S. and China," in Cohen, ed., *Frontiers*, pp. 136–37, 140; Tucker, *Patterns*, pp. 80–99, 166–67, 185. On China and Interim Aid, see Tucker, pp. 464–74; Stueck, *Road to Confrontation*, p. 53. On post-UNRRA aid, see *FRUS 1947*, 7:1,293–1,358; Tang Tsou, *America's Failure*, p. 463.

62. At the same time, the aid act relieved the administration of responsibility for distributing military matériel or for advising KMT troops, so that the Americans could avoid close involvement in the civil war. On China Aid Act of 1948, see *FRUS 1948*, 8:442–505; Stueck, *Road to Confrontation*, pp. 58–59; Tang Tsou, *America's Failure*, p. 475.

63. Stuart to SecState, *FRUS 1948*, 8:515–17; Tang Tsou, *America's Failure*, pp. 477–78.

64. Quotation from Stueck, *Road to Confrontation*, p. 55, also see pp. 54–56.

65. The White House rejected suggestions by the Joint Chiefs of Staff and General Albert C. Wedemeyer for the use of American officers in advising Nationalist troops. The military record of the KMT did not improve during the remainder of 1948. In the last major battles in North China and Manchuria

during the fall of 1948, U.S. observers almost unanimously agreed that KMT defeats were due to inept generalship by Chiang and his Whampoa clique and to the collapse of Nationalist morale, rather than to a shortage of matériel. See Stueck, pp. 56–57; Tang Tsou, *America's Failure*, pp. 482–84.

66. Tang Tsou, *America's Failure*, p. 443; Stueck, *Road to Confrontation*, p. 63.

67. See Clubb to SecState, Nov. 24, 1948, *FRUS 1948*, 8:652–53; Clubb to SecState, Nov. 26, 1948, p. 653; Lapham to Hoffman, Nov. 26, 1948, pp. 654–58; Cleveland to Lapham, Dec. 2, 1948, pp. 658–62; Stuart to SecState, Dec. 4, 1948, pp. 662–63; Cabot (Lapham) to ECA (Davis and Ivy), Dec. 14, 1948, pp. 663–65; Butterworth to Lovett, Dec. 18, 1948, pp. 665–66; Butterworth to Lovett, Dec. 28, 1948, pp. 666–67; Butterworth to Lovett, Dec. 30, 1948, pp. 667–68.

68. Quotation from Cleveland to Lapham, Jan. 7, 1949, *FRUS 1949*, 9:612. In a Cabinet meeting a week later, Lovett and Hoffman debated the issue once again. Despite Hoffman's best efforts, Lovett persuaded the President and the Cabinet to cut off aid to areas controlled by the Chinese Communists or any coalition government that included the Communists. The ECA would, however, distribute supplies already ashore in Communist-controlled areas. As an ECA official later observed, the Truman administration had reduced U.S.-CCP ties to whatever meager contacts American missionaries and businessmen could maintain. For Cabinet debate between Lovett and Hoffman, see Butterworth to Lovett, Jan. 10, 1949, p. 613; Butterworth Memo for the Record, Jan. 14, 1949, pp. 614–15. For observation by ECA official, see Lapham to Hoffman, March 9, 1949, p. 627. For Hoffman's views, see Memo to President on 33rd Meeting of NSC, Feb. 4, 1949, Papers of HST-PSF-Subject File: NSC Meetings, File "Memos for President—Meeting Discussions (1949)," HSTL.

69. Stueck, *Road to Confrontation*, pp. 118–19; Warren I. Cohen, "Acheson, His Advisers, and China, 1949–1950," in Borg and Heinrichs, eds., *Uncertain Years*, pp. 24–39.

70. The JCS agreed with Acheson that China was not crucial to U.S. security interests and that the United States should avoid a land war in Asia at all costs, but were less sanguine about the possibility of a Sino-Soviet rift. General MacArthur, in contrast, wished to extend aid to the KMT without any strings attached and to oppose Communism everywhere short of committing U.S. troops to the mainland. See Gaddis, "Strategic Perspective," pp. 92–93. Due to Truman's disinterest in Chinese affairs, Acheson assumed primary responsibility for U.S. policy toward that country. See Tucker, *Patterns*, pp. 173–83, 191–93.

71. Acheson also headed off Congressional pressures for a major aid program to rescue the Nationalists, of which the proposal by Senator Patrick McCarran (R-Nevada) for $1.5 billion in aid to the KMT was the most notorious. On China Aid Act extension, see *FRUS 1948*, 8:668–85; Memo by Office of Far Eastern Affairs, Jan. 14, 1949, *FRUS 1949*, 9:599–601; Butterworth Memo, n.d., pp. 601–06; ECA Memo, n.d. [April 1949], pp. 606–07; Butterworth to SecState, March 15, 1949, p. 607; Editorial Note, p. 610. On McCarran proposal, see Acheson to Connally, March 15, 1949, pp. 607–09, 607n. On KMT requests for major assistance, see pp. 671–99, 729–816.

72. On June 1, Edmund Clubb, the American Consul in Peking, informed Washington that Chou En-lai, then a key member of the Central Committee and Politburo of the Chinese Communist Party, had expressed through an intermediary a desire to pursue the establishment of economic relations with the United States. The Chinese contact reportedly portrayed Chou as the leader of a moderate, nationalist, and pro-Western faction within the CCP leadership that sought U.S. aid and trade. Clubb favored following up on Chou's overture, but Ambassador Stuart demanded concrete action by the CCP to demonstrate its independence from Moscow. "They betray not slightest trace of contumacy against Soviet leadership, but rather sympathetic unquestioning acceptance of it," Stuart cabled home. President Truman directed the State Department "not to indicate any softening toward the Communists but to insist on judging their intentions by their actions." Mao's virulent attacks upon the United States and his warm praise of Stalin in speeches during June 1949 probably killed whatever chance remained of further American contact with Chou. As Clubb suggested, however, Mao may have felt forced to take so assertive a stand in order to put to rest Soviet suspicions of Chinese Titoism. Stuart quotation from Stuart to Sec-State, June 6, 1949, *FRUS 1949*, 8:369. For Stuart's views, see, e.g., Stuart to SecState, June 7, 1949, pp. 372–73; Stuart to SecState, June 9, 1949, pp. 377–78; Stuart to SecState, June 15, 1949, p. 385; Stuart to SecState, June 22, 1949, pp. 395–96; Stuart to SecState, July 6, 1949, pp. 405–07. For Clubb's views, see e.g., Clubb to SecState, June 1, 1949, pp. 375–60; Clubb to SecState, June 2, 1949, pp. 363–64; Clubb to SecState, June 11, 1949, pp. 379–81; Clubb to SecState, June 20, 1949, pp. 392–94; Clubb to SecState, June 27, 1949, pp. 398–99; Clubb to SecState, June 30, 1949, pp. 401–03. For Washington's abortive message to Chou, see Webb to Clubb, June 14, 1949, pp. 384–85. Truman quotation from Webb Memcon, June 16, 1949, p. 389. For Clubb's interpretation of Mao's speeches, see Clubb to SecState, June 22, 1949, pp. 394–95. Scholars have vigorously debated the authenticity and sincerity of Chou's démarche (and a similar overture to Stuart in late June 1949), the CCP's relationship with the Soviet Union, and the possibility of closer U.S.-CCP ties before the Korean War. Compare Michael H. Hunt, "Mao Tse-Tung and the Issue of Accommodation with the United States, 1948–1950," in Borg and Heinrichs, eds., *Uncertain Years*, pp. 185–233, with Steven M. Goldstein, "Chinese Communist Policy Toward the United States: Opportunities and Constraints, 1944–1950," in Borg and Heinrichs, pp. 235–78, and Tucker, *Patterns*, pp. 174–75.

73. Souers Memo, with attached NSC 41, Feb. 28, 1949, *FRUS 1949*, 9:826–34. Truman approved NSC 41 on March 3, 1949. See Souers to NSC, March 3, 1949, p. 834.

74. When the State and Commerce Departments, at the behest of the Pentagon, sought in June 1949 to bring export controls against the CCP in conformity with the "R" procedure in effect in Europe, the British continued to drag their feet, arguing that the Western countries should concentrate on a few key import commodities, such as oil. On British investment in China and "foot in door" quotation, see British Embassy to Department of State, April 5, 1949, *FRUS 1949*, 9:839. On the British position, see, e.g., pp. 837–41; Sprouse

Memcon, Feb. 10, 1949, pp. 823–26; Douglas (Martin and McIntyre) to SecState (State and Commerce), June 24, 1949, pp. 861–63; Magill Memcon, Sept. 9, 1949, pp. 871–75. On U.S. efforts to strengthen controls, see Acheson (Commerce and State) to Douglas (Martin and McIntyre), June 22, 1949, pp. 859–60. On Acheson-Bevin talks, see pp. 880–84, and Tucker, *Patterns*, pp. 20–28. In reviewing NSC 41 in November 1949, the State Department (in NSC 41/1) confirmed that the CCP, due to severe economic problems partly caused by Western sanctions, was susceptible to economic pressure. Despite the disappointing response of its allies, therefore, the United States should unilaterally implement the strict R procedure of controls, even if this ended up penalizing American exporters and curtailing Japanese recovery. See Lay to NSC (NSC 41/1), Nov. 7, 1949, *FRUS 1949*, 9:889–96.

75. The State Department sought to minimize oil sales to the CCP in order to keep the CCP dependent upon U.S. supplies while avoiding the need for an embargo. See Acheson to Cabot, Feb. 11, 1949, *FRUS 1949*, 9:1,002; Acheson to Cabot, April 1, 1949, pp. 1,002–03; McBride Memcon, April 4, 1949, pp. 1,004–06; Cabot to SecState, April 18, 1949, pp. 1,107–08; Cabot to SecState, April 28, 1949, p. 1,009; Acheson to Cabot, April 30, 1949, p. 1,012; Freeman to Allison, June 24, 1949, pp. 1,015–16; Acheson to Douglas, June 24, 1949, pp. 1,016–17; Douglas to Acheson, June 27, 1949, pp. 1,017–18. On CCP attitude toward oil companies, see Stuart to SecState, May 11, 1949, pp. 1,012–13; Cabot to SecState, July 13, 1949, pp. 1,019–20. Truman and the Commerce and Defense Departments wished to adopt even stricter controls toward the CCP than did the State Department. See Merchant to SecState, Aug. 19, 1949, pp. 1,022–24; McWilliams to Rusk, Aug. 22, 1949, p. 1,024. On State Department contacts with oil companies, see Butterworth to SecState, Sept. 7, 1949, p. 1,027; Magill Memcon, Oct. 14, 1949, pp. 1,028–29; McConaughy to SecState, Nov. 14, 1949, pp. 1,030–31; Brown Memcon, Nov. 22, 1949, pp. 1,031–33; Brown Memcon, March 9, 1950, *FRUS 1950*, 6:622–25. On conflict between Commerce and State, see Eakens Memcon, Dec. 7, 1949, *FRUS 1949*, 9:1,034–35. On U.S. business with China, see Tucker, *Patterns*, pp. 112–33.

76. On linkage between Sino-Japanese trade and Sino-American consular issues, see, e.g., West to MacArthur, May 7, 1949, *FRUS 1949*, 9:977–79; Acheson to Clubb, May 8, 1949, p. 980; Clubb to SecState, July 9, 1949, pp. 991–92; Acheson to Clubb, Sept. 19, 1949, pp. 995–96. Sino-Japanese trade from May to November 1949 totalled only about $15 million, most of which consisted of barter trade. See Sebald to SecState, Dec. 9, 1949, pp. 1,000–01.

77. See Souers to NSC, with attached NSC 48/2, Dec. 30, 1949, *FRUS 1949*, 7(2):1,215–20; Department of Army to MacArthur, Jan. 13, 1950, *FRUS 1950*, 6:619–20; Acheson to Sawyer, Feb. 3, 1950, pp. 621–22. For history of U.S. trade policy toward CCP, see Bishop to Jessup, June 6, 1950, pp. 636–38.

78. The JCS adopted an ambiguous position on Taiwan. While they favored further measures after December 1949 to defend the island against a Communist takeover, they did not advocate direct U.S. military intervention to save it at this point. In a January 1950 meeting with Senators William F. Knowland (R-Calif.) and Alexander H. Smith (R-N.J.), Acheson stated that the President and the Joint Chiefs of Staff had decided that the retention of Taiwan was "not of *vital*

importance to our security." See Acheson Memcon, Jan. 5, 1950, *FRUS 1950*, 6:260; also pp. 258–63; Rusk Memcon, Jan. 2, 1950, pp. 256–57; Strong to SecState, Jan. 2, 1950, pp. 257–58; J. K. Fall Memcon on "Formosa Problem," Jan. 4, 1950, Acheson Papers, File "Memos of Conversation Jan. 1950," HSTL; Stueck, *Road to Confrontation*, pp. 137, 140–41; Tucker, *Patterns*, pp. 184–87, 193–94; Gaddis, "Strategic Perspective," pp. 92–93.

79. For Truman statement, see *Public Papers, Truman, 1950*, p. 11. Also see Stueck, *Road to Confrontation*, p. 142; Cohen, "Acheson and China," in Borg and Heinrichs, eds., *Uncertain Years*, p. 51. John Paton Davies of the Policy Planning Staff expressed the prevailing attitude of the administration toward China in a February 1950 memo. Davies believed that meaningful negotiations with the CCP leadership were impossible in the short term, but once the Chinese suffered economic hardship and experienced Soviet tutelage firsthand, a nationalist faction within the CCP might revolt against the Stalinist faction and come to terms with the West. See Davies Memo, Feb. 2, 1950, *FRUS 1950*, 6:305–06.

80. Accompanying the treaty were two agreements: Soviet relinquishment of rights (won at Yalta) to Chinese ports and railroads, and a five-year, $300 million aid package. See Levine, "Soviet Policy on China," pp. 300–01; Tucker, *Patterns*, pp. 31–32, 54–55. For Acheson's views on Sino-Soviet split, see, e.g., Memo to President on 50th Meeting of NSC, Dec. 30, 1949, Papers of HST-PSF-Subject File: NSC Meetings, File "Memos for President—Meeting Discussions (1949)," HSTL.

81. For interdepartmental debate on military sales to the KMT, see Acheson to Johnson, March 7, 1950, *FRUS 1950*, 6:316–17; Acheson to Johnson, April 14, 1950, pp. 325–26; Rusk to Acheson, April 26, 1950, pp. 333–35; Johnson to Acheson, May 6, 1950, p. 339; Dulles Memcon, May 25, 1950, pp. 343–44; Burns to Rusk, May 29, 1950, pp. 346–47; Acheson to Johnson, June 1, 1950, pp. 351–52. On Rusk's views, see Howe to Armstrong, May 31, 1950, pp. 347–51. Also see Stueck, *Road to Confrontation*, pp. 142–43, 146, 149–51.

82. Quotations from Dean Acheson, "Crisis in Asia—An Examination of U.S. Policy," speech delivered before National Press Club, in *DSB* (Jan. 23, 1950), 22:112, 115, 116–17.

9. Natural Resources and National Security

1. Eckes, *Minerals*, pp. 5–8, 50.

2. *Ibid.*, pp. 31–55.

3. *Ibid.*, pp. 51–52, 119.

4. *Ibid.*, p. 121.

5. On minerals, see *ibid.*, p. 122; on exponents of "have-not" thesis, pp. 122–25. On U.S. supplies of Allied oil, see Gerald Nash, *United States Oil Policy, 1870–1964: Business and Government in Twentieth Century America*, pp. 157–58. Quotation from George H. Thornley, President of World Trade Foundation of America, to William L. Clayton, Jan. 25, 1946, with attached WTFA article, "Selected Industries and Products Dependent upon Imported Materials," Jan.

24, 1946, Clayton-Thorp Papers, File "W," HSTL. The Krug commission, which Truman appointed to study the impact of the Marshall Plan on U.S. resources, also highlighted the growing U.S. dependence on imported raw materials.

6. Eckes, *Minerals*, pp. 125–27. Cf. Harry Magdoff, *The Age of Imperialism: The Economics of U.S. Foreign Policy*, pp. 45–54, and Richard J. Barnet and Ronald E. Muller, *Global Reach: The Power of the Multinational Corporations* (New York: Simon & Schuster, 1974), pp. 126–28.

7. A Pentagon report at the end of 1948 showed that total authorized funds through FY'49 equalled $1.45 billion, far short of the $3.69 billion necessary to achieve minimum stockpile objectives. See Office of Secretary of Defense, "Status of Stockpiling Program," Dec. 20, 1948, Papers of HST-PSF-Subject File, File "Agencies-Military-President's program-Army, Navy, and Air appropriations," HSTL. Also see Eckes, *Minerals*, pp. 129–45; quotation on p. 149.

8. See Memo to President on 12th Meeting of NSC, June 4, 1948, Papers of HST-PSF-Subject File: NSC Meetings, File "Memo for President—Meeting Discussions (1948)," HSTL; Eckes, *Minerals*, pp. 153–57.

9. CIA, "Soviet Objectives in Latin America," ORE 16/1, Nov. 1, 1947, Papers of HST-PSF-Intelligence File, File "Central Intelligence Repts. O.R.E. 1947 No. 15–39," HSTL. Also see Eckes, *Minerals*, pp. 147–57.

10. On Venezuela, see Carrigan to SecState, April 15, 1948, *FRUS 1948*, 9:759–60; Forrestal to SecState, April 24, 1948, pp. 760–61; Carrigan to SecState, April 30, 1948, p. 761; Donnelly to SecState, Sept. 14, 1948, p. 766; Lovett to Embassy in Venezuela, Oct. 29, 1948, pp. 769–70; NSC 29, "Security of Strategically Important Industrial Operations in Foreign Countries," Sept. 3, 1948, Papers of HST-PSF–Subject File: National Security Council Meetings, File "N.S.C. Meeting No. 19, 9–2–48," HSTL. Also see Eckes, *Minerals*, p. 151.

11. A State Department representative replied in December 1947 that Washington was requiring greater European production of strategic materials (especially in colonies and dependencies) to satisfy European and U.S. industrial needs and to augment the U.S. stockpile. See Knowland to Marshall, Sept. 26, 1947, Recovery Series, File "840.50 Recovery/9–2047—9–3047," NA; and C. Tyler Wood to Knowland, Dec. 15, 1947. Senator Henry Cabot Lodge (R-Mass.) insisted upon the same *quid pro quo*; see Senator A. H. Vandenberg to Marshall, Oct. 20, 1947, with attached (Lodge) "Memorandum on European Aid," n.d., Recovery Series, File "840.50 Recovery/10–1747—10–2047," NA. See also Robert A. Lovett to Julius Krug, June 2, 1948, Recovery Series, File "840.50 Recovery/1–148—1–948," NA. The Marshall Plan legislation did not provide for the ironclad guarantees of U.S. access to raw material sources after ERP ended that some American officials, such as oil expert Walter J. Levy, desired. See Walter J. Levy to Paul Nitze and C. H. Bonesteel, "Comments on U.S. Statement on Strategic Materials," Jan. 27, 1948, Recovery Series, File "840.50 Recovery/1–2548—2848," NA. On ECA legislation, see Eckes, *Minerals*, pp. 157–60.

12. E.g., see Haldore Hanson to W. Walton Butterworth, "Interpretation of the European Recovery Program to the Far East," Nov. 2, 1947, Recovery Series, File "840.50 Recovery/11–147—11–1347," NA. The State Department

also criticized the British in the spring of 1948 for promoting new developmental schemes in British Africa (Tanganyika, Uganda, Nigeria) at the same time that the U.K. was requesting U.S. dollars for domestic reconstruction. But as the American Counselor for Economic Affairs in London pointed out, the British could not very easily recover without restoring colonial production of food and raw materials, especially since the erection of the Iron Curtain had blocked traditional sources of such supplies in Eastern Europe. See Don C. Bliss to Edward T. Wailes, April 16, 1948, Recovery Series, Confidential Decimal File 1945–49, File "840.50 Recovery/4–148," NA.

13. On Portugal, see W. J. Galloway Memcon, "Economic Cooperation Agreement," June 8, 1947, Recovery Series, Confidential Decimal File 1945–49, File "840.50 Recovery/6–148," NA. On Southern Rhodesia, see Evan Just to Donald D. Kennedy, Sept. 16, 1948, and H. P. Bramble to Robert Lovett, Nov. 13, 1948, File "840.50 Recovery/8–148," NA.

14. The U.S. received only $82 million in strategic materials by the end of 1951 (as against total ERP expenditures of about $13 billion), and investment in new minerals projects ($33 million by ECA and $105 million in counterpart) yielded very little in the way of repayments in kind. See Eckes, *Minerals*, pp. 157–60; Arkes, *Bureaucracy*, pp. 279–85.

15. Robert A. Packenham, *Liberal America and the Third World: Political Development Ideas in Foreign Aid and Social Science*, pp. 35–38.

16. On U.S. and LDC perspectives on development, see T. C. Achilles Memcon, July 15, 1948, Recovery Series, Confidential Decimal File, 1945–49, File "840.50 Recovery/6–148," NA; David A. Baldwin, *Economic Development and American Foreign Policy, 1943–62*, pp. 93–95; John H. Adler, "The Fiscal and Monetary Implementation of Development Programs," p. 600. On early discussion of ITO and LDCs, see, e.g., Stevenson to SecState, *FRUS 1946*, 1:1,292; Wilcox to SecState, Dec. 27, 1946, pp. 1,360–66. The U.S. objected in particular to preference systems, exchange controls, export subsidies, quantitative restrictions (QRs), and subsidies to state enterprises. The U.S. delegation decided in February 1948 to avoid a showdown with Latin American countries on QRs because if the U.S. had been outvoted, the Soviets and local Communist organizations might have been able to exploit the situation. See Dennison to Carter, Dec. 13, 1947, *FRUS 1948*, 1(2):809–16; Lovett (Daniels and Smith) to Embassy in Cuba, Dec. 30, 1947, pp. 818–19; U.S. Delegation in Havana Draft Telegram, Jan. 14, 1948, pp. 830–33; Briggs to SecState, Jan. 28, 1948, pp. 837–38; Wilcox to Clayton, Feb. 4, 1948, pp. 844–46; Nufer Memo, Feb. 6, 1948, pp. 849–50. The National Foreign Trade Council opposed the ITO because it allegedly stressed governmental foreign aid over private investment as the most desirable means of development, and because the proposed ITO charter did not adequately protect foreign investment. See Mira Wilkins, *The Maturing Enterprise: American Business Abroad from 1914 to 1970*, p. 288.

17. On FCN and double taxation treaties, see State Department Bulletin, Aug. 23, 1948, *FRUS 1948*, 1(2):950; State Department Bulletin, Aug. 25, 1948, pp. 950–52; Loree to SecState, Feb. 8, 1949, *FRUS 1949*, 1:631–35; Marshall (Thorp) to Loree, March 15, 1949, pp. 635–36. The NAC's revised draft of the FCN treaty in June 1949 included these criteria for aid to the LDCs:

equitable treatment of foreign enterprise, full and prompt compensation of nationalized property, and abstention from the imposition of exchange restrictions on transfer of capital or earnings, except in times of balance-of-payments stringency. The NAC also instructed the State Department to seek retroactivity of these provisions for existing U.S. investment. On foreign resistance to U.S. provisions in the FCNs, see Current Economic Developments, May 2, 1949, pp. 636–38; NAC Staff Committee to NAC, June 13, 1949, pp. 639–40; Current Economic Developments, Nov. 7, 1949, pp. 647–50. On NAC draft of new FCN, see Minutes of NAC Meeting #130, June 14, 1949, pp. 640–47. On failure of FCNs, see Eckes, *Minerals*, p. 162.

18. Baldwin, *Development*, pp. 16–22.

19. *Ibid.*, pp. 31–50; Wilkins, *Enterprise*, p. 289. For statement of U.S. aid and investment policy, see Marshall to Truman, Aug. 20, 1948, *FRUS 1948*, 1(2):952–58. Truman approved the statement on August 23.

20. U.S. investment in overseas oil grew 143 percent from 1946 to 1950 while investment in mining and manufacturing grew 38 percent and 58 percent, respectively, during the same years. American companies generally favored Canada over Latin American countries, which suffered from a reputation for "creeping expropriation." From 1943 to 1950, U.S. investment in Latin American manufacturing doubled, but total U.S. investment in Canadian industries ($1.9 billion) continued to exceed that for all of Latin America ($780 million) in 1950. See Wilkins, *Enterprise*, pp. 282–83, 301–24; Baldwin, *Development*, pp. 67–70.

21. Baldwin, *Development*, pp. 65–66.

22. "False economy" quotation from Memo to President on 60th Meeting of NSC, July 7, 1950, Papers of HST-PSF-Subject File: NSC Meetings, File "Memos for Pres.—Meeting Discussion (1950)," HSTL. "Know-how" quotation from Ayers' undated transcript of Truman off-the-record Remarks before Businessmen's Dinner Forum, Washington, D.C., Oct. 20, 1949; "specific origin" quotation from Ayers' Memo of Conversation, n.d. [1952], Ayers Papers, File "For. Policy (folder 1)," HSTL. On Cabinet meeting, see Ayers Diary, Jan. 22, 1949, Ayers Papers, File "Diary 1949," HSTL. Also see Truman, *Trial and Hope*, p. 231.

23. Unsigned "Memorandum for the President," Dec. 20, 1948, Papers of Walter Salant, File "Point IV File," HSTL. Hereafter cited as "Salant Papers." Salant identifies this memo as originating in the State Department in a letter to Jerry N. Hess, May 7, 1973.

24. Acheson quotation from Acheson, *Present*, p. 337. Clark Clifford, the counsel to the President, had developed Point IV for use in the presidential address with the help of Council of Economic Advisers member Walter S. Salant despite the lukewarm reaction of Acting Secretary of State Robert A. Lovett and Paul Nitze of the Policy Planning Staff. On Acheson and Point IV, see *ibid.*, pp. 350–51. On Salant's role, see Salant to Hess, May 7, 1973; and Salant Memo, "Foreign Investment and American Foreign Policy," Jan. 11, 1949, Salant Papers, File "Point IV File," HSTL. On early State Department planning and Acheson's first press conference, see Francis H. Russell to Clark Clifford, Jan. 26, 1949, with attached Prepared Statement (for Acheson, not used), n.d.,

Clifford Papers, File "Point IV: President's Inaugural Address, 1949," HSTL; and State Department Press Release, Jan. 26, 1949, *FRUS 1949*, 1:758–59.

25. Lloyd quotation from David D. Lloyd, "Progress on Point IV," March 29, 1949, Clifford Papers, File "Point IV: President's Inaugural Address, 1949," HSTL. Acheson quotation from attached (Acheson to Truman) Memo, "Summary of Attached Document Entitled Objectives and Nature of the Point IV Program," n.d. [March 1949]. For evidence of bureaucratic delay in the planning of Point IV, see Acheson to Pace, Feb. 2, 1949, *FRUS 1949*, 1:761–62; Minutes of State Department Meeting, Feb. 3, 1949, pp. 762–64; Weigle Memo, Feb. 9, 1949, pp. 769–70; Minutes of State Department Meeting, Feb. 18, 1949, pp. 770–73; Acheson to Truman, March 14, 1949, pp. 774–83; Salant to Nourse, May 9, 1949, Salant Papers, File "International Relations," HSTL.

26. On business pressure, see e.g., U.S. Associates, International Chamber of Commerce, "Report on . . . Point IV," April 6, 1949; and Earl Bunting to Clark Clifford, May 20, 1949, with attached NAM Report, "The Bold New Plan," May 1949, Clifford Papers, File "Point IV: Miscellaneous," HSTL. On NAC, see Minutes of NAC Meeting #123, April 14, 1949, *FRUS 1949*, 1:784–86, 786n. On Truman address, see Harry S. Truman, "Special Message to the Congress Recommending Point 4 Legislation," June 24, 1949, *Public Papers, Truman, 1949*, pp. 329–33. Truman told his staff that the proposal for guarantees of private investment was the one part of his speech that could cause political trouble, but "Acheson . . . wanted it and he [Truman] let it stay in." See Ayers' Diary, June 27, 1949, Ayers Papers, File "Diary 1949," HSTL.

27. For Acheson quotation, see Acheson, *Present*, p. 351. On administrative problems, see, e.g., Editorial Note, *FRUS 1950*, 1:851–52; Gordon to Howell, May 31, 1950, pp. 852–56; Halle to Barber, May 18, 1950, pp. 856–59; Memorandum of Understanding between State Department and ECA, April 11, 1950, pp. 861–62; Dennison to Kotschnig, May 8, 1950, pp. 862–64, 864n. On Congressional criticism of Point IV, see State Department Memo, June 20, 1950, pp. 846–51.

28. H. W. Singer, "The Distribution of Gains between Investing and Borrowing Countries," pp. 474–78, quotation on p. 479. Officials of the Truman administration were not entirely unaware of these problems. E.g., see Willard L. Thorp, "Some Basic Policy Issues in Economic Development," pp. 408–14. On "dependency" thesis, see Walter LaFeber, *Inevitable Revolutions: The United States in Central America*, pp. 16–17.

29. Truman remarks before American Society of Civil Engineers, Nov. 2, 1949, *Public Papers, Truman, 1949*, p. 547. Also see Truman, *Trial and Hope*, p. 232.

30. On containment and Point IV, see Truman, *Trial and Hope*, p. 239. Packenham, *Third World*, pp. 47–48, quotation on p. 46.

31. Packenham identifies three American "doctrines" during the 1947 to 1968 period. The third, "explicit democratic" approach refers to the use of aid to achieve human rights objectives in the Third World and pertains best to the early Kennedy presidency. This study uses the term "approach" rather than "doctrine" because official thinking on economic development during the Truman years lacked the coherence and precision of a doctrine (*Third World*, pp. 109–110).

32. David Green, *The Containment of Latin America: A History of the Myths and Realities of the Good Neighbor Policy*, pp. viii–ix, 1–208 passim; R. Harrison Wagner, *United States Policy Toward Latin America: A Study in Domestic and International Politics*, pp. 12–17.

33. The Roosevelt administration also gave military aid to Latin America. Lend-Lease totalled $262 million, including $150 million to Brazil. On Lend-Lease and the wartime Latin American economies, see Green, *Latin America*, pp. 95–103, 112, 179–81; LaFeber, *Central America*, p. 90; Wagner, *U.S. Policy Toward Latin America*, pp. 46–47.

34. U.S. statistics from Commerce Department, *HSUS*, p. 870. British statistics from Raymond F. Mikesell, *Foreign Investments in Latin America* (Washington, D.C.: Pan American Union, 1955), p. 10, also see pp. 5–9; and Green, *Latin America*, pp. 269–76.

35. On Bogota Conference and Economic Agreement, see Acheson (Thorp) Circular Memo, March 7, 1949, *FRUS 1949*, 2:424–27; Editorial Note, p. 429; Miller to SecState, *FRUS 1950*, 2:675–79; LaFeber, *Central America*, pp. 95–96; Green, *Latin America*, pp. 276–90. Truman's faith in the efficacy of private development is illustrated in a letter that he wrote his wife following a visit to the Caribbean in February 1948. The islands' "beauty is a revelation and the people the kindliest yet," he wrote. "Some day the idle rich will discover the climate and the beaches and then the prosperity of those parts will be assured." See Truman to Bess Wallace Truman, Feb. 26, 1948, Papers of HST-PSF-Family Correspondence File, File " . . . February 1948," HSTL. See also John C. Wiley, "Memorandum," Bogota, Nov. 8, 1945, Papers of HST-PSF-Subject File: Foreign Affairs File, File "South America," HSTL.

36. On Rio Pact, see Green, *Latin America*, pp. 276–90; LaFeber, *Central America*, pp. 92–94, and p. 17.

37. Joseph Page, *Peron: A Biography*, pp. 73–74, 77–78.

38. *Ibid.*, pp. 95–105, 146–49, 168–72.

39. The U.S. oil companies refused to grant generous wage increases to Argentine workers while accepting smaller price increases for oil products than the state oil company had won. Peron told U.S. diplomats that his country would continue to sell its grain at high world market prices until the United States provided agricultural machinery, shipping facilities, and gasoline at "fair market" prices. On U.S. relations with Argentina during 1945 and 1946, see Green, *Latin America*, pp. 237–54, 287–88; Ernest R. May, "The 'Bureaucratic Politics' Approach: U.S.-Argentine Relations, 1942–1947," in Julio Cotler and Richard R. Fagan, eds., *Latin America and the United States: The Changing Political Realities*, pp. 130–38. On American oil companies in Argentina, see *FRUS 1947*, 8:278–304; on wheat issue, pp. 304–16. On alleged Argentine discrimination against U.S. business, see, e.g., Virginia Prewett Memo, Oct. 14, 1946, Papers of HST-PSF-Subject File: Foreign Affairs File, File "Argentina: Folder 3," HSTL.

40. On ECA pledges of aid, see Ray to SecState, Sept. 13, 1948, *FRUS 1948*, 9:290–92; Lovett Memcon, Dec. 11, 1948, pp. 307–09; Lovett to Embassy in Argentina, Dec. 23, 1948, pp. 309–10. Also see C. B. Lyon Memcon (dictated by George C. Marshall), Oct. 5, 1948, Recovery Series, Confidential Decimal File 1945–49, File "840.50 Recovery/10–148," NA. Despite pressure from U.S. busi-

nessmen, the State Department and ECA also acquiesced in Argentine state-trading and discrimination against U.S. imports. See Norman Armour, "Proposals of the American Chamber of Commerce in Buenos Aires re Offshore Procurement under the ERP," May 12, 1948, Recovery Series, File "840.50 Recovery/5–1248—5–1748," NA; T. R. Martin, "Offshore Procurement for ECA," April 28, 1948, Recovery Series, File "840.50 Recovery/4–2848—4–3048," NA; Robert F. Loree, Chairman of National Foreign Trade Council, to Paul G. Hoffmann, Administrator of ECA, April 27, 1948, Recovery Series, File "840.50 Recovery/5–2048—5–2548," NA; Hoffmann to Loree, May 6, 1948; E. P. Thomas, President of NFTC, to Hoffmann, May 25, 1948; Willard L. Thorp to Loree, n.d. On U.S. reneging on ECA agreement, see Ray to SecState, Feb. 24, 1949, *FRUS 1949*, 2:481–82; Acheson (Bruce) to Embassy in Argentina, Feb. 25, 1949, pp. 482–83. Also see Page, *Peron*, pp. 172–73; Wagner, *U.S. Policy Toward Latin America*, p. 48.

41. On renewed economic crisis in Argentina, see Bruce (Ray) to SecState, Jan. 4, 1949, *FRUS 1949*, 2:473–78; Tewksbury to Bruce, Jan. 25, 1949, pp. 478–80; Ray to SecState, Feb. 9, 1949, p. 481.

42. By trying to force too hard a bargain on the price of Argentine exports, the ECA, in the estimation of the U.S. Ambassador in Buenos Aires, was partially to blame for the bilateral trade agreement that Argentina concluded with Britain during this period. On Argentine expropriation threat and demand for aid, see Ray to SecState, March 9, 1949, *FRUS 1949*, 2:485–86; Ray to SecState, March 14, 1949, pp. 486–87; Ray to SecState, March 16, 1949, p. 488; Ray to SecState, March 18, 1949, p. 489; Ray to SecState, March 23, 1949, pp. 489–90; Dearborn Memo, May 23, 1949, pp. 500–04. On Acheson, see Acheson to Embassy in Argentina, March 31, 1949, pp. 494–95; Acheson to Embassy in Argentina, April 15, 1949, pp. 495–97; Acheson to Embassy in Argentina, April 29, 1949, pp. 497–98. On ECA, see Bruce to SecState, June 10, 1949, pp. 506–07. On Anglo-Argentine trade, see Sawyer to Webb, June 7, 1949, pp. 504–05; Webb to Sawyer, June 21, 1949, pp. 508–09. The Standard Oil Company of New Jersey claimed that British practices under this agreement would force U.S. oil companies in Argentina out of business. See Steelman Memo, Jan. 28, 1950, with attached SONJ Memo, "Dollar-Sterling Oil Problem," Jan. 26, 1950, Papers of HST-PSF-General File, File "Oil," HSTL.

43. On perceptions of Peron as moderate, see e.g., Dearborn Memo, Jan. 20, 1948, *FRUS 1948*, 9:279–81; Ray to Briggs, Feb. 20, 1948, pp. 281–83. On Peron's pledge, see e.g., Bruce to SecState, April 28, 1948, pp. 284–88; Bruce to SecState, June 3, 1948, pp. 288–90. Also see Page, *Peron*, pp. 184–85.

44. Kennan quotation cited in LaFeber, *Central America*, p. 107. In late April 1950, Argentina reached a settlement with U.S. meatpacking and oil companies, and the NAC reciprocated by extending $125 million in Eximbank credits toward partial liquidation of Argentina's commercial arrears, contingent upon Argentina's retirement of its remaining commercial debts and upon further steps to encourage private investment. See Nufer Memcon, Dec. 6, 1949, *FRUS 1949*, 2:516–17; Griffis to SecState, Dec. 30, 1949, pp. 518–24; White Memcon, Feb. 9, 1950, *FRUS 1950*, 2:691–92; Griffis to Miller, Feb. 15, 1950, pp. 693–95; Griffis to Department of State, March 1, 1950, pp. 696–701; Webb (Miller) to Embassy in Argentina, March 17, 1950, pp. 704–05; Griffis to De-

partment of State, March 17, 1950, pp. 705–07; Acheson (Miller) to Embassy in Argentina, March 24, 1950, p. 707; Acheson (Miller) to Embassy in Argentina, March 30, 1950, pp. 707–08; White Memo, April 20, 1950, pp. 709–10; Mallory to SecState, April 24, 1950, pp. 710, 710n.; Acheson to Embassy in Argentina, April 26, 1950, p. 711; Corbett Memcon, April 28, 1950, pp. 711–13; Minutes of NAC Meeting #156, May 16, 1950, pp. 717–24; Acheson Circular Memo, June 7, 1950, pp. 727–28; Maleady Memcon, June 19, 1950, pp. 728–30, 730n.; Brigfeld Memo of Telephone Conversation, Sept. 26, 1950, pp. 734–35. Brazil felt betrayed by the U.S. reconciliation with Axis-sympathizer Argentina, setting the stage for a deterioration in U.S.-Brazilian relations after the war. See Stanley E. Hilton, "The United States, Brazil, and the Cold War, 1945–1960: End of the Special Relationship," pp. 599–606. On internal sources of Argentine recession, see Page, *Peron*, pp. 174–75, 186.

45. Statistics on U.S. aid to Latin America and Western Europe from Commerce Department, *HSUS*, pp. 875, 874 respectively. Statistics on 1948–1957 period from LaFeber, *Central America*, p. 95. Although Washington regularly encouraged the Latin American countries to apply for small credits from the Eximbank, a high-level U.S. official in the IMF privately admitted in June 1949 that the tough policies of the Fund had a direct impact upon "the magnitude of dollar funds for developmental purposes available to countries outside of the ERP area." He added that if developmental funds available from the Eximbank and IBRD "turn out to be small, . . . we will be confronted by countries whose position may be pretty desperate." See Southard to Snyder and Martin, "Fund Drawings vs. Developmental Loans," June 13, 1949, Snyder Papers, File "International Monetary Fund and Bank—Gen'l corres. and applications, 1946–1952," HSTL.

46. See Michael B. Stoff, *Oil, War, and American Security: The Search for a National Policy on Foreign Oil, 1941–1947*, pp. 71–73; Aaron David Miller, *Search for Security: Saudi Arabian Oil and American Foreign Policy, 1939–1949*, pp. 122–24; Craufurd D. Goodwin, "Truman Administration Policies Toward Particular Energy Sources," in Goodwin, *Energy Policy in Perspective: Today's Problems, Yesterday's Solutions*, pp. 76–77; Wittner, *Intervention*, p. 18.

47. Anderson, *Aramco*, pp. ix, 25–28.

48. *Ibid.*, pp. 29–33.

49. By 1975, the estimates had risen to 663 billion barrels for the Mideast and 242 billion for the United States. Although the numbers had risen, the ratio remained roughly the same (*ibid.*, pp. 38–39). Quotation from Acheson to SecState, Oct. 9, 1945, with attached Merriam to Henderson, n.d. [August 1945], *FRUS 1945*, 8:45.

50. On PRC, see Anderson, *Aramco*, pp. 50–67; Stoff, *Oil*, pp. 70–80; Miller, *Search for Security*, pp. 92–99; Stephen D. Krasner, *Defending the National Interest: Raw Materials Investments and U.S. Foreign Policy*, pp. 189–99.

51. On Anglo-American Oil Agreements, see Anderson, *Aramco*, pp. 68–107; Stoff, *Oil*, pp. 151–95; Miller, *Search for Security*, pp. 100–06; Krasner, *National Interest*, pp. 199–205; Wittner, *Intervention*, pp. 21–22.

52. Anderson, *Aramco*, pp. 143–44, Forrestal quotation on p. 142. Also see Nash, *U.S. Oil Policy*, pp. 188–89; Miller, *Search for Security*, p. 150.

53. During the fall of 1946, Socony and Jersey, with the support of the State

Department, had also renounced the 1928 "Red Line Agreement," a multinational accord restricting oil production in Asia Minor and the Arabian peninsula, excluding Kuwait. This freed the two U.S. corporations to join Aramco. On Red Line, Aramco merger, and pipeline, see Stoff, *Oil*, pp. 93n., 195–208; Anderson, *Aramco*, pp. 140–59, 171, quotation on p. 142. On U.S. governmental support of the oil companies, see also *FRUS 1947*, 5:628–68; *FRUS 1949*, 6:91–164, 1,573–1,629 passim; Miller, *Search for Security*, pp. 150–62, 173–84; and "The American Drive for Oil Abroad, 1938–50," Session 105 of American Historical Association Convention (with Michael B. Stoff, Clayton R. Koppes, Irvine H. Anderson, and Lloyd C. Gardner), Dec. 30, 1980, Washington, D.C. (transcript in my possession).

54. On fifty-fifty agreement, see Anderson, *Aramco*, pp. 187–96; on U.S. recognition of Israel, p. 169.

55. For debate over antitrust and tax issues, cf. *ibid.*, pp. 146, 194–96, 202–03; and Krasner, *National Interest*, pp. 205–13.

56. On U.S. aid to Saudi Arabia, see Anderson, *Aramco*, pp. 136–40; Miller, *Search for Security*, pp. 135–38, 142–44; *FRUS 1946*, 7:738–50; *FRUS 1947*, 5:1,329–42.

57. By the spring of 1950 the Marine battalion was no longer available for Saudi oil demolition. See Memo to President on 57th Meeting of NSC, May 18, 1950, HST-PSF-Subject File: NSC Meetings, File "Memos for Pres.—Meeting Discussions (1950)," HSTL. On U.S. military capabilities, see Anderson, *Aramco*, pp. 162–66. On Istanbul Conference, see McGhee Statement, Nov. 30, 1949, *FRUS 1949*, 6:178–79, also see pp. 168–77.

58. Anderson, *Aramco*, p. 202.

59. Stoff, *Oil*, pp. 207–08, quotation on p. 214.

60. See Goodwin, "Truman Administration Policies," pp. 84–90, 103–14; Stuart Symington Memo, "Petroleum Imports," n.d. [forwarded to Truman on June 26, 1950], Papers of HST-PSF-General File, File "Oil," HSTL; Charles Maylon to Truman, Aug. 22, 1950, with attached Interior Memo, "Independent Refiners," July 19, 1950; R. H. S. Eakens Memo, "Oil Imports," Aug. 31, 1949, Acheson Papers, File "Memos of Conversation August-September 1949," HSTL.

61. On synfuels, see Goodwin, "Truman Administration Policies," pp. 146–67. On shortcomings of stockpiling program, see Eckes, *Minerals*, pp. 140–45, 157–59.

62. Quotation from unsigned memo, "The Following Notes . . . ," n.d. [early 1952?], Records of the President's Materials Policy Commission 1951–52, File "Correspondence-Staff: Staff Studies-typewritten copies," HSTL. Hereafter cited as "Records of PMPC."

63. On the PMPC and materials policy, see Craufurd D. Goodwin, "The Truman Administration: Toward a National Energy Policy," in Goodwin, *Energy Policy*, pp. 52–61; Eckes, *Minerals*, pp. 175–98; Krasner, *National Interest*, pp. 50–51. For the main conclusions of the PMPC, see President's Materials Policy Commission, *Resources for Freedom, Volume 1: Foundations for Growth and Security*, pp. 1–21; H. D. Coombs, "Probable Findings and Recommendations of the Commission," n.d. [1952?], Records of PMPC, File "Correspondence-Staff:

Staff Studies-typewritten copies," HSTL. On debate over private vs. public investment, see William C. Ackerman, "Summary of Minutes," Feb. 26, 1951, File "Administrative File: PMPC-Commission Meetings," HSTL; Ackerman, "Summary of Minutes," March 13, 1951; Glenn H. Craig to Isaiah Frank, "Draft Report of President's Materials Policy Commission," April 15, 1952; Harold W. Sheehan to Ackerman, "Draft IV . . . ," May 27, 1952.

64. Eckes, *Minerals*, pp. 261–64.

10. The Waning of Economic Containment

1. See Yergin, *Shattered Peace*, p. 5. Melvyn Leffler adds, "Although the desire of the national military establishment for large increments in defense expenditures did not prevail in the tight budgetary environment and presidential election year of 1948, the mode of thinking about national security that subsequently accelerated the arms race and precipitated military interventionism in Asia already was widespread among defense officials" ("American Conception of National Security").

2. E.g., see Spanier, *American Foreign Policy*, p. 54.

3. On "militarization" thesis, see, e.g., Yergin, *Shattered Peace*, passim. For economic thesis on NATO's origins, see, e.g., Block, *Economic Disorder*, pp. 103–07; Kolko, *Limits*, chapter 18 passim.

4. For Bevin initiative, see Inverchapel to Marshall, Jan. 13, 1948, *FRUS 1948*, 3:3–6. "Plain truth" quotation from Inverchapel to Lovett, Jan. 27, 1948, p. 14. Also see Inverchapel to Lovett, Feb. 6, 1948, pp. 19–20. For Franco-German thesis on NATO's origins, see Timothy P. Ireland, *Creating the Entangling Alliance: The Origins of the North Atlantic Treaty Organization*, passim, and on European initiative, pp. 48–79.

5. Quotation from Kennan to Lovett, Feb. 24, 1948, with attached PPS/23, *FRUS 1948*, 1(2):510. Also see Kennan to Marshall, Jan. 20, 1948, *FRUS 1948*, 3:7–8; Jan. 21, 1948, pp. 9–12.

6. Marshall quotation from Marshall to Inverchapel, March 12, 1948, *FRUS 1948*, 3:48; also see Hickerson to Marshall, March 8, 1948, pp. 40–42. On Truman, see Truman address before Congress, March 17, 1948, pp. 54–55. NSC quotation from Souers to NSC, NSC 7, March 20, 1948, *FRUS 1948*, 1(2):548, 550. The "Pentagon talks" resulted in recommendations for the expansion of the Western Union to include the Scandanavian countries; the eventual inclusion of Germany, Austria, and Spain; U.S.-U.K. guarantees to Greece, Turkey, and Iran; and continuing political and military consultations between the U.S. and Western Union. See Minutes of 6th Meeting of Pentagon Talks, April 1, 1948, *FRUS 1948*, 3:71–75.

7. Opposition to a NATO-like organization came from several quarters, most notably Kennan, who did not participate in many of the decisions in this period due to a trip to Japan and a subsequent illness in March-April 1948. Kennan's ability to counter the strong tide in Washington favoring U.S. association with Western Union was also tempered by the fact that in his absence, the PPS in

PPS/27 had endorsed U.S. military consultations leading to a pact with the West European countries. See PPS/27, March 23, 1948, *FRUS 1948*, 3:61–64; Kennan to Lovett, April 29, 1948, pp. 109–10. The NSC substantially adopted the viewpoint of PPS/27 on Western Union. See NSC 9, April 13, 1948, pp. 85–88. For Kennan's misgivings about NATO, see also Kennan, *Memoirs*, pp. 396–414. For JCS Comments on NSC 7, see Forrestal to NSC, April 17, 1948, *FRUS 1948*, 1(2):561–64; Rearden, *OSD*, chapter 13. For Lovett quotation, see Memo to the President on 11th Meeting of NSC, May 21, 1948, Papers of HST-PSF-Subject File: NSC Meetings, File "Memo for President—Meeting Discussions (1948)," HSTL.

8. The Europeans, the NSC also decided, would have to pay for the lion's share of their own rearmament. By limiting American aid to members of continuous and effective security pacts, the Vandenberg Resolution gave the administration the discretionary authority to withhold military aid or a security guarantee from certain countries, such as Turkey, which sought to join the alliance before the U.S. favored its membership. On the administration's consultation with Congress, see Lovett Memcon, April 11, 1948, *FRUS 1948*, 3:82–84; Lovett Memcon, April 18, 1948, pp. 92–96; Lovett Memcon, April 27, 1948, pp. 104–08. For Vandenberg Resolution, see Senate Resolution 239, June 11, 1948, pp. 135–36. On discretionary authority, see Lovett Memcon, May 25, 1948, pp. 130–31; Lovett Memcon, July 21, 1948, pp. 196–98. On NSC approval of an Atlantic pact along the lines of the Vandenberg Resolution, see NSC 9/3, June 28, 1948, pp. 140–41. On military aid, see NSC 14/1, July 1, 1948, *FRUS 1948*, 1(2):585–88; Kaplan, *NATO*, pp. 14–15, 19–23; Yergin, *Shattered Peace*, pp. 354, 363–64.

9. Harriman quotation from Harriman to Marshall and Forrestal, July 14, 1948, *FRUS 1948*, 3:184. Also see Draper Memcon with Harriman in Paris on July 17, 1948, Memo Dated July 19, 1948, Papers of HST-PSF-Subject File, File "*Cabinet:* Army, Secretary of the," HSTL. Marshall quotation from Marshall to Lovett (Forrestal), Nov. 8, 1948, *FRUS 1948*, 1(2):655. For Marshall on B-29s, see Memo to President on 15th Meeting of NSC, July 16, 1948, Papers of HST-PSF-Subject File: NSC Meetings, File "Memo for President—Meeting Discussions (1948)," HSTL. "Psychological" quotation from memo of 3rd Meeting of Working Group, Washington Exploratory Talks, July 15, 1948, *FRUS 1948*, 3:186. Also see Bohlen Memcon, Aug. 6, 1948, p. 206; Marshall to Truman, Aug. 23, 1948, pp. 221–22; memo, "Washington Exploratory Conversations on Security," Sept. 9, 1948, pp. 237–48; memo by Brussels Pact Ambassadors to Department of State, Oct. 29, 1948, p. 270; Kennan to Marshall and Lovett, with attached PPS Report, Nov. 24, pp. 284–85; Lovett to Harriman, Dec. 3, 1948, p. 305; Kaplan, *NATO*, p. 35. On Acheson's relations with Congress regarding the NAT, see Acheson, *Present*, pp. 364–76; on SFRC testimony, pp. 375–76. On Congressional debate on the NAT, see Ireland, *Alliance*, pp. 119–48.

10. Quotation from FACC Policy Paper, Feb. 7, 1949, *FRUS 1949*, 1:254, 255. On MAP and security organization, see Ireland, *Alliance*, pp. 153–63. Harriman also linked U.S. support of Western Union to the success of the ERP. See Harriman to Lovett, Nov. 12, 1948, Recovery Series, Confidential Decimal File 1945–49, File "840.50 Recovery/11-148," NA. For fears that military aid

could stall European recovery, see, e.g., Minutes of Third Meeting of Washington Exploratory Talks, July 17, 1948, *FRUS 1948*, 3:157–58.

11. Nitze quotation from Nitze to FASC, Jan. 31, 1949, *FRUS 1949*, 4:55; also see pp. 54, 56–57. "Rearmament" and "dilemma" quotations from Kaplan, *NATO*, pp. 42, 72.

12. Although the Congress authorized $1.3 billion in military aid for FY 1950 (with about $1 billion earmarked for NATO countries), it required the NATO countries to reach an integrated defense plan (achieved in January 1950) before the Executive could release the bulk of authorized MAP funds. Other amendments limited the funds available to accelerate arms production in Europe. By delaying final passage of the Mutual Defense Assistance Act to October 1949, the Congress further slowed Western rearmament. See Kaplan, *NATO*, pp. 41–49, 68, 77.

13. Quotation from Kaplan, pp. 71–72. While the Defense Department was perhaps the natural candidate to administer this program, Secretary of Defense Johnson showed little interest in MAP and in any case carried less weight in the administration than Acheson. The Defense Department, moreover, recognized the important political, economic, and psychological dimensions of military aid (Kaplan, pp. 40, 49).

14. Congress authorized $1.3 billion in military aid world-wide ($52 million expended) and $4.4 billion in economic aid ($3.4 billion expended) for FY 1950 (Kaplan, p. 116, also see pp. 72–77). Ireland quotation from Ireland, *Alliance*, p. 183.

15. See Robert J. Donovan, "Truman's Perspective," in Francis H. Heller, ed., *Economics and the Truman Administration*, p. 18; Forrestal to Walter G. Andrews, Dec. 13, 1948, in Millis, *Forrestal Diaries*, p. 536.

16. Quotation from David Alan Rosenberg, "The Origins of Overkill: Nuclear Weapons and American Strategy, 1945–1960," p. 16; also see his "American Atomic Strategy and the Hydrogen Bomb Decision," and Lynn Eden, "Capitalist Conflict and the State: The Making of United States Military Policy in 1948," in Charles Bright and Susan Harding, eds., *Statemaking and Social Movements: Essays in History and Theory*, passim.

17. According to Truman, the administration's priorities were "efficiency, economy and getting a dollar's worth of value for each dollar expended." See Truman to Forrestal, May 13, 1948, Clifford Papers, File "National Military Establishment-miscellaneous," HSTL.

18. In October 1948 Forrestal argued for a defense budget of $17.5 billion, compared with Truman's $14.4 billion, for FY '50. See Forrestal to Marshall, Oct. 31, 1948, *ibid.* In December, Forrestal requested, but failed to achieve, a $16.9 billion budget (compared with the JCS' request for $23 billion). "Productive potential" quotation from Bohlen to Carter, Nov. 7, 1948, *FRUS 1948*, 1(2):654. Marshall quotation from Marshall to Lovett (Forrestal), Nov. 8, 1948, p. 655. Also see Forrestal to Marshall, Oct. 31, 1948, pp. 644–47; Lovett to Marshall, Nov. 1, 1948, pp. 647–48; Lovett to Marshall, Nov. 2, 1948, pp. 648–54; Millis, *Forrestal Diaries*, pp. 492–95, 498–99, 501–05, 508–11, 535–36, 538; Schilling, "Politics of National Defense," in Schilling, ed., *Strategy*, pp. 100–266, passim; Rearden, *OSD*, chapter 9.

19. Souers to NSC, NSC 52, July 5, 1949, with attached Truman to Souers, July 1, 1949, *FRUS 1949*, 1:350, 351.

20. Lay to NSC, July 8, 1949, NSC 52/1, with attached Pace "Summary Tabulation," July 8, 1949, pp. 352–57.

21. The NSC approved the BOB's cut of the ECA budget (from $4.2 to $3 billion), but hoped to maintain MAP at about $1–1.5 billion. Altogether, the NSC adopted a package of foreign and military programs costing $19–20 billion. Quotation on Defense Department from Rearden, *OSD*, chapter 10, p. 33. Nourse quotation from Memo to President on 46th Meeting of NSC, Sept. 30, 1949, Papers of HST-PSF-Subject File: NSC Meetings, File "Memos for President—Meeting Discussions (1949)," HSTL. On CEA, see also Clarence Yin-Hsieh Lo, "The Truman Administration's Military Budgets during the Korean War," p. 150; Nourse Memo, Sept. 30, 1949, *FRUS 1949*, 1:394–96. Quotation by NSC from NSC to Truman, NSC 52/3, Sept. 29, 1949, p. 387; also see pp. 388–93. On Treasury Department, see Memo by Acting Secretary of Treasury, Sept. 29, 1949, pp. 393–94. On nuclear weapons production, see Rosenberg, "Overkill," pp. 21–22. Also see Robert J. Donovan, *Tumultuous Years: The Presidency of Harry S. Truman, 1949–1953*, p. 132.

22. Lawton to Truman, "Current Issues Regarding the 1952 and 1953 Budgets," April 19, 1950, Papers of HST-PSF-Subject File, File "BOB: Budget Data—FY 1952–1953," HSTL.

23. CEA Members Nourse and Keyserling, who agreed on very little else, both contended that Truman, rather than Forrestal and Johnson, was primarily responsible for the low defense budgets before the Korean War. See Oral History Interviews with Edwin G. Nourse, 1972, HSTL, pp. 45–49, and Leon P. Keyserling, 1975, HSTL, pp. 116–18. Cf. Leon H. Keyserling, "The View from the Council of Economic Advisers," in Heller, ed., *Economics*, pp. 89–90.

24. William S. Hill, Jr., "The Business Community and National Defense: Corporate Leaders and the Military," pp. 18, 20–21, 491, quotation on p. 16; Collins, *Business Response*, pp. 127–41; Paterson, "Economic Cold War," p. 41.

25. Hill, "Business Community," pp. 32, 51–59, 68; Collins, *Business Response*, pp. 139–41. For a representative businessman's views on the proper role of the federal government in the postwar economy, see Walter D. Fuller (president of Curtis Publishing Co.), "American Business After the War," in *The United States After War*, pp. 95–124.

26. See Hill, "Business Community": on munitions procurement, p. 165; on aviation and shipbuilding, pp. 19, 69, 76, 88–89, 97–99, 110, 206–13, 230, 234, 247, 284; and Yergin, *Shattered Peace*, pp. 268–69, 341–43, 359–63.

27. See Hill, "Business Community": on steel, pp. 166, 179, 326, 409; on electronics, pp. 180–84, 195–97, 274, 357; on machine tools, p. 355.

28. *Ibid.*, pp. 333, 336, 342–43, 348–50, 399, 415, Sawyer quotation on p. 348. On aircraft industry, see Lo, "Military Budgets," p. 144.

29. Hill, "Business Community," pp. 429, 434–35, quotation on p. 437.

30. Gregg Herken, *The Winning Weapon: The Atomic Bomb in the Cold War, 1945–1950*, pp. 303–05; John Lewis Gaddis, *Strategies of Containment: A Critical Appraisal of Postwar American National Security Policy*, pp. 84–85.

31. For Kennan quotation, see Minutes of 148th Meeting of PPS, Oct. 11,

1949, *FRUS 1949*, 1:401–02. Also see Minutes of 171st Meeting of PPS, Dec. 16, 1949, pp. 414–15; Gaddis, *Strategies*, p. 71.

32. Quotation from Minutes of 148th Meeting of PPS, Oct. 11, 1949, *FRUS 1949*, 1:402. Acheson also noted that the administration would need to decide by January 1950 whether to expand the U.S. atomic weapons program, depending upon negotiations with the Soviets on international control (p. 403).

33. "Islam" quotation from Acheson, *Present*, p. 490. Quotation on Pentagon from 171st Meeting of PPS, Dec. 16, 1949, *FRUS 1949*, 1:415; also see p. 416. "Drift" quotation from Lo, "Military Budgets," p. 168.

34. "Danger" from Record of Meeting of PPS, Feb. 2, 1950, *FRUS 1950*, 1:142–43. "Soviet moves" from Nitze Memo, Feb. 8, 1950, pp. 145–46. For Nitze's evidence of a new Communist offensive, see "Recent Soviet and Soviet-Satellite Moves," addendum to Nitze memo above, Papers of HST-PSF-Foreign Affairs File, File "Russia 1949–1952," HSTL. Also see Samuel F. Wells, Jr., "Sounding the Tocsin: NSC 68 and the Soviet Threat," pp. 119, 126–27.

35. Quotations from Kennan to Acheson, Feb. 19, 1950, *FRUS 1950*, 1:160, 164, also see pp. 160–67. On differences between Kennan and architects of NSC 68, see Gaddis, *Strategies*, pp. 90–104.

36. Quotation from Thorp to Acheson, April 5, 1950, *FRUS 1950*, 1:219.

37. Acheson Memcon, March 24, 1950, *ibid.*, p. 207.

38. *Ibid.* Also see Wells, "Tocsin," p. 126.

39. Quotations from NSC 68, April 7, 1950, *FRUS 1950*, 1:238, 240, 253, 261; also see pp. 242, 245–46, 249–52, 282–85. For a summary of NSC 68, see Wells, "Tocsin," pp. 131–35.

40. Quotation from NSC 68, April 7, 1950, *FRUS 1950*, 1:285; also see pp. 256–58, 286; and Gaddis, *Strategies*, pp. 93–94.

41. Quotation from Acheson, *Present*, p. 488, also see pp. 489–90; Wells, "Tocsin," p. 124; Lo, "Military Budgets," pp. 137–38.

42. The BOB claimed that the total war effort achieved in 1944 had caused the deterioration of capital assets and inflationary pressures that the government could suppress only over the short term. "Cost" quotation from Truman to Lay, April 12, 1950, *FRUS 1950*, 1:235. Also see Memo to President on 55th Meeting of NSC, April 21, 1950, Papers of HST-PSF-Subject File: NSC Meetings, File "Memos for Pres.—Meeting Discussions (1950)," HSTL. On CEA, see Dearborn to Lay, May 8, 1950, *FRUS 1950*, 1:311. For evidence of conflict between Nourse and Keyserling on defense budgets, see Nourse's daily diary, 1946–1949, in Nourse Papers, HSTL; Keyserling Interview, pp. 112–15; Nourse Interview, pp. 76–77. The NSRB also strongly supported NSC 68; see NSRB Memo, May 29, 1950, *FRUS 1950*, 1:316–21. On BOB, see Schaub to Lay, May 8, 1950, pp. 304–05. On Webb, see McWilliams Memcon, June 6, 1950, p. 324. "Defense budget" quotation from Press Conference, May 4, 1950, *Public Papers, Truman, 1950*, p. 286. For Johnson quotation, see Battle Memo of Telephone Conversation, June 5, 1950, Acheson Papers, File "Memos of Conversation May/June 1950," HSTL. In testimony before a Joint Session of the Senate Foreign Relations and Armed Services Committees, Acheson had stated that he expected the defense budget to be increased. In a later conversation with James Lay, Acheson "mentioned NSC 68 as an example of progressive forward-think-

ing and . . . said that this paper would have gotten us well along toward strengthening the United States even if the Korean Crisis had not come up." See Battle Memo of Conversation, Jan. 27, 1951, Acheson Papers, File "Memos of Conversation January 1951," HSTL. Also see Wells, "Tocsin," pp. 137–38; Rearden, OSD, chapter 17, pp. 1–2, 15–19.

43. NSC 68 did not substantially differ in its recommendations from NSC 20/4 in November 1948, the earlier assessment of Soviet-American relations of which NSC 68 was a review. The tone of NSC 68, however, was new in that the threat of Soviet attack was magnified; in this sense, the Soviet bomb was probably an important factor. In retrospect, it is clear that NSC 68 grossly exaggerated the Soviet threat and distorted the nature of Soviet Communism. Estimates of Soviet ground forces, atomic weapons and deliverability were greatly overrated while U.S. retaliatory capacity and mobilization potential were understated. The Soviets commenced a major military buildup only after the post-Korea U.S. rearmament had begun in earnest. Quotation from Wells, "Tocsin," p. 139, see also pp. 138–39, 152–57; and Acheson, Present, p. 488. Statistics on FY '50 budget from W. J. McNeil to Louis Johnson, July 5, 1950, Papers of HST-PSF-Subject File, File "Bureau of the Budget: Budget-military—1945–53," HSTL.

44. Lay Memcon, May 12, 1950, FRUS 1950, 1:313.

45. Quotations from Memo to President on 72nd Meeting of NSC, Nov. 24, 1950, Papers of HST-PSF-Subject File: NSC Meetings, File "Memos for Pres.—Meeting Discussions (1950)," HSTL; Memo to President on 75th Meeting of NSC, Dec. 15, 1950; Keyserling Memo, Dec. 8, 1950, FRUS 1950, 1:430. Also see pp. 427–31; and Butler Memo, Dec. 13, 1950, pp. 466–67; NSC Report to President, Dec. 14, 1950, pp. 468–70; Memo to President on 105th Meeting of NSC, Oct. 18, 1951, Papers of HST-PSF-Subject File: NSC Meetings, File "Memos for Pres.—Meeting Discussions (1951)," HSTL; Lo, "Military Budgets," p. 152.

46. Congress, which had authorized $1.23 billion for MAP before the Korean invasion, increased the total to $5 billion after war broke out. ECA, meanwhile, was cut by $208 million in June 1950. See Kaplan, NATO, pp. 104–05; Commerce Department, HSUS, p. 87; Paterson, Confrontation, p. 232. U.S. military aid, incidentally, was not designed to close the dollar gap in Western Europe. See Lo, "Military Budgets," pp. 136, 154, 162.

47. For relegation of multilateralist objectives to a secondary status, see conclusions to NSC 104, cited below; Lo, "Military Budgets," p. 176. The State Department and ECA usually took a softer line on export controls than did the National Security Resources Board and the Defense and Commerce Departments. See CIA Report #313, Aug. 8, 1950, Papers of HST-PSF-Intelligence File, File "Central Intelligence—Memorandum 1950–1952," HSTL; NSC 69/1, "Export Controls and Security Policy," Aug. 21, 1950, Papers of HST-PSF-Subject File: NSC Meetings, File "NSC Meeting No. 66 8–24–50," HSTL; NSC 91, "East-West Trade," Oct. 30, 1950, File "NSC Meeting No. 70 11–2–50," HSTL; NSC 102, "Export Control Policy toward the Soviet Bloc," Jan. 19, 1951, File "NSC Meeting No. 83 2–14–51," HSTL; NSC 104, "U.S. Policies and Programs in the Economic Field Which May Affect the War Potential of the Soviet Bloc," Feb. 12, 1951, File "NSC Meeting No. 84 2–21–51," HSTL. Also see Kaplan, NATO, pp. 62–65.

11. Conclusion

1. Forrestal to Chan Gurney, Dec. 8, 1947, in Millis, *Forrestal Diaries*, pp. 350–51.

2. "Washington," Thomas Paterson adds, "attempted to exploit Europe's weakness for its advantage and must share a substantial responsibility for the division of the world into competing blocs" (*Confrontation*, p. 260).

3. Quotation from Truman to Eugene P. Thomas, Oct. 17, 1946, cited in Paterson, *Confrontation*, p. 5n.

4. In fact, exports constituted a much more important part of the national economy during the 1889–1917 period, when they averaged more than 6.5 percent of GNP, than they did during the Truman presidency. The same generalizations hold true if one compares imports as a percentage of GNP, or exports and imports as a percentage of the production of movable goods, for the 1920s and the 1945–1960 period. See Commerce, *HSUS*, p. 887. Cf. Magdoff, *Age of Imperialism*, pp. 173–201.

5. Quotation from Truman Memo, n.d., Papers of HST-PSF-Subject File, File "Bureau of Budget: Budget-misc. 1945–53," HSTL.

6. For a European perspective on U.S. sanctions, see Albert Bressand, French Institute for International Relations, *Ramses 1982: The State of the World Economy* (Cambridge, Mass.: Ballinger, 1982), pp. 101–11.

7. On Truman-Eisenhower era, see Robert A. Pollard and Samuel F. Wells, Jr., "1945–1960: The Era of American Economic Hegemony," in William H. Becker and Samuel F. Wells, Jr., *Economics and World Power: An Assessment of American Diplomacy Since 1789*, pp. 333–90; Burton I. Kaufman, *Trade and Aid: Eisenhower's Foreign Economic Policy, 1953–1961*, passim. On U.S. economic policies since Kennedy, see David P. Calleo, *The Imperious Economy*, passim; James Chace, *Solvency: An Essay on American Foreign Policy*, passim.

8. Gaddis, *Strategies*, p. 359. The defense figures exclude veterans' benefits.

9. For critiques of free trade, see Robert B. Reich, "Beyond Free Trade," *Foreign Affairs* (Spring 1983), 61:773–804; Wolfgang Hager, "Let Us Now Praise Trade Protectionism," *Washington Post*, May 15, 1983. On Pacific Rim countries, see *Washington Post*, April 22, 1984.

10. For the orthodox view on foreign trade, see William E. Brock, "No, Let Us Praise Free Trade," *Washington Post*, June 13, 1983.

11. Robert A. Pastor, *Congress and the Politics of U.S. Foreign Economic Policy*, p. 331.

12. Calleo, *Imperious Economy*, p. 157.

Selected Bibliography

ARCHIVAL AND MANUSCRIPT COLLECTIONS

WASHINGTON, D.C. NATIONAL ARCHIVES. DIPLOMATIC BRANCH. RECORD GROUP 59.

Clayton, William
Pasvolsky, Leo
Office of the Assistant Secretary and Under Secretary of State for Economic Affairs, 1941–48, 1950 (Dean Acheson, Willard Thorp)
Office of European Affairs, 1934–1947 (Matthews-Hickerson Papers)
Pauley Reparations Mission
Policy Planning Staff
840.50 Recovery Series (Marshall Plan)

INDEPENDENCE, MISSOURI. HARRY S. TRUMAN LIBRARY.

Acheson, Dean
Ayers, Eben A.
Blaisdell, Thomas C., Jr.
Clayton-Thorp Papers
Clifford, Clark M.
Connelly, Matthew J.
Elsey, George M.
Jones, Joseph M.
Nourse, Edwin G.
Rosenman, Samuel I.
Salant, Walter S.
Snyder, John W.
Truman, Harry S.
 (1) President's Secretary's Files
  (a) Subject File: Agencies; Bureau of the Budget; Cabinet; Foreign Affairs; NSC Atomic; NSC Meetings

(b) General File
(c) Intelligence File
(2) White House Central Files, Confidential File
(3) Family Correspondence File, Correspondence from Harry S.
Truman to Bess Wallace Truman, 1945–1959
Webb, James E.
President's Air Policy Commission (Finletter Commission)
President's Materials Policy Commission (Paley Commission)
Oral History Interviews: Keyserling, Leon (1975); Nourse, Edwin G.
(1972)

CLEMSON, SOUTH CAROLINA. ROBERT MULDROW COOPER
LIBRARY.

Byrnes, James F.

PUBLIC DOCUMENTS AND GOVERNMENT PUBLICATIONS

United Nations. Economic and Social Council. Economic Commission
for Europe. Research and Planning Division. *A Survey of the Economic Situation and Prospects of Europe.* Washington, D.C.: GPO,
1948.
____ Department of Economic Affairs. *Economic Report: Salient Fea-
tures of the World Economic Structure, 1945–47.* Lake Success, N.Y.:
n.p., 1948.
U.S. Congress. Library of Congress. European Affairs Division. *War
and Postwar Greece: An Analysis Based on Greek Writings.*
Washington, D.C.: GPO, 1952.
____ Senate. Committee on Banking and Currency. *Study of Export-
Import Bank and World Bank.* 83rd Cong., 2d sess., 1954.
____ Senate. Committee on Foreign Relations. *Assistance to Greece and
Turkey. Hearings on S. 938.* 80th Cong., 1st sess., 1947.
____ Senate. Committee on Foreign Relations. *Legislative Origins of the
Truman Doctrine. Historical Series. Assistance to Greece and Turkey.
Hearings held in Executive Session on S. 938.* 80th Cong., 1st sess.,
1947 (released 1973).
____ Senate. Committee on Foreign Relations. *Foreign Relief Aid: 1947.
Historical Series. Hearings held in Executive Session on H. Res. 153
and S. 1774.* 80th Cong., 1st sess., 1947 (released 1973).
____ Senate. Committee on Foreign Relations. *European Recovery Pro-
gram. Hearings on S. 2202. Part 1.* 80th Cong., 2d sess., 1948.
____ Senate. Committee on Foreign Relations. *Foreign Relief Assistance*

Act of 1948. Historical Series. Hearings Held in Executive Session. 80th Cong., 2d sess., 1948 (released 1973).

U.S. Department of Commerce. Bureau of Foreign and Domestic Commerce. Office of International Trade. *Foreign Trade of the United States 1936–1949.* Washington, D.C.: GPO, 1951.

———— Bureau of the Census. *Historical Statistics of the United States: Colonial Times to 1970, Part 2.* Bicentennial Edition. Washington, D.C.: GPO, 1975.

U.S. Department of State. *Bulletin.* Washington, D.C.: GPO, 1944–50. Vols. 11–22 (1944–50).

———— *Foreign Relations of the United States.* Washington, D.C.: GPO, 1964–1977. Annual volumes, 1943–1950.

———— *Foreign Relations of the United States: The Conferences at Malta and Yalta.* Washington, D.C.: GPO, 1955.

———— *Foreign Relations of the United States: The Conference of Berlin (The Potsdam Conference).* 2 vols. Washington, D.C.: GPO, 1960.

U.S. Office of the President. *Public Papers of the Presidents of the United States.* Washington, D.C.: Office of the *Federal Register,* National Archives and Records Service, 1961–1965. Harry S. Truman, 1945–1950.

———— President's Committee on Foreign Aid. *European Recovery and American Aid.* Washington: GPO, 1947.

———— President's Materials Policy Commission. *Resources for Freedom.* Volume I: *Foundations for Growth and Security.* Washington, D.C.: GPO, 1952.

BOOKS, ARTICLES, AND UNPUBLISHED PAPERS

Acheson, A. L. K., J. F. Chant, and M. F. J. Prachowny, eds. *Bretton Woods Revisited.* Buffalo: University of Toronto Press, 1972.

Acheson, Dean. *Present at the Creation: My Years in the State Department.* New York: New American Library, Signet Books, 1970.

Adenauer, Konrad. *Memoirs 1945–1953.* London: Weidenfeld and Nicolson, 1966.

Adler, John H. "The Fiscal and Monetary Implementation of Development Programs." *American Economic Review Papers and Proceedings* (May 1952), 42:584–600.

Adler, Les K. and Thomas G. Paterson. "Red Fascism: The Merger of Nazi Germany and Soviet Russia in the American Image of Totalitarianism, 1930's–1950's," *American Historical Review* (April 1970), 75:1,146–64.

Adler, Selig. *The Isolationist Impulse: Its Twentieth Century Reaction.*
New York: Crowell-Collier, Collier Books, 1961.

Ames, Edward. "International Trade Without Markets—The Soviet
Bloc Case." *American Economic Review* (December 1954),
44:791–807.

Anderson, Irvine H. *Aramco, the United States, and Saudi Arabia: A
Study of the Dynamics of Foreign Oil Policy, 1933–1950.* Princeton,
N.J.: Princeton University Press, 1981.

Arkes, Hadley. *Bureaucracy, the Marshall Plan, and the National Interest.* Princeton, N.J.: Princeton University Press, 1972.

Baldwin, David A. *Economic Development and American Foreign Policy,
1943–52.* Chicago: University of Chicago Press, 1966.

Baykov, Alexander. *Soviet Foreign Trade.* Princeton, N.J.: Princeton
University Press, 1946.

Becker, William H. and Samuel F. Wells, Jr., eds. *Economics and World
Power: An Assessment of American Diplomacy Since 1789.* The Polit-
ical Economy of International Change Series. New York: Columbia
University Press, 1984.

Bennett, Martin Toscan. "Japanese Reparations: Fact or Fantasy?"
Pacific Affairs (June 1948), 21:185–94.

Bergsten, C. Fred. "International Economic Relations." *Transatlantic
Perspectives* (February 1982), 6:2–5.

Bernstein, Barton J., ed. *Politics and Policies of the Truman Administration.* Chicago: Quadrangle Books, 1970.

Bidwell, Percy W. "Imports in the American Economy." *Foreign Affairs*
(October 1945), 24:85–98.

Block, Fred L. *The Origins of International Economic Disorder: A Study
of United States International Monetary Policy from World War II to
the Present.* Berkeley: University of California Press, 1977.

Blum, John Morton, ed. *From the Morgenthau Diaries.* Vol. 3: *Years of
War, 1941–1945.* Boston: Houghton Mifflin, 1967.

Bohlen, Charles E. *Witness to History 1929–1969.* New York: Norton,
1973.

Bonn, M. J. "The Economics of Fear." *Annals of the American Academy
of Political and Social Science* (July 1946), 246:130–42.

Borden, William S. "The Pacific Alliance: The United States and Japanese Trade Recovery, 1947–1954." Ph.D. dissertation, University
of Wisconsin, 1981.

Borg, Dorothy and Waldo Heinrichs, eds. *Uncertain Years: Chinese-
American Relations, 1947–1950.* New York: Columbia University
Press, 1980.

Brenn, Bruce M. "U.S. Reparations Policy Toward Japan: September
1945 to May 1949." In Richard K. Beardsley, ed., *Studies in Japanese History and Politics,* pp. 71–113. Center for Japanese Studies,

Occasional Papers No. 10. Ann Arbor: University of Michigan Press, 1967.

Bright, Charles and Susan Harding, eds. *Statemaking and Social Movements: Essays in History and Theory.* Ann Arbor: University of Michigan Press, forthcoming.

Buhite, Russell D. *Soviet-American Relations in Asia, 1945–1954.* Norman: University of Oklahoma Press, 1981.

Calleo, David P. *The Imperious Economy.* Cambridge, Mass.: Harvard University Press, 1982.

Cecil, Robert. "Potsdam and its Legends." *International Affairs* (Chatham House) (July 1970), 46:455–65.

Chace, James. *Solvency: An Essay on American Foreign Policy.* New York: Vintage Books, 1981.

Clay, Henry. "Britain's Declining Role in World Trade." *Foreign Affairs* (April 1946), 24:411–28.

Clay, Lucius D. *Decision in Germany.* Westport, Conn.: Greenwood Press, 1970.

Clemens, Walter C., Jr. "The Soviet World Faces West, 1945–1970." *International Affairs* (Chatham House) (July 1970), 46:475–89.

Cohen, Warren I., ed. *New Frontiers in American-East Asian Relations: Essays Presented to Dorothy Borg.* New York: Columbia University Press, 1983.

Collins, Robert M. *The Business Response to Keynes, 1929–1964.* New York: Columbia University Press, 1981.

Cooper, Richard M. *The Economics of Interdependence: Economic Policy in the Atlantic Community.* Council on Foreign Relations, Atlantic Policy Series. New York: McGraw-Hill, 1968.

Cotler, Julio and Richard R. Fagen, eds. *Latin America and the United States: The Changing Political Realities.* Stanford, Calif.: Stanford University Press, 1974.

Cuff, R. D. and J. L. Granatstein. *American Dollars—Canadian Prosperity: Canadian-American Economic Relations 1945–1950.* Toronto: Samuel-Stevens, 1978.

Davis, Lynn. *The Cold War Begins: Soviet-American Conflict over Eastern Europe.* Princeton, N.J.: Princeton University Press, 1974.

DeConde, Alexander, ed. *Isolation and Security.* Durham, N.C.: Duke University Press, 1957.

Dennett, Raymond, and Joseph E. Johnson, eds. *Negotiating with the Russians.* Boston: World Peace Foundation, 1965.

Deutscher, Isaac. *Stalin: A Political Biography.* 2d ed., enl. New York: Oxford University Press, Galaxy Books, 1970.

Diebold, William, Jr. *Trade and Payments in Western Europe: A Study in Economic Cooperation, 1947–51.* Council on Foreign Relations Series. New York: Harper, 1952.

Divine, Robert A. "The Cold War and the Election of 1948." *Journal of American History* (June 1972), 59:90–110.

Djilas, Milovan. *Conversations with Stalin.* New York: Harcourt, Brace & World, Harvest Books, 1962.

Domar, Evsey D. "The Varga Controversy." *American Economic Review* (March 1950), 40:132–51.

Donovan, Robert J. *Conflict and Crisis: The Presidency of Harry S Truman, 1945–48.* New York: Norton, 1977.

——— *Tumultuous Years: The Presidency of Harry S Truman, 1949–1953.* New York: Norton, 1982.

Dorn, Walter L. "The Debate over American Occupation Policy in Germany in 1944–1945." *Political Science Quarterly* (December 1957), 72:481–501.

Dower, J. W. *Empire and Aftermath: Yoshida Shigeru and the Japanese Experience, 1878–1954.* Cambridge, Mass.: Harvard University Press, 1979.

Eckes, Alfred E., Jr. "Open Door Expansionism Reconsidered: The World War II Experience." *Journal of American History* (March 1973), 59:909–24.

——— *A Search for Solvency: Bretton Woods and the International Monetary System, 1944–71.* Austin: University of Texas Press, 1975.

——— *The United States and the Global Struggle for Minerals.* Austin: University of Texas Press, 1979.

Feis, Herbert. "Political Aspects of Foreign Loans." *Foreign Affairs* (July 1945), 23:609–19.

——— "The Future of British Imperial Preferences." *Foreign Affairs* (April 1946), 24:661–74.

——— "The Conflict over Trade Ideologies." *Foreign Affairs* (January 1947), 25:217–28.

——— *Between War and Peace: The Potsdam Conference.* Princeton, N.J.: Princeton University Press, 1960.

Fenoaltea, Sergio. "Italy at Work: Achievements and Needs." *Foreign Affairs* (July 1946), 24:715–22.

Ferrell, Robert H., ed. *Dear Bess: The Letters from Harry to Bess Truman, 1910–1959.* New York: Norton, 1983.

Fontaine, André. "Potsdam: A French View." *International Affairs* (Chatham House) (July 1970), 46:466–74.

Freeland, Richard M. *The Truman Doctrine and the Origins of McCarthyism: Foreign Policy, Domestic Politics, and Internal Security, 1946–1948.* New York: Schocken Books, 1974.

Fuller, Walter D. "American Business After the War." In *The United States After War.* Cornell University Summer Session Lectures. Freeport, N.Y.: Books for Libraries Press, Essay Index Reprint Series, 1969.

Gaddis, John Lewis. *The United States and the Origins of the Cold War, 1941–1947*. New York: Columbia University Press, 1972.

_____ "Was the Truman Doctrine a Real Turning Point?" *Foreign Affairs* (January 1974), 52: 386–402.

_____ *Strategies of Containment: A Critical Appraisal of Postwar American National Security Policy*. New York: Oxford University Press, 1982.

_____ "The Emerging Post-Revisionist Synthesis on the Origins of the Cold War." *Diplomatic History* (Summer 1983), 7:171–90.

_____ "The United States and the Question of a Sphere of Influence in Europe, 1945–1949." Paper delivered before Oslo International Symposium on European Atlantic Defense, 1947–1953, Oslo, Norway, August 7–11, 1983.

Gallup, George H. *The Gallup Poll: Public Opinion, 1935–1971*. Vol. 1: *1935–1948*. New York: Random House, 1972.

Gardner, Lloyd C. *Architects of Illusion: Men and Ideas in American Foreign Policy, 1941–1949*. Chicago: Quadrangle Books, 1972.

Gardner, Richard N. *Sterling-Dollar Diplomacy: The Origins and Prospects of Our International Economic Order*. Rev. and enl. New York: McGraw-Hill, 1969.

Gimbel, John. *The American Occupation of Germany: Politics and the Military, 1945–1949*. Stanford, Calif.: Stanford University Press, 1968.

_____ "On the Implementation of the Potsdam Agreement: An Essay on U.S. Postwar German Policy." *Political Science Quarterly* (June 1972), 87:242–69.

_____ *The Origins of the Marshall Plan*. Stanford, Calif.: Stanford University Press, 1976.

Goodwin, Craufurd D., ed. *Energy Policy in Perspective: Today's Problems, Yesterday's Solutions*. Washington, D.C.: Brookings Institution, 1981.

Green, David. *The Containment of Latin America: A History of the Myths and Realities of the Good Neighbor Policy*. Chicago: Quadrangle Books, 1971.

Griswold, A. Whitney. *The Far Eastern Policy of the United States*. New York: Harcourt, Brace, 1938.

Hadley, Eleanor M. *Antitrust in Japan*. Princeton, N.J.: Princeton University Press, 1970.

_____ "Japan: Competition or Private Collectivism?" *Far Eastern Survey* (December 14, 1949), 18:289–94.

Hall, H. Duncan. "The British Commonwealth as a Great Power." *Foreign Affairs* (July 1945), 23:594–608.

Halle, Louis J. *The Cold War as History*. New York: Harper & Row, 1967.

Hamby, Alonzo B. "Henry A. Wallace, the Liberals, and Soviet-American Relations." *Review of Politics* (April 1968), 30:153–59.

—— "The Liberals, Truman, and FDR as Symbol and Myth." *Journal of American History* (March 1970), 56:859–67.

Hammond, Thomas T., ed. *Witnesses to the Origins of the Cold War.* Seattle: University of Washington Press, 1982.

Harriman, W. Averell and Elie Abel. *Special Envoy to Churchill and Stalin, 1941–1946.* New York: Random House, 1975.

Harrington, Daniel F. "Kennan, Bohlen, and the Riga Axioms." *Diplomatic History* (Fall 1978), 2:423–37.

Harris, Seymour E., ed. *Foreign Economic Policy of the United States.* Cambridge, Mass.: Harvard University Press, 1948.

Hartmann, Susan M. *Truman and the 80th Congress.* Columbia: University of Missouri Press, 1971.

Hathaway, Robert M. *Ambiguous Partnership: Britain and America, 1944–1947.* New York: Columbia University Press, 1981.

Heller, Francis H., ed. *Economics and the Truman Administration.* Lawrence: Regents Press of Kansas, 1981.

Herken, Gregg. *The Winning Weapon: The Atomic Bomb in the Cold War, 1945–1950.* New York: Vintage Books, 1981.

Herring, George C., Jr. "Lend-Lease to Russia and the Origins of the Cold War, 1944–1945." *Journal of American History* (June 1969), 56:93–114.

—— "The United States and British Bankruptcy: Responsibilities Deferred." *Political Science Quarterly* (June 1976), 86:260–80.

Hess, Gary R. "The Iranian Crisis of 1945–46 and the Cold War." *Political Science Quarterly* (March 1974), 89:117–46.

Hill, William S., Jr. "The Business Community and National Defense: Corporate Leaders and the Military." Ph.D. dissertation, Stanford University, 1980.

Hilton, Stanley E. "The United States, Brazil, and the Cold War, 1945–1960: End of the Special Relationship." *Journal of American History* (December 1981), 68:599–624.

Hitchens, Harold L. "Influences on the Congressional Decision to Pass the Marshall Plan." *Western Political Quarterly* (March 1968), 21:51–68.

Hogan, Michael J. *Informal Entente: The Private Structure of Cooperation in Anglo-American Economic Diplomacy, 1918–1928.* Columbia: University of Missouri Press, 1977.

—— "The Search for a 'Creative Peace': The United States, European Unity, and the Origins of the Marshall Plan." *Diplomatic History* (Summer 1982), 6:267–85.

Hollerman, Leon. "International Economic Controls in Occupied Japan." *Journal of Asian Studies* (August 1979), 38:707–19.

Holloway, David. *The Soviet Union and the Arms Race.* New Haven: Yale University Press, 1983.

Hughes, H. Stuart. *The United States and Italy.* Rev. ed. American Foreign Policy Library. Cambridge, Mass.: Harvard University Press, 1965.

Iatrides, John O. *Revolt in Athens: The Greek Communist "Second Round," 1944–1945.* Princeton, N.J.: Princeton University Press, 1972.

Igarishi, Takeshi. "George Kennan and the Redirection of American Occupation Policy for Japan: The Formulation of National Security Council Paper 13/2." Paper delivered before Amherst College Conference on the Allied Occupation of Japan, August 20–23, 1980.

―――― "The Ordeal of the Containment Policy—George Kennan and the Redirection of American Occupation Policy for Japan." Paper delivered at the Japan Seminar at the University of Maryland at College Park, February 28, 1981.

Inaba, Shuzo. "Reparations and Japan's Economy." *Contemporary Japan* (1952), 21 (1/3):108–113.

Ireland, Timothy P. *Creating the Entangling Alliance: The Origins of the North Atlantic Treaty Organization.* Westport, Conn.: Greenwood Press, 1981.

Iriye, Akira. *The Cold War in Asia: A Historical Introduction.* Englewood Cliffs, N.J.: Prentice-Hall, 1974.

Jackson, Scott. "Prologue to the Marshall Plan: The Origins of the American Commitment for a European Recovery Program." *Journal of American History* (March 1979), 65:1043–68.

Jones, Byrd L. "The Role of Keynesians in Wartime Policy and Postwar Planning, 1940–1946." *American Economic Review: Papers and Proceedings* (May 1972), 62:125–33.

Jones, Joseph M. *The Fifteen Weeks: February 21–June 5, 1947.* New York: Viking Press, 1955.

Kaiser, David E. *Economic Diplomacy and the Origins of the Second World War: Germany, Britain, France, and Eastern Europe, 1930–1939.* Princeton, N.J.: Princeton University Press, 1980.

Kaplan, Lawrence S. *A Community of Interests: NATO and the Military Assistance Program, 1948–1951.* Washington, D.C.: GPO, 1980.

Kaser, Michael. *Comecon: Integration Problems of the Planned Economies.* New York: Oxford University Press, 1967.

Kaufman, Burton I. *Trade and Aid: Eisenhower's Foreign Economic Policy, 1953–1961.* Baltimore, Md.: Johns Hopkins University Press, 1982.

Kennan, George F. *Memoirs: 1925–1950.* Boston: Atlantic Monthly

Press, 1967.

—— "The Sources of Soviet Conduct." *Foreign Affairs* (July 1947), 25: 566–82.

Kindleberger, Charles P. "U.S. Foreign Economic Policy 1776–1976." *Foreign Affairs* (January 1977), 55:395–417.

Knight, Jonathon. "American Statecraft and the 1946 Black Sea Straits Controversy." *Political Science Quarterly* (Fall 1975), 90:451–75.

Kolko, Gabriel. *The Politics of War: The World and United States Foreign Policy, 1943–1945.* New York: Random House, Vintage Books, 1970.

Kolko, Joyce and Gabriel. *The Limits of Power: The World and United States Foreign Policy, 1945–1954.* New York: Harper & Row, 1972.

Kousoulas, D. George. "The Truman Doctrine and the Stalin-Tito Rift: A Reappraisal." *South Atlantic Quarterly* (Summer 1973), 72:427–39.

Krasner, Stephen D. *Defending the National Interest: Raw Materials Investments and U.S. Foreign Policy.* Princeton, N.J.: Princeton University Press, 1978.

Kuklick, Bruce. *American Policy and the Division of Germany: The Clash with Russia over Reparations.* Ithaca, N.Y.: Cornell University Press, 1972.

—— "The Division of Germany and American Policy on Reparations." *Western Political Quarterly* (June 1970), 23:276–93.

Kuniholm, Bruce Robellet. *The Origins of the Cold War in the Near East: Great Power Conflict and Diplomacy in Iran, Turkey, and Greece.* Princeton, N.J.: Princeton University Press, 1980.

LaFeber, Walter. *America, Russia, and the Cold War, 1945–1975.* 3d ed., rev. New York: Wiley, 1976.

—— *Inevitable Revolutions: The United States in Central America.* New York: Norton, 1983.

Laloy, Jean L. "Stalin and Europe: Policy Objectives at the End of World War II." Seminar on February 2, 1979 at the Woodrow Wilson International Center for Scholars, Washington, D.C. Transcript.

Leffler, Melvyn P. "The American Conception of National Security and the Beginnings of the Cold War, 1945–1948." *American Historical Review* (April 1984), 89:346–81.

Leigh, Michael. "Is There a Revisionist Thesis on the Origins of the Cold War?" *Political Science Quarterly* (March 1974), 89:101–16.

Lo, Clarence Yin-Hsieh. "The Truman Administration's Military Budgets during the Korean War." Ph.D. dissertation, University of California at Berkeley, 1978.

Lundestad, Geir. *The American Non-Policy Towards Eastern Europe, 1943–1947: Universalism in an Area Not of Essential Interest to the*

United States. New York: Humanities Press, 1975.

—— "Empire by Invitation? The United States and Western Europe, 1945–1952." Paper delivered at conference on "Reconstruction and the Restoration of Democracy: U.S.-European Relations 1945–1952." Salzburg, Austria, April 16–17, 1983.

McCagg, William O., Jr. *Stalin Embattled 1943–1948.* Detroit: Wayne State University Press, 1978.

McCoy, Donald R. "Republican Opposition During Wartime, 1941–1945." *Mid-America* (July 1967), 49:174–89.

McInnis, Edgar, Richard Hiscocks, and Robert Spencer, eds. *The Shaping of Postwar Germany.* London: Dent, 1960.

MacIsaac, David. "The Air Force and Strategic Thought." Working Paper #8, International Security Studies Program. Presented June 21, 1979, at the Woodrow Wilson International Center for Scholars, Washington, D.C.

McLellan, David S. *Dean Acheson: The State Department Years.* New York: Dodd, Mead, 1976.

—— "The 'Operational Code' Approach to the Study of Political Leaders: Dean Acheson's Philosophical and Instrumental Beliefs." *Canadian Journal of Political Science* (March 1971), 4:52–75.

McNeill, William Hardy. *The Greek Dilemma: War and Aftermath.* Philadelphia: Lippincott, 1947.

Magdoff, Harry. *The Age of Imperialism: The Economics of U.S. Foreign Policy.* New York: Monthly Review Press, Modern Reader Paperbacks, 1969.

Maier, Charles S. "Revisionism and the Interpretation of Cold War Origins." *Perspectives in American History* (1970), 4:313–47.

—— "The Politics of Productivity: Foundations of American International Economic Policy after World War II." *International Organization* (Autumn 1977), 31:607–33.

—— "The Postwar Eras and the Conditions for Stability in Twentieth Century Western Europe." *American Historical Review* (April 1981), 86:327–52.

—— Comments on Michael J. Hogan, "The United States, European Unity, and the Origins of the Marshall Plan." Seminar on November 4, 1981, at Woodrow Wilson International Center for Scholars, Washington, D.C. Transcript.

—— "'You People in Europe': Regional Concepts and National Roles Within the Marshall Plan." 1981.

Mark, Eduard. "American Policy Toward Eastern Europe and the Origins of the Cold War, 1941–1946." *Journal of American History* (September 1981), 68:313–36.

Mason, Edward S. and Robert E. Asher. *The World Bank Since Bretton Woods.* Washington, D.C.: Brookings Institution, 1973.

Mastny, Vojtech. "The Cassandra in the Foreign Commissariat: Maxim Litvinov and the Cold War." *Foreign Affairs* (January 1976), 54:366–76.

—— *Russia's Road to the Cold War: Diplomacy, Warfare, and the Politics of Communism, 1941–1945.* New York: Columbia University Press, 1979.

Mayne, Richard. *The Recovery of Europe: From Devastation to Unity.* New York: Harper & Row, 1970.

Messer, Robert L. *The End of an Alliance: James F. Byrnes, Roosevelt, Truman, and the Origins of the Cold War.* Chapel Hill: University of North Carolina Press, 1982.

Mikesell, Raymond F. "The Role of the International Monetary Agreements in a World of Planned Economies." *Journal of Political Economy* (Dec. 1947), 55:497–512.

Mikhailov, Nikolai. "The Soviet Peacetime Economy." *Foreign Affairs* (July 1946), 24:633–37.

Miller, Aaron David. *Search for Security: Saudi Arabian Oil and American Foreign Policy, 1939–1949.* Chapel Hill: University of North Carolina Press, 1980.

Millis, Walter, ed. *The Forrestal Diaries.* New York: Viking Press, 1951.

Moore, Ray A. "Reflections on the Occupation of Japan." *Journal of Asian Studies* (August 1979), 38:721–34.

Morgenthau, Henry, Jr. "Bretton Woods and International Cooperation." *Foreign Affairs* (January 1945), 23:182–94.

—— "Postwar Treatment of Germany." *Annals of the American Academy of Political and Social Science* (July 1946), 246:125–29.

Nagai, Yonosuke and Akira Iriye, eds. *The Origins of the Cold War in Asia.* New York: Columbia University Press, 1977.

Nash, Gerald. *United States Oil Policy, 1870–1964: Business and Government in Twentieth Century America.* Pittsburgh, Pa.: University of Pittsburgh Press, 1968.

Neu, Charles E. *The Troubled Encounter: The United States and Japan.* New York: Wiley, 1975.

Nove, Alec. *An Economic History of the U.S.S.R.* Baltimore, Md.: Penguin Press, Pelican Books, 1972.

Oneal, John R. *Foreign Policy Making in Times of Crisis.* Columbus: Ohio State University Press, 1982.

Packenham, Robert A. *Liberal America and the Third World: Political Development Ideas in Foreign Aid and Social Science.* Princeton, N.J.: Princeton University Press, 1973.

Page, Joseph. *Peron: A Biography.* New York: Random House, 1983.

Pastor, Robert A. *Congress and the Politics of U.S. Foreign Economic Policy.* Berkeley: University of California Press, 1982.

Paterson, Thomas Graham. "The Economic Cold War: American Business and Economic Foreign Policy, 1945–1950." Ph.D. dissertation, University of California at Berkeley, 1968.

———. *Soviet-American Confrontation: Postwar Reconstruction and the Origins of the Cold War.* Baltimore: Johns Hopkins University Press, 1973.

———. *On Every Front: The Making of the Cold War.* New York: Norton, 1979.

Patterson, James T. *Mr. Republican: A Biography of Robert A. Taft.* Boston: Houghton Mifflin, 1972.

Penrose, E. F. *Economic Planning for the Peace.* Princeton, N. J.: Princeton University Press, 1953.

Perlmutter, Oscar William. "The 'Neo-Realism' of Dean Acheson." *Review of Politics* (January 1964), 26:100–23.

Pfau, Richard. "Containment in Iran, 1946: The Shift to an Active Policy." *Diplomatic History* (Fall 1977), 1:359–72.

Polk, Judd and Gardner Patterson. "The British Loan." *Foreign Affairs* (April 1946), 24:429–40.

Price, Harry Bayard. *The Marshall Plan and its Meaning.* Ithaca, N.Y.: Cornell University Press, 1955.

Pubrantz, Jerry. "Marxism-Leninism and Soviet-American Economic Relations Since Stalin." *Law and Contemporary Problems* (Autumn 1972), 87:535–47.

Ratchford, B. U. and William D. Ross. *Berlin Reparations Assignment: Round One of the German Peace Settlement.* Chapel Hill: University of North Carolina Press, 1947.

Rearden, Steven L. "The History of the Office of the Secretary of Defense." Volume 1: "The Formative Years, 1947–1950." Washington, D.C.: JCS Joint Secretariat, Historical Division, forthcoming.

Reday, Joseph Z. "Reparations from Japan." *Far Eastern Survey* (June 19, 1949), 18:145–51.

Reischauer, Edwin O. *The United States and Japan.* 3d ed., rev. American Foreign Policy Library. Cambridge, Mass.: Harvard University Press, 1965.

Rendell, Robert S. "Export Financing and the Role of the Export-Import Bank of the United States." *Journal of International Law and Economics* (1976), 2:91–146.

Resis, Albert. "The Churchill-Stalin Secret 'Percentages' Agreement on the Balkans, Moscow, October 1944." *American Historical Review* (April 1978), 83:368–87.

Rosenberg, David Alan. "American Atomic Strategy and the Hydrogen Bomb Decision." *Journal of American History* (June 1979), 66:62–87.

———. "U.S. Nuclear Stockpile, 1945 to 1950." *Bulletin of Atomic Scien-*

tists (May 1982), 38:25–30.

—— "The Origins of Overkill: Nuclear Weapons and American Strategy, 1945–1960." *International Security* (Spring 1983), 7:3–71.

Rowland, Benjamin M., ed. *Balance of Power or Hegemony: The Interwar Monetary System.* New York: New York University Press for the Lehrman Institute, 1976.

S., K. R. "Economic Planning in Eastern Europe." Part 1 of "The Russian Sphere in Europe." *The World Today (Chatham House Review)* (October 1947), 3:432–45.

Santis, Hugh de. "Conflicting Images of the USSR: American Career Diplomats and the Balkans, 1944–1946." *Political Science Quarterly* (Fall 1979), 94:475–94.

Schaller, Michael. *The U.S. Crusade in China, 1938–1945.* New York: Columbia University Press, 1979.

—— "Securing the Great Crescent: Occupied Japan and the Origins of Containment in Southeast Asia." *Journal of American History* (September 1982), 69:392–414.

Schilling, Warner R., Paul Y. Hammond, and Glenn H. Snyder. *Strategy, Politics, and Defense Budgets.* New York: Columbia University Press, 1962.

Schmitt, Hans A., ed. *U.S. Occupation in Europe after World War II.* Lawrence: Regents Press of Kansas, 1978.

Schnabel, James F. *The History of the Joint Chiefs of Staff.* Vol. 1: *The Joint Chiefs of Staff and National Policy, 1945–1947.* Washington, D.C.: JCS Joint Secretariat, Historical Division, 1979.

Schonberger, Howard. "The Japan Lobby in American Diplomacy, 1947–1952." *Pacific Historical Review* (1977), 46(3):327–59.

Schwartz, Harry. *Russia's Soviet Economy.* Englewood Cliffs, N.J.: Prentice-Hall, 1954.

Sherry, Michael S. *Preparing for the Next War: American Plans for Postwar Defense, 1941–45.* New Haven, Conn.: Yale University Press, 1977.

Sherwin, Martin J. *A World Destroyed: The Atomic Bomb and the Grand Alliance.* New York: Knopf, 1975.

Shlaim, Avi. *The United States and the Berlin Blockade, 1948–1949: A Study in Crisis Decision-Making.* Berkeley: University of California Press, 1983.

Singer, H. W. "The Distribution of Gains Between Investing and Borrowing Countries." *American Economic Review Papers and Proceedings* (May 1950), 40:473–85.

Slusser, Robert, ed. *Soviet Economic Policy in Postwar Germany: A Collection of Papers by Former Soviet Officials.* New York: Research Program on the U.S.S.R., 1953.

Smith, Gaddis. *Dean Acheson.* New York: Cooper Square Publishers, 1972.

Smith, Jean Edward, ed. *The Papers of General Lucius D. Clay.* Vol. 1: *Germany 1945–1949.* Bloomington: Indiana University Press, 1974.

Snowden, J. K., ed. *The German Question 1945–1973: Continuity in Change.* London: Bradford University Press, 1975.

Spanier, John. *American Foreign Policy Since World War II.* 6th ed. New York: Praeger, 1973.

Steel, Ronald. *Walter Lippmann and the American Century.* New York: Vintage Books, 1980.

Stein, Harold, ed. *American Civil-Military Decisions: A Book of Case Studies.* Birmingham: University of Alabama Press, 1963.

Stein, Herbert. *The Fiscal Revolution in America.* Chicago: University of Chicago Press, 1969.

Stockwin, J. A. A. *Japan: Divided Politics in a Growth Economy.* London: Weidenfeld & Nicolson, 1975.

Stoff, Michael B. *Oil, War, and American Security: The Search for a National Policy on Foreign Oil, 1941–1947.* Yale Historical Publications Miscellany #125. New Haven, Conn.: Yale University Press, 1980.

Stueck, William Whitney, Jr. *The Road to Confrontation: American Policy Toward China and Korea, 1947–1950.* Chapel Hill: University of North Carolina Press, 1981.

Stupak, Ronald J. *The Shaping of Foreign Policy: The Role of the Secretary of State as Seen by Dean Acheson.* New York: Odyssey Press, 1969.

Sweezy, Alan. "The Keynesians and Government Policy, 1933–1939." *American Economic Review: Papers and Proceedings* (May 1972), 62:116–24.

Taubman, William. *Stalin's American Policy: From Entente to Detente to Cold War.* New York: Norton, 1982.

Thorp, Willard L. "Some Basic Policy Issues in Economic Development." *American Economic Review: Papers and Proceedings* (May 1951), 41:407–17.

Truman, Harry S. *Memoirs.* Vol. 1: *Year of Decisions.* Garden City, N.Y.: Doubleday, 1955.

—— *Memoirs.* Vol. 2: *Years of Trial and Hope.* Garden City, N.Y.: Doubleday, 1956.

Tsou, Tang. *America's Failure in China, 1941–1950.* Chicago: University of Chicago Press, 1963.

Tuchman, Barbara W. *Stilwell and the American Experience in China, 1911–45.* New York: MacMillan, 1970.

Tucker, Nancy Bernkopf. *Patterns in the Dust: Chinese-American Rela-*

tions and the Recognition Controversy, 1949–1950. New York: Columbia University Press, 1983.

Ulam, Adam. *Expansion and Coexistence: Soviet Foreign Policy, 1917–1973.* 2d ed., enl. New York: Praeger, 1974.

Van Dormael, Armand. *Bretton Woods: Birth of a Monetary System.* New York: Holmes & Meier, 1978.

Vandenberg, Arthur H., Jr., ed. *The Private Papers of Senator Vandenberg.* Boston: Houghton Mifflin, 1952.

Varga, E. "Anglo-American Rivalry and Partnership: A Marxist View." *Foreign Affairs* (July 1947), 25:583–95.

Vinson, Fred M. "After the Savannah Conference." *Foreign Affairs* (July 1946), 24:622–32.

Wagner, R. Harrison. *United States Policy Toward Latin America: A Study in Domestic and International Politics.* Stanford, Calif.: Stanford University Press, 1970.

—— "The Decision to Divide Germany and the Origins of the Cold War." *International Studies Quarterly* (June 1980), 24:155–90.

Ward, Barbara. "Europe Debates Nationalization." *Foreign Affairs* (October 1946), 25:44–58.

Warner, Geoffrey. "The Division of Germany 1946–1948." *International Affairs* (Chatham House) (January 1975), 51:60–70.

Wells, Samuel F., Jr. "Sounding the Tocsin: NSC 68 and the Soviet Threat." *International Security* (Fall 1979), 4:116–48.

Werth, Alexander. *France 1940–1955.* New York: Holt, 1956.

—— *Russia at War, 1941–1945.* New York: Avon Books, Discus Books, 1964.

Westerfield, H. Bradford. *Foreign Policy and Party Politics: Pearl Harbor to Korea.* New Haven, Conn.: Yale University Press, 1955.

Wexler, Imanuel. *The Marshall Plan Revisited: The European Recovery Program in Economic Perspective.* Westport, Conn.: Greenwood Press, 1983.

White, H. D. "The Monetary Fund: Some Criticisms Examined." *Foreign Affairs* (January 1945), 23:195–210.

Wilkins, Mira. *The Maturing Enterprise: American Business Abroad from 1914 to 1970.* Cambridge, Mass.: Harvard University Press, 1974.

Williams, William Appleman. *The Tragedy of American Diplomacy.* Rev. and enl. New York: Dell, Delta Books, 1962.

Wittner, Lawrence S. *American Intervention in Greece, 1943–1949.* New York: Columbia University Press, 1981.

Wright, C. Ben. "Mr. 'X' and Containment." *Slavic Review* (March 1976), 35:1–31.

Wright, Gordon. *The Ordeal of Total War, 1939–1945.* Rise of Modern

Europe Series. New York: Harper & Row, Harper Torchbooks, 1968.

Yamamura, Kozo. "Zaibatsu, Prewar and Zaibatsu, Postwar." *Journal of Asian Studies* (August 1964), 23:539–54.

Yergin, Daniel. *Shattered Peace: The Origins of the Cold War and the National Security State*. Boston: Houghton Mifflin, 1978.

Zevin, Robert B. "An Interpretation of American Imperialism." *Journal of Economic History* (March 1972), 32:316–60.

Index

ACC, *see* Allied Control Council

Acheson, Dean: anti-Communism and, 71; appointed Secretary of State, 189–90; and Argentina, 212; atomic weapons, 235–38, 341n32; and Communist China, 172; containment policy, 55, 125; Delta Council speech, 135, 304n2; demobilization, 21; on economic integration, 2, 8; foreign policy priorities, 126–27; on German reconstruction, 295n61; and Greece, 116–19; legacy of, ix, 251; and Marshall, 126; and Middle East, 113; and Nationalist China, 193–94; and NATO, 226; and Near East, 121; NSC-68, 239, 341n42; occupation of Japan, 174–75, 319n16; Point IV, 206–7, 331n24; and Poland, 42–44; Press Club speech (1950), 194–96; rearmament and, 241; reparations suspension, 94–95; Soviet threat, 231–32; Taiwan, 190, 193; on Truman Doctrine, 124–25; on Tsaldaris, 118, 299n33; urges MFN status for Soviet Union, 52, 278n52

Adenauer, Konrad, 98, 157

Advanced technology, 252

Africa, British and Portuguese colonies in, 202, 330n12

Agreement for Intra-European Payments and Compensations (AIEPC), 160

Agriculture: Germany, 85–86; Italy, 77–78; Marshall Plan impact, 165

Air Force, 230

Air Policy Commission, 233

Air power, 155, 233–34, 268n34, 312n67

Aircraft industry, 233–34

Albania, 115–16

Allied Control Council (ACC), 94, 96–98; German economy and government, 102–3, 106; Japan, 175–77

Allis-Chalmers Manufacturing Company, 161–62

American Bankers Association, 16

American Council on Japan, 322n47

American Farm Bureau Federation, 146

American Federation of Labor, 146

American Mining Congress, 200

American Society of Civil Engineers, 208

Anderson, Irvine H., 215

Anglo-American Financial Agreement (December 1945), 69–70, 146–47

Anglo-American Oil Agreements, 215

Anti-Communism: Marshall Plan and, 147–49, 152; Truman Doctrine and, 124, 129–31, 135; U.S. foreign policy and, 71–72

Arabian-American Oil Company, *see* Aramco

Aramco, 216–19

Argentina, U.S. relations with, 211–13, 221

Armed forces, Soviet Union, *see* Soviet Union, defense spending

Armed forces, U.S., *see* Demobilization; Military headings, specific branches

Army personnel shortages, 154

Army-Navy Munitions Board, 199–201

Asia, *see* East Asia; Northeast Asia; Southeast Asia, specific countries

Atlantic Charter (1941): containment policies, 53; Eastern Europe, 57–58; multilateralism and, 11; U.S. commitment to, 49

Attlee, Clement R., 69, 108

374